THE
NEW BOOK
OF
KNOWLEDGE
ANNUAL

THE NEW BOOK OF KNOWLEDGE ANNUAL 2007

HIGHLIGHTING EVENTS OF 2006

⌒The Young People's Book of the Year⌒

Scholastic Library Publishing, Inc.
Danbury, Connecticut

ISBN 0-439-90024-7

ISSN 0196-0148

The Library of Congress Catalog Card Number: 79-26807

STAFF

FERN L. MAMBERG
EDITORIAL DIRECTOR

DEBBIE A. LOFASO
CREATIVE DIRECTOR

JOHN PERRITANO
SENIOR EDITOR

SUSAN PETRUZZI
PHOTO RESEARCHER

LIGHTHOUSE INDEXING PLUS
INDEXER

TERESA KLUK
PRODUCTION MANAGER

YOUNG PEOPLE'S PUBLICATIONS

VIRGINIA QUINN MCCARTHY
EDITOR IN CHIEF

EDITORIAL STAFF

ELAINE HENDERSON
Executive Editor

MICHAEL JIMENEZ
Senior Art Director

SARA A. BOAK
MATTHEW ZIEM
KEVIN M. MAYER
EVELYN SAMORÉ
PATRICIA A. BEHAN
PATRICIA RAETHER
ROSEMARIE KENT

CONTENTS

CONTRIBUTORS

BEAMAN, Patricia
Adjunct Professor, New York University Tisch School of the Arts; Artist-in-Residence, Wesleyan University; Soloist and Teacher, the New York Baroque Dance Company

BALLET

BUGAJSKI, Janusz
Director, New European Democracies Project, Center for Strategic and International Studies; Author, *Cold Peace: Russia's New Imperialism; Political Parties of Eastern Europe: A Guide to Politics in the Post-Communist Era; Nations in Turmoil: Conflict and Cooperation in Eastern Europe*

(REVIEWER) MONTENEGRO; SERBIA

EADINGTON, William R.
Professor of Economics and Director of the Institute for the Study of Gambling and Commercial Gaming, University of Nevada, Reno; Coauthor, *Gambling: Views from the Social Sciences; The Business of Gaming*

GAMBLING

GENAT, Robert L.
Author, *Drag Racers; Mopar Muscle; Hot Rod Milestones; The Birth of Hot Rodding; Challenger & 'Cuda;* Founder, Zone Five Photo; Member, the Motor Press Guild and the American Auto Racing Writers and Broadcasters Association

AUTOMOBILE RACING

GUTSCH, William A., Jr.
Chairman, American Museum–Hayden Planetarium; Author, *The Search for Extraterrestrial Life; 1001 Things Everyone Should Know About the Universe*

(REVIEWER) GALAXIES; SPACE PROBES; UNIVERSE

HANCOCK, Ian F.
Professor of Linguistics, The University of Texas at Austin; Director, the Program of Romani Studies and the Romani Archives and Documentation Center, The University of Texas at Austin; Author, *We Are the Romani People;* Coauthor, *A History of the Romani People*

ROMANIES

HUGHES, Meredith Sayles
Managing Director, The Food Museum
at *foodmuseum.com;* Author, *Plants We
Eat* series

GRAPES AND BERRIES

KURTZ, Henry I.
Author, *The Art of the Toy Soldier;
John and Sebastian Cabot*
DR. JACKSON'S CROSS-COUNTRY JAUNT

PASCOE, Elaine
Author, *South Africa: Troubled Land;
Neighbors at Odds: U.S. Policy in Latin
America; Racial Prejudice; Fooled You!
Fakes and Hoaxes Through the Years;
Freedom of Expression: The Right to
Speak Out in America*

AROUND THE WORLD

PATENT, Dorothy Hinshaw
Faculty Affiliate, University of Mon-
tana; Coauthor, *Biodiversity; Big Cats;
Gray Wolf, Red Wolf; Garden of the
Spirit Bear; Prairie Dogs*
RATS AND MICE; RODENTS; SQUIRRELS,
WOODCHUCKS, AND CHIPMUNKS

PIPER, Jon K.
Professor, Department of Biology,
Bethel College; Coauthor, *Farming in
Nature's Image: An Ecological Ap-
proach to Agriculture*

GRASSES AND GRASSLANDS

ROBINSON, Clay A.
Professor of Soil Science, West Texas
A&M University

SOILS

TESAR, Jenny
Author, *Science on the Edge: Stem Cells;
Endangered Habitats; Global Warming;
Scientific Crime Investigation; The Waste
Crisis; Shrinking Forests; What on Earth
Is a Meerkat?;* Coauthor, *Discover Sci-
ence Almanac*

SPACE BRIEFS

VAN RYZIN, Robert
Editor, *Coins* magazine; Author, *Striking Impressions: A Visual Guide to Collecting U.S. Coins*

COIN COLLECTING

IN THE PAGES OF THIS BOOK . . .

How closely did you follow the events of 2006? Do you remember the people who made news during the year? What about the trends—what was in and what was out? Who won in sports? What were the top songs, films, and television shows? What important anniversaries were celebrated? All these helped to make up your world in 2006—a year that was like no other.

Here's a quiz that will tell you how much you know about your world—about what took place during the past year and about other things, as well. If you're stumped by a question, don't worry. You'll find all the answers in the pages of this book. (The page numbers after the questions will tell you where to look.)

In January 2006 (Sandra Day O'Connor/ Samuel A. Alito, Jr./Henry M. Paulson) became a U.S. Supreme Court Associate Justice. (*18; 70*)

In August, the team from _____ won the 2006 Little League World Series. (*183*)

Which TV stars won Emmy Awards in 2006 for best actor and actress in a drama series? (*272*)

In February, adventurer Steve Fossett set a new world record for the longest nonstop unrefueled flight in a plane called (*WorldSpan/GlobalFlyer/Spirit of Bournemouth*). (*20*)

In April, Hu Jintao, the president of _____, met with President George W. Bush in the White House. (*24*)

Which National League baseball team won its tenth World Series in October? (*180*)

The 125th anniversary of the assassination of President (James A. Garfield/Abraham Lincoln/John F. Kennedy) was marked in 2006. (*216*)

The year 2006 celebrated the 75th year in which "The Star-Spangled Banner" was the official national anthem of the United States. "The Star-Spangled Banner" was written during the War of _____ . (*228*)

How many times has ice-skater Sasha Cohen won the gold medal at the U.S. Figure Skating Championships? (*194*)

Rufus, a colored (collie/Irish setter/bull terrier), was named America's top dog at the Westminster Kennel Club dog show in February. (*97*)

The 2006 Winter Olympic Games were held in the city of Turin, in the country of _____ . (*20, 168*)

What is noteworthy about the passenger ship *Freedom of the Seas,* which was christened in May? (*27*)

(*Whittington/Criss Cross/Rosa*), a novel about teenage friends in a small town, won the 2006 Newbery Medal as the best American book for young readers. (*300*)

In 2006, scientists announced that Pluto would no longer be considered a true planet. They said it will now be called a _____ planet. (*32, 135*)

In June, 13-year-old Katharine Close won the 2006 Scripps National Spelling Bee by spelling the word "ursprache." What does the word mean? (*245*)

In July, the United States, Canada, and Mexico designated 13 wildlife refuges to protect (viceroy/swallowtail/monarch) butterflies along their migration route. (*99*)

The Miami _____ defeated the Dallas Mavericks to win the 2006 National Basketball Association title. (*184*)

In 2006, a cable network devoted to music videos celebrated its 25th anniversary. Can you name that network? (*285*)

April 18 marked the 100th anniversary of the (Chicago/Boston/San Francisco) earthquake. (*124*)

In June, President George W. Bush created the world's largest protected marine area, in waters near the U.S. state of _____ . (*29*)

In 2006, Montenegro declared its independence from Serbia, making it the world's youngest nation. Both Montenegro and Serbia had been part of what country? (*28, 318, 319*)

In March, the U.S. government issued a newly designed ($5/$10/$20) bill. (*23*)

The 2006 Academy Award for Best Motion Picture went to _____ . (*260*)

The National Baseball Hall of Fame's first female inductee was chosen in 2006. Can you name her? (*69*)

On June 12, Senator (Robert C. Byrd/Joe Lieberman/Hillary Clinton) became the longest-serving senator in U.S. history—having served 17,327 days. (*71*)

The documentary film *An Inconvenient Truth,* produced by former Democratic senator and presidential candidate Al Gore, was about the threat of global _____ . (*113, 267*)

A made-for-TV musical on the Disney Channel turned into a worldwide hit in 2006. Name the movie. (*252, 280*)

Golfer (Jim Furyk/Phil Mickelson/Tiger Woods) won both the British Open and the PGA Championship in 2006. (*190*)

On May 1, New York City's most famous skyscraper, the _____, celebrated its 75th anniversary. (*222*)

In the November midterm elections, which political party won control of the U.S. Congress for the first time in twelve years? (*39*)

At the end of 2006, about 140,000 U.S. troops were still in the country of (Iran/Lebanon/Iraq). (*42*)

Roger Federer, the top-ranked male tennis player, won three Grand Slam singles events in 2006—Wimbledon, the Australian Open, and _____ . (*196*)

The Whiskers family—a family of animals—starred on TV during the year. What kind of animals were they? (*85*)

In 2006, Americans celebrated the 300th anniversary of the birth of the great American statesman, scientist, inventor, and writer (Thomas Jefferson/James Madison/Benjamin Franklin). (*202*)

In October, the Asian country of _____ announced it had tested a nuclear bomb. (*36, 60*)

At the 2006 Kids' Choice Awards, which TV show did 25 million kids select as their favorite? (*243*)

The Census Bureau announced that the U.S. population had reached (200/300/400) million on October 17, 2006. (*36*)

On December 31, Kofi Annan of Ghana retired as Secretary-General of the United Nations. He was replaced on January 1, 2007, by Ban Ki-moon of _____ . (*36, 68*)

THE WORLD IN 2006

Travelers wait at Gatwick Airport, outside London, on August 10, 2006, after British officials disrupted a terrorist plot. The terrorists had planned to blow up planes flying to the United States. Inset: Containers of liquids and gels were confiscated at airports in the United States. Officials banned all liquids and gels from carry-on luggage because the terrorists had planned to smuggle liquid bombs onto planes in such containers.

THE YEAR AT A GLANCE

War in Iraq, threats of international terrorism and the spread of nuclear weapons, and a humanitarian tragedy in the African nation of Sudan were some of the problems facing the world in 2006. There was growing alarm, too, about the continued warming of the world's climate. But the year also had many high points and memorable moments.

THE WAR IN IRAQ

Concern over the future of Iraq was rising in 2006. Three years after a U.S. invasion drove Iraqi dictator Saddam Hussein from power, violence still plagued the country. The Iraqi government couldn't rein in the conflict. Nor could the United States, which still had 140,000 troops stationed in Iraq.

Iraqis had gone to the polls in December 2005 and had chosen a new parliament, the first under a new democratic constitution. The results, announced early in 2006, gave the most seats to Shi'ite Muslims, the country's largest ethnic group. But the Shi'ites still needed the support of other groups— Sunni Muslims and Kurds—to govern. It took months to form a "national unity" government that included those groups. Despite this encouraging step, there was a sharp increase in violence during the year.

Sunni Muslim rebels and foreign-born terrorists attacked U.S. soldiers and Iraqi security forces. Increasingly, they used car bombs and other terrorist tactics that targeted Iraqi civilians. And there was growing conflict between Sunnis and Shi'ites. Shi'te militias roamed the streets in some areas, carrying out revenge killings. The conviction of Saddam Hussein for crimes against humanity and his execution, on December 30, didn't lessen the violence. Iraq seemed to be heading toward civil war.

The continuing violence—and the inability of Iraqi or U.S. leaders to control it—led to a broad debate over the course of U.S. policy. On one side, there were those who urged the U.S. government to begin withdrawing troops. This, they hoped, might force the Iraqis to take charge of their future. On the other side, some people thought the United States should send more troops to stop the fighting. And there were many proposals that fell somewhere between the two extremes. All were still being debated at year's end.

THE THREAT OF TERRORISM

The U.S. government viewed the war in Iraq as a key part of its war on terrorism. However, the war also fueled the anger of Islamic radicals—and that was producing more potential terrorists. Islamic militants staged attacks around the world in 2006. British authorities thwarted what might have been the most serious of these plots. In August, they arrested a group of people—most British-born Muslims—who were planning to blow up passenger planes flying from Great Britain to the United States.

Afghanistan has been a front in the war on terror ever since the terrorist group Al Qaeda staged the September 11, 2001, terrorist attacks against the United States. After the attacks, the United States invaded Afghanistan. The goal was to destroy Al Qaeda, which was based there, and drive out the Taliban, the Islamic militia that ruled most of Afghanistan and had sheltered the terrorists. The Taliban was driven from power, and Afghanistan seemed on the way to democracy. But in 2006 the situation seemed to be taking a turn for the worse. Al Qaeda's leaders were still at large, hiding along the Afghanistan-Pakistan border. And the Taliban was trying for a comeback, mounting a growing number of attacks against Western and Afghan forces.

The rise of radical Islam also gave a new twist to the long-running conflict between Israel and the Palestinian Arabs. The conflict dates to 1948, when Israel was founded as a Jewish homeland in the mostly Arab territory of Palestine. Between bouts of fighting, there has been some progress toward peace. Palestinians have achieved self-government in the West Bank and the Gaza Strip, territories Israel has controlled since 1967. But in January 2006, Palestinians elected a new parliament, and the results of the vote took most of the world by surprise. Hamas, a radical Islamic party and terrorist group, gained control of the legislature. Hamas has sworn to destroy Israel and has carried out many terrorist attacks against Israelis, so this ended any hope of immediate peace.

Hezbollah, a radical Shi'ite group based in Lebanon, set off a conflict with Israel by kidnapping two Israeli soldiers in July. Israeli airstrikes, troops, and

tanks struck back at Hezbollah inside Lebanon. A U.N.-sponsored truce stopped the conflict after a month. Hezbollah then began a bid for more power in Lebanon. In December, the group's members took to the streets, demanding that the elected government resign.

Iran, a major backer of Hezbollah and other radical groups, caused concern in 2006 when it ignored a U.N. demand to suspend its nuclear program. Iran insisted that the program was aimed at producing fuel for nuclear-power plants. But most people thought the goal was nuclear weapons. If Iran had such weapons, it might use them against Israel or give them to terrorists.

OTHER WORLD EVENTS

Nuclear weapons also put North Korea in the news. In October, the North Koreans announced that they had tested a nuclear bomb. As with Iran, the concern was that North Korea might sell nuclear weapons to terrorists or use them against neighboring countries, such as South Korea and Japan. The

U.N. Security Council condemned the test and imposed economic sanctions against North Korea.

Darfur, a dry corner of the African nation of Sudan, was the scene of a continuing tragedy. Fighting there pitted government troops and Arab militias against non-Arab rebels. And the region's non-Arab civilians were the victims of atrocious violence and hardship. As the death toll mounted, aid agencies struggled to help tens of thousands of refugees. The conflict seemed likely to spill over into neighboring countries.

While wars and crises grabbed headlines during the year, a number of worrisome trends also came in for attention. The worldwide climate change called global warming was one. Scientists pointed to mounting evidence that Earth's climate was warming rapidly. And they said that people were driving the trend through the use of gasoline, oil, coal, and other fossil fuels. These fuels produce carbon dioxide and other gases that trap the heat in the atmosphere. Experts warned that unless people take major steps to conserve energy and change to new technologies, the effects could be devastating.

Avian influenza, or bird flu, was another worldwide concern. Although the disease primarily affects birds, health officials worried that it might begin to spread rapidly among people. That might set off a worldwide epidemic, or pandemic. Officials kept a close eye on outbreaks in 2006.

After ten years as Secretary-General of the United Nations, Kofi Annan retired at the end of the year. U.N. members chose South Korean statesman Ban Ki-moon to succeed the diplomat from Ghana.

IN THE UNITED STATES AND CANADA

Canadian voters also chose new leadership in 2006. The Conservative Party defeated the Liberal Party in parliamentary elections in January, so Conservative leader Stephen Harper replaced Liberal leader Paul Martin as prime minister.

The war in Iraq was a major issue in U.S. congressional elections in November. Voters were dissatisfied with the way President George W. Bush and the Republican administration had handled the war. At the polls, voters gave Democrats control of both houses of Congress for the first time in twelve years. Representative

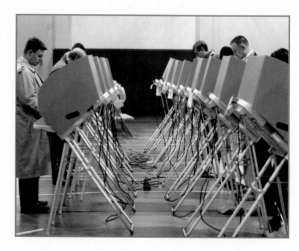

Nancy Pelosi of California, the Democratic leader in the House of Representatives, became the first woman in U.S. history to be chosen as Speaker of the House. Democrats also made big gains at the state level, replacing Republicans as governors of six states. And they picked up almost 300 seats in state legislatures.

The war wasn't the only issue that caused controversy in the months leading up to the election. Congress debated several new proposals that would tighten control of U.S. borders. The goal was to stop immigrants from entering the country without official approval. But in the end, no bill was passed.

Parts of the U.S. Gulf Coast were still recovering from Hurricane Katrina, which devastated the region in August 2005. Rebuilding was slow, especially in the city of New Orleans, which had suffered severe flooding. Many people were unable to return to their damaged homes.

ON THE BRIGHT SIDE

Construction of the *International Space Station* (*ISS*) resumed for the first time since 2003, when the loss of the space-shuttle *Columbia* caused the United States to ground its shuttle fleet. In July, September, and December 2006, shuttles completed successful missions to the space station.

Special events and exhibitions honored several major anniversaries in 2006. The year marked the 400th birthday of the famous Dutch artist Rembrandt van Rijn and the 250th birthday of the great composer Wolfgang Amadeus Mozart. And Americans celebrated the 300th birthday of Benjamin Franklin, the multi-talented patriot who helped found the United States.

The entertainment industry continued to adapt to new technology. Digital recording, the Internet, and other developments were changing the way artists produced and distributed their movies, TV shows, and music to audiences. And just five years after its introduction in 2001, the iPod was everywhere. People liked the ease with which this and similar MP3 players let them download music from the Internet and take it with them wherever they went.

The 20th Winter Olympic Games brought competitors and spectators from all over the world to Turin, Italy, in February. Athletes from 80 countries took part. Germany took home the most medals, 29, including 11 gold. Americans won 25 medals, 9 of them gold. The Americans excelled in the snowboarding events, winning three of the six gold medals. Canadians won 24 medals, including 7 gold. Canadian speed-skater Cindy Klassen won an amazing five medals. This was more than any other Canadian had ever won in a single Winter Olympics.

JANUARY

12 More than 360 Muslim pilgrims died in a human stampede near Mecca, Saudi Arabia. Hundreds more were injured. They were on their annual weeklong *hajj*, or pilgrimage, to the Muslim holy city.

23 In Canada's parliamentary elections, the Conservative Party defeated the Liberal Party, which had governed Canada for 13 years. Following the elections, Conservative leader Stephen Harper became prime minister. He succeeded Paul Martin, who had been prime minister since 2003.

25 Hamas, a radical Islamic party considered a terrorist group by many Western nations, won the parliamentary elections in Palestine's West Bank and Gaza Strip. Hamas took 76 of the 132 seats in the legislature, making it the dominant party in the Palestine National Authority (PNA). (Hamas leader Ismail Haniya was chosen prime minister of the PNA on February 19.)

31 Samuel A. Alito, Jr., a federal appeals court judge of Philadelphia, was confirmed by the U.S. Senate as a Supreme Court Associate Justice. He replaced Sandra Day O'Connor, who had served on the High Court since 1981.

Government changes in January: In national elections in **Chile,** Michelle Bachelet was elected president. She replaced Ricardo Lagos Escobar, who had been president since 2000. . . .In **Kuwait,** Sabah al-Ahmad al-Jabir al-Sabah was named emir and head of state. He replaced Jabir al-Ahmad al-Sabah, who

Hundreds of thousands of Muslim pilgrims pray at a mosque in the holy city of Mecca, during their weeklong *hajj* in January. Every year, Muslims come from all over the world for the ritual.

President George W. Bush delivers his sixth State of the Union address to Congress. Behind him are Vice President Dick Cheney (left) and Speaker of the House Dennis Hastert.

President George Bush's State of the Union Address

"Tonight the state of our Union is strong—and together we will make it stronger." That was the message President George W. Bush brought to the U.S. Congress on January 31, in his 2006 State of the Union address. The State of the Union address, which is given every year to Congress, is a chance for the president to outline his plans for the year ahead. Here are some highlights of Bush's address:

World affairs: Bush said that the United States was committed to ending tyranny around the world, calling "radical Islam" the greatest threat to freedom. He called for more democracy in the Middle East, and he warned the government of Iran not to seek nuclear weapons. Regarding Iraq, he said, "We must keep our word, defeat our enemies, and stand behind the American military in this vital mission."

Finances: The president said that short-term tax cuts passed earlier in his presidency had helped make the U.S. economy healthy, and he called on Congress to make the tax cuts permanent. Yet tax cuts and the cost of the Iraq war had created huge deficits in the federal budget. The president asked Congress to cut or end more than 140 government programs to help close the gap.

Energy and education: Bush called for more research into new energy technologies to help cut the need for foreign oil. And calling for more focus on math and science in schools, he proposed training 70,000 high-school teachers to lead advanced-placement courses in those subjects.

had been emir since 1977. . . .In **Portugal,** Anibal António Cavaco Silva was elected president. He succeeded Jorge Sampaio, who had held the position since 1996. . . .In **Taiwan,** Su Tseng-chang was appointed premier. He succeeded Frank Hsieh, who had been premier since 2005.

FEBRUARY

3 More than 1,000 people died when an Egyptian ferry sank in the Red Sea while traveling between Saudi Arabia and Egypt. It was the worst maritime disaster in Egyptian history.

11 Adventurer Steve Fossett set a new world record for the longest non-stop, unrefueled flight. Flying in the *GlobalFlyer*, a lightweight experimental plane, Fossett flew from the Kennedy Space Center in Florida to Bournemouth, England—a distance of 25,766 miles (41,467 kilometers). His time in the air was 76 hours, 42 minutes, 55 seconds. Fossett has broken 110 world records in airplanes, balloons, gliders, and ships.

17 The village of Guinsaugon, in Southern Leyte, the Philippines, was wiped out by a huge mudslide. In some places, the mud was 115 feet (35 meters) deep. About 1,000 people were killed.

26 The 20th Winter Olympic Games ended in Turin, Italy, after 16 days of competition. German athletes won the most medals (29), followed by the United States (25), Canada (24), Austria (23), and Russia (22).

Government changes in February: In **Haiti,** René Garcia Préval was elected president. He succeeded Boniface Alexandre, who had been president since 2004. . . .Feleti Sevele was appointed premier of **Tonga.** He replaced Lavaka ata Ulukalala, who had been premier since 2000.

American adventurer Steve Fossett, who set yet another aviation record in February, poses with one of his Guinness World Records certificates.

Scientists have found dozens of new and rare species of plants and animals in a remote mountain area on the island of New Guinea. One of the animals was this rare golden-mantled tree kangaroo, which was so tame that scientists could pick it up and carry it back to their camp. Another was Berlepsch's six-wired bird of paradise (above), named for the six long, skinny, wirelike feathers on its head.

A Lost World—Found

Scientists from the United States, Indonesia, and Australia announced that they had discovered about 40 new animal and plant species on the island of New Guinea, in Southeast Asia. Rare tree kangaroos, mammals that lay eggs, birds and frogs never seen before—these are some of the wonders that were found in the island's Foja Mountains. Shrouded in mist and covered with tropical forests, these remote mountains are like a lost world.

The scientists had spent several weeks in late 2005 exploring the mountains, which are in the part of the island controlled by Indonesia. There are no roads into the region, so the scientists were dropped off by helicopter.

One of the scientists' biggest discoveries was a new bird species, a kind of honeyeater. It was the first new bird found in New Guinea since 1939. They also found several new mammals, four new butterflies, and 20 new frogs, including one less than half an inch (1.2 centimeters) long. They saw rhododendron plants with white flowers almost 6 inches (15 centimeters) across, the largest on record.

The scientists spotted Berlepsch's six-wired birds of paradise, birds so rare that they hadn't been seen in 100 years. They also saw a long-beaked echidna, a little mammal that's very unusual because it lays eggs. And they found the rare golden-mantled tree kangaroo, which had never been seen in Indonesia before.

There are probably many more rare plants and animals in the mountains, the scientists say. Their trip to this lost world shows how important it is to protect unspoiled wild places.

MARCH

4 U.S. President George W. Bush ended a four-day trip to South Asia. His first stop was in Afghanistan, where he met with that country's president, Hamid Karzai; and he visited the new U.S. embassy in Kabul, the nation's capital. In India, Bush and Indian Prime Minister Manmohan Singh announced a deal that would allow India to buy U.S. nuclear fuel and nuclear-reactor components. In return, India agreed to keep its military and civilian nuclear programs separate, and allow its civilian plants to be inspected. Bush's final stop was in Pakistan, where he urged President Pervez Musharraf to continue his fight against terrorism.

16 President George W. Bush nominated Idaho Governor Dirk Kempthorne as U.S. Secretary of the Interior. He replaced Gale Norton, who had been Interior Secretary since 2001. (Kempthorne was confirmed by the U.S. Senate on May 10.)

Government changes in March: In presidential elections in **Benin,** Yayi Boni was elected president. He replaced Mathieu Kerekou, who had been president from 1972 to 1991 and 1996 to 2006. . . .In **Israel,** following the parliamentary victory of his Kadima Party, Ehud Olmert became prime minister. (Olmert had been acting prime minister since January 4, after Prime Minister Ariel Sharon suffered a massive stroke. Sharon had been prime minister since 2001.). . . .In **Jamaica,** Portia Simpson Miller was appointed prime minister. She succeeded Percival J. Patterson, who had been prime minister since 1992.

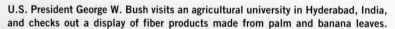

U.S. President George W. Bush visits an agricultural university in Hyderabad, India, and checks out a display of fiber products made from palm and banana leaves.

Does this new $10 bill look like a phony? The background colors of orange, yellow, and red and other security features are meant to discourage counterfeiters.

A New, Colorful $10 Bill

On March 2, the U.S. government issued a newly designed $10 bill—the third bill to be redesigned in the past several years. New $20 and $50 bills were issued in 2003 and 2004, and a new $100 bill is planned. The main purpose of the new bills is to stop counterfeiters.

The colors of the new bills are a break with tradition. U.S. currency was always green in the past. Now different colors are being used for different denominations. This will help people tell the bills apart, and it will make the bills harder to counterfeit.

The new $10 bill has background colors of pale orange, yellow, and red. On the face of the bill, the words "We the People" (from the U.S. Constitution) are printed in faint red in the background. Small yellow 10's appear in the background on both sides of the bill. Like the old ten, the new one has a portrait of Alexander Hamilton on its face, and the U.S. Treasury Building on the back. Hamilton was the first Secretary of the Treasury. The portrait has been moved up, and some details have been changed in both pictures.

Next to the portrait, a symbol of freedom—the torch carried by the Statue of Liberty—appears twice. It's in the background to the left of Hamilton's portrait and in a metallic red image to the right. Symbols of freedom had also been added to the redesigned $20 bill (the American eagle) and the $50 bill (the stars and stripes).

The new $10 bills have three security features. Each has a watermark—a faint image that's part of the paper—that you can see by holding the bill up to the light. The bill also has a security thread, a thin strip of plastic embedded in the paper. The thread shows the bill's denomination in tiny print. The third security feature is color-shifting ink. The numeral 10 in the lower right corner of the bill's face changes from copper to green when the bill is tilted. These three features are hard for counterfeiters to copy. If they aren't present, you know you have a phony ten!

APRIL

8 A mission to rotate crews aboard the *International Space Station* (*ISS*) ended as a Russian *Soyuz* spacecraft landed in Kazakhstan, in central Asia. The new *ISS* crew consisted of Pavel Vinogradov of Russia and Jeffrey Williams of the United States. Brazilian astronaut Marcos Pontes had accompanied them into space. But he returned to Earth eight days later with the former *ISS* crew, American astronaut William McArthur and Russian cosmonaut Valery Tokarev.

21 Chinese President Hu Jintao ended a four-day visit to the United States. His trip included a meeting with President George W. Bush at the White House. This was the first time a Chinese president had visited the White House since 1997. The two leaders discussed trade between the two nations and the Iranian and North Korean nuclear-weapons programs.

Government changes in April: Nouri Kamel al-Maliki was sworn in as premier of **Iraq.** He replaced Ibrahim al-Jaafari, who had been premier under the Iraqi provisional government since 2005. . . . Following parliamentary elections in **Italy,** Romano Prodi became premier. He replaced Silvio Berlusconi, who had been premier since 2001. . . .**In South Korea,** Han Myeong Sook was named premier, becoming that nation's first female leader. She replaced Lee Hai Chan, who had served since 2004.

TV-Turnoff Week was celebrated April 24–30. It was the twelfth time this event (which is sponsored by the nonprofit group TV-Turnoff Network) urged kids—and adults—to "Turn off TV, turn on life." On average, American kids are glued to the tube for 1,023 hours a year—more time than they spend in school! Couch-potato kids miss out on many things, in-cluding sports and other activities that burn calories and keep them from becoming overweight.

On the anniversary of the Chernobyl nuclear disaster, Ukrainians demonstrate against their country's plans to build 22 new nuclear power plants.

Chernobyl: Twenty Years After the Tragedy

On April 26, 1986, one of four nuclear reactors in the Chernobyl nuclear plant, in what was then the Soviet republic of Ukraine, exploded and caught fire. Radioactive dust spewed into the environment for ten days, contaminating large areas of the Soviet Union and northern Europe. It was the world's worst nuclear power plant disaster. The twentieth anniversary of that event was marked in April 2006.

Thirty-one people died at the site of the disaster, and 500 more were hospitalized. After the radioactive material spewed into the air, some of it settled to the earth in Ukraine and the neighboring republic of Russia, but hardest hit was the republic of Belarus. More than 300,000 people were forced to evacuate the heavily contaminated areas closest to the site.

The World Health Organization said that 9,000 people would probably die from exposure to the radiation. That number could be much higher—it may never be known precisely how many people have died prematurely or suffered illnesses as a result of the accident.

In Kiev, the capital of the now-independent country of Ukraine, church bells tolled twenty times beginning at 1:23 in the morning of April 26, 2006. That was the exact time the Chernobyl nuclear reactor had exploded twenty years earlier. Memorials and candlelight vigils were held throughout the country, as well as in Belarus and Russia. And scientists gathered for a three-day conference to discuss what could be learned from the Chernobyl disaster.

"Chernobyl must not be a mourning place," said Ukrainian President Viktor Yushchenko at one memorial service. "It must become a place of hope."

MAY

8 President George W. Bush named U.S. Air Force Lieutenant General Michael Hayden as head of the Central Intelligence Agency (CIA). Hayden replaced Porter Goss, who had resigned.

13 U.S. Secretary of State Condoleezza Rice stated that the United States would restore full diplomatic relations with Libya. The move came after Libya announced it would halt its nuclear-weapons program. Rice also said that Libya would be removed from the State Department list of countries that sponsor terrorism. The United States had broken off diplomatic relations with Libya in 1980.

27 A powerful earthquake struck central Java in Indonesia. The quake caused massive destruction, killing more than 6,200 people and leaving 1.5 million people homeless.

30 President George W. Bush nominated Henry M. Paulson, Jr., as U.S. Secretary of the Treasury. Paulson, the head of the investment bank Goldman Sachs, replaced John Snow, who had held the position since 2003. (Paulson was confirmed by the U.S. Senate on June 28.)

Government changes in May: In **Comoros**, Ahmed Abdallah Mohamed Sambi won the presidential election. He replaced Azaly Assoumani, who had been the leader of the country since 1999. . . .Following national elections in **Costa Rica**, Oscar Arias Sanchez (winner of the 1987 Nobel Peace Prize) was sworn in as president. He succeeded Abel Pacheco, who had served since 2002. . . . In the **Solomon Islands**, Manasseh Sogavare became prime minister. He replaced Allan Kemakeza, who had held the office since 2001.

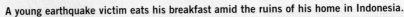

A young earthquake victim eats his breakfast amid the ruins of his home in Indonesia.

Freedom of the Seas, the largest passenger ship in the world, makes its way down New York Harbor after being christened. At right, visitors tour the cruise ship's luxurious promenade.

Freedom of the Seas

Freedom of the Seas—the world's largest passenger ship—was christened on May 12, 2006. The ceremony was held at Bayonne, New Jersey, south of the Statue of Liberty in New York Harbor. (The ship's maiden voyage, from Miami to the Caribbean, began on June 9.)

Freedom of the Seas grabbed the title "world's largest ship" from the *Queen Mary 2*, which had made its maiden voyage in January 2005. *Freedom* is 18 decks high and 1,111.5 feet (338.8 meters) long. It can carry 4,000 passengers, compared to the *QM2's* 3,000.

This colossal ship was built for Royal Caribbean International—at a cost of $947 million. Much of that money was spent on spectacular amenities for those who want to cruise in luxury. The ship boasts flat-screen TV's in every stateroom, shipwide wi-fi capabilities, a water park, a rock-climbing wall, an ice-skating rink, a miniature golf course, a basketball court, and a boxing ring. Kids will enjoy the H2O Zone, a pool area featuring spray cannons, water jets, and interactive fountains.

There are other huge ships ahead for the 10 million North Americans who take cruises every year. *Liberty of the Seas*, the sister ship of *Freedom of the Seas*, will be completed in 2007. And a third Royal Caribbean ship, *Independence of the Seas*, is scheduled to be launched in 2008.

JUNE

3 Montenegro declared its independence from Serbia. They were the last two of the former Yugoslavia's six republics to remain united after the other republics declared their independence in 1991 and 1992. The people of Montenegro had voted for independence on May 21.

13 President George W. Bush made a brief surprise visit to Baghdad, the capital of war-torn Iraq. He met with Iraq's new premier, Nouri Kamel al-Maliki, and his Cabinet in a show of support, and he addressed a crowd of civilians and U.S. military personnel.

21 President George W. Bush met in Vienna, Austria, with Austrian Chancellor Wolfgang Schuessel and other leaders of the European Union (EU). They discussed international trade, ways to prevent Iran from building nuclear weapons, and the U.S. prison camp for terrorists at Guantanamo Bay, Cuba. Bush then flew to Budapest, Hungary, to take part in the 50th commemoration of the 1956 Hungarian uprising against the Soviet Union's domination of that country.

Government changes in June: Geir H. Haarde was named premier of **Iceland.** He succeeded Halldor Asgrimsson, who had been premier since 2004. . . .In **Laos,** Choummaly Sayasone was appointed president; he replaced Khamtai Siphan-

The shells of tiny mollusks—like the ones shown below—are common today. On June 23, archaeologists announced that the same kinds of shells had been found in Israel and Algeria. But these shells were 100,000 years old, and they had been used as decorative beads. The two shells found in Israel (inset; four views of each shell) had holes in them. Scientists believe the holes were made so the shells could be strung together into necklaces. The scientists said this meant that modern human behavior, such as the wearing of ornamentation, developed earlier than had been thought.

Protecting Hawaii's Marine Life

On June 15, President George W. Bush signed a proclamation creating the Northwestern Hawaiian Islands Marine National Monument. By doing this, he created the world's largest protected marine area.

The new national monument is the largest conservation region in the United States. It covers an area of 140,000 square miles (363,000 square kilometers). That's larger than every state in the United States except Alaska, California, Montana, and Texas. The monument stretches from Nihoa Island, near the main islands of Hawaii, northwest to Kure Atoll, a distance of nearly 1,400 miles (2,250 kilometers). It includes ten islands and atolls and the surrounding waters, reefs, and shoals. One of the atolls, Midway, isn't part of the Northwestern Hawaiian Islands, but it's part of the national monument.

Bush's plan for the national monument included a number of major conservation measures. It immediately banned the dumping of waste in the region, and the extraction of resources other than fish. Commercial and sport fishing will be phased out by 2011.

The waters surrounding the Northwestern Hawaiian Islands contain the country's largest coral-reef system. Animals found there include whales, dolphins, seals, and sea lions, as well as a variety of marine birds, reptiles, and fish. The huge coral-reef system is also a nesting ground to more than 7,000 species of animals, including the endangered Hawaiian monk seal and the threatened Hawaiian Islands green sea turtle. A quarter of the species can't be found anywhere else on Earth.

Animal life on the Northwestern Hawaiian Islands: a family of Laysan albatross, a blue parrotfish, a Hawaiian monk seal.

don, who had held the office since 1998. Bouasone Bouphavanh was appointed premier; he replaced Boungnang Volachit, who had served since 2001....In national elections in **Peru,** Alan García was elected president. He succeeded Alejandro Toledo, who had served since 2001....In **Vietnam,** Nguyen Tan Dung was named premier. He succeeded Phan Van Khai, who had been premier since 1997.

JULY

12 Violence erupted along the Israel-Lebanon border when Hezbollah, a militant Shi'ite organization, attacked Israel. Hezbollah forces killed eight Israeli soldiers and captured two more. Israel retaliated with air, sea, and artillery bombardments against Hezbollah strongholds and other targets in southern Lebanon, and Hezbollah fired hundreds of rockets into northern Israel. Israeli troops then entered Lebanon, and fighting raged through the end of the month.

17 The space shuttle *Discovery* completed a 13-day mission to the *International Space Station* (*ISS*). The *Discovery* crew consisted of Commander Steve Lindsey, pilot Mark Kelly, and mission specialists Mike Fossum, Lisa Nowak, Stephanie Wilson, and Piers Sellers. German astronaut Thomas Reiter was also aboard. He stayed on the *ISS*, joining Pavel Vinogradov of Russia and Jeffrey Williams of the United States.

17 A powerful earthquake in the Indian Ocean triggered a tsunami that crashed ashore on the southern coast of the Indonesian island of Java. The large, rapidly moving ocean wave killed more than 600 people.

17 Leaders of the major industrialized nations, known as the Group of Eight (G-8), ended a three-day meeting in St. Petersburg, Russia. This was the first time that a G-8 meeting had been held in Russia. The G-8 consists of Canada, France, Germany, Great Britain, Italy, Japan, Russia, and the United States. The group's discussions focused on energy, especially high oil prices; world trade; and infectious diseases such as bird flu.

Government changes in July: In general elections in **Mexico**, Felipe Calderón was elected president. (Because of the closeness of the vote and a protest by his opponent, Calderón wasn't formally declared president until September.)

Leaders of the Group of Eight attend a meeting at Konstantinovsky Palace, outside St. Petersburg, Russia.

The summer heat wave caused numerous power outages. Here, a freeway traffic sign in Los Angeles urges people to save energy.

A Record Heat Wave

Beginning in mid-July and continuing into August, record high temperatures scorched most of the United States and much of southern Canada. More than 200 people died in the United States, about half of them in California.

California was the state hardest hit. There, in Death Valley, the thermometer hit 125°F (52°C) on July 17! The heat wave then traveled east and north. In the northern plains states, it blistered Bismarck, North Dakota, with temperatures as high as 112°F (44°C). And in Canada, Lytton, British Columbia, suffered through three straight days of heat that topped 107°F (42°C).

Other cities affected included Phoenix, Arizona (118°F/48°C); Woodland Hills, California (119°F/48°C); and New York City (110°F/43°C).

In many areas, the intense heat was accompanied by windstorms and thunderstorms, causing significant damage. Water lines ruptured, roads buckled, and power generators failed. Hundreds of thousands of people went without power—and without air conditioning.

Europe didn't escape the heat wave. That continent's heat wave, which began at the end of June, also reached triple-digit numbers in July in some countries. Hardest hit were Great Britain, the Netherlands, Belgium, Germany, and Ireland, where July was the hottest month ever recorded.

Calderón replaced Vicente Fox Quesada, who had been president since 2000. . . .In **Poland**, Jaroslaw Kaczynski, the twin brother of President Lech Kaczynski, was named premier. He replaced Kazimierz Marcinkiewicz, who had been premier since 2005.

31

AUGUST

10   A typhoon struck China's southeastern provinces of Zhejiang, Fujian, and Jiangxi. The heavy rains and winds of more than 170 miles (274 kilometers) an hour killed more than 400 people. The storm also sank 1,000 ships and destroyed some 50,000 houses. Total damage was estimated at $1.5 billion.

10–11   British law-enforcement officers arrested 24 people, most of them British-born Muslims. They were accused of planning to blow up airplanes flying from Great Britain to the United States.

24   The International Astronomical Union (IAU) announced that Pluto was no longer classified as a true, or classic, planet. It was given the new designation of "dwarf planet."

Government changes in August: As a result of parliamentary elections in the **Czech Republic**, Mirek Topolanek became premier. He succeeded Jiri Paroubek, who had served as premier since 2005. . . .Following parliamentary elections in **Tuvalu**, Apisai Ielemia was named prime minister. He replaced Maatia Toafa, who had held the office since 2004.

In London's Trafalgar Square, newspapers headlined the terrorist plot to blow up aircraft flying from Great Britain to the United States. Authorities said it would have been the deadliest terrorist attack since September 11, 2001.

Hurricane Katrina: One Year Later

A year after Hurricane Katrina cut a swath of destruction along the U.S. Gulf Coast, much of the region was still struggling to rebuild. And tens of thousands of people who had fled the August 29, 2005, storm still couldn't return to their homes.

Workers had cleared away tons of debris in storm-damaged areas, but the cleanup had gone faster in some areas than in others. In Biloxi and Gulfport, Mississippi, for example, many neighborhoods were quickly ready to rebuild. But people faced special challenges in New Orleans, Louisiana, which sits below sea level.

Katrina had breached the levee system that protects New Orleans from flooding. Floodwaters had covered 80 percent of the city and wrecked entire city blocks in low-lying, mostly poor areas. City officials said that 5,500 homes and businesses would have to be torn down because hurricane damage had made them unsafe.

The levees were repaired, but people worried whether they would be able to withstand future storms. At least some of the breaches had resulted from serious flaws in the design and construction of the levees.

One year after the devastation caused by Hurricane Katrina, workers were still cleaning up in New Orleans. And the population of the city had dropped by nearly 60 percent.

But the picture wasn't all grim. By August 2006, federal aid had begun to reach Gulf Coast homeowners to help them rebuild. And while the population of New Orleans was still less than half what it had been before the storm, the city was coming back to life. Roads and bridges were repaired, many businesses reopened, and tourists were returning. And a number of schools reopened.

Officials said the full cost of rebuilding along the Gulf Coast might eventually be as high as $300 billion. And some areas might never be rebuilt. Experts question whether it makes sense to build in areas that are at high risk for storms and floods.

SEPTEMBER

5 President George W. Bush nominated Mary E. Peters, a former administrator of the Federal Highway Administration (FHWA), to be U.S. Secretary of Transportation. She replaced Norman Y. Mineta, who had served in that office since 2001. (The U.S. Senate confirmed Peters's appointment on September 30.)

21 Scientists announced that they had found the 3.3-million-year-old fossil remains of a 3-year-old girl. They were the earliest, best-preserved remains of an early human child ever found. The fossil, found in Ethiopia, belongs to the species *Australopithecus afarensis*. That's the same species as the fossil known as Lucy, which was discovered in 1974 and is the most famous fossil of an early human. The new fossil was nicknamed "Lucy's Baby."

21 A 12-day mission to the *International Space Station* (*ISS*) ended when the space shuttle *Atlantis* returned to Kennedy Space Center. The purpose of the mission was to bring new parts for the construction of the *ISS*. The *Atlantis* crew consisted of Commander Brent Jett, pilot Chris Ferguson, mission specialists Joseph Tanner, Daniel Burbank, Heidemarie Stefanyshyn-Piper, and Canadian astronaut Steven MacLean.

30 By the end of the month, nearly 200 people had become ill and three had died after eating fresh bagged spinach that was contaminated with *E. coli* bacteria. The spinach had been grown and processed in the Salinas Valley in California.

Government changes in September: In **Japan,** the parliament elected Shinzo Abe as premier. He succeeded Junichiro Koizumi, who had been premier since 2001. . . In national elections in **Sweden,** Fredrik Reinfeldt was elected premier. He replaced

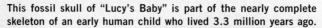

This fossil skull of "Lucy's Baby" is part of the nearly complete skeleton of an early human child who lived 3.3 million years ago.

IN LOVING MEMORY OF THE BRAVE AND INNOCENT LIVES LOST ON SEPTEMBER 11, 2001

Five years later: A banner near Ground Zero displaying the names of victims reminds people to "Never Forget" September 11, 2001. Inset: A drawing of the proposed Freedom Tower and three new skyscrapers.

September 11, 2006:
A Day of Remembrance

Americans observed a day of remembrance on September 11, 2006, the fifth anniversary of the 9/11 terrorist attacks. On that date in 2001, terrorists hijacked four passenger jets, crashing two of them into the World Trade Center in New York City, destroying the twin towers. The third plane struck the Pentagon outside of Washington, D.C., and the fourth went down in a field in Pennsylvania. Altogether, about 3,000 people were killed.

Solemn ceremonies were held at the three sites to mark the anniversary. Friends and family members of the victims heard tributes to those who had died and listened as their names were read aloud. Thousands gathered in lower Manhattan at Ground Zero, the site where the twin towers once stood. They observed two moments of silence, 17 minutes apart, marking the precise times that the terrorists had flown the hijacked planes into the twin towers.

Originally the World Trade Center had seven buildings at the site, including the twin towers. All seven were destroyed in the attack or were so heavily damaged that they were later torn down. The site is still mostly empty. But one building, 7 World Trade Center, has been rebuilt. Construction has started on two others: the Freedom Tower, which will eventually rise 1,776 feet; and a modern Transportation Hub. And designs for three more skyscrapers were unveiled in time for the fifth anniversary.

Göran Persson, who had been premier since 1996. . . .In **Thailand,** Premier Thaksin Shinawatra was overthrown in a military coup. He was replaced by retired Army Commander Surayud Chulanont. . . .In **Tonga,** Crown Prince Tupouto'a became King George Tupou V upon the death of his father, King Taufa'ahau Tupou IV, who had been king since 1965.

OCTOBER

9   North Korea set off an underground nuclear test, despite being warned against such an action by the United Nations Security Council. It was the first such test since 1998, when both Pakistan and India detonated a number of underground nuclear weapons. The Security Council voted 15–0 to place sanctions on North Korea.

13   Ban Ki-moon of South Korea was named the next Secretary-General of the United Nations, for a five-year term. He will replace Kofi Annan on January 1, 2007.

15   A 6.7-magnitude earthquake struck Hawaii. Centered off the western shore of Hawaii Island, the quake caused property damage, landslides, and power outages. There were some injuries, but no deaths were reported.

16   Russian and American scientists announced that they had created a new element—Element 118 on the periodic table of elements. It's the heaviest element ever made. Scientists hope this will help them learn more about the nature of atoms.

Government change in October: In general elections in **Estonia,** Toomas Hendrik Ilves was named president. He replaced Arnold Ruutel, who had been president since 2001.

According to the U.S. Census Bureau, the population of the United States hit 300 million on October 17, at 7:46 A.M. The Census Bureau based its calculations on the fact that a baby is born every 7 seconds, someone dies every 13 seconds, and an immigrant enters the country every 31 seconds.

The 2006 Nobel Prizes

Chemistry: Roger D. Kornberg of the United States for his studies of how genes instruct cells to produce proteins. Kornberg showed how information from genes is copied into molecules called messenger RNA. The RNA molecules carry the information to the cells' protein-making machinery. Proteins enable the cell to carry out its functions. Defects in the protein-making process are involved in illnesses such as heart disease and cancer. (Kornberg's father, Arthur, shared the 1959 Nobel medicine prize for earlier studies of genetic information.)

Economics: Edmund S. Phelps of the United States for his work in explaining the interaction of wages, unemployment, and inflation. The explanation says that wages and inflation tend to rise together, pushing each other up, until the unemployment rate reaches a "natural" level. Then prices no longer rise. Governments use this idea in setting interest rates and other policies.

Literature: Orhan Pamuk of Turkey for his novels. In works such as *Snow* and *My Name Is Red,* the Nobel committee said, Pamuk "created new symbols for the clash and interlacing of cultures." Pamuk is as well known for his political stands as for his lyrical prose. In 2005 he faced trial for "insulting Turkishness" for comments he made about Turkey's treatment of Armenians during World War I. The charges were dropped in January 2006.

Turkish writer Orhan Pamukwon won the Nobel Prize for Literature. He is shown here in front of a poster of himself.

Peace: Muhammad Yunus of Bangladesh and his Grameen Bank for their "efforts to create economic and social development from below." Yunus and the bank pioneered microcredit—tiny loans—as a tool for fighting poverty. Since 1974 the bank has given millions of such loans to impoverished Bangladeshis. The loans have allowed people to buy livestock, tools, and other things they need to make a living. The program has become a model for other developing countries. "Lasting peace cannot be achieved unless large population groups find ways in which to break out of poverty," the Nobel committee said.

Physics: John C. Mather and George F. Smoot of the United States for work that shed light on the origin of the universe. Mather and Smoot discovered patterns of background cosmic radiation that appear to confirm what scientists have long suspected—that the universe was born in a gigantic explosion, the Big Bang. Their work has also allowed better understanding of how galaxies and stars first formed.

Physiology or Medicine: Andrew Z. Fire and Craig C. Mello of the United States for discovering how to block the effects of specific genes. The method they discovered, called RNA interference, occurs naturally. It takes place when certain molecules in cells cause the destruction of messenger RNA from a specific gene. That gene's instructions thus don't reach the cell's protein-making machinery. The discovery has opened a new route for the treatment of diseases such as AIDS, heart disease, and cancer.

NOVEMBER

8 President George W. Bush named Robert M. Gates to be Secretary of Defense. Gates replaced Donald Rumsfeld, who had served in that position since 2001. (The U.S. Senate confirmed the nomination on December 6.)

12 Gerald R. Ford became the longest-living president in U.S. history. As of this date, he had lived 93 years and 121 days—one day longer than President Ronald Reagan had lived when he died in June 2004. (Ford, the 38th president, was the only president who was never elected to the White House.)

20 The U.S. Mint announced that it would issue a series of one-dollar coins featuring all the deceased presidents of the United States. The first coin, displaying George Washington, will be put into circulation in February 2007. The other coins will follow at three-month intervals. The reverse of each coin will feature the Statue of Liberty.

21 President George W. Bush returned from a weeklong trip to Asia, where he met with the leaders of Singapore, Vietnam, and Indonesia. His goals were to assure those countries of U.S. commitment to the region, and to gain support in his effort to halt North Korea's nuclear-weapons program. Bush also met twice with Russian President Vladimir Putin, once at a stopover at a Moscow airport, and again in Hanoi, Vietnam.

Government changes in November: In national elections in **Ecuador,** Rafael Correa was elected president. He replaced Alfredo Palacio, who had held that office since 2005. . . .In national elections in **Nicaragua,** Daniel Ortega was elected president. He replaced Enrique Bolaños, who had been president since 2002.

Gold-colored $1 coins featuring the first four presidents of the United States will be issued in 2007, starting with George Washington. Officials at the U.S. Mint hope that collectors will snap up the coins and all the rest of the coins in the series—just as they have been doing with the new U.S. state quarters.

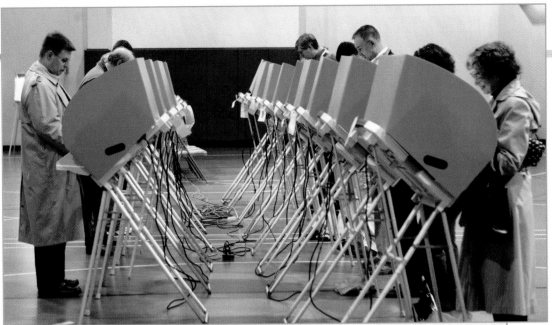

Some 68 million Americans voted on November 7. Here, voters are e-voting on electronic voting machines.

America Votes: 2006

In national elections on November 7, the Democratic Party won control of the U.S. Congress for the first time in twelve years. Democrats also made big gains at the state level.

There were two major reasons for the Democratic gains. Voters were unhappy about the war in Iraq, where almost 3,000 Americans had been killed with no end in sight to the fighting. Voters were also concerned about the number of Republicans who had been involved in scandals.

Democrats picked up six Senate seats. Two people who ran as Independents—Joseph Lieberman of Connecticut and Bernard Sanders of Vermont—also won Senate seats. Because they both align with the Democratic Party, the elections gave Democrats a 51–49 edge in the Senate when the new Congress meets in January 2007. In the House of Representatives, the Democrats gained 30 seats, giving them 233 seats to the Republicans' 202 seats in the new Congress.

Democrats will replace Republicans as governors of six states—Arkansas, Colorado, Maryland, Massachusetts, New York, and Ohio. With these new seats, the Democrats will hold 28 of the 50 state governorships.

The Democratic victory led to a number of "firsts" in U.S. electoral history:

• The number of women serving in the U.S. Congress rose to a record high—16 in the Senate, and 71 in the House.

• California Congresswoman Nancy Pelosi was chosen the first woman to serve as Speaker of the House of Representatives.

• Keith Ellison of Minnesota became the first Muslim elected to a seat in Congress.

• Deval Patrick became the first African American to be elected governor of Massachusetts—and only the second African American ever to be elected governor in the country.

DECEMBER

1 A typhoon struck the island of Luzon in the Philippines. The powerful storm caused flash floods and massive mudslides that buried entire villages. More than 400 people were killed.

4 John Bolton, U.S. ambassador to the United Nations since August 1, 2005, announced his resignation.

22 The space shuttle *Discovery* completed a 13-day mission to the *International Space Station* (*ISS*). The *Discovery* crew consisted of Commander Mark Polansky; pilot William Oefelein; mission specialists Robert Curbeam, Joan Higginbotham, Nicholas Patrick, and Christer Fuglesang of Sweden; and *ISS* Flight Engineer Sunita Williams. Williams stayed on the *ISS*, replacing German astronaut Thomas Reiter, who returned to Earth aboard the *Discovery*.

Government changes in December: Jigme Singye Wangchuck, king of **Bhutan** since 1972, resigned. He was succeeded by his son, who took the title King Jigme Khesar Namgyel Wangchuck.

Gerald R. Ford, the 38th president of the United States, died on December 26. He was 93 years old, and had lived longer than any other president in U.S. history.

Ford, a Michigan Republican, became president under unusual circumstances. In fact, he was the first—and only—person to become president without having been elected president or vice president.

Ford had served in the U.S. House of Representatives for 25 years, and was House minority leader for eight of those years. In 1973, when Spiro T. Agnew, President Richard M. Nixon's vice president, resigned because of a scandal, Nixon picked Ford to be vice president.

Just ten months later, on August 9, 1974, President Nixon resigned during the Watergate scandal, and Vice President Ford succeeded to the presidency. It was the first time in U.S. history that a vice president had assumed the presidency because of the resignation of the chief executive.

A month after being sworn in, Ford, out of compassion for Nixon and a wish to end the Watergate controversy, pardoned the disgraced former president for offenses he might have committed against the United States. He also gave conditional amnesty to Vietnam War resisters. That war, so unpopular in the United States, ended in 1975 when the South Vietnam government fell to Communist North Vietnam.

In 1976, America's bicentennial year, Ford won the Republican presidential nomination, but he lost the election to Democrat Jimmy Carter. His short presidency—it had lasted just 896 days—was over. Ford has been praised for his integrity and basic decency.

...and Looking Ahead to 2007

Here are a few anniversaries that will be noted in 2007:

● The 400th anniversary of the founding of Jamestown (Virginia), the first permanent British settlement in North America, on May 14, 1607.

● The 200th anniversary of the birth of Robert E. Lee on January 19, 1807. Lee was the last commander-in-chief of the Confederate armies during the U.S. Civil War (1861–65).

● The 200th anniversary of the maiden voyage of Robert Fulton's steamboat, the *Claremont*, on August 17, 1807. The trip—from New York City to Albany, New York, on the Hudson River—proved that steamboats could be commercially successful.

● The 125th anniversary of the birth of Franklin D. Roosevelt, the 32nd president of the United States, on January 30, 1882; and the 75th anniversary of his election to the first of his four terms on November 8, 1932.

● The 75th anniversary of Amelia Earhart's historic flight across the Atlantic on May 20–21, 1932. She was the first woman to fly solo across the ocean. Five years later, the world-famous aviator and her navigator disappeared over the Pacific Ocean while attempting the first round-the-world flight at the Equator.

● The 50th anniversary of the launch of *Sputnik I*, the world's first artificial satellite, on October 4, 1957. That launch, by the Soviet Union, ushered in the Space Age.

The Mahdi Army, the most powerful and radical Shi'ite militia in Iraq, was responsible for much of the violence against Sunni Muslims during the year.

THE WAR IN IRAQ

The year 2006 began hopefully in Iraq, with a major step toward democracy. But hopes were soon swallowed by a rising tide of violence. At year's end, Iraq seemed well on the way to all-out civil war—and Americans were divided over what to do about the problem.

The United States, with Great Britain and a small number of allies, invaded Iraq in March 2003 to overthrow Saddam Hussein, Iraq's brutal dictator. U.S. leaders said that Saddam was hiding weapons of mass destruction and had links to Al Qaeda, the terrorist group behind the September 11, 2001, attacks on the United States. The war drove him from power, and he was later arrested. However, no weapons of mass destruction or evidence of ties to Al Qaeda were ever found. And in the wake of the invasion, fighting continued. About 140,000 U.S. troops were still in Iraq through 2006, trying to establish order.

A NEW GOVERNMENT

The election of a new parliament, the first under a constitution adopted in 2005, was a major step toward democracy for Iraq. The results of the election were announced in January 2006. They showed that the vote had split along ethnic and religious lines.

Shi'ite Muslim parties won 128 of the 275 seats in the new parliament. Shi'ites, who live mainly in southern Iraq, form the country's largest group but were persecuted under Saddam Hussein. Kurdish parties won 53 seats. The Kurds live in northern Iraq and were also persecuted by Saddam. But since the 1990's they have enjoyed self-government, under international protection.

The largest Sunni Muslim party won 44 seats. Sunnis make up about 20 percent of the population and controlled Iraq under Saddam. A second Sunni party won 11 seats. And a nonreligious party headed by former prime minister Ayad Allawi won 25 seats.

The new parliament's first job was to pick a prime minister, who would in turn name a Cabinet. Because Shi'ites won the most seats, they were guaranteed a leading role. But they fell just short of winning a majority in parliament, so they needed the support of other parties to govern.

It took six months for the parties to reach agreement on the makeup of the new government. In May they finally named Nouri Kamel al-Maliki, a hard-line Shi'ite Muslim, as prime minister. Maliki had been exiled to Syria when Saddam Hussein ruled Iraq but had returned after the U.S. invasion in 2003. He belonged to the Islamic Dawa Party, the leading Shi'ite group.

For his Cabinet, Maliki picked a group of ministers who included members of Iraq's other main ethnic groups, the Kurds and Sunnis, as well as Shi'ites. The hope was that this new "national unity" government would be able to stop the violence between members of these groups.

Nouri Kamel al-Maliki, a hard-line Shi'ite Muslim, became prime minister in May. He included Kurds and Sunnis in his Cabinet, but the violence continued.

Jill Carroll talks to reporters following her release by Iraqi captors. She was held hostage nearly three months.

Jill Carroll: Kidnapped

The kidnapping of an American journalist in Iraq caused an international outcry in 2006. Gunmen ambushed Jill Carroll, a reporter for *The Christian Science Monitor* and other news organizations, on January 7 in a Baghdad neighborhood. They took her captive and killed her translator.

A previously unknown group called the Revenge Brigades claimed responsibility for the kidnapping. They said Carroll would be killed unless all women prisoners in Iraq were released by February 26. She appeared twice in videos broadcast on Arab television, begging for her life.

The deadline passed, and there was no more news. Carroll's family, her friends, her employers, and government leaders continued to plead for her release. And unlike many other victims of violence in Iraq, she survived. During her captivity she was moved from place to place repeatedly. Although she feared being killed at any moment, she wasn't mistreated.

Carroll's ordeal ended on March 30, when her captors dropped her off near the offices of the Iraqi Islamic Party. She walked inside, and people there called American officials. She had no idea why she had been let go. "I'm just happy to be free. I want to be with my family," she said.

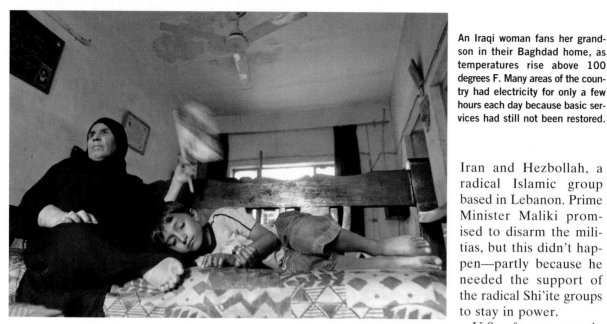

An Iraqi woman fans her grandson in their Baghdad home, as temperatures rise above 100 degrees F. Many areas of the country had electricity for only a few hours each day because basic services had still not been restored.

GROWING VIOLENCE

Violence was a major reason for the delay in forming the new government. In the north and west, Sunni Muslim rebels continued to launch attacks almost daily, targeting U.S. and Iraqi troops and civilians. And throughout the country, fighting increased between Sunnis and Shi'ites. Only Kurdish areas were quiet.

A sharp spike in the violence began on February 22, when terrorists blew up the golden dome of an important Shi'ite shrine in the city of Samarra. Angry Shi'ites took to the streets and attacked Sunnis, and Sunnis fought back. About 400 people were killed in several days of fighting.

The Sunnis and Shi'ites of Iraq have a long history of resentment against each other. But outsiders were adding fuel to the conflict between them. One such person was Abu Musab al-Zarqawi, a Jordanian-born terrorist. As head of Al Qaeda in Iraq, Zarqawi directed horrifying attacks, including suicide bombings, kidnappings, and beheadings; and he tried to fan the flames of the conflict between Sunnis and Shi'ites. In early June he was killed in a U.S. bombing raid.

But others kept the violence going. On the Shi'ite side were militias like the Mahdi Army and the Badr Brigades. These fighters were thought to be getting support from Iran and Hezbollah, a radical Islamic group based in Lebanon. Prime Minister Maliki promised to disarm the militias, but this didn't happen—partly because he needed the support of the radical Shi'ite groups to stay in power.

U.S. forces mostly tried to stay out of the fighting between Sunnis and Shi'ites, urging them to work out their differences. The United States pressed the new Iraqi government to take a bigger role in stopping the violence, and the U.S. military continued to help train and equip Iraqi soldiers and police. The idea was that when Iraqi forces were able to secure their own country, the Americans could go home. But as the U.S. forces turned over more security operations to Iraqis, the violence rose. By August 2006 the United States was moving more troops into Baghdad, the capital, which had become increasingly dangerous. Plans to cut the number of U.S. troops in Iraq were scrapped.

As the gulf between Sunnis and Shi'ites grew, frightened families fled homes in mixed neighborhoods. Fighting broke out between rival Shi'ite groups, too. Violence throughout the country was killing more than 100 Iraqis a day. U.S. troops were also casualties. By the end of the year, the number of American soldiers killed since the start of the war had reached 3,000.

Efforts to rebuild Iraq also suffered as a result of the extreme violence. Electrical networks and oil-production facilities were constantly sabotaged. Since the 2003 invasion, the United States had completed several thousand reconstruction projects in the country, including new schools, health clinics, and roads. But some of the money originally earmarked for rebuilding had to go instead to training Iraqi security forces and building prisons. As much as 25 percent of the cost of every reconstruction project went toward providing security against rebel attacks. And corruption, fraud, and waste were common.

Despite spending more than $18 billion, then, the U.S. reconstruction effort fell short. Many areas had electricity for only part of each day. Water, sewer, and other basic services were limited. Iraqi oil production in 2006 was still less than it had been before the invasion, reducing what should have been a major source of income for this oil-rich country.

DEBATE IN THE UNITED STATES

In the United States, the war became an issue in the congressional elections in November 2006. Unhappiness over Iraq and the way Republican President George W. Bush and his administration had handled the war helped Democrats take control of both houses of Congress.

As more and more people questioned the war, Bush took some steps to answer the criticism. He proposed a series of benchmarks, or goals, for the Iraqi government to meet in establishing security. The military began a review of U.S. strategy in Iraq. And in November, Defense Secretary Donald Rumsfeld, who had directed the war effort, resigned.

Many people hoped that the Iraq Study Group, a special commission made up of experts from both major political parties, would come up with an answer. That group's report, presented in December, called for a gradual pullback of all U.S. combat troops in Iraq by early 2008. It also recommended placing many more U.S. training teams with Iraqi Army units, in the hope of making them better able to fight alone. Above all, it called for a broad diplomatic effort in the Middle East, in order to find a lasting solution—specifically, it called for the United States to engage in direct talks with Iran and

Holding a Koran, Saddam Hussein yells at the court as he receives his verdict of guilty and his sentence of death.

Death of a Tyrant

In November 2006, a panel of five Iraqi judges convicted Saddam Hussein, Iraq's former dictator, of crimes against humanity. In nine months of testimony, the judges heard chilling details of how Saddam had brutally crushed a Shi'ite town in the 1980's. They sentenced him to death by hanging.

The verdict prompted wild celebrations in Shi'ite areas—and anger in Sunni areas where Saddam still had support. U.S. and Iraqi forces were braced for violence. Fighting broke out in several areas, but it was soon halted.

Under Iraqi law, a death sentence is automatically appealed. While Saddam's appeal was pending, he was put on trial in a separate case, on charges of killing at least 50,000 people in attacks on Kurdish areas in 1987 and 1988. Then, on December 23, an appeals court approved his death sentence and ordered that it be carried out within 30 days. Just a week later, on December 30, Saddam Hussein was hanged.

Syria. The recommendations weren't binding, and it wasn't immediately clear if they would be put into practice.

By the end of the year, U.S. troops had been fighting in Iraq for three years and nine months, longer than the time of American involvement in World War II.

THE ARAB-ISRAELI CONFLICT

Arabs and Israelis have been at odds since 1948, when the United Nations created Israel as a Jewish homeland in the mostly Arab territory of Palestine. This long dispute has caused many deaths, and it's the source of deep anger and bitterness on both sides.

In 2006, tensions flared again as Israel struggled with radical Arab groups. The conflict had two focal points: the Palestinian-controlled territories of the West Bank and the Gaza Strip; and the nation of Lebanon, which lies to Israel's north.

THE PALESTINIAN PROBLEM

The original U.N. plan for Palestine called for two nations: one Jewish, one Arab. But the Arab state never came to be. Arab countries rejected the plan, and they attacked Israel. Israel then won a series of Arab-Israeli wars. In 1967, during one of the wars, Israel gained control of the Gaza Strip (along the Mediterranean coast), the West Bank (on the west side of the Jordan River), and other areas where Palestinian Arabs live.

For years, Palestinians launched terrorist attacks against Israelis. Israel responded with military force. But in 1993, after a series of peace talks brokered by the United States, the Palestinians won limited self-rule in parts of the West Bank and Gaza Strip. They set up a government, the Palestinian National Authority (PNA). Then progress toward peace stalled, and violence erupted again.

There was new hope in 2005. Mahmoud Abbas, a moderate, was elected president of the PNA. He and Israeli Prime Minister Ariel Sharon declared a truce. Israeli troops and settlers left the Gaza Strip.

But hope for peace sank in January 2006, when Palestinians elected a new parliament. Hamas, a radical Islamic party that has sworn to destroy Israel, won 76 of the 132 seats in the legislature. Abbas was still president, but he had much less power once his party, Fatah, no longer controlled parliament. Hamas picked a new PNA prime minister, Ismail Haniya, and a Cabinet. They controlled security, finance, and other government functions.

Why did Hamas win? Fatah had run the PNA since its founding, and many Palestinians felt that the party hadn't done a good job. Crime and unemployment were high, and officials were corrupt. Meanwhile, Hamas had spent years building support by setting up schools, hospitals, and charities.

Although Palestinians saw Hamas as part of their community, Israelis and Americans saw it as a terrorist group. Israeli and U.S. leaders

Palestinian President Mahmoud Abbas (below), was undermined when the radical Islamic group Hamas won parliamentary elections and named Ismail Haniya (left) as prime minister. Ehud Olmert (right) became Israel's new prime minister in April.

said they wouldn't deal with Hamas unless the group accepted Israel and rejected terrorism. But Hamas leaders vowed never to recognize Israel's right to exist.

Violence soon grew. Gaza militants fired rockets into southern Israel. And in June militants kidnapped an Israeli soldier. Israel then closed Gaza's borders. Gaza's economy ground to a halt. Israel also saw a change in govern-

Syria and Iran, both nations that deny Israel's right to exist, arm and support Hezbollah. In the past, they have used Hezbollah to put pressure on Israel. The government of Lebanon, which Syria controlled until last year, has tolerated the militants.

Hezbollah sparked the 2006 conflict by kidnapping two Israeli soldiers on July 12. Israel answered with airstrikes against Hezbollah

Lebanon became a battleground when fighting broke out between Israel and the militant Islamic group Hezbollah in July. Above: An Israeli tank crew stands by as Israeli missiles strike a village in southern Lebanon.

ment in 2006. Sharon had suffered a severe stroke, and his deputy Ehud Olmert stepped in. Olmert was formally named prime minister in April, after parliamentary elections.

In September, Olmert and Abbas agreed to a cease-fire in Gaza. And Olmert offered major concessions if the Palestinians would commit to peace and return to talks. But Hamas and Fatah were unable to agree on negotiating with Israel.

FIGHTING IN LEBANON

In July, fighting broke out between Israel and Hezbollah, a militant Islamic group based in southern Lebanon. Lebanon is a convenient base for launching terrorist attacks against Israel. For more than 20 years, Israel patrolled a narrow strip of land in southern Lebanon to keep terrorists away from the border. But Israeli troops left Lebanon in 2000, and Hezbollah quickly moved in.

bases. Because Hezbollah fighters took up positions in towns and villages, civilian casualties were high. An estimated 500,000 people fled their homes in southern Lebanon to escape the fighting. Israelis also fled their homes, as Hezbollah fired rockets at Israeli towns near the border and northern cities such as Haifa.

As the rocket attacks continued, Israeli troops and tanks crossed into Lebanon. Hezbollah fighters put up stiff resistance. In a month of fighting, 800 people died. Then Israel, the government of Lebanon, and Hezbollah agreed to a U.N.-sponsored cease-fire plan. It called for 30,000 Lebanese and United Nations troops to take charge in southern Lebanon.

The fighting raised concern for Lebanon's future. This country had suffered through years of civil war and had only just begun to recover. But once the cease-fire was in place, Hezbollah began to push for more power, putting Lebanon's democratic government at risk.

IMMIGRATION: A CONTROVERSIAL PROBLEM

Most Americans think of their nation as a land of opportunity, welcoming newcomers from abroad. That's the promise represented by the Statue of Liberty, in New York City. Immigrants have shaped the United States throughout its history—but they haven't always been welcomed with open arms. At times, Americans have hotly debated the question of how many immigrants should be allowed into the country, and from where.

The year 2006 was one of those times. Congress debated new proposals that would tighten control of U.S. borders, in the hope of stopping people from entering the country without official approval. And in cities throughout the country, there were huge demonstrations calling for fair treatment of immigrants.

A NATION OF IMMIGRANTS

It's often said that the United States is a nation of immigrants. That's because Americans all came from somewhere else or are descended from someone who did. Even the American Indians, who have lived in what is today the United States longer than anyone, are descended from people who came from Asia thousands of years ago.

The first European settlers came to America for a variety of reasons. Some were seeking riches. Others were fleeing religious persecution.

But most came in the hope of finding a better way of life and more economic opportunities than they had in the countries they left behind. Today, immigrants come to the United States for many of the same reasons.

Over its 230-year history, the United States has seen several great waves of immigration. The mid-1800's brought one such wave. Nearly 1.5 million Irish immigrants came to escape famine and poverty after a blight caused potato crops, on which they depended, to fail several years in a row. More than a million Germans also arrived, fleeing political upheavals in Europe. On the West Coast, the discovery of gold in California and the building of the transcontinental railroad created a demand for labor. Chinese workers arrived to fill the need.

The biggest wave of immigration took place in the late 1800's and early 1900's. Millions of people arrived during this period, mostly from

*Give me your tired, your poor,
Your huddled masses yearning
to breathe free,
The wretched refuse of your
teeming shore.
Send these, the homeless,
tempest-tost, to me,
I lift my lamp beside the
golden door!*

These words, from an 1883 poem by Emma Lazarus, are engraved on a bronze plaque inside the statue's pedestal.

In the early 1900's, millions of immigrants from southern and eastern Europe arrived in the United States, including this Jewish man (above) and Italian family (right).

southern and eastern Europe. Among them were Italians, Slavs, Greeks, and Poles. Many Jews arrived from Eastern Europe, where they faced persecution. Out west, many people immigrated from Japan and other Asian countries to work on large farms. New immigrants made up about 15 percent of the U.S. population during this period.

Most immigrants faced a difficult period of adjustment. They often had to take low-paying jobs, and they weren't always welcome. Sometimes American workers feared that immigrants would take their jobs; sometimes people resented the newcomers out of prejudice. From time to time there were calls to limit immigration of one ethnic group or another. In 1882 the U.S. Congress passed the Chinese Exclusion Act, which suspended new immigration by Chinese workers.

In 1921, Congress passed the Quota Act. This law limited annual immigration from any country to 3 percent of the number of people of that nationality living in the United States in 1910. The law was amended several times, but it remained the basis of U.S. immigration policy for more than 40 years. In 1965, Congress finally scrapped the quota system and adopted a new set of immigration guidelines. The new guidelines set limits on the total number of immigrants allowed into the country each year and gave priority to three groups: refugees, who left their homelands because of war or persecution; people who had special skills; and people who had close relatives in the United States.

Under the new policy, most immigrants to the United States have come from Latin America and Asia rather than from Europe. Many Asians arrived as refugees in the 1970's, after wars in Vietnam, Cambodia, and Laos. Latin Americans have arrived mainly from Mexico and countries of Central America and the Caribbean. In 1995 the number of immigrants allowed to enter the country each year was increased from 290,000 to 675,000.

ILLEGAL IMMIGRATION

People who aren't citizens of a country—called aliens—need official government permission to enter and stay in that country. The United States admits aliens in three categories: refugees, temporary visitors, and resident aliens. Temporary visitors come to travel, attend school, or do business. They get permits called visas, which allow them to stay for a limited time. Resident aliens are non-citizens living permanently in the United States. Like citizens, resident aliens hold jobs, own property, and pay taxes. But they can't vote or hold most public offices, and if they break the law they may be deported (required to leave the country). Resident aliens over age 18 must carry an identification card, generally known as a green card.

The United States limits the number of green cards that it issues, and there aren't enough for everyone who wants to come to live in the country. Some people decide to ignore the law and come anyway. People who enter without permission or stay beyond the terms of their visas are called illegal, or undocumented, aliens.

It's thought that there are about 11 million illegal aliens in the United States, but no one knows the true number. Most of these people came for the same reasons that have traditionally drawn immigrants to the country—the hope of finding freedom and a better way of life. Many illegal aliens work in low-paying jobs, as farm workers, maids, cooks, and unskilled laborers. Many have lived in the United States for years.

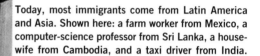

Today, most immigrants come from Latin America and Asia. Shown here: a farm worker from Mexico, a computer-science professor from Sri Lanka, a housewife from Cambodia, and a taxi driver from India.

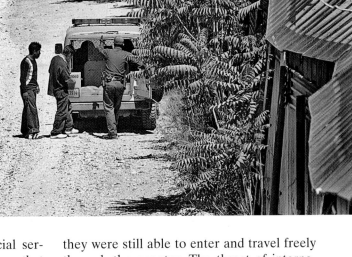

Right: Many barriers have been erected along the long Mexican-U.S. border, where most illegal immigrants enter the country. Above: Border Patrol agents in Arizona escort a group of illegal immigrants back to the border.

Some Americans see the illegal immigrants as no different from other immigrants. They, too, are people who have come hoping to find a better life. Some industries depend on them because they are willing to work for low wages. Many farmers rely on migrant workers to pick crops, for example, and many of these workers don't have green cards. But other Americans say that illegal immigrants take jobs from U.S. workers and place a strain on public services. They may use medical facilities and other kinds of social services, for example, without paying the taxes that support those services.

Illegal immigration has been an issue in the past. The Immigration Reform and Control Act of 1986 set penalties for people who employ illegal aliens. It also gave legal status to many illegal aliens then living in the United States. But people continued to enter the country without permission, and the penalties for employing illegal aliens were seldom applied.

The terrorist attacks of September 11, 2001, put a spotlight on the problem. Three of the 19 hijackers who carried out those attacks were in the United States illegally, on expired visas. One had a student visa but had never shown up for class. Several others were on an official "watch list" of suspected terrorists, but they were still able to enter and travel freely through the country. The threat of international terrorism prompted calls for stronger immigration laws—and stricter enforcement of those laws.

Most Americans agree that the United States needs better immigration controls. At the very least, it's important to keep out terrorists and other criminals. But how?

COMPETING PROPOSALS

Several immigration proposals were on the table in 2006. Each one had supporters and opponents.

In December 2005, the House of Representatives passed a bill that called for strong border security. This bill would have made it a felony—a major crime—to be in the country

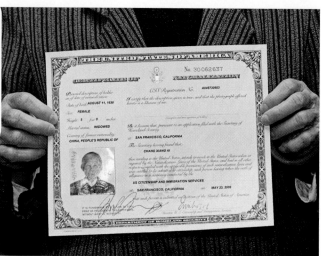

Resident aliens in the United States are non-citizens living permanently in the United States. They must carry an identification card, known as a green card (above). When an immigrant becomes a U.S. citizen, he or she receives a certificate of naturalization (right).

without permission. Anyone who helped an illegal immigrant would have faced criminal charges, too. The bill also called for a 700-mile (1,127-kilometer) fence along the Mexican-U.S. border, where most illegal immigrants enter. The House rejected calls for a guest-worker program, which would have allowed workers to enter the United States temporarily to perform specific jobs.

The House bill sparked huge demonstrations by supporters of immigration. The biggest protest took place in March in Los Angeles, where some 500,000 people, young and old, rallied peacefully to call for fair treatment of immigrants. There were demonstrations in other cities as well. Supporters of immigration

also called for a "National Day of Action" on April 10, and there were huge rallies in New York City; in Phoenix, Arizona; and in many other cities. About 180,000 people marched in Washington, D.C. Then, on May 1, supporters called for "A Day Without Immigrants"—a national boycott. The idea was to show how important immigrants are to the U.S. economy. Immigrants were urged to stay out of work, shops, and school. Hundreds of thousands did, and once again there were huge rallies and marches around the country.

The Senate passed its own immigration reform bill in May. The Senate version would have tightened border security with stronger barriers and more border patrols, but it wouldn't

Top 10 Ethnicities of Immigrants Who Passed Through Ellis Island (1899–1931)

1. Italian
2. Jewish
3. German
4. Polish
5. Scandinavian
6. English
7. Irish
8. Scottish
9. Slovak
10. French

Top 10 Countries of Origin of Legal Immigrants to the U.S. (2005)

1. Mexico
2. India
3. China
4. Philippines
5. Cuba
6. Vietnam
7. Dominican Republic
8. Korea
9. Colombia
10. Ukraine

Sources: Statue of Liberty and Ellis Island Immigration Museum; Department of Homeland Security

have penalized people who helped illegal aliens for humanitarian reasons—by giving them food or shelter, for example. The Senate bill also opened the way to legal status for illegal immigrants who had been in the country for more than five years. These immigrants would have to hold jobs, pass criminal background checks, learn English, and pay fines and back taxes. Eventually they would have the right to apply for citizenship.

President George W. Bush supported this approach. But conservative Republicans in both the Senate and the House were against the plan to offer legal status. They said it amounted to amnesty for illegal aliens and would reward

tems, cameras, ground sensors, aerial vehicles, and wireless communications systems.

In August, the Homeland Security Department pointed with pride to the fact that the number of illegal immigrants entering from Mexico was down significantly for the first time in several years. But not everyone was happy with that result. The tighter security had kept many illegal migrant farm workers from entering the country, as they do most years, to pick crops. In many areas, fall fruit crops rotted before they could be picked and shipped to market. Growers from all the major farming states protested by rallying in Washington, D.C., carrying baskets of fruit to the front lawn of the Capitol.

Hundreds of thousands of legal and illegal immigrants and their supporters took part in "A Day Without Immigrants." It was meant to show how important immigrants are to the U.S. economy.

people who had broken the law by entering the country without permission. Republicans in the House decided to hold hearings to try to build support for their view before working with the Senate on a compromise.

Although action on legislation stalled, the government took other steps to tighten control of the Mexican-U.S. border. The president ordered 6,000 National Guard troops to the area, to assist the Border Patrol agents whose job it is to block illegal immigration. Plans were put forward for high-tech security—radar sys-

Illegal immigration became an issue in campaigns for congressional elections held in November 2006. Just before the elections, Congress passed and the president signed a law approving construction of the fence along the Mexican-U.S. border. Action on other proposals was put off.

The debates and demonstrations of 2006 brought the problems of border security and illegal immigration to everyone's attention. But it was clear that the problem wouldn't be easily solved.

Violence in the region of Darfur, Sudan, has left more than 200,000 people dead. And more than 2.5 million people have been forced to flee their villages for squalid, overcrowded camps in Sudan and Chad. Here, displaced villagers in a refugee camp in Darfur line up to fill their water containers.

THE TRAGEDY OF DARFUR

Violence and hardship continued to plague the people of Darfur, a region in the African nation of Sudan, throughout 2006. In more than three years of fighting, at least 200,000 and perhaps as many as 400,000 people have been killed in this region. Another 2.5 million people have been driven from their homes. And aid agencies have been struggling to help the refugees.

Darfur is in western Sudan, and is larger than California. The problems of this poor, arid region are rooted in disputes between two groups of people who live there. Some people have condemned the violence as genocide—a systematic effort by one group of people to kill all the members of a different group. Everyone agrees that the situation in Darfur is a tragedy.

"DEVILS ON HORSEBACK"

Sudan has suffered through civil wars almost from the time of its independence in 1956. Most of the fighting has been between northern Muslims, who control the government, and non-Muslim Africans in the south, who have had few rights. In 2005, the government and the southern rebels signed a peace agreement giving greater self-government to the south.

The conflict in Darfur, however, has continued to rage. This region is home to two main ethnic groups. One group is made up of people mostly of Arab descent, who traditionally are nomadic traders and camel herders. The other group is made up of darker-skinned Africans, who are mostly farmers. Both groups are Muslims.

Some years ago, Arab nomads began to raid farming villages. Sudan's government did nothing to stop the raids. In fact, there was clear evidence that the government was hiring and arming the Arab raiders—even though the government denied that it was doing this. The armed groups, or militias, became known as the janjaweed, which means "devils on horseback."

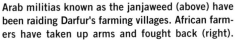
Arab militias known as the janjaweed (above) have been raiding Darfur's farming villages. African farmers have taken up arms and fought back (right).

The African farmers took up arms and fought back. In February 2003, African rebels seized several towns in Darfur. They demanded economic help and a greater say in government. And they demanded that the government disarm the janjaweed.

Instead, the government took military action against the African rebels. And the janjaweed stepped up its attacks against civilians. Mounted on horses and camels, they swooped down on villages, burning houses and killing men, women, and children. Tens of thousands of survivors fled, leaving everything behind.

International agencies set up refugee camps in Darfur and in the neighboring country of Chad, just over Sudan's western border. As the number of people in the camps swelled, they became crowded and dangerous places. In addition, many victims of the conflict were stuck in areas where government restrictions forbade aid workers to go—or where conditions were too dangerous for them to travel. Thus people continued to die from disease and starvation, as well as from the ongoing violence.

The African Union called on Sudan to disarm the janjaweed militias, and it helped work out a formal cease-fire between the government and the rebels in 2004. Several thousand soldiers representing the African Union were sent into Darfur as observers. But the cease-fire didn't hold, and the African Union troops were too few to stop the fighting.

VIOLENCE GROWS

Violence in Darfur expanded in 2006. Arab militias even spread the fighting into Chad, attacking refugee camps and villages there. There were also reports that Sudan was supporting rebels who were fighting the government in Chad, which Sudan said was backing the Darfur rebels. And fighting broke out among the Darfur rebels themselves, between factions representing different tribal groups.

The United Nations offered to take over command of the African Union observer force in Darfur and expand it from 7,000 troops into a peacekeeping force of more than 20,000. But Sudan's government said that it wouldn't accept such a force until it reached a peace agreement with the rebels. Thus the U.N. and the African Union sponsored peace talks between rebel and government officials, who met in Nigeria in the spring of 2006.

The talks led to a peace agreement between the government and the Sudanese Liberation Army (SLA), the largest of the three main rebel factions. Under the terms of the agreement, signed on May 5, both the janjaweed and the rebels were to disarm. But the peace agreement never took hold. In fact, violence among the African rebels increased, as the SLA fought with rebel groups that opposed the agreement. Pro-government militiamen launched new attacks on Darfuris, and fighting between the government and Darfur rebels spilled into both Chad and the Central African Republic.

Sudan continued to block plans for a U.N. peacekeeping force, insisting that the U.N. must only fund and support an African Union force. There was progress in mid-November, at an AU meeting in Ethiopia. Sudanese officials agreed to hold new talks with all the rebel and militia groups. And they agreed in principle to a broader U.N. role in an expanded peacekeeping force. But there was still no agreement on the size or makeup of that force.

Aid agencies, such as the U.N. World Food Programme, have been struggling to help the refugees.

AID EFFORTS FALTER

Meanwhile, attempts to bring aid to victims of the conflict ran into problems. During 2006, aid agencies were feeding almost three million people a day in refugee camps in Darfur, nearly half the population. But the U.N. World Food Programme announced in May that it would have to cut in half the amount of food it gave to Darfur refugees, to the level of 1,050 calories per person per day. The program had run short of money because the nations of the world had donated only a third of the money needed, even though they had promised much more. "You start wondering, what will it take?" one aid official said. "How bad does it have to get before the international community acts?"

The government of Sudan came under intense criticism for failing to distribute some of its vast stores of grain to help the refugees. Finally it agreed to do so, and the food that was cut was restored. But the aid effort was still in financial

The African Union sent several thousand soldiers to Darfur to monitor a cease-fire. But the troops were too few to stop the fighting.

trouble. The United Nations Children's Fund (UNICEF) had to cut back on its childhood nutrition programs. And medical clinics in some of the refugee camps were forced to close because they were running out of money, too.

On top of that, Arab militias and some rebel groups were attacking aid workers. There were about 14,000 aid workers in the region, including about 1,000 from other countries. But aid workers were increasingly threatened by fighters and bandits, who hijacked their vehicles and sometimes killed them. This kept help from reaching many people, and malnutrition and disease began to increase. Officials feared that the effort to bring aid to Darfur's people might collapse altogether.

U.S. government agencies, charities, and private individuals have provided millions of dollars in aid for Darfur's people. U.S. negotiators helped work out the peace agreement in May 2006, and the United States has backed calls for stronger peacekeeping missions. But at year's end it seemed that much more would be needed on the part of people around the world to stop the violence in this troubled region.

Mia Farrow, a goodwill ambassador for UNICEF, is surrounded by children at a Darfur refugee camp.

Rallying to Help Darfur

Movie stars, music stars, and other celebrities are followed by reporters and photographers wherever they go. They get constant attention. And sometimes they use that attention for good ends. A number of celebrities have helped to put an international spotlight on Darfur. Among them were actor George Clooney and actress Mia Farrow, who both took steps to call attention to the situation in 2006.

Clooney addressed a huge rally on April 30 on the National Mall in Washington, D.C. Thousands of people turned out for this event, called the Rally to Stop Genocide. Besides celebrities like Clooney, the speakers included Illinois Senator Barack Obama; human rights activist Elie Wiesel, a recipient of the Nobel Peace Prize; Olympic speed-skater Joey Cheek, who donated his medal winnings to the Darfur cause; and Russell Simmons, the founder of Def Jam Records. They called on the United States to do more to end the violence in Darfur.

Farrow went to Darfur in June 2006 as a goodwill ambassador for UNICEF. She traveled to some of the 200 camps set up for Darfur refugees, to draw attention to their plight. The people in these camps were getting food and other help, but they weren't safe. Often they had to travel outside the camps to find water and wood for cooking fires, and then they risked being attacked by janjaweed militias. "Everywhere I went, women asked for 'water, water, water.' They were desperate for wells inside the camps so they wouldn't get attacked looking for water," Farrow reported.

Thousands of less famous people also took up the cause in 2006, holding rallies and candlelight vigils to show their concern. They were determined not to let the world forget the ongoing tragedy in Darfur.

IDENTITY THEFT

Imagine this: As a high-school senior, you are accepted at the college of your choice. The tuition is more than you can afford, so you apply for a student loan. It's the first time you've applied for a loan of any kind. But the lender says you have a bad credit history. Your loan application is rejected!

How could this happen? Through identity theft. This crime occurs when someone steals personal information, such as a Social Security Number (SSN). The thief then uses the information in some fraudulent way, such as charging merchandise, taking money from bank accounts, or getting a loan or a driver's license.

Identity theft is a serious problem. A report released by the U.S. Department of Justice in 2006 showed that 3.6 million households—about 3 percent of all households in the nation—were victims of identity theft during just one six-month period in 2004. Their losses added up to a whopping $3.2 billion!

Adults are the most common victims of identity theft. But kids aren't safe. They have SSN's and other information thieves can use. And when a minor's identity is stolen, the problem may go undetected for years. The victim may not find out until he or she is old enough to apply for a job, a driver's license, or a loan.

PHISHERS AND DUMPSTER DIVERS

How can thieves steal your identity? Here are just a few of the ways:

■ They steal your personal mail. Bank and credit-card statements, credit-card offers, new checks, and tax statements all have information ID thieves can use. Some thieves even fill out change-of-address forms at the post office, to divert mail to another location.

■ They rummage through your trash to find discarded mail, such as credit-card offers and statements. This practice is called "dumpster diving."

■ They steal your wallet or purse or take personal information from your home.

■ They trick you into giving them personal information. This is called "phishing" online and "pretexting" when it's done by phone. The thieves pretend to be taking a survey or pose as representatives of banks. They ask for your SSN, bank-account numbers, and passwords.

■ They get information from banks and other companies by hacking into computer systems or by bribing or tricking employees.

■ They steal bank or cellphone passwords and account numbers by watching as people enter the numbers on their phones or at ATM's.

■ They use fraud to get personal information from consumer-reporting companies. These companies compile credit histories on individuals. Anyone who pays bills has a credit history. It shows whether the person makes payments on time. A thief may get a copy of the report by claiming to be a lender, landlord, or employer who wants to check a credit history.

Identity thieves go through garbage to find discarded mail containing personal information. They also steal Social Security Numbers. And they create fake drivers' licenses.

Once thieves have the information they want, they go to town. They may get new forms of ID, such as a driver's license with your name—and a thief's photo. They may use counterfeit checks or debit cards to drain your bank account. They may open new credit-card accounts in your name or run up charges on existing accounts. They may set up phone or wireless service or take out loans in your name. Of course, they don't pay the bills. Then the bad debts are reported on your credit history.

PROTECT YOURSELF

You can't prevent ID theft completely. But you can reduce your risk. Here are eight ways.

■ Never give out personal information on the phone, through the mail, or online unless you know for sure whom you're dealing with. Don't post information that could be used by an ID thief on blogs or social networking sites.

■ Give your Social Security Number only when absolutely necessary.

■ Don't carry your Social Security card. Carry only cards and ID you'll need when you go out.

■ Be careful when responding to promotional offers. ID thieves may create phony offers to get your personal information.

■ Be careful with mail and trash. Drop off outgoing mail at the post office or a secure collection box, and pick up mail promptly from your mailbox. Tear or shred any trash with personal information.

■ Equip your computer with up-to-date antivirus and security software.

■ Use strong passwords on bank, phone, and credit accounts. A strong password has a combination of letters (upper and lower case), numbers, and symbols.

■ Check bills and bank statements for unusual activity. And check your credit report. The Federal Trade Commission (FTC) has instructions for doing this online at *www.ftc.gov/credit*. If you're a minor, it isn't legal for you to enter into credit agreements. Thus consumer-reporting agencies should have no record of you. If they do, someone may be using your information illegally.

If you think your personal information has been stolen, act fast. Take the steps listed below. Quick action can limit the damage done by these clever thieves.

IF YOU ARE A VICTIM

ID theft can be costly, and it can take months to straighten out. These steps can minimize the damage.

■ If you think your personal information was stolen, place a fraud alert on your credit report. (To find out how, visit the FTC Web site at *www.consumer.gov/idtheft*.) This can help stop someone from opening new credit accounts in your name.

■ Close bank and credit accounts that may have been tampered with. When you open new ones, be sure to place passwords on them.

■ If a driver's license or other form of ID has been lost or stolen, cancel the document and get a replacement.

■ Report theft or misuse of personal information to the police, and file a report with the FTC.

More and more cases of identity theft are turning up each year. That's why it's smart to protect your personal information and to act quickly if you think you may have been a victim of this crime.

North Korea's nuclear-bomb test in October made headlines around the world. That test and Iran's bid to become a nuclear power were of worldwide concern in 2006.

AROUND THE WORLD

What would happen if nuclear weapons were to come into the hands of terrorists or rogue nations that might threaten other countries with them? That was one worry that faced the world during 2006—but it was far from the only one. Here are some of the events that made headlines during the year.

NORTH KOREA'S BOMB TEST

North Korea created alarm worldwide on October 9 by announcing that it had tested a nuclear bomb. This was the first time that the secretive Asian country had offered any evidence of its claim to have nuclear weapons.

With the test, North Korea declared itself a member of the "nuclear club"—the small group of nations that have these weapons. North Korea's underground explosion registered around the world at seismic monitoring stations, which record tremors in the earth. However, experts said that it was quite small for a nuclear blast. Thus it wasn't immediately clear whether North Korea's test had been successful.

Successful or not, governments around the world condemned the nuclear test as an act that threatened international peace and stability. One of the world's most isolated countries, North Korea has been ruled by a Communist dictatorship since the end of World War II. In the 1950's, North Korea fought a bitter war with South Korea, which is a democracy today. The two sides never signed a peace treaty, just a cease-fire; and North Korea has often threatened to abandon the cease-fire. Since the United States is a strong ally of South Korea, that would set off a conflict that could reach beyond the region.

The North Koreans have been trying to develop nuclear weapons for many years. In 1994, they agreed to stop their weapons program. But they continued in secret, and in 2003 they admitted to the secret program. They claim to need nuclear weapons to defend their country against the United States, although U.S. officials have said repeatedly that they have no intention of attacking North Korea. Many people worry that North Korea may sell its nuclear weapons, perhaps to terrorists; or use them against South Korea or another neighbor, such as Japan.

The North Koreans have also tried to develop long-range missiles that would be able to travel as far as the western United States. They test-fired such a missile in July 2006, but it failed and crashed within seconds of the launch. Five smaller missiles were also tested in July.

While the United States and other nations took the missile tests seriously, the October nuclear test brought a bigger reaction. The United Nations Security Council passed a resolution condemning the test and calling for economic sanctions against North Korea. The sanctions included bans on the sale or transfer of materials that North Korea could use to make missiles or nuclear or other unconventional weapons, and on exports of weapons from North Korea. It gave nations the right to inspect cargo headed to or from the country. But to prevent a veto by China and Russia, both allies of North Korea, the Security Council ruled out the use of force in making the sanctions stick.

The Security Council also banned sales of luxury goods to North Korea. This was intended to punish the small elite that governs the country, and not the majority of North Koreans. Most North Koreans are desperately poor and rely on food and other basics from abroad.

The resolution also ordered North Korea not to conduct further nuclear or missile tests. And it called on the North Koreans to sit down at the negotiating table with other countries. Five nations—South Korea, China, Japan, Russia, and the United States—had begun holding talks with the North Koreans in 2003, in the hope of getting them to give up their weapons program. But North Korea had walked out of the talks repeatedly and hadn't returned since 2005.

It was possible that North Korea's 2006 threats and tests were a way of getting the world's attention—and perhaps increased economic aid. But that didn't make the situation any less dangerous. North Korea might not yet have nuclear-armed missiles, but it was clearly trying to reach that goal.

IRAN'S NUCLEAR PROGRAM

There was growing concern about Iran's nuclear program, too. On August 31, Iran defied a United Nations deadline to stop enriching uranium, a key step in making nu-

Left: Iranian President Mahmoud Ahmadinejad, at the opening of a nuclear facility. He defended Iran's right to enrich uranium, a key step in making a fuel that can be used for nuclear power—or nuclear weapons. Below: Iranian women rally to his support.

nuclear energy
is our
obvious right

clear fuel. The fuel can be used for nuclear weapons or for nuclear-power plants, and Iran has insisted that its goals are peaceful. But most experts believe that the goal of Iran's program is producing weapons. That's a concern particularly for the United States and other Western countries. Iran's Islamic government has declared the West to be its enemy, and it has supported terrorist groups.

U.S. officials have said they want to solve the problem through diplomacy. Military action—bombing Iran's nuclear sites, for example—would be ineffective and might rally support for the Iranian government, which is run by conservative Muslim clerics. The United States hasn't had formal diplomatic relations with Iran since Islamists took over the government in 1979, so it has been working with European countries to get Iran to give up its nuclear ambitions.

These efforts began in 2003, when inspectors from the U.N. International Atomic Energy Agency (IAEA) found that the Iranians were hiding a uranium-enrichment program.

In August, British police arrested 24 people who were plotting to blow up planes flying from Britain to the United States. Here, a police officer guards the British Airways terminal at JFK International Airport in New York City.

But talks with Iran fell apart in 2005, and the problem was brought to the U.N. Security Council in February 2006. The Security Council told Iran to halt its enrichment program, but Iran refused. In fact, Iranian President Mahmoud Ahmadinejad announced that his country had obtained new centrifuges, advanced machines that could process uranium more quickly. This brought Iran another step closer to large-scale production of nuclear fuel—and, perhaps, building a nuclear weapon.

The United States wanted the Security Council to penalize Iran by imposing sanctions, such as restrictions on travel and trade. But two key Security Council members, Russia and China, weren't willing to do this right away. Instead, the Security Council set a deadline of August 31 for Iran to stop enrichment. And the United States joined other countries in offering Iran incentives, such as better diplomatic relations and access to technology, if it would do so.

The deadline passed with Iran insisting on keeping its nuclear program. In December, the Security Council imposed sanctions meant to block Iran's access to materials and technology used in uranium processing and missile building. But it wasn't clear that the sanctions would halt Iran's quest for nuclear technology.

Iran's past support of terrorism made its nuclear ambitions especially worrisome. If Iran—or North Korea— were to supply nuclear weapons to terrorists, the results would be disastrous.

INTERNATIONAL TERRORISM

A report prepared by U.S. intelligence services and released in September 2006 stated that growing Islamic radicalism was producing more potential terrorists, raising the risk of attacks around the world. The report said the increase was fueled in part by opposition to the U.S. war in Iraq, which had become a rallying point for extremists.

Terrorists staged a number of devastating attacks during the year. In April, bombs killed eighteen people at a Red Sea resort in Egypt. It was the third time since 2004 that terrorists had attacked in the area. Authorities said that the bombers probably had ties to the Islamic terrorist group Al Qaeda, which carried out the September 11, 2001, attacks in the United States. Then, on July 11, seven bombs exploded on commuter trains in Mumbai, India, during rush hour. No group claimed responsibility for that attack, which killed 186 people.

Several other plots were uncovered before they could be carried out. In June, Canadian authorities arrested a group of 17 Muslim men and boys suspected of plotting to bomb major buildings in the Toronto area. The group also planned to storm the Parliament building in Ottawa and take hostages, officials said.

An even deadlier plot was discovered in Britain. In August, British law-enforcement officers arrested 24 people who, they said, planned to blow up passenger planes bound from Great Britain to the United States. The plotters hoped to smuggle liquid explosives aboard the planes, officials said. Most of those arrested were British-born Muslims of Pakistani heritage. Several arrests were also made in Pakistan. Had the plot been carried out, it would have been the deadliest terrorist attack since 2001.

In Great Britain and the United States, authorities raised terror-alert systems to their highest levels. Airports imposed strict security measures, including bans on liquids and gels in airplane cabins. This led to long delays and lots of confusion for passengers, but most were just glad that the plot had been foiled.

The attacks and plots renewed debate over the steps that nations could take to protect their people from international terrorism. In the United States, some people were concerned that certain government antiterrorism programs threatened civil lib-

In May, Nepal's King Gyanendra was stripped of his power by the nation's parliament. Here, less than three weeks later, a Hindu holy man wishes the king a happy birthday.

Nepal: Hopes for Peace

Sandwiched between India and Tibet in the Himalayas, the world's highest mountain range, the little kingdom of Nepal was long considered a mysterious land. Modern transportation and communication have ended Nepal's isolation, and the country has seen growing political turmoil. Since 1996, Maoist rebels have been trying to do away with the monarchy and establish a Communist republic. Thousands of people have been killed. In 2006, however, the conflict seemed to be nearing an end as Nepal's king agreed to give up most of his powers.

King Gyanendra was named to the Nepalese throne in 2001. He accused the government of inefficiency and said it had failed to end the Maoist rebellion. He tried to extend his control by dismissing the prime minister, dissolving parliament, and suspending elections. With the backing of the military, he took over all the powers of the government in 2005.

But the king's tough approach didn't end the fighting; in fact, it sparked weeks of violent protests. In April 2006, Gyanendra was finally forced to restore parliament, and an interim government was formed. The government declared a cease-fire and began talks with the rebels, to bring them into the political process. And parliament passed a series of regulations stripping the king of his powers.

There were still reports of violence, but Nepal was calmer than it had been for years.

Some 440 suspected terrorists were still held at the U.S. Navy base at Guantanamo Bay, Cuba, in 2006. President George W. Bush was criticized for his administration's treatment of these and other suspected terrorists arrested overseas.

There were questions about how the prisoners had been treated and when, if ever, they would be charged with crimes or released.

The administration said it wanted to bring some of the suspects before special military tribunals. But the U.S. Supreme Court ruled in August that the planned tribunals would limit the rights of the accused in ways that violated both the code of military justice and the Geneva Conventions, an international treaty that governs the treatment of military prisoners. The president then won approval from Congress for a slightly modified tribunal plan. In the fall, fourteen "high-level" terrorism suspects were brought to Guantanamo from locations in other countries where U.S. authorities had held them in secret. Tribunals were expected to hear their cases in 2007.

erties without making the country any safer. In one controversial program, government officials claimed the right to listen in on phone calls from overseas without first getting a court warrant. A federal judge ruled that the program was unconstitutional, but the government said it would appeal the ruling.

President George W. Bush also faced criticism for his administration's treatment of suspected terrorists arrested overseas. The United States was holding some 440 people at the U.S. Navy base in Guantanamo Bay, Cuba, and many had been there since 2002.

Police examine the wreckage of a car used in a suicide bombing in the city of Kandahar in Afghanistan. Taliban and Al Qaeda attacks in Afghanistan increased during the year.

TROUBLE IN AFGHANISTAN

Many of the people held in Guantanamo had originally been picked up in Afghanistan, where the United States and its allies launched a military action in October 2001. The assault was aimed at Al Qaeda, the terrorist group that staged the September 11 attacks against the United States; and at the Taliban, the Islamic militia that then ruled most of Afghanistan. The Taliban had sheltered Osama bin Laden, the head of Al Qaeda, and other leaders of the group.

The allied forces quickly drove the Taliban from power, and for many Afghans that was cause for great joy. The Taliban had imposed strict religious rules, banning music and barring women from work and school. Afghans chose a new leader, Hamid Karzai. And the United States and other donors pledged $4.5 billion to help rebuild the country, which had been torn by many years of civil war. Afghanistan seemed to be turning into a new democracy with a promising future.

But five years later, the picture didn't look so bright. Osama bin Laden and other top leaders of Al Qaeda and the Taliban were still at large, hiding in the wild mountains along the border with Pakistan. Fighters loyal to those groups often attacked Western troops as well as aid and reconstruction workers, slowing the pace of rebuilding. The number of attacks increased in 2006, and the Afghan security forces weren't strong enough to deal with the threat. About 31,000 Western troops, including 12,000 from the United States, were there to help, under the command of the North Atlantic Treaty Organization (NATO). Another 8,000 U.S. troops were hunting for terrorists and providing security for reconstruction efforts.

Danish cartoons showing the Muslim Prophet Mohammed in an unfavorable light set off protests around the world in early 2006.

The worst fighting was in the southeast, and the Afghan government accused Pakistan of tolerating Taliban and terrorists in the border region. But other parts of the country faced challenges, too. Trade in illegal drugs was flourishing as Afghan farmers increasingly grew opium poppies, the source of opium and heroin.

Many Afghans were growing tired of the presence of foreign soldiers in their country—and polls showed that many Americans were tired of the war, too. But analysts said that only stronger efforts could bring peace and stability to Afghanistan.

MUSLIM PROTESTS

A handful of political cartoons set off a storm of protest worldwide early in 2006. The cartoons, first published in a Danish newspaper in September 2005, were caricatures of the Prophet Mohammed, the founder of Islam. Muslim traditions forbid any illustration of the prophet, and several of these drawings showed Mohammed in an unfavorable light. One cartoon depicted the prophet wearing a turban in the shape of a bomb. Muslims were deeply insulted.

The cartoons didn't cause a stir outside Denmark for several months. Then Muslim countries in the Middle East began to boycott Danish goods, and Muslims began to hold rallies protesting the cartoons. Muslim

East Timor: Fresh Conflict

The little Southeast Asian nation of East Timor—only slightly larger than the state of Connecticut—saw some big trouble in 2006. And this wasn't the first time conflict had come to East Timor, which is one of the poorest countries in the world.

East Timor takes up half the island of Timor, in the Indonesian archipelago. Once a colony of Portugal, it declared independence in 1975—and was promptly occupied by Indonesia. The East Timorese fought the occupation for more than 20 years, and in 1999 they voted overwhelmingly for independence in a U.N.-supervised referendum. But a period of violence followed the vote, as pro-Indonesia militias drove people from their homes and destroyed houses, schools, and water and electrical systems. An international peacekeeping force, led by Australia, put a stop to the violence.

East Timor formally became independent in 2002, but since then tensions have grown between people in eastern and western parts of the country. In April 2006 those tensions erupted in violence. At least 30 people died, and more than 100,000 people fled their homes to escape the fighting. Troops and police from Australia, New Zealand, Malaysia, and Portugal helped restore order. But months

Violence in East Timor forced thousands into refugee camps. Here, an Australian peacekeeper disperses a crowd of angry youths in a camp in Dili, the nation's capital.

later, there was still low-level fighting. And more than 50,000 refugees were still living in makeshift camps in and around Dili, the capital.

In July, José Ramos-Horta was named prime minister. Ramos-Horta shared the Nobel Peace Prize in 1996 for his work in raising world awareness of East Timor's troubles in the 1990's. Now it was hoped that he could unify the country. A major part of his job was to rebuild the army and police forces, which had been involved in the violence. He also called on East Timor's rival political factions to hold talks. If tensions remained high, he warned, violence could erupt again before national elections, scheduled for May 2007.

leaders demanded that the government of Denmark apologize. Danish officials tried to explain that their government doesn't control what Danish newspapers print. (Governments of some Muslim countries do control the press.)

The Danish newspaper that ran the cartoons apologized for causing offense. However, the paper stood by its right to print the cartoons. Meanwhile, protests grew larger and more violent. In cities across Asia, Africa, and the Middle East, protesters burned Danish flags and shouted anti-Western slogans. The worst violence took

place in Nigeria. There, more than 100 people died in clashes between Muslims and Christians. In Syria, demonstrators burned the Norwegian and Danish embassies.

Moderate Muslim leaders called for calm. Denmark said that it would host a conference to promote understanding between Muslims and the West. Several newspapers in Europe reprinted the cartoons, to show support for press freedom. But most newspapers in Europe and the United States didn't—they didn't want to inflame the situation.

The furor was one of several incidents during the year that highlighted differences between Western and Muslim cultures. In Western countries, most people see free speech as an important part of democracy. Open debate helps people make good decisions. Thus it's okay for the press or anyone else to criticize government and religion, as long as no one is harmed. Few people would favor banning political cartoons, even if the cartoons offend some people.

But often there is no clear line between what's acceptable and what is not. Does freedom of speech come with responsibilities to not insult or mock religion? And who should decide what is acceptable? In some countries, the government decides. The U.S. Constitution lets individuals decide what to say or print, but individuals must be responsible for their actions.

A doctor in Padua, Italy, carefully inspects a chicken for signs of bird flu. The deadly disease spread from Asia to Europe and Africa in 2006.

BIRD-FLU WORRIES

Health officials worldwide continued to monitor avian influenza, or bird flu, in 2006. This disease primarily affects birds, but there were concerns that it might begin to spread rapidly among people and set off a worldwide epidemic, or pandemic.

Like all kinds of influenza, bird flu is caused by a virus. Several kinds of flu viruses occur naturally among birds, but concern has focused on a strain called H5N1, first identified in 1996. Many wild birds carry the virus without getting sick. But domestic birds such as chickens and ducks get very sick and may die when they catch the flu. Since 2003, millions of chickens and other birds in Southeast Asia have died from the flu or been killed in hopes of preventing its spread. In 2006 the virus was reported for the first time in India, Africa, and Western Europe.

While the bird-flu virus doesn't usually infect humans, some people have caught bird flu—and more than half of these people have died of the disease. Vietnam and Thailand have seen a number of bird-flu cases in past years, but in 2006 the disease seemed to be under control in those countries. More than 40 people died of bird flu in Indonesia, however. And there were deaths in other countries, including Egypt, Iraq, and Turkey.

People catch bird flu mostly from handling infected poultry. But scientists have confirmed that at least one death resulted from human-to-human spread, and they suspect that the disease spread among family members in several other cases. They still don't think the bird-flu virus can spread widely among people. But they are concerned because flu viruses change, or mutate, quickly and often. If this virus mutates so that it spreads more easily from person to person, an influenza pandemic could begin.

Researchers hope to develop a vaccine against the virus before that happens. In addition, health workers are learning how to detect bird flu and control outbreaks among birds as well as people. Vietnam and China have vaccinated millions of chickens against the virus, for example, and Thailand has set up a successful system of monitoring and culling to stop outbreaks.

The work is important because past flu pandemics have been deadly. The worst, in 1918–19, killed more than 500,000 people in the United States and perhaps as many as 50 million worldwide.

ELAINE PASCOE
Author, *Freedom of Expression: The Right to Speak Out in America*

NEWSMAKERS

Kofi Annan, 68, retired as Secretary-General of the United Nations on December 31, 2006, after two five-year terms. A soft-spoken diplomat from Ghana, Annan was the first black African ever elected to the post. During his years as Secretary-General, the U.N. expanded its peacekeeping operations. It now has 84,000 peacekeeping troops around the world. The U.N. also took new steps to promote economic development and fight disease. Annan won wide praise for his skills as the world's top diplomat. He was less successful in making reforms within the U.N., which critics say is inefficient and corrupt.

The United Nations chose South Korean statesman **Ban Ki-moon,** 62, as its next Secretary-General. When he took office on January 1, 2007, he became the eighth Secretary-General and the first from Asia since the 1960's. By tradition, the job rotates among the regions of the world.

Ban will oversee an organization with 192 member nations and a $20 billion annual budget. He's an experienced diplomat and has served as South Korea's foreign minister and national security adviser. Those positions gave him lots of experience with North Korea. And dealing with North Korea, which is developing nuclear weapons, will be a top priority in his new job.

In July, **Effa Manley** (1897–1981) became the first woman ever elected to the National Baseball Hall of Fame. Manley (right, with baseball great Don Newcombe) was one of 17 people from the Negro Leagues honored in 2006.

The Negro Leagues were formed by African-American teams before 1947, back when baseball was a segregated sport. With her husband, Abe Manley, Effa Manley co-owned the Newark Eagles from 1936 to 1948. She managed all the business details—scheduling, travel, payroll, contracts, and promotion. The Eagles' high point came in 1946, when they won the Negro League World Series. Manley, who was white but married an African American and was accepted as a black woman, also campaigned for civil rights. Later she co-wrote a book on the history of the Negro Leagues. She also urged the Baseball Hall of Fame to recognize more players from those leagues. Until 2006, only 18 were in the Hall.

Canadians chose a new leader and a new direction in 2006. In elections on January 23, the Conservative Party defeated the Liberal Party, which had led Canada for 13 years. Conservative leader **Stephen Harper,** 46, thus replaced Liberal leader Paul Martin as prime minister.

Harper, an economist, represented Alberta in parliament from 1993 to 1997. In 2002 he went back to parliament as head of the Canadian Alliance, which later merged with another party to form the Conservative Party. Unlike Martin, Harper supported the U.S. invasion of Iraq in 2003. In the 2006 campaign he promised to cut taxes, fight crime, and increase military spending.

Samuel A. Alito, Jr., was sworn in as an Associate Justice of the U.S. Supreme Court in January 2006. Alito, 55, replaced Sandra Day O'Connor, who retired. Alito had worked in government and in federal courts for most of his career. In the 1980's, in the administration of President Ronald Reagan, he worked on cases brought before the Supreme Court and gave advice on constitutional questions. In 1990 he became a judge on the U.S. Court of Appeals for the Third Circuit, where he became known for his conservative opinions.

After President George W. Bush nominated him to the Supreme Court, the Senate held confirmation hearings. Most Senate Democrats said Alito was too conservative and would tip the balance of the Court to the right. But Republicans were in the majority, and they backed Bush's choice.

In January 2006, voters in Chile elected their first woman president—**Michelle Bachelet,** 54. Her story is inspiring. "I was a victim of hatred, and I have dedicated my life to reversing that hatred," she says.

As a young girl, Bachelet lived briefly near Washington, D.C., where her father worked at the Chilean embassy. The family returned to Chile in 1963. Ten years later, a U.S.-backed coup overthrew Chile's leftist president Salvador Allende. General Augusto Pinochet took power. His agents tortured and killed Bachelet's father, who had supported Allende. Bachelet, then a medical student, was also arrested and tortured, as was her mother. After five years in exile, she returned to Chile in 1979 and worked in a clinic for children.

In 1990, Pinochet's harsh rule ended. Democracy returned. Bachelet became active in politics, as a member of the Socialist Party. In 2000, Chile elected a Socialist president, and Bachelet landed key government jobs. That experience prepared her for the presidency.

The work of **Muhammad Yunus** of Bangladesh is proof that small actions can accomplish great things. Yunus, 66, and his Grameen Bank won the 2006 Nobel Peace Prize for figuring out a new way to fight poverty—with microcredit, or tiny loans, to the poorest of the poor.

In the mid-1970's Yunus, then a professor of economics at Chittagong University, made his first loans—a total of $27—to 42 poor villagers. The money, all repaid, helped them get on their feet. That success led him to found Grameen Bank, which makes small loans to poor people so they can buy livestock, tools, and other things they need to make a living. The bank has inspired similar programs worldwide, which together have helped more than 100 million people in 130 countries. Yunus planned to invest part of his share of the $1.4-million Nobel award in Bangladesh, by founding an eye hospital and a company that would produce low-cost nutritious foods for the poor.

U.S. Senator **Robert C. Byrd** of West Virginia achieved a landmark on June 12, 2006. That day was his 17,327th in office—making Byrd, 88, the longest-serving senator in U.S. history. And he wasn't finished. In November, he won election to a ninth Senate term. He will be 95 when it ends.

Byrd was the adopted son of a coal miner and grew up in poverty. He served in the West Virginia assembly and the U.S. House of Representatives before winning his Senate seat in 1958. A Democrat, he served as Senate majority leader (1977–81 and 1987–89) and as president pro tempore (1989–95). Over his many years of service he became known for his fiery speeches, in which he often quoted poetry or cited Roman history. He also became a respected expert on the Senate's history and rules and a staunch defender of its traditions.

This African chameleon has a very special hunting weapon—its tongue. When a chameleon wants to dine, it shoots its sticky-tipped tongue forward with lightning speed and grabs hold of an insect. Powerful muscles controlling the tongue draw it back with the prey attached—and the prehistoric-looking lizard gulps down its meal. Fully extended, a chameleon's tongue may be longer than its body!

WHOOO GIVES A HOOT!

In the Sonoran Desert in southwestern Arizona, a lizard scurries across the desert floor. From atop a saguaro cactus, 30 feet (9 meters) tall, a hunter swoops silently down and snatches the lizard in its powerful talons. Back on the cactus, the hunter swallows its prey in one gulp.

The hunter is a cactus ferruginous pygmy owl, a bird that remained at the center of an environmental controversy in 2006. This bird is a member of one of the most fascinating but, to most people, least-known bird families. There are more than 130 kinds of owls worldwide, and 20 in North America. Although we rarely see or hear owls, these creatures play an important role in the natural world and are often helpful to people.

OWLS OF MANY KINDS

Owls are found in every part of the world except Antarctica and a few remote islands, and in nearly every kind of habitat. Snowy owls are at home in the Arctic tundra. Burrowing owls inhabit grassland. Elf owls live in deserts. Woodland owls of many types live from the cool pine forests of the north to the tropical rain forests. Screech owls live in towns and cities.

Owls also vary enormously in size. The smallest owls are the elf owl of the southwestern United States and the least pygmy owl of Central and South America. They are only about 5 inches (12 centimeters) long—about the size of a sparrow. The largest owl is the eagle owl of Europe, Asia, and northern Africa. It measures about 30 inches (76 centimeters) long.

Big or small, all owls are meat-eating predators—they hunt for their food. And all have many physical features in common. One of these is their general shape: a large head with a hooked beak, and no neck to speak of. All owls also have large feet with sharp claws, which are powerful weapons for catching prey and fighting enemies. The outer toe can be moved forward, backward, and outward to grasp and hold a victim.

An owl's huge eyes are another distinctive feature—they are much larger than those of other birds, and they can see in the dimmest light. In addition, the eyes are set to face forward (like your eyes) rather than to the sides (like most birds' eyes). This allows the owl to judge distance, an essential ability when it dives to catch its prey. But an owl cannot move its eyes from side to side. Instead, the owl turns its head. Some owls can turn their heads more than 270 degrees to one side or the other.

Owls also have a remarkable sense of hearing. An owl's face is shaped like a disk, and this shape helps funnel sounds to ear openings at the sides of its head. (The tufts of feathers on some owls' heads aren't ears but just a kind of decoration.) An owl's hearing is far more sensitive than human hearing. A great gray owl, for example, can hear a mouse running through tunnels under a foot of snow. And many owls can tell with pinpoint accuracy where a sound is coming from. Thus they can hunt in almost total darkness.

An owl can't move its eyes from side to side. But it can turn its head more than 270 degrees!

HOOTING NIGHT HUNTERS

Owls need these super senses of sight and hearing because most are nocturnal—they hunt by night. Only a few types of owls hunt during the day. This is one reason why they are rarely seen by people. Another reason is that owls have soft, fluffy plumage that blends with their surroundings. Snowy owls are mostly white, just like their snow-covered habitat. Woodland owls are usually brown or gray, while owls that live in open country are pale or yellowish in color.

This camouflage coloring makes the owls nearly invisible to their

An owl's wing feathers have fuzzy edges and are more flexible than those of other birds. They hardly make a sound when an owl flies.

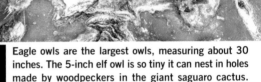

Eagle owls are the largest owls, measuring about 30 inches. The 5-inch elf owl is so tiny it can nest in holes made by woodpeckers in the giant saguaro cactus.

catch sixteen mice, three gophers, a rat, and a squirrel in just 25 minutes. Some small owls eat mainly insects, and some large owls can catch chickens and rabbits. A few kinds of owls catch fish, snatching them from the surface of the water. The oriental hawk owl eats crabs, and some eagle owls prefer frogs. But mice and other small rodents are the favorite foods of most kinds of owls.

Not all owls call "whoo, whoo." But many owl calls are strange and startling, ranging from bone-chilling hoots to unearthly shrieks. The screech owl, which is the most common owl in North America, whistles. The barking owl of Australia can growl like a dog. Other owl calls include snores, hissess, coughs, and chirps.

These calls all serve the same functions as the calls of other birds—to stake out territory; attract mates; or indicate fear, anger, or hunger. Many of the calls aren't very loud, but some calls carry over surprisingly long distances. The deep, booming call of the snowy owl can be heard up to 7 miles (11 kilometers) away in the thin Arctic air.

prey. And owls are among the world's most stealthy hunters—because they fly silently. The wing feathers of most birds have stiff edges that make a whooshing noise as the birds fly. But an owl's more flexible wing feathers have fuzzy edges, and they hardly make a sound.

Owls are such efficient hunters that they have little trouble finding their prey in the dark. One barn owl was actually seen to

Owls live in many different habitats. Burrowing owls (above) inhabit grassland and nest in underground tunnels made by small animals. The snowy owl (right) makes its home in the Arctic tundra. The screech owl (below) lives in towns and cities.

NESTS AND YOUNG

Most owls don't build nests. Some use nests abandoned by eagles, crows, and other birds. Some lay their eggs in holes in trees. The tiny elf owl nests in holes in the giant saguaro cactus—holes made by woodpeckers and flickers. Burrowing owls usually nest in underground tunnels made by prairie dogs, ground squirrels, or other animals, although the owls can dig their own burrows.

A female owl lays from one to a dozen eggs. She sits on the eggs until they hatch, while her mate shares the food he catches with her. Depending on the species, it takes from 21 to 42 days for the eggs to hatch. The baby owls (called nestlings or owlets) are born with their eyes and ears closed. The eyes and ears open when the birds are about a week old.

OWLS AND PEOPLE

Owls are often thought of as strange, even scary. In myths and legends, they have been associated with the supernatural. Their nocturnal habits, silent flight, strange calls, and huge piercing eyes contribute to this misconception. Perhaps the spookiest owl of all is the barn owl, which is common in farm areas. This pale-colored owl sometimes seems to glow with a ghostly light. In fact, the glow is caused by a phosphorescent mold that the bird picks up in its roost.

77

WHAT'S ON THE MENU?

Owls, like the barn owl pictured here, usually swallow their prey whole—fur, bones, and all. But an owl can't digest fur and bone. Instead, indigestible materials are packed into pellets inside the owl's stomach. Every so often, the owl burps up a pellet, or bolus, and it's dropped on the ground.

Owl pellets look like fuzzy lumps. The pellets can be taken apart to see what was on the owl's menu. Scientists first soak the pellet in warm water, and then gently pull it apart with tweezers. They might find skulls, jaws, and other bones; beaks and teeth; fur and feathers; the exoskeletons (or shells) of insects; and even the tiny bristles of earthworms.

Owl pellets have yielded important discoveries in the past. By studying fossilized pellets, scientists have been able to learn about the diet of prehistoric owls. And in Europe in the early 1900's, owl pellets helped prove to doubting farmers that owls weren't killing poultry and songbirds. Instead, the owls were helping the farmers—by killing rodents and insects that would otherwise destroy crops.

On the other hand, owls are often portrayed as cute figures in cartoons and advertisements. This may be because, with its forward-facing eyes and the "ear" tufts of some species, an owl's face looks a bit like a human face—or, at least, more so than the faces of most birds do.

And people have always found much to admire about these wonderful birds. In ancient times, the hunting ability of owls was greatly valued. In fact, relatives of the burrowing owl that nested near the Acropolis in Athens became the military mascot of that ancient Greek city-state. (These owls can still be found in the same area.) A legend tells that the Athenians were able to defeat the Persians at the battle of Marathon because a flock of owls swooped down on the Persian soldiers, confusing them and allowing the Greeks to gain an advantage.

The owl also became an emblem of Athena, the Greek goddess of war and wisdom and the protector of the city of Athens. Thus owls became associated with wisdom. But the Athenians weren't the only people to make this connection.

Perhaps because of their large heads and eyes, owls are often thought to be especially intelligent. Scientists say they are no smarter than other birds. But their skill as hunters makes them valuable in controlling pests. A pair of barn owls can eat about 1,300 rats a year. Thus farmers in many areas set out nesting boxes to attract owls, to control pests that would otherwise eat crops. Today some cities are doing this. In New York City, for example, officials relocated barn owls to some of the city's parks after setting up nesting boxes there.

Despite their helpful role, owls have often been hunted by people. And owls are sometimes killed unintentionally by pesticides or poisons put out to kill rats and mice. But today the greatest danger facing many kinds of owls is the destruction of their habitats. To survive, each breeding pair of owls needs a territory of a certain size—large enough to provide the food the pair and its young need. As people take over land for farming and development, less is left for the owls.

The cactus ferruginous pygmy owl is just one of seven kinds of owls that are in danger of dying out for this reason. Cactus ferruginous pygmy owls live only in Arizona, Texas, and Mexico. Those that live in Arizona have been at the center of a controversy for a number of years.

These owls, which were once common, were placed on the U.S. Endangered Species list in 1997. Under the law, it became illegal to kill or harm them—but despite the protection their numbers kept falling. In 1999 there were 41 adult cactus ferruginous pygmy owls in Arizona; in 2006, there were just 13.

The problem, wildlife officials said, was development. Southern Arizona is a fast-growing region, and people have been taking over wild areas for housing, logging, livestock grazing, and other uses. The wild desert scrublands where the owls lived and raised their young started to disappear.

A plan was created to set aside 1.2 million acres (485,623 hectares) in southern Arizona as "critical habitat" for the cactus ferruginous pygmy owls. People who wanted

The cactus ferruginous pygmy owls that live in Arizona are in danger of dying out.

to build houses or use this land in other ways would have to show that their actions wouldn't affect the owls.

Builders complained that the plan would basically ban development of the land, which is mostly privately owned. That, they said, was unfair. Builders also said that the owls in Arizona were the same as the owls in Texas and Mexico; and since those owls were plentiful, the Arizona cactus ferruginous pygmy owls shouldn't even be on the endangered list.

Then, in 2005, the administration of President George W. Bush proposed that the cactus ferruginous pygmy owls in Arizona be taken off the Endangered Species list. In 2006, the U.S. Fish and Wildlife Service did just that. But environmentalists said they would continue their fight to keep the cactus ferruginous pygmy owl protected in Arizona.

AND THE WINNER IS . . .

What contests could these odd-looking animals win? Wacky as they all seem, each one is a prizewinner—in its own way.

The **king vulture** (above) could win the lumpy-nose award. Its large, powerful bill is decorated with a fleshy yellow crest. Like other vultures, the king vulture is a scavenger. It lives in the tropical forests of South America and eats carrion—the flesh of dead animals. That may sound ghastly, but in fact the king vulture serves a useful purpose as part of nature's clean-up crew.

The male **elephant seal** (inset) could take top prize for nose size. The seal shown here is still young, and his nose is still growing. As a full-grown adult, he'll weigh as much as 8,000 pounds (3,700 kilograms) and have a really monstrous nose. Elephant seals are found in coastal waters from Alaska to Baja California, and around the southern tip of South America. In breeding season, males gather harems of females on the beaches and defend them vigorously against other males.

The **hoatzin** (opposite page, top left) is a shoo-in for the wild-hair prize. Of course, since the hoatzin is a bird, its "do" is made up of feathers, not hair. This chicken-sized bird lives in the jungles of South America. It's sometimes called the stinkbird—because it has bad breath! The hoatzin eats leaves, shoots, and buds; these plant parts are high in fiber. Like a cow, the bird has a special chamber in its stomach where bacteria digest the plant fibers. That produces a lot of stinky gases, which the hoatzin burps up.

The male **mandrill** (top right) deserves the colorful-face award. His is a face no one can forget— bright blue cheeks, shading to purple and violet, flanking a scarlet nose. When the mandrill is frightened, angry, or excited, the colors become even brighter. The largest monkey of the African forests, the male mandrill can weigh 100 pounds (45 kilograms). Females are smaller and not so loudly colored.

The **axolotl** (above) could win a space-alien look-alike contest. It looks like something from Mars, but it's actually from Mexico. Its name means "water toy" or "water dog" in the Aztec Indian language. The axolotl is a salamander, and those feathery stalks around its head are gills. They allow the axolotl to breathe underwater.

Salamanders are amphibians, and they all spend at least part of their lives in water. Most grow up and move onto land. They change from water-dwelling larvae into land-dwelling, air-breathing adults, a process called metamorphosis. But the axolotl is one salamander that doesn't change. It just gets bigger and bigger—up to 12 inches (30 centimeters) long. And it spends its whole life in the water, never moving onto land.

Meerkats are little African animals that start each day standing on their hind legs and basking in the warm rays of the sun.

MEERKATS: UNITED THEY STAND

If meerkats had a motto, it would have to be "Go team!" That's because a meerkat's life is all about teamwork. These clever little African animals live in groups and cooperate in everything. They hunt for food together, groom each other, and baby-sit. And they take turns acting as lookouts for the group—standing on their hind legs, sometimes for hours, in the hot African sun.

Meerkats are spunky and charming, and people find them hard to resist. In fact, one of the hit shows on cable television in 2006 was *Meerkat Manor*, which followed the life of a meerkat family in

A meerkat uses its upright stance to act as guard for the rest of the colony.

weekly episodes. But meerkats don't act the way they do to be cute.

Meerkats live in semidesert areas of southern Africa. Life is hard in these dry areas, and there are many predators that would love to dine on a tasty little meerkat. By banding together, meerkats survive.

DIGGERS AND HUNTERS

The meerkat has another name—suricate. But "meerkat" is the better-known term. Meerkat means "marsh cat" in Afrikaans, a language spoken in South Africa. Despite the name, meerkats don't live in marshes, and they aren't cats. They are members of the mongoose family.

A meerkat is roughly the size of a large squirrel. Its

body is about 1 foot (30 centimeters) long, and its tapering tail is a bit shorter than that. The animal's coarse fur is gray-brown, with a yellowish tinge and brownish bands along the back and tail. The ears and the tip of the tail are black. Dark-rimmed eyes, a pointy nose, and long powerful claws complete the picture.

Bands, or colonies, of meerkats live in underground burrows, which they sometimes share with ground squirrels and other animals. With their long claws, meerkats are excellent diggers. The tunnels and chambers of their burrows may extend many yards and have several entrances. There may be as many as 40 meerkats in a colony, but many groups have fewer members. The members are generally related, forming an extended family.

Meerkats tumble out of their burrows at sunrise and start the day with one of their favorite activities: a sunbath. The animals stand together in a group, with their bellies turned toward the warming rays of the sun. They look almost human. Soon, though, it's time to begin the day's work—an endless search for the insects, lizards, eggs, plant bulbs, and small rodents, snakes, and birds that meerkats love to eat.

A group of meerkats hunts for food over a territory that may cover several square miles. The group forages in a different section of the territory each day. When they have eaten everything they can find in the territory—which may even take months—they move to a new territory and dig a new burrow.

The meerkats scurry along on all fours, sniffing and scratching the dry ground and exploring every nook and cranny in their search. When a meerkat sniffs out a beetle or some other tidbit, it digs furiously until it finds the prize. Only when the prey is completely uncovered does the meerkat kill and eat it.

ON GUARD

While it's digging for food, with its head and claws buried in the ground, a meerkat is all but defenseless. It would be an easy mark for any predator. But that's where teamwork

Meerkats make good baby-sitters. While a mother meerkat hunts for food, another adult will stay with her babies—tending, grooming, and cuddling the youngsters.

comes in. At least one meerkat is always on guard as the group hunts. This meerkat stands upright and scans the area constantly, looking for jackals and other predators on the ground and for eagles and vultures in the sky. The meerkats take turns on guard duty, so they all have a chance to eat.

Meerkats have keen noses and excellent eyesight, and they can spot eagles that are no more than specks in the sky. They aren't very good climbers, but they willingly clamber onto rocks and up trees to get a better view when they are on guard. And they don't seem to mind standing upright, even on their toes, for long periods of time. The meerkat's

This meerkat is gobbling one of its favorite foods: a luscious scorpion! Yum!

In the hottest part of the day, the meerkats find shelter in the shade of a bush or a tree. While one of the group stands guard, the others sit or lie down to rest. They may cuddle or groom each other. Those that have the energy may play, tumbling rowdily in the dirt.

At day's end the band returns to the burrow for the night. One by one, the meerkats crawl in, pile on top of each other, and curl up. Finally a mound of meerkats is sleeping soundly.

tail helps. When the animal stands upright, it stiffens its tail and uses it for support.

When a guard meerkat senses danger, it utters a long warning peep or bark. The other meerkats quickly run for cover. If there's no cover handy, they stand and fight. These little animals can be surprisingly fierce. They bunch together in tight formation, fluff out their fur, stick their tails up in the air, and growl and hiss. Then, together, they advance on their enemy in a stiff-legged gait, jumping into the air with each stride. The effect is alarming, and many predators run away. If the predator doesn't run, the meerkats continue their advance. They scream and hiss and may even bite.

Meerkats prefer to run from large predators or very dangerous ones, such as eagles. But they often gang up on smaller predators, including snakes, to drive them out of the territory. Meerkats act in much the same way when a rival group tries to enter their territory. After driving the intruders off, the victorious meerkats may mill around excitedly for a few minutes, chattering and hugging each other.

Meerkats seem to enjoy doing most everything together—even sleeping.

BABY-SITTERS

Meerkats cooperate in more than hunting and defense. They also work together to raise their young.

Baby meerkats, or pups, are born in litters, usually of two to five. Their ears and eyes are closed for the first 10 to 14 days of life, and they stay in the burrow. The mother nurses them. But other meerkats help—by baby-sitting. While the mother goes out with the group to forage for food, another adult stays with the babies, often for the whole day. Other adults also help groom and cuddle the young.

By the time young meerkats are six weeks old, the mother has begun to bring them solid food. They learn about solid food by snatching bits from her mouth. In fact, the pups may refuse to eat even the tastiest

"Say a few words for your fans," this scientist seems to be saying. Meerkats make a wide variety of sounds.

morsel unless they have first obtained it from their mother this way.

As they get older, the pups go out with the group on foraging expeditions. Each youngster tags along with an older meerkat, learning the ins and outs of hunting. Adult meerkats don't generally share food with each other, but they willingly share it with the youngsters. And they teach the youngsters how to deal with live prey, including dangerous but tasty scorpions.

A study released in 2006 reported how meerkats teach pups to handle scorpions, which have a poisonous sting. At first, the adults give the pups only dead scorpions. Later they let the pups handle live scorpions without stings. When they can handle those, the pups get their scorpions complete with stings. The researchers who did the study say it marks clear evidence of teaching in mammals other than humans.

Perhaps because they're found only in southern Africa, meerkats weren't studied very much until recent times. Now scientists are learning a lot more about these animals and

The Whiskers family on *Meerkat Manor* is probably pretty similar to this furry family of meerkats.

Meerkat Manor

Can the Whiskers family make peace with the rival Lazuli family? Can Tosca make amends with Flower? Will Shakespeare survive a poisonous snakebite?

Fans of the cable television show *Meerkat Manor* tuned in week after week for answers to those and more questions in 2006. The show was like a soap opera with furry stars—a family of meerkats, named the Whiskers, struggling to survive in Africa's Kalahari Desert. There were family quarrels, secret romances, and a feud with a neighboring meerkat family.

Just like the characters in a soap opera, each meerkat had a distinct personality. Zaphod, the top male, would defend the Whiskers at all costs. But the real boss of the clan was Flower, the dominant female. She stopped at nothing to get her way, even driving other females out of the clan. Shakespeare was a hero who rescued his young brother Mitch from near death. Mozart was the clan's chief baby-sitter, a natural caregiver who stayed by Shakespeare's side when he was bitten by a poisonous snake.

The little animals provided more than enough drama to carry *Meerkat Manor* into a second season. Fans couldn't get enough of this furry reality show.

their complex society. Researchers are studying how meerkats communicate with each other, too. Meerkats make a wide variety of sounds—murmurs, grunts, barks, peeps, trills, growls, shrieks—and scientists aren't sure what they all mean.

It's likely that researchers will enjoy finding out more about meerkats. Clever and comical, meerkats would make any scientist smile.

85

This blind, blond, furry crustacean is just one of several recently discovered new animal species. It's being called the "Yeti crab."

THE EVER-CHANGING ANIMAL KINGDOM

There are more than 1 million known species of animals on Earth, and scientists are still finding more. Most new species are found in places where few researchers have ventured before—in the dark depths of the ocean, in caves beneath Earth's surface, and in dense, unexplored tropical forests.

The discoveries of several new species were announced in 2006.

A FURRY CRUSTACEAN

Divers searching the floor of the South Pacific Ocean found a creature that looks like a lobster or a crab—but it's covered with silky, blond fur! They're calling it the "Yeti crab." Yeti is a mythical hairy monster said to haunt the Himalayan Mountains.

New species of creepy crawlies found in California caves: a daddy longlegs spider (top) and a pseudoscorpion (above).

Like all lobsters and crabs, the creature is a crustacean. But it's so different that scientists have created a separate crustacean family for it—Kiwaidae. The name comes from *Kiwa*, who is the goddess of crustaceans in Polynesian mythology. The scientific name of the furry crab itself is *Kiwa hirsuta*. *Hirsuta* means "hairy" in Latin.

Scientists aren't yet sure of the purpose of the animal's silky hairs, called setae. They do know, however, that the hairs are full of bacteria, which might serve as food for the crustacean or help it survive in some other way. The Yeti crab has another odd feature: It's blind. It was found 900 miles (1,448 kilometers) south of Easter Island in waters

This odd mammal lived in the days of the dinosaurs.

7,540 feet (2,271 meters) beneath the ocean's surface. No sunlight reaches the dark depths where it lives, so it has no need for sight.

CREEPY CAVE CRAWLERS

Blaze-orange spiders. . .see-through sow bugs. . .a daddy longlegs with a mouth bigger than its body. Those are some of the 27 new kinds of animals that scientists have found in caves at two national parks in California. A team of scientists has been studying 30 caves at Sequoia and Kings Canyon national parks for several years. They expected to find a few new creatures. But they were amazed by the number they actually discovered.

Many of the animals live only in the caves. Some live only in one specific cave. None have been officially named. Sequoia and Kings Canyon national parks have a total of 238 known caves. Imagine what surprises may be waiting in those yet to be explored!

AN ODD FOSSIL MAMMAL

Scientists in China found a new species of animal—that is, the fossil remains of a strange mammal that lived 164 million years ago, in the days of the dinosaurs.

The animal wasn't the ancestor of any existing species of animal. It was about the size of a small house cat and looked something like a cross between a modern beaver, a platypus, and a river otter. The creature had fur, a broad scaly tail, webbed feet for swimming, and sharp teeth

Glow Pigs

Here's a new animal that wasn't discovered—it was created in a lab.

Scientists in Taiwan have bred pigs that actually glow in the dark! In daylight the pigs' eyes, teeth, and trotters look green. Their skin has a greenish tinge. In the dark, under a blue light, the pigs glow vivid green. And it's not just the skin that's green. The pig is green from inside out—including its heart and other internal organs.

Otherwise, the pigs look normal. The scientists produced the glow pigs by adding genetic material from fluorescent jellyfish to pig embryos. Their purpose wasn't to make glow-in-the-dark bacon. Instead, they hope to use the pigs for research into human diseases.

for catching and eating fish. It swam in rivers and lakes in northern China, and probably lived in nests built in burrows along the shore.

Scientists say it is the earliest swimming mammal ever found. It had long been thought that the mammals that lived when dinosaurs roamed Earth were tiny creatures that lived only on land. Now scientists are rethinking that idea. It seems that prehistoric animals are full of surprises, too.

Two male moose competing for the attentions of a female use their huge antlers as battering rams. Antlers are among the many remarkable weapons used by animals for fighting and hunting.

WILDLIFE WEAPONS

It's the winter mating season, and the two giant male moose are vying for the attentions of a female moose. They stare at each other, snorting and pawing the ground. Suddenly, they run full tilt at each other. Their huge antlers collide, making a loud crunching noise that can be heard throughout the woods. They back off and then charge again, and again, and again. Finally, the weaker moose loses heart and runs off.

The moose uses its antlers to batter or stab its rival. But other animals may bite, scratch, sting, or shock their enemies. They may bombard them with hot gas, burning acid, or a smelly spray.

To capture their food, most hunting animals use their teeth and claws, but many other kinds of weapons are also used. Some animals catch their prey by poisoning them, electrocuting them, or even by shooting at them.

FIGHTING TOOTH . . .

Hunting animals usually have strong jaws and sharp teeth. If you look at the jaws of a dog or a cat, you will see four long pointed teeth—two in the upper jaw and two in the lower. These are called canine teeth, or fangs. Canines are the chief weapons of many hunting animals. Like daggers, they are used for stabbing and slashing.

Monkeys and apes also have long canine teeth, but they use them mainly for self-defense. A monkey threatens an enemy by opening its mouth and flashing its dangerous canines.

Animals such as elephants, walruses, and wild pigs are armed with tusks—extra-long teeth that grow out of an animal's mouth. An African elephant will defend her helpless calf from lions and leopards by charging and stabbing with her tusks. She can kill any enemy instantly with one powerful thrust. Tusks are used for digging up food as well as for fighting.

Fish have a greater variety of teeth than any other group of animals. Since they have no limbs to help them grasp their prey, they must rely on their teeth to seize and hold whatever they catch. Some fish have teeth not only in their jaws but also on their tongues or even far back in their throats.

A shark's teeth have jagged edges and pointed tips, like steak knives. Most sharks have several rows of teeth, lined up one behind another. New teeth are growing in all the time. When the teeth in the front row are old and worn, they drop out. Then the teeth in the row behind move in to take their place. During a ten-year period, a tiger shark will grow, use, and shed as many as 24,000 teeth.

. . . AND NAIL

A cat's claws can be as dangerous as its teeth. Lions, tigers, and all other cats use their claws to hook their prey and pull it down. Because of the way a cat's claws are curved, they make very effective weapons. Once they dig into the flesh, the victim's struggling only serves to draw them in deeper.

Except for the cheetah, all cats can pull their claws back into their toes. A cat usually keeps its claws pulled in, so they won't be blunted by the hard ground. When it climbs or fights, it pushes its claws out.

A leopard's sharp fangs are deadly weapons that it uses to capture cattle, birds, and other prey. Walruses are armed with powerful tusks, which they use for digging up food as well as for fighting.

Other animals with claws—such as dogs, bears, and raccoons—cannot pull them in. They use their claws mainly for digging or climbing rather than hunting or fighting. Even so, their claws can still cause plenty of damage. A bear fights by striking an enemy with its front paws. When it hits its target, its heavy claws can rip and tear.

Birds of prey hunt with the pointed talons on their feet. An eagle will swoop down from the sky, snatch up a rabbit with its talons, and carry it away. Some birds, such as the flightless ostrich, defend themselves with their feet. An ostrich has long muscular legs with two toes on each foot. The big toe is armed with a thick sharp nail. The ostrich fights by kicking. Its kick can be more dangerous than that of a horse.

Hoofed animals also fight by kicking. A zebra can smash an enemy's teeth with a well-aimed kick.

LOCKING HORNS

Horns are used for self-defense by grazing animals like goats, sheep, cattle, and antelope. The horns of a Rocky Mountain goat are short and curved. A mother goat protecting her kid has been known to kill a bear by stabbing it in the heart. A male bighorn sheep has thick, heavy, tightly curled horns, which it uses as battering rams.

In Africa, an antelope called the gemsbok has horns like swords that may be 4 feet (1.2 meters) long. When a gemsbok attacks, it lowers its head between its legs, so the sharp tips of its horns are pointing at the enemy. A charging gemsbok can scoop up a lion with its horns and throw the lion over its back.

Antlers are found among most members of the deer family. Unlike horns, which keep on growing throughout an animal's life, antlers last only for a few months each year. They start growing in the spring, reach their full size during the winter, then drop off. The following spring, the animal grows a new set of antlers.

The pointed tips of fully grown antlers are as sharp as pitchforks. Antlers serve as

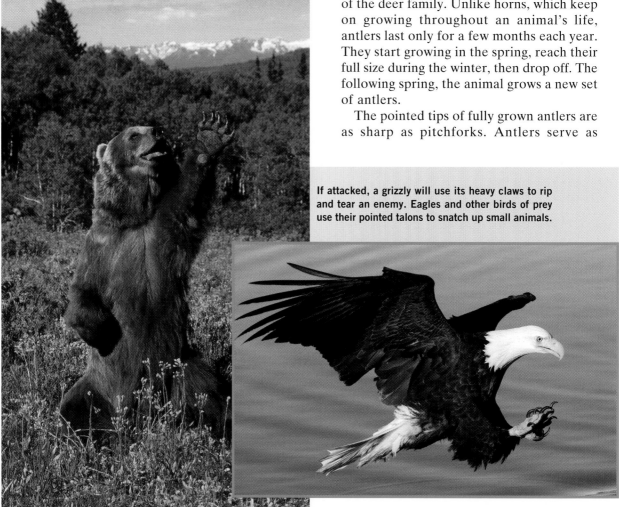

If attacked, a grizzly will use its heavy claws to rip and tear an enemy. Eagles and other birds of prey use their pointed talons to snatch up small animals.

Beware! When a porcupine is threatened, its quills stand on end like thousands of sharp needles. A porcupine fish has spines that are similar to a porcupine's quills. The spines lie flat. But when the fish is scared, it gulps water and swells up like a thorn-covered balloon. Its spines stick out in all directions, ready to stab any attacker.

weapons only during the winter mating season, when rival males fight over females. They are also used to fight off enemies such as wolves. But once they have dropped off, the animal must rely for protection on speed and its hooves.

STICKING IT TO THEM

A porcupine seems to know that it is well protected as it waddles slowly through the forest with its nose to the ground. Buried beneath its long fur are 30,000 dangerous quills that keep most enemies at a distance.

Quills are stiff hairs growing out of the porcupine's skin. They are as sharp as needles and may be 4 inches (10 centimeters) long. The pointed tip of each quill has tiny barbs, or hooks, that curve backward, like the barbs on harpoons.

Usually the quills lie flat against the porcupine's body. But when a porcupine is frightened, its quills stand on end. Twisting about on its short legs, the porcupine keeps its rear toward the enemy and whips its bristling tail back and forth. As a warning, it hisses and gnashes its teeth.

A porcupine can't shoot its quills, but it can swat an enemy with its tail. When the tail hits its target, it drives hundreds of quills into the enemy. As the victim backs away, the quills are pulled out of the porcupine and stay buried in the victim's body. Once a quill has stabbed an enemy, the barbed tip works its way into the flesh. A badly wounded animal can die of its injuries.

Some fish have spines similar to a porcupine's quills. The spines of a porcupine fish resemble the prickly thorns of a rose bush. Usually, a porcupine fish swims about with its spines lying flat against its body. But when it is alarmed, it gulps water and swells up like a prickly balloon. Its spines stick out in all directions, ready to stab any enemy.

THE POISONERS

Poison is used as a weapon for hunting or self-defense by many kinds of fish, snakes, and insects, as well as other animals. The poison,

them in place. It fights by twisting about in the water, jabbing at the enemy with its spines. Fishermen must handle catfish with great care to avoid being stung.

The deadliest of all venomous fish is the ugly little stonefish, found off the coast of Australia. A stonefish lies hidden among stones and debris in shallow water, waiting to leap forward and snap up its prey. Its body is covered with warts and coated with algae and slime, making it almost invisible.

Eighteen jagged spines jut out from its body. These fish are considered as deadly as

Some animals use poisons to protect themselves. The ugly little stonefish has jagged spines on its back containing the deadliest of all fish poisons.

or venom, is produced by special glands in the animal's body. The animal injects its venom by biting or stinging.

Many fish are armed with venomous spines, which they use only for self-defense. A catfish has a sharp spine in the fin on its back and two more spines in the fins on its sides. All three spines are barbed, like a porcupine's quills. They are connected to glands that pump poison into an enemy's wounds. When a catfish is alarmed, it lifts its spines and locks

cobras. Swimmers in Australia have died within an hour after stepping on a stonefish.

Venomous snakes use their poison to capture food, as well as in self-defense. They can strike and kill with lightning speed. A rattlesnake has two hollow fangs in its upper jaw. Each fang is connected to a poison gland in the rattler's cheek. When the snake sinks its fangs into a victim, its cheeks squeeze against the poison glands. Poison squirts into the wound through tiny holes in the tips of the

Chemical warfare is another animal weapon. The bombardier beetle defends itself by spraying enemies with an irritating gas that shoots out from the tail end of its body.

fangs. A rattlesnake bite can kill a rabbit in a few minutes. It can also kill a person unless the victim receives quick medical aid.

The biggest venomous snakes are cobras, which live in Africa and Asia. A king cobra may be 18 feet (5.5 meters) long. A cobra warns its enemies by rearing up, hissing loudly, and spreading the skin of its neck into a wide hood. Some cobras can spit their poison through small holes in the front of their fangs. They are said to aim at the eyes of their enemies.

Spiders capture food just as some snakes do—with a poisonous bite. Like a rattlesnake, a spider has two sharp fangs connected to poison glands in its head. All spiders are poisonous, but only a few, like the black widow, are dangerous to humans. Most spiders are so small that their fangs cannot pierce human skin.

Hornets, wasps, and bees have poisonous stingers at the tips of their tails. A bee's venom is similar to a snake's, but it isn't as dangerous because it's released in much smaller amounts. Some ants also have poisonous stingers in their tails, which they use to kill enemies and capture the creatures

they eat. Ants can also bite with their powerful ice-tong jaws. An ant will often bite an enemy, then turn around and squirt poison into the wound.

CHEMICAL WARFARE

A skunk cannot really injure an enemy. Yet it is armed with one of nature's most effective weapons—a bad-smelling chemical spray. Most animals get out of the way when they see a skunk coming.

A skunk always gives warning before it fires. It lowers its head and drums on the ground with its front paws. It may click its teeth and growl or hiss. If the enemy doesn't retreat, the skunk lifts its bushy tail. That's the last warning. Suddenly the skunk twists around into a U-shaped position. It aims its tail at the enemy and lets go with its stinking spray.

Skunk spray comes from two stink glands beneath the skunk's tail. Each gland is connected to a small tube that lies hidden under the skin. When the skunk fires, the tubes pop out like a pair of nozzles. They squirt two streams of thick, oily fluid that join together in a misty spray.

Most frogs eat insects, which they catch with their long, sticky tongues. But the champion tongue-flicker is the African chameleon. This reptile takes aim, whips out its *really* long, sticky tongue, and seizes its prey.

A skunk can aim straight ahead, to either side, or up into the air. It can shoot its spray more than 10 feet (3 meters), even more if the spray is carried by the wind. The strong smell of skunk spray can make a person or animal sick. If the spray hits the eyes, they will sting and burn until tears wash the spray out.

Skunks aren't the only animals that use odor as a weapon. Snakes, weasels, minks, wolverines, and several other animals have scent glands similar to a skunk's but not as powerful.

Some insects are also equipped for chemical warfare. When they are threatened, they release a fluid or gas that stinks, burns, or stings. A stinkbug drives off enemies by giving off a repulsive smell. Some ants can spray a burning acid. The bombardier beetle attacks enemies by blasting them with hot gas that shoots out from the tail end of its body. It can give off as many as 20 consecutive sprays.

SHOCKING WEAPONS

Fish are the only animals that have the power to shock their enemies. About 250 kinds of fish can send an electrical charge into the water. The most powerful of these is the electric eel, which lives in South American rivers.

In the eel's tail are bundles of cells that produce electricity in much the same way as an electric battery. As the eel swims along, it gives off a weak current that helps it find its way in muddy river waters. When it finds food or is alarmed, it can deliver an electric shock of up to 650 volts. That's enough power to stun the fish and frogs it feeds on and to jolt enemies like alligators.

THE TONGUE LASSO

Frogs and toads use their long sticky tongues as hunting weapons. They catch insects by flicking out their tongues. The champion tongue-flicker, however, is a reptile, the African chameleon. Usually, a chameleon's tongue is folded up inside its mouth. When it spots an insect, it creeps forward, takes aim, opens its mouth, and fires. Its tongue, longer than its body, shoots out like a spring uncoiling. The swollen tip of the tongue is coated with a sticky fluid that can trap big insects as well as small reptiles and birds. After hitting its target, the chameleon hauls its meal back into its mouth.

THE WATER GUN

Of all the animals that use weapons, the archerfish is in a class by itself. It shoots water bullets at its prey. These little fish live in Australia and Southeast Asia. They hunt by waiting below the surface of a pond, with the tips of their mouths sticking out of the water. When an archerfish sees an insect or spider on

The sharpshooter of the animal world is the amazing archerfish. It can capture a spider a few feet away by blasting it with a stream of water bullets.

a leaf or plant stem, it closes its gills and forces water into its mouth. Then it presses its tongue against the roof of its mouth and fires droplets of water in a rapid stream.

An archerfish can score a bull's-eye from several feet away. The fast jet of water knocks the insect or spider off its perch. It falls into the pond, where it's seized and swallowed by the sharpshooting archerfish.

Few animals have a weapon as unusual as that of the archerfish. But every animal uses the weapons it was born with—to hunt and to protect itself—so it can stay alive for another day.

ANIMALS IN THE NEWS

What's cuter than a baby giant panda? More baby pandas! And lots of baby pandas were posing for photos in 2006. At zoos and centers where scientists are working to save these rare animals, there's been a **panda population boom!**

The giant panda is one of the world's most endangered animals. Scientists in China are raising pandas in captivity in hopes of increasing their numbers. In 2005 a record 16 cubs (top) were born at a panda research center in Wolong, in southern China. And in 2006 twin pandas at another Chinese center, near Chengdu, each gave birth to twins. China also released a captive-bred panda into the wild for the first time. A 4-year-old male, it was set free in a forest of bamboo—the giant panda's main food.

Baby pandas also frolicked in the United States. Two cuddly cubs were born at U.S. zoos in 2005: a male at the National Zoo in Washington, D.C., and a female at the San Diego Zoo in California. The male cub (above left, with his mom) was named Tai Shan, which means "peaceful mountain." The female cub (above right) was named Su Lin, which means "a little bit of something very cute."

A third cub was born at Zoo Atlanta in Georgia in September 2006. Following Chinese tradition, the new cub, a female, wouldn't be named for 100 days.

Rufus, a colored bull terrier, won the best-in-show award at the 2006 Westminster Kennel Club show in New York City in February. Westminster is the most famous dog show in the United States, and Rufus was the first colored bull terrier to win the top prize.

Bull terriers were first bred in England in the 1800's, as fighting dogs. Today they are bred and trained to be family pets. This breed's most distinctive feature is its head—the size of a football and shaped like an egg. The Westminster judges thought Rufus's head was perfect. They placed him over 2,622 entries, representing 165 breeds and varieties. Rufus, whose full name is Champion Rocky Top's Sundance Kid, enjoyed a steak dinner after his win.

Manatees cruise warm bays and calm coastal waters in Florida. Protected by state and federal laws, the number of these gentle giants has grown from about 1,000 to more than 3,000 since the late 1970's. As a result, in 2006 Florida changed the manatee's status from "endangered" (at great risk of dying out) to "threatened" (at risk, but not in immediate danger). The federal government was also reviewing the manatee's status. But conservationists objected to this change in status, saying that manatees still face great danger from collisions with boats, pollution, and other threats.

The world lost two giant tortoises, both zoo favorites, in 2006—but no one could say they died young. **Harriet** (above), a tortoise at the Australia Zoo, lived an amazing 175 years. And **Adwaitya** (right), a tortoise at a zoo in Calcutta, India, was even older. He may have been more than 250!

Adwaitya was from the Aldabra Atoll (part of the Seychelles Islands) in the Indian Ocean. No one knows just when he was born, but British sailors brought him to India sometime in the 1700's. Harriet was from the Galápagos Islands off the coast of South America. Some people say she was taken from her home by the British naturalist Charles Darwin, who stopped at the islands in 1835. Others dispute this.

The tortoises' lives stretched from the era of sailing ships to the era of space flight. But it's doubtful that they paid much attention.

The thoroughbred racehorse **Barbaro** captured the hearts of animal lovers in 2006. In May, Barbaro won the Kentucky Derby, the most famous U.S. horse race and the first of three that make up racing's Triple Crown. But in the second race, the Preakness, his right hind leg fractured—a tragic and possibly fatal injury. Barbaro was rushed to the University of Pennsylvania large animal hospital, where veterinarian Dean Richardson (right, with Barbaro in August) set the break. Barbaro began a long recovery, and fans showered him with get-well cards and gifts of carrots and apples.

In July 2006, Canada, Mexico, and the United States designated 13 wildlife refuges as protected areas for **monarch butterflies**. The idea is to form a network of places along the monarchs' migration routes where monarch habitat will be preserved and restored.

Millions of monarch butterflies make one of the world's great migrations each fall. Monarchs from eastern Canada and the United States head south to Mexico, flying some 2,800 miles (4,500 kilometers), to winter in the forests of the Sierra Madre mountains. Monarchs west of the Rocky Mountains fly a shorter distance to eucalyptus groves in southern California. They fly north in the spring.

But illegal logging is shrinking the Mexican forests, development is doing the same to the eucalyptus groves, and pesticides are killing the milkweed plant on which monarch caterpillars feed.

Early land animals evolved from fish—but how was the switch from water to land made? In 2006 scientists announced that they had found an important piece of the puzzle: fossils of a strange fish that swam in water and walked on land. They called it a "missing link" between fishes and the first four-legged land animals.

The fish was named **Tiktaalik roseae**. Tiktaalik means "large freshwater fish" in the Inuit language of Canada's far north, where the fossils were found. This area is cold and icy today, but it was warm when the fish lived—375 million years ago. Tiktaalik was a big fish, up to 9 feet (2.7 meters) long, with fins, scales, and other fish features. And it was a meat eater, with sharp teeth. It probably spent most of its time in shallow freshwater streams and swamps. But scientists think it could move on land like a seal, pushing along with its front fins. Those front fins had bones that were like early versions of shoulder, elbow, wrist, and finger bones. One scientist called them "fins that could do push-ups."

Tiktaalik had other unusual features. Its skull was flat, like a crocodile's. Its neck and ribs were more like those of early four-legged land animals than like those of other fishes. All these features mark Tiktaalik's place in evolution—a place between water and land. (Above: fossils of the prehistoric fish. Inset: A drawing of what Tiktaalik probably looked like.)

Beluga whales (above) and about 100,000 other animals were on view at the new **Georgia Aquarium** in Atlanta, Georgia, in 2006. "Amazing," "fantastic," and "magical" were some of the words that visitors were using to describe the aquarium, which opened in November 2005.

The Georgia Aquarium is the largest aquarium in the world, with more than 60 ocean and freshwater habitats arranged in five galleries. Two belugas and a group of African black-footed penguins (inset) are among the animals in Cold Water Quest, a gallery that presents the life of cold oceans. A gallery devoted to coral reefs includes one of the largest living-reef exhibits in the world, home to living corals and thousands of colorful reef fishes. Other galleries display fishes and animals from African, South American, and Asian rivers; and from Georgia's coastal waters.

The aquarium's showpiece is in the Ocean Voyager gallery. It's a huge saltwater tank holding more than 6 million gallons of water. Visitors can walk through an underwater see-through tunnel or stand in front of a giant window to see inside. The tank's most amazing residents are two whale sharks, named Ralph and Norton. These giant fish can grow to be as big as school buses!

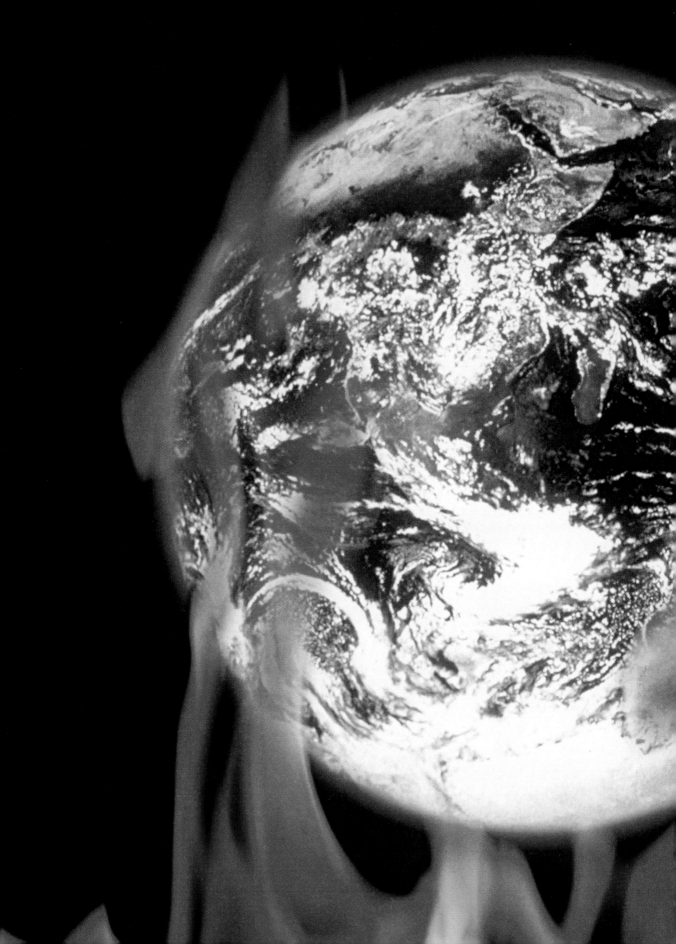

SCIENCE

Hot enough for you? In 2006 there was growing concern over global warming—a worldwide trend that's making Earth's climate hotter. While the climate has gone through many cycles of warming and cooling in the past, most scientists agree that the current trend doesn't fit any natural cycle. They say that people are largely responsible for the warming trend, mainly through the use of fossil fuels that release carbon dioxide and other gases into the air when burned. These gases act like the glass in a greenhouse, trapping heat from the sun and causing world temperatures to rise. Scientists warn that global warming is likely to have far-reaching effects. And it will take bold actions by people all over the world to slow the trend.

ALL IN A DREAM

You're the soccer team's best player, and you're late for the championship game. But it's not your fault: Your mom's car broke down—and you've been running for what seems like hours to get to the school soccer field. As you race toward the field you see the scoreboard: The rival team is winning 4–0. As you reach the bench, the coach glares at you and yells, "Where the heck were you?" Your heart is pounding so hard you can barely answer the coach. Just then the referee blows his whistle—and the game is over!

But what's this? That's not the referee's whistle. It's your alarm clock. You're not at the soccer field; you're home in bed. And you didn't miss the soccer game—you were only dreaming!

Dreams take the real world and turn it upside down. All sorts of unpredictable and impossible things can happen: You may meet old friends who have moved far away or relatives who passed on long ago. Your pet dog may talk. You may suddenly find the solution to a problem that's been troubling you for days. Your deepest wishes may be granted—or you may be chased by a bug-eyed monster. You may even fly!

Why do we dream? Do the events in the dreams have meaning? People have been fascinated by these questions since ancient times. Long ago, some people thought that dreams might be messages from the gods. Others thought that dreams were predictions of future events.

Few people hold such beliefs today. In recent times, scientists have studied dreams and learned much about them. Dreams, most experts believe, are messages from our subconscious. Buried feelings and fears are called up and interwoven with events that take place during the day. But in sleep, these messages are often disguised—and that's what makes dreams so fascinating.

STUDYING DREAMS

"To sleep: perchance to dream," says the prince in Shakespeare's play *Hamlet*. Scientists say there's no chance about it: Everybody dreams! Even people who say they never dream actually do—they just don't remember their dreams.

How do scientists know? They have watched people dream in sleep laboratories. At a sleep laboratory, volunteers are hooked up to electronic monitoring equipment. An electroencephalograph, or EEG, records brain waves—the electrical impulses that are constantly given off by the brain. Other machines monitor eye movements and heart and breathing rates.

The volunteers' job is easy—they simply go to sleep. But all night long, scientists keep watch on the monitoring equipment. Brain waves vary with the brain's activity, so watching the EEG tells scientists what's going on while the volunteer is sleeping. Heart rate and other physical signs also vary throughout the night.

In addition to EEG's, researchers are using diagnostic imaging to learn about dreams. These procedures are functional magnetic resonance imaging (fMRI) and positron emission tomography (PET). Like X-rays, these procedures allow doctors to "see" inside the body. Both the MRI and the PET have been used to scan the brains of people who are awake. Now they are being used to scan the brains of people who are asleep and dreaming. Researchers are actually able to "see" those parts of the brain involved in dreams.

By studying sleeping volunteers, researchers have learned that there are different kinds of sleep. Every night, you go through a number of sleep cycles. Each cycle lasts about 90 minutes and is made up of a period of deep sleep and a period of light sleep. Near the end of the cycle comes a period of what scientists call rapid eye movement, or REM, sleep.

Some Dreams Do Come True!

Do dreams really come true? Sometimes they do. And when they are the dreams of famous people, everyone gets to know about them.

❨ **Paul McCartney**, the guitarist/singer/songwriter for the Beatles, has written hundreds of songs. One of the most popular is "Yesterday" (1965). According to the *Guinness World Records* book, it's been played over the air more than 6 million times in the United States alone! And according to McCartney, he didn't just write the song—he dreamed it! "I woke up with a lovely tune in my head," he said. "I liked the melody a lot, but because I'd dreamed it, I couldn't believe I'd written it. . .But I had the tune, which was the most magic thing!"

❨ **Stephen King** is known as the King of Horror. His horror stories have sent chills up the spines of millions of fans. One of King's most popular novels was *Misery*, which was published in 1987. The movie, which followed in 1990, starred James Caan in the role of a writer who was held prisoner by a maniacal admirer (Kathy Bates). How did King get the idea for this frightening tale? He dreamed it when he fell asleep on an airplane! King says that the ideas for some of his other novels also came to him in dreams.

❨ **Jack Nicklaus** is one of the greatest golfers of all times. He's the only golfer ever to win 18 major golf tournaments. But would he have had such phenomenal success if he hadn't had a particular dream? In 1964, just two years after he turned pro, Nicklaus was in a terrible slump. Then, one night he dreamed he was playing a great game—and that he was holding his golf club differently. After waking up, Nicklaus returned to the golf course, changed the way he gripped the club, and dramatically improved his golf game. The rest is history. "But that's how it happened," Nicklaus said. "It's kinda crazy, isn't it?"

❨ **Mary Wollstonecraft Shelley** was the author of one of the most famous horror stories ever written: *Frankenstein*. In 1816, 19-year-old Mary, her future husband English poet Percy Bysshe Shelley, and their friend the poet Lord Byron decided to compete to see who could create the best ghost story. She went to bed thinking about the story. The next morning she awoke from a frightening dream about a monster. "I have found it!" she thought. "What terrified me will terrify others." And the cause of that terror was the monster Frankenstein! Mary's very first novel, *Frankenstein*, brought her lasting fame.

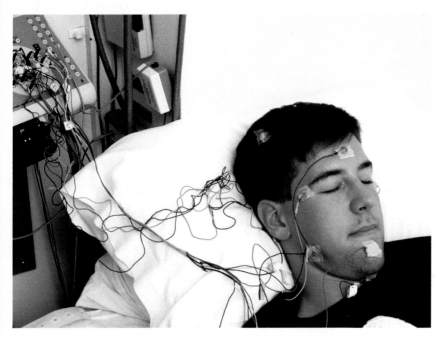

A volunteer is hooked up to electronic monitoring equipment at a sleep lab. By studying brain waves and other physical signs, scientists learn about sleep and dreams.

During REM sleep, a person's eyes move back and forth as if he or she were watching something. Brain waves show patterns that resemble those seen in a person who is awake. The sleeper's heart and breathing rates may increase. And by waking volunteers during REM sleep, researchers have learned that this is when most dreams occur.

Over eight hours of sleep, most people have three to five dreams, each lasting five to fifty minutes. Usually, most of the dreams are forgotten by morning. But by waking volunteers in the middle of a dream and asking them about it, researchers have learned a lot about dreams.

For example, while many people think they dream in black and white, dreams are almost always in color. Apparently the memory of the colors in our dreams fades even more quickly than the memory of the dreams themselves.

People usually hear as well as see in their dreams. Dreams may even involve the senses of smell and touch. Blind people dream as much as sighted people, but their dreams are made up of sounds, smells, and sensations. During REM sleep, their eyes don't move.

In many dreams, the dreamer simply watches the action. In others, the dreamer plays a part. While sleeping, people seldom move or act out their dreams. That's because messages from the brain to the muscles are blocked during REM sleep.

Whether we watch the action or take part in it, many of our dreams involve people and places with which we're familiar. Often, dreams seem to be related to events that took place during the day and especially the hours just before sleep. But in dreams, people may behave strangely, and familiar places may be oddly changed. Events often make no sense, although during the dream they may seem logical. Other dreams, however, are so realistic that on awakening, the dreamer can't believe the events didn't really happen.

Knowing these facts about dreams doesn't explain what purpose dreams serve or why people dream what they do. But researchers have plenty of theories.

THE LANGUAGE OF DREAMS

One of the best-known theories of the meaning of dreams was developed by Austrian physician Sigmund Freud, in the 1890's. Freud originated psychoanalysis, a method of helping people with emotional problems. Part of Freud's complex dream theory stated that dreams are a way in which people fulfill subconscious wishes—wishes that they don't even know they have. The wish fulfillment happens indirectly, through symbols. That is, the images in dreams stand for ideas or things that are too stressful for the dreamer to picture directly and thus must be disguised.

Some researchers have proposed theories that are almost the opposite of Freud's. According to one of these theories, dreams mean nothing at all. During sleep, the cerebral cortex (the part of the brain that's involved in thought) is stimulated randomly. Thus dreams are just meaningless images, called up by chance.

However, most researchers believe that dreams have at least some meaning. And while many experts disagree with parts of Freud's dream theory, it is generally agreed that the mysterious images we see in sleep are symbols. If you dream about another person, for example, he or she may represent a character trait in yourself. Animals often stand for instincts and emotions. Colors may reflect your inner feelings—bright, sharp colors may indicate intense feelings, while black may indicate sadness.

Even the dream's setting is important. A house, for example, is supposed to be a symbol of the self. The basement stands for the unconscious, while the upper floors stand for the conscious mind. If you dream about a house with a lot of empty, unused rooms, your dream may be telling you that you're not using all your talents.

Everyone's dreams are unique. But certain experiences seem to occur in almost everyone's dreams at one time or another. And these experiences, too, may have symbolic meanings.

If you dream you are falling, for example, your dream may show that you feel insecure. If you dream you can't find something important, such as money or a set of keys, it may show that you don't want to accept grown-up responsibility. And a dream about failing an exam may show that you feel unprepared for life's demands.

But many people who interpret dreams say that a dream's true meaning depends on the dreamer. Symbols are just a starting point in decoding a dream—you have to think about the dream and decide how it relates to your situation.

Sometimes dreams can help solve problems. Thus some dream experts suggest that if you are troubled by a problem that you can't solve, you should focus on it just before you go to sleep. Supposedly, the brilliant scientist Albert Einstein found the key to his famous theory of relativity in a dream!

How to Remember Your Dreams

Everyone has dreams, but most people remember little about them. However, you can take steps to improve your dream-recall.

❨ Keep a pencil and paper or a recorder near your bed.

❨ Just before you get into bed, review the day's events in your mind.

❨ When you're in bed and about to go to sleep, keep telling yourself, "I'll remember my dreams. I'll remember my dreams."

❨ When you wake up—even if it's in the middle of the night—don't move. Recall as much as you can about your dream.

❨ Then write down or record your dream.

❨ Note any feelings you may have about the dream—were you frightened, happy, lonely, worried?

❨ Note the most important images in the dream, and where it took place.

With practice, using these steps will make your dream-recall much better. And remembering your dreams can lead to an understanding of them—and of your own thoughts and feelings.

Record high temperatures that have been recorded over the past 20 years reflect a worldwide climate trend called global warming. The fossil fuels used in electric power plants are a major cause of global warming.

GLOBAL WARMING: TURNING UP THE HEAT

Did you swelter through the summer of 2006? Most people in the United States did, as a series of brutal heat waves baked wide sections of the country. The summer heat waves followed an unusually warm spring. For the continental United States, the first half of 2006 was the warmest first half of any year since good records were first kept, in 1895, according to scientists at the National Oceanographic and Atmospheric Administration (NOAA). And the year 2005 was also one of the hottest on record.

In fact, 19 of the past 20 years rank among the hottest on record. Scientists say the record temperatures reflect a worldwide climate trend called global warming. Earth's climate has gone through many cycles of warming and cooling in the past. But most scientists agree that the current rapid warming trend doesn't fit any natural cycle. Instead, they say, people are largely responsible.

THE GREENHOUSE EFFECT

The warming is taking place through a process called the greenhouse effect. Certain gases in the air, especially carbon dioxide, absorb heat from the sun and prevent it from escaping back into space. The gases act like the glass in a greenhouse, trapping heat from the sun. As a natural process, the greenhouse effect helps regulate temperature on Earth, allowing life to flourish. Now, however, scientists are concerned that human activities are turning up the heat.

When people burn gasoline, oil, coal, and other fossil fuels, carbon dioxide and other greenhouse gases are released into the air. As the use of these fuels has grown, greenhouse gases have begun to build up in the atmosphere. Concentrations of carbon dioxide in the atmosphere have increased sharply since the start of the Industrial Revolution (in the early 1800's), when fossil fuels began to be widely used. Climate scientists have confirmed this by studying cores from ancient glaciers in Greenland and Antarctica. Bubbles of air trapped in the ice provided samples of the atmosphere up to 650,000 years old. The scientists analyzed the samples and found that the level of carbon dioxide is now 27 percent higher than at any previous time. And by the end of this century, levels could be double the pre-industrial level.

With more greenhouse gases, the atmosphere is trapping more heat from the sun. And world temperatures are rising. On average, global surface temperatures rose about 1°F (0.6°C) in the 20th century, with much of the increase coming in the last 25 years. Using computer models that simulate the behavior of the climate, many scientists predict that average temperatures will increase another 3 to 7°F (1.5 to 4°C) by 2100. This is a bigger, faster increase than the world has ever seen.

Scientists don't expect the warming to be uniform around the globe. Land areas will warm much faster than oceans, and areas in northern high latitudes will see the greatest change. But

An elementary school in Laurel, Maryland, adopted a program that encouraged students to track the amount of trash they were disposing of during Wednesday lunches.

Green Is Cool

What can you do to fight global warming? Be "green" by using less energy. That will cut back greenhouse gas emissions. You and your family can take lots of simple steps to do this. With energy prices soaring in recent years, these actions may also save you money.

■ Replace incandescent lightbulbs with fluorescent bulbs, which use much less electricity. Coal-fired electric power plants are especially big producers of greenhouse emissions. According to one estimate, if every U.S. household replaced just three 60-watt bulbs with fluorescents, that would be equal to taking 3.5 million cars off the road.

■ Recycle more. Reducing your family's trash output by one large bag every two weeks can reduce greenhouse gas emissions by more than half a ton a year.

■ Use less energy to heat your home by turning the thermostat down. Lowering the thermostat by just 2 degrees can cut household emissions of carbon dioxide by 6 percent. Blocking air leaks and installing insulation help, too.

■ Use a microwave oven for cooking. Microwave ovens cook food faster, so they use about one third the energy that traditional ovens use.

■ Use appliances wisely. Wash clothes in cold water, and run dishwashers on "energy saving" cycles.

■ Leave the car at home. Walk, ride a bike, or use public transportation when you can.

The Arctic has been severely affected by global warming. For example, the shrinking sea ice is making it difficult for polar bears to hunt for seals, which are a major source of food for the bears.

Scientists say that warming temperatures will affect all parts of the world. Some species of butterflies and frogs may become extinct, while ragweed, mosquitoes, and poison ivy will thrive.

all parts of the world will feel the effects of the warming. And the changes are already taking place.

WARMER AT THE POLES

The effects of global warming are being seen most dramatically at and near the North and South Poles. The Arctic region is warming nearly twice as fast as the rest of the planet, according to a study completed by an international team of scientists in 2004. And the change is taking place quickly. In Alaska and western Canada, average winter temperatures have gone up 5 to 7 degrees in the past 50 years.

The change has already brought problems. In some places, permafrost—a layer of permanently frozen soil that lies just below the surface—has started to melt. This has softened the ground, buckling roads and causing trees and buildings to tip. Warmer temperatures are also thinning glaciers and the sea ice that hugs the Arctic coasts. The ice no longer reaches as far out from the shore as it once did, so the coasts have less protection from

storms. Waves are wearing away the shores. Scientists say that if global warming continues, half the ice that normally covers the Arctic Ocean in summer will melt by 2100.

The shrinking sea ice is also causing problems for Arctic animals such as polar bears. Polar bears prowl the sea ice hunting for seals. Without the ice, they are trapped on shore and can't reach their prey. There have even been reports of polar bears drowning as they tried to swim from ice floe to ice floe across stretches of open water.

As the North and South Poles warm, everything from weather patterns to ocean currents will be affected, researchers say. That's because the poles act like Earth's air conditioners. Cold air and water flow from the poles toward the equator. Melting ice at the poles also contributes to global warming through something that scientists call a feedback loop. Normally, the brilliant white polar ice caps reflect about 90 percent of the sun's light and heat. As they shrink, more of the sun's heat falls on dark water and the land, which absorb it and grow warmer.

WARMER ALL OVER

Global warming is already being blamed for shifting weather patterns, floods, and droughts. Warm temperatures in the Atlantic Ocean helped create powerful hurricanes in

2005. Global warming may also have helped bring severe drought to the Amazon region in South America.

In western North America, the change is also contributing to drought. Warmer winter temperatures mean that less snow falls in mountain areas. Rivers that are normally fed by spring snowmelt are running low. This causes water shortages in areas that depend on these rivers. It also affects production of hydroelectric power. And researchers blame climate change for hot, dry conditions that have produced a surge in wildfires in the mountains of the West since the 1980's.

Different parts of the world are likely to experience different effects from global warming. Some places will have more precipitation. Other places will have less. As glaciers and sea ice continue to melt, coastal areas will face flooding from rising sea levels. Seas have risen about 6 to 8 inches (15 to 20 centimeters) worldwide over the last century, and the rate of rise has increased in the last decade. Melting glaciers and warmer ocean waters could raise sea levels worldwide as much as 3 feet (1 meter) by 2100. Rising sea levels would begin to flood low-lying areas. If warming continues beyond then and melts all of Greenland's ice sheet, sea levels could rise as much as 23 feet (7 meters), bringing huge changes to coastal areas. Much of coastal Florida and most of the Asian nation of Bangladesh would be under water, for example.

Warming temperatures would also damage forests and other wildlife habitats. Frogs, butterflies, and many other animals are already under pressure from climate change. One recent study estimated that more than a million species could be driven to extinction by 2050. On the other hand, many insect pests thrive in warm temperatures. Among them are fire ants, mosquitoes, and beetles that attack evergreen forests. Their numbers are expected to increase.

The effects of climate change could show up in suburban backyards, too. One recent study showed that high levels of carbon dioxide in the air have led

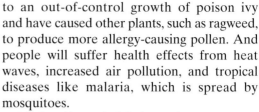

Thinking Big!

Over the years, scientists have come up with some far-out ideas to fight global warming. Here are a few of them:

⬥ Build huge orbiting sunshades to shield Earth from some of the sun's light and heat.

⬥ Place trillions of small lenses in orbit to bend sunlight away from the planet.

⬥ Seed the upper atmosphere with sunlight-scattering particles to reflect sunlight back into space.

⬥ Fertilize the sea with iron to create vast blooms of algae. The plants would soak up tons of carbon dioxide and, as they died, carry the excess carbon to the bottom of the ocean.

So far, none of these ideas has been tried. Mainstream scientists have dismissed most of them as impractical, impossible, or dangerous. Cutting greenhouse gas emissions is still the best way to fight global warming, they say. But as the world continues to warm, people may be willing to look at far-out solutions to climate change.

Wind turbines, such as these in California, provide energy without causing a buildup of greenhouse gases.

to an out-of-control growth of poison ivy and have caused other plants, such as ragweed, to produce more allergy-causing pollen. And people will suffer health effects from heat waves, increased air pollution, and tropical diseases like malaria, which is spread by mosquitoes.

All the effects of global warming may not be bad. Warmer temperatures could mean a longer growing season in cold-winter climates. And high carbon-dioxide levels may act like a fertilizer for crops, and not just weeds like poison ivy. In some areas, then, crop production might increase. Also, reduced sea ice could allow more shipping and fishing in Arctic waters. But most climate experts expect the harmful effects of climate change to outweigh any benefits.

WHAT CAN BE DONE?

The best way to fight global warming is to reduce the amount of carbon dioxide and other greenhouse gases that people put into the atmosphere every day. The fossil fuels used in cars and electric power plants are the biggest sources of these gases. New technologies—hydrogen fuel cells for cars and wind, nuclear, or other energy sources for power—could drastically cut the use of these fuels, and that would cut greenhouse gas emissions. These energy sources aren't commonly used now, and it would take time to make them widely available. Environmentalists have called on governments to do more to encourage their use and to raise mileage standards for cars and trucks, so they use less fuel. Meanwhile, people should take steps to use less energy and produce fewer greenhouse gas emissions in their daily lives.

However, getting people to conserve energy and change to new technologies isn't easy. So far, the experts say, too little is being done. At least 160 nations have

A billboard in Montreal, Canada—the site of an international conference on climate change in late 2005—shows children's artwork supporting the Kyoto Protocol, a treaty that limits carbon-dioxide emissions.

ratified the Kyoto Protocol, an international treaty that calls on countries to limit or cut their carbon-dioxide emissions. But the United States isn't on board, and the United States (which has about 5 percent of the world's population) churns out about 25 percent of the world's carbon-dioxide emissions. U.S. President George W. Bush has said that meeting the targets called for in the treaty would slow economic growth by raising energy costs.

U.S. officials have also complained that the treaty doesn't require developing nations such as China and India to cut emissions. These countries have argued that they can't afford to make the same cuts as wealthy nations. The Kyoto Protocol will expire in 2012. In December 2005, delegates from 185 countries met in Montreal, Canada, for an international conference on climate change. But they reached no new agreements.

To many people, the threat of global warming seems far off and unimportant. That's because most people haven't yet suffered any harm from climate change. Environmentalists and others have been trying to raise awareness of the problem. In 2006 a documentary film, *An Inconvenient Truth*, produced by former senator and presidential candidate Al Gore, brought the threat of global warming to the attention of many

Americans. And more people are coming to see the need for action. Many business leaders, for example, now recognize that the effects of global warming will be more costly than the expense of cutting greenhouse gas emissions.

Private groups are also taking action. In August 2006, the Clinton Foundation, a nonprofit organization headed by former U.S. President Bill Clinton, said it would fund a program to cut greenhouse gas emissions in cities. Cities produce about 70 percent of the gases. The program would help cities measure their emissions and buy energy-saving products to reduce them.

It may not be possible to completely stop global warming, climate scientists say. Even if everyone stops producing greenhouse gases today—something that's not likely to happen—the buildup that has already taken place will cause temperatures to keep rising for some time. Carbon dioxide and other greenhouse gases break down very slowly in the atmosphere. Thus people will have to adapt to climate change, with steps like planting drought-resistant crops and moving away from low-lying coastal areas.

But it's not too late to keep global warming from becoming a catastrophe, the experts say. If people take action now, some of the worst effects may be prevented.

NOW YOU SEE IT. . .NOW YOU DON'T

Your eyes and brain work together to give you lots of information about your surroundings. A lens in each eye focuses an image on the retina at the back of the eye. Cells in the retina (called rods and cones) send messages along nerves to the brain, which analyzes and interprets the messages. But sometimes the brain has trouble interpreting the messages. It "sees" things that aren't really there. Look at the pictures on these pages. Each of them tries to trick your brain!

Which blue circle is the largest? Actually, all three are the same size. You can prove this by measuring their diameters. The borders surrounding the circles confuse your brain—they distract attention from the blue circles. Because the borders differ, the circles appear to be unequal.

This same principle makes a full moon look much larger when it is near the horizon than when it is high in the sky. Seeing the moon near trees and other objects tricks the brain.

Close your right eye and stare at the cross. Move the drawing closer to your eyes. At a certain point, the red dot disappears.

This happens when the dot's image falls on part of the retina called the blind spot. This area doesn't send messages to the brain. Because the brain doesn't receive the information it needs, it takes a guess. It fills the space with slanted lines.

Look at one of the dark squares in this drawing. Do you see dancing gray spots where the white lines cross one another?

Contrast makes colors seem to be brighter. White looks brighter when it's next to a dark color than when it's next to white or another light color. In the drawing, the white of the lines between the dark squares seems whiter than the white where two lines cross.

Now look directly at one of the dancing gray spots. You can't! The spots disappear when you try to look directly at them. They form in your peripheral vision only when you focus on a dark square.

In this drawing, where is the middle prong attached?

The drawing provides contradictory information. The left part of the drawing looks like three pipes. The right part looks like a flat box. But the two parts together don't make sense. The brain is confused because it is unable to visualize a three-dimensional object.

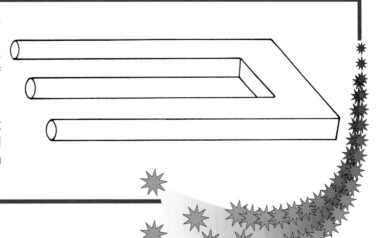

Look at the green stripes in this picture. Are those on the left lighter than those on the right?

They seem to be, but they are actually exactly the same. Contrast between a color and its background can make the color seem lighter or darker. The green stripes on the left lie against a light orange background. Those on the right lie against a dark black background.

Test a similar concept in your home. Turn on a light at night when the room is dark. Then turn it on when the room is filled with sunlight. The light seems brighter at night because of the contrast between light and darkness.

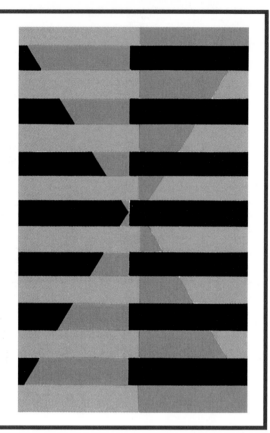

Are the seven slanted lines in this picture parallel to each other or do they diverge?

Your brain probably thinks the lines diverge, when in reality they are parallel. You can check this with a ruler. Lay the ruler along one of the slanted lines; then slide it to each of the other lines.

Your brain sees the lines as diverging because it's confused by the short "hatch marks." Extra pieces of information such as these hatch marks are called "visual noise."

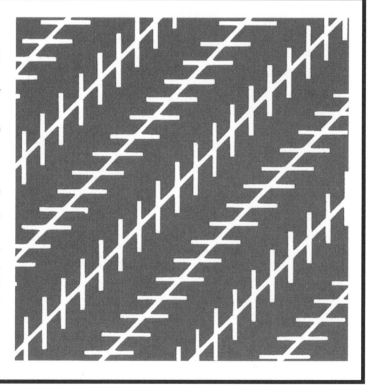

Does this drawing seem to vibrate? It's the shimmering-star illusion.

The brain sees motion that isn't there. This happens because the brain can't decide if it's looking at radiating black lines or radiating white lines. It keeps switching from one image to the other.

Flipbooks also give the illusion of motion. You are actually looking at individual pictures. But each one flashes past your eyes so rapidly that you seem to "see" motion. Animated cartoons depend on the same illusion.

Do you see two faces in profile? Or do you see a wide-topped vase?

It all depends on whether your brain interprets the picture as showing two dark objects against a light background—or one light object against a dark background.

The picture has no perspective; thus there are no distance cues. Both possibilities are equally likely, so your brain is confused. It has trouble deciding what is background and what is foreground. It switches rapidly back and forth between the two images.

You never see both images at the same time. The brain can construct only one image at a time.

THE QUEEN OF FLOWERS

"Of all the flowers, methinks a rose is best."
William Shakespeare

Since ancient times, poets have praised roses as symbols of beauty and love. Songwriters have compared beautiful women to roses. Artists have created magnificent paintings of roses, and roses have served as symbols of royalty. The ancient Greek poet Sappho gave the rose its proper title: the Queen of Flowers. And even today, the rose ranks as the world's most popular flower.

THE ROSE PLANT

There are more than 100 species of wild roses—and many thousands of varieties that have been specially cultivated. All the roses are members of a single genus, *Rosa*. This genus is part of a much larger family, Rosaceae, which includes many important trees, shrubs, and herbs. Apple, pear, peach, and cherry trees are members of this family.

While there are many kinds of roses, they all have certain characteristics in common.

The plants are shrubby, with woody stems and sharp thorns. Each leaf is composed of an odd number of separate leaflets, usually five to seven. The flowers are rings of soft, often fragrant petals, borne singly or in groups.

After the flower's petals drop, its base develops into a small fruit—the rose hip—which contains the plant's seeds. Rose hips look like tiny apples. When they are ripe, they are red, orange, yellow, or brown, depending on the variety.

There are several important differences between wild roses and the garden types. The wild roses are mostly thorny shrubs or climbers. Their white, pink, or red flowers usually have five petals, arranged in a single layer. And most wild roses have a single period of bloom, usually in spring or early summer.

Garden roses, on the other hand, grow in many different ways—upright, as shrubs; climbing over trellises; and even as trees. Some kinds bloom twice a year, and many bloom repeatedly from spring to frost. Their

The roses in French Empress Josephine's garden were painted by artist Pierre Joseph Redouté. His detailed watercolors are still important reference works.

Rosa Sulfurea   *Rosier jaune de souffre*

The Poetry of Roses

Roses have long been the subject of song and poetry. Walter Wingate, a Scottish poet who lived from 1865 to 1918, wrote this poem:

Roses

A sea of broom was on the brae,
A heaven of speedwell lit the way;
But ever as I passed along
Of roses only was my song—
　　　　　Roses, roses, roses!

They spread their petals, pink and white
Full stretch to feast upon the light;
They pushed each other on the spray
Like children mad with holiday—
　　　　　Roses, roses, roses!

But as when summer noon is high
A fearful cloud bedims the sky,
A sudden memory of pain
Arises from the bright refrain—
　　　　　Roses, roses, roses!

I watch a figure to and fro
'Mong summer roses long ago,
Herself a rose as blythe as they—
Alas! how soon they pass away—
　　　　　Roses, roses, roses!

Glossary
broom: shrubs
brae: hillside
speedwell: snapdragons
blythe: lighthearted

flowers have many petals, arranged in several layers. And they come in a great range of colors, including pink, red, white, yellow, peach, and lavender.

ROSES FOR EVERY GARDEN

Special varieties of roses have been grown for gardens since ancient times. Today there are varieties for different climates, different soils, and different uses. These thousands of roses have been developed over centuries by crossing different species and varieties. A cross occurs when the pollen produced by a rose of one plant is transferred to the egg-producing structure of a blossom on another plant. If the egg is fertilized it develops into a seed. The seed contains genetic material from both parents. When it's planted, it develops into a new variety.

Wind and insects are nature's agents of cross-breeding. Even more important are human agents—people who cross existing rose varieties in the hope of creating ever more perfect plants. The mechanics of cross-breeding are fairly simple, and many amateur gardeners try their hand at it. But only rarely does a cross result in an outstanding new variety.

After the rose's petals drop, its base develops into a fleshy berrylike fruit—called a rose hip. The rose hip contains the plant's seeds and is an important source of vitamin C.

Here are some of the major kinds of garden roses:

🌿**Old-garden roses** include some varieties, such as damask and gallica, that have been around since before the time of Christ. Some other old-garden roses are moss roses, named for the mosslike fuzz on their

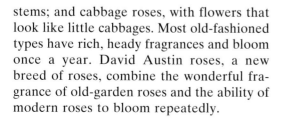

Roses are prized for their beauty and their many garden uses. They grow as ramblers, uprights, shrubs, even as trees. And they come in almost any color—except true blue.

🌹 **Tea roses** were named for their scent, which resembles that of freshly crushed tea leaves. Along with another variety, called China roses, tea roses originated around 1800. They have a long blooming season but aren't very hardy.

🌹 **Hybrid tea roses** are the roses that are usually sold by florists. These varieties were developed by crossing tea roses with other types of roses in the late 1800's.

🌹 **Polyanthas** were developed at about the same time as the hybrid teas. But while hybrid teas bear flowers on long stems, polyanthas are low-growing plants that produce clusters of small flowers. Just like the hybrid teas, though, the plants are everblooming.

stems; and cabbage roses, with flowers that look like little cabbages. Most old-fashioned types have rich, heady fragrances and bloom once a year. David Austin roses, a new breed of roses, combine the wonderful fragrance of old-garden roses and the ability of modern roses to bloom repeatedly.

121

Floribundas were created by crossing hybrid teas and polyanthas. They are shrubbier and have larger flowers than the polyanthas. Their name—a Latin word meaning "flowers in abundance"—tells something important about them: Floribundas carry quantities of blossoms from early summer until frost.

Grandifloras resemble both the hybrid teas and floribundas. The flowers look like those of the hybrid tea, but they are borne in clusters like those of the floribundas.

Miniature roses are dainty plants ranging from 4 to 18 inches (10 to 46 centimeters) in height. Some have flowers no bigger than a penny. Their small size makes them well suited to rock gardens, window boxes. and indoor containers. But their flowers have very little fragrance.

Climbing roses and ramblers don't really climb. Instead, they have long trailing stems that can be trained to grow over walls and fences. There are many types of climbing roses. Some have large flowers, and some small; some bloom once a year, and others are everblooming.

Tree roses don't grow naturally—they are created by gardeners. The desired rose variety is grafted onto a tall stout stem, or standard, with healthy roots. The rose plant then gets all its nourishment through the standard. Most rose trees are between 2 and 5 feet (60 and 150 centimeters) tall.

ROSES IN HISTORY AND LEGEND

Since roses have been popular through the ages, they are rich in history and legend. For example, the ancient Greeks had numerous stories concerning the origin of roses. Many had to do with Aphrodite, the goddess of love and beauty. According to one legend, the goddess Cybele created the first rose. She was jealous of Aphrodite and wanted to be sure that there would be something on Earth more beautiful than her rival.

Another legend told how red roses came to be. The goddess Aphrodite learned that her beloved Adonis was wounded. As she rushed to him, she ran through a hedge of roses. The thorns pricked her skin, drawing blood that stained the flowers red forever.

Say It With a Rose

Our language and literature are filled with expressions that use roses to make comments about life and people. Here's a sample of such sayings, together with their meanings.

Gather ye rosebuds while ye may: Take advantage of opportunities that exist today because they may not exist tomorrow.

No rose without a thorn: Something always detracts from pleasure.

Seek roses in December: Search for the impossible. (This expression is from a poem by English poet Lord Byron, written before refrigeration and other modern inventions made it possible to buy roses at any time of the year.)

A rose by any other name would smell as sweet: A change of name doesn't change the qualities of a person, object, or idea.

Everything's coming up roses: Everything is going along beautifully.

A bed of roses: A soft, comfortable life.

Looking at the world through rose-colored glasses: Being overly optimistic and ignoring obvious faults and problems.

To the ancient Egyptians and Romans, roses were symbols of luxury. At Cleopatra's palace in Egypt, the floors were strewn with rose petals. When she entertained Mark Antony, the carpet of petals was knee-deep. The Roman emperor Nero was one of the most extravagant rose-lovers of all time. His guests rested on pillows stuffed with rose petals, while fountains sprayed rose water into the air.

Roses have also been political symbols. In England during the 1400's, two royal groups, the House of York and the House of Lancaster, battled for the crown in what became known as the War of the Roses. York took the white rose as its symbol, and Lancaster used the red rose. The fighting lasted more than 30 years, until 1487. Then Henry VII, a Lancastrian, married Elizabeth of York. The red and white roses were joined in the Tudor Rose, which became the national flower.

Roses found a royal patron in the early 1800's in France. Empress Josephine, the wife of Napoleon I, established one of history's greatest rose collections and did much to popularize rose growing. Her garden contained some 250 different types of roses. Their beauty was recorded by the French artist Pierre Joseph Redouté, whose detailed watercolors are still important reference works.

A PLANT WITH MANY USES

Even in ancient times people knew that roses could provide more than beauty. The ancient Romans used rose petals and hips to make delicious wines and jellies, and to flavor honey. And they turned roses into medicines that were said to cure every imaginable ailment. Belief in the medicinal value of roses continued through the Middle Ages.

The Arabs, on the other hand, simmered rose petals and turned them into an important cooking ingredient. Today rose water is also used in colognes and cosmetics.

Another fragrant rose product is rose oil, which is made by putting petals from fresh, fragrant blooms into olive oil. After a day or two, the petals are mashed and their oil is strained. Then the process is repeated, using the same

The Language of Roses

During England's Victorian era (1837–1901), flowers had meanings of their own. Dictionaries were even written to explain the meanings. A red rose, for example, symbolized love. But every other rose variety or color had its own meaning, too. Here are some of them.

Blue rose—*mystery*
Bouquet of roses—*gratitude*
Burgundy rose—*beauty*
Coral rose—*desire*
Damask rose—*freshness, beautiful complexion*
Dark crimson rose—*mourning*
Hibiscus rose—*delicate beauty*
Lavender rose—*enchantment*
Orange rose—*passion*
Pink rose—*perfect happiness*
Peach rose—*modesty*
Purple rose—*loving protection*
Red rose—*deep love*
Red and white roses together—*unity*
Rosebud—*beauty and youth*
Tea rose—*remembrance*
Thornless rose—*love at first sight*
White rose—*innocence, purity*
Yellow rose—*friendship*

oil, with ten or more batches of petals. The fragrant oil is used in perfumes, scented candles, and other sweet-smelling items.

Roses are no longer used in medicines, but they do have healthful properties. Rose hips are very high in vitamin C. Hips from plants that haven't been sprayed with pesticides are used to make tea, jelly, and even wine. The Queen of Flowers not only brings beauty, it may bring good health as well.

The Call=Chronicle=Examiner

SAN FRANCISCO, THURSDAY, APRIL 19, 1906.

EARTHQUAKE AND FIRE: SAN FRANCISCO IN RUINS

The 1906 earthquake and fire in San Francisco was one of the worst natural disasters in U.S. history.

THE GREAT SAN FRANCISCO EARTHQUAKE

"The shock came, and hurled my bed against an opposite wall. I sprang up, and, holding firmly to the foot-board managed to keep on my feet to the door. The shock was constantly growing heavier; rumbles, crackling noises, and falling objects already commenced the din. The door refused to open. The earthquake had wedged it in the door-frame."

Those words were written by a survivor of one of the greatest disasters in U.S. history: the 1906 San Francisco, California, earthquake and fire. April 18, 2006, marked the 100th anniversary of that quake. The disaster was an important event in U.S. history, and not only because it almost destroyed San Francisco. It was also important for the wealth of scientific knowledge learned from it.

A CITY SHAKES

The quake struck at 5:12 A.M., an hour when most people were still in bed. The earth shook violently for almost a full minute. The quake probably measured 7.7 to 7.8 on the scale that scientists use today to rate earthquake magnitude. People felt the shaking from southern Oregon to points south of Los Angeles and inland as far as central Nevada. San Francisco was near the epicenter, the underground point where the earthquake originated, so it was hit hard.

The woman who wrote the account above described how, after the jammed bedroom door finally sprang open, she, her husband, and their son survived the terrifying event. They clung desperately to doorways in their fourth-

124

floor apartment as the floor rolled under their feet and parts of the building came crashing down around them:

"It grew constantly worse, the noise deafening; the crash of dishes, falling pictures, the rattle of the flat tin roof, bookcases being overturned, the piano hurled across the parlor, the groaning and straining of the building itself, broken glass and falling plaster, made such a roar that no one noise could be distinguished.

"We never knew when the chimney came tearing through; we never knew when a great marine picture weighing one hundred and twenty-five pounds crashed down, not eight feet away from us. . . .I never expected to come out alive."

This family was lucky—most of their building was still standing when the ground stopped shaking. The worst damage took place in "filled" areas of the city. These places had once been swamps, but the city had dumped earth there to create dry land for new buildings. The new land shook like jelly, and buildings fell.

The severe shaking caused damage outside the city, too, in many other places affected by the quake. But in San Francisco, this was just the beginning of the disaster. The quake also broke gas lines, shorted electrical circuits, and overturned wood- and coal-burning stoves. Fires broke out. Because the city's water lines were also broken, firefighters couldn't put out the blazes. They were helpless as fires spread out of control for three days, burning almost 500 city blocks.

Fires even threatened to destroy the U.S. Mint building, where 60 percent of U.S. gold and silver coins were produced. Inside the Mint's vaults was a third of the nation's gold supply. Mint employees and a handful of soldiers worked feverishly to save the stockpile from flames hot enough to melt steel, using water from a well in the building's courtyard. They succeeded.

Together, the quake and fire destroyed some 28,000 buildings. More than 2,500 people died. And an estimated 225,000 people out of a population of 400,000 were left homeless. But amazingly, San Francisco bounced back. The city was rebuilt. It celebrated its recovery in 1915 by hosting a world's fair, the Panama-Pacific International Exposition.

Measuring Earthquakes

Scientists detect and measure earthquakes with seismographs, instruments that record motion in the ground. Seismic stations all around the world monitor Earth for vibrations that radiate out from the site of a quake. Their reports allow scientists to pinpoint the location of the earthquake and rate its strength. (Below, a scientist reads a seismograph chart.)

An earthquake's magnitude is its strength at its epicenter, or source. The Richter Scale, developed in the 1930's by Charles Richter, uses a mathematical formula to rate magnitude. In recent years new magnitude scales have been developed, but they are all extensions of Richter's idea. Here are the categories that the United States Geological Survey uses in rating earthquake magnitude.

Great:	8.0 or more
Major:	7.0 - 7.9
Strong:	6.0 - 6.9
Moderate:	5.0 - 5.9
Light:	4.0 - 4.9
Minor:	3.0 - 3.9

Each full number on the magnitude scale represents a tenfold increase in the strength of a quake. Thus a quake with a magnitude of 7.0 is ten times as strong as a 6.0 quake.

Then and Now: The destruction in 1906—the Call Building at right was greatly damaged. Today—the Central Tower Building is located at the site of the former Call Building.

LESSONS FROM 1906

The San Francisco earthquake set off a flurry of scientific investigation. At the time, scientists understood little about earthquakes or about how and where they occur. But they made detailed observations of the 1906 quake and its effects, not just in San Francisco but also in other places affected by the disaster.

Among other things, they learned that damage to buildings in an earthquake is strongly related to both the design and construction of the structure and to the type of soil on which it stands. Damp, loose soils made up of fine sand and sediment can actually behave like fluids during a quake, flowing and rolling in waves.

The scientists also saw how the earthquake had displaced the ground surface—by as much as 20 feet (6 meters) in some places. Their observations laid the foundation for the modern idea of how earthquakes occur.

Earthquakes are common in places where the great plates that make up Earth's surface collide. California is one such place. Due to forces deep within Earth, the surface plates are constantly in motion. The movement is very slow. But over millions of years, it has shifted continents and changed the surface of Earth.

Where plates grind against each other, as they do along the western coast of North America, enormous pressure builds up along their edges. Finally the edges of the plates shift, or rebound, releasing the pressure in an earthquake. The

In 1906, the earth ruptured for a distance of 290 miles along a deep crack called the San Andreas fault (below). Scientists say that such severe earthquakes occur along the San Andreas fault about every 200 years.

sudden release sends out shaking movements, or seismic waves. Some of these seismic waves, called surface waves, travel over the surface of Earth. Others, called body waves, travel down through Earth's interior.

In 1906 the earth ruptured for a distance of 290 miles (470 kilometers) along a deep crack called the San Andreas fault. After studying the pattern of damage caused by the quake, scientists understood for the first time that faults such as this give rise to earthquakes. Before then, most people thought that earthquakes created the faults.

THE NEXT "BIG ONE"?

The 1906 earthquake wasn't the last to hit San Francisco, although it remains the biggest. In 1989 a magnitude 7.1 earthquake killed 67 people and caused serious damage. Once again, the city bounced back.

Scientists estimate that earthquakes as severe as the 1906 event occur along the San Andreas fault every 200 years or so. San Francisco is also at risk for earthquakes from several other faults in the region. No one knows when the next "big one" will hit—but most scientists say it will come someday. And they are watching for it. Using instruments called seismographs, scientists now monitor earth movements at sites throughout California and in other earthquake-prone regions of the world. They use other instruments to track the stresses and distortion of Earth's surface that occur as pressure builds along a fault.

Computers analyze the data from these surveys and help scientists create a detailed picture of the location and activity of faults. This research has helped scientists understand which faults are likely to produce strong earthquakes, what the long-term probabilities for such quakes are, and how severe they are likely to be. In earthquake-prone regions, they have also identified areas where loose soils or other factors make building especially risky. And they have learned to design and construct buildings, bridges, and other structures that can better withstand earthquakes.

Scientists still can't predict exactly when the next major earthquake will strike, in California or anywhere else. But they have a much clearer picture of the risks and what can be done to reduce them.

A young girl in an "earthquake cottage" takes part in a re-enactment of the 1906 disaster.

Remembering a Disaster

San Francisco marked the anniversary of the 1906 earthquake and fire with a host of special events.

■ There were concerts and performances, exhibits of photographs and artifacts from the time of the earthquake and fire, and walking tours of earthquake faults and other landmarks. Special programs raised public awareness of earthquake dangers and how to prepare for them.

■ At the Presidio, a national park, people could visit a re-creation of a refugee camp, made up of tents and shacks called "earthquake cottages." Such camps housed more than 200,000 homeless San Franciscans in the months after the quake, as they struggled to rebuild their lives.

■ The Exploratorium, the city's famous science museum, used the history and scientific lessons of the 1906 earthquake and fire as a jumping-off point for a series of quake-related events and exhibits. These ranged from programs covering the science of earthquakes, to a demonstration by real rescue dogs, to a quivering, large-scale model of San Francisco sculpted from Jell-O. Visitors could also see historic films from 1905 and 1906 and watch earthquakes pop up on an international map as they occurred throughout the world.

■ At 5:12 A.M. on April 18, 2006, thousands of San Franciscans gathered on Market Street in the heart of the city. As sirens blared, they recalled the historic earthquake that struck the city at that moment exactly 100 years before.

Crystals are the basic structures that make up most inorganic solids. Usually, the crystalline structure can only be seen with a microscope. But some crystals, like the multicolored tourmaline shown above, develop so that their basic crystal structure is revealed.

MAKING THINGS CRYSTAL CLEAR

Diamonds, sapphires, emeralds, rubies—these names call up visions of beautiful objects glittering in the light and glowing with color. These gems are all crystals, and their beauty and rarity has made them precious. But there are many other kinds of crystals. And because certain crystals have special properties, they are widely used in science and industry. In fact, crystals are probably working for you right now—in your watch, in your television, or in your computer.

Crystals are actually all around us—metals, rocks, salt, snowflakes, and even grains of sand consist of crystals. Crystals are the basic structures that make up most inorganic (nonliving) solids. The structures are formed by tiny particles—atoms or molecules, depending on the substance. These particles link up together in an orderly geometric pattern that's repeated over and over again. Usually this pattern, or crystalline structure, is so small that it can be seen only with the help of a powerful microscope.

HOW CRYSTALS FORM

Almost any inorganic substance can form crystals under the right conditions. Two well-known exceptions are glass and plastic.

Crystals form from molten (melted) or dissolved substances as a result of evaporation or changes in temperature or pressure. A few atoms or molecules in a substance cluster together, forming a basic crystalline pattern called a "unit cell." These particles attract more particles of the substance, which join the crystal by forming additional—and identical—unit cells. Together, the cells form a network called a lattice. As more and more unit cells are stacked together, the crystal grows larger and larger. Different substances form crystals of different shapes.

A crystal that's large enough to see—a small quartz crystal, for example—may contain hundreds of millions of unit cells. When a crystal grows freely, without bumping into other crystals, it may develop smooth, mirrorlike faces and sharp, well-defined angles that reveal its basic structure. This is because no matter how large a crystal grows, the angles between its faces always stay the same.

In nature, crystals form under various conditions. Snowflakes begin when water vapor

Good-Vibe Crystals

Are you tense and nervous? Feeling tired and run-down? Upset about an argument you had with a friend? According to some people, the answer to your problems just might be a crystal.

In recent years, crystals have become a fad among people who believe that the stones have special powers. The theory is that the crystals have electromagnetic currents that are in tune with energy fields in the human body. Wearing or meditating on a crystal can supposedly influence the body's energy fields—sharpening your thoughts, solving your problems, and even curing illness. In addition, believers say, certain crystals have specific effects. Amethyst and topaz can soothe your nerves. Clear quartz can boost your energy. Rose quartz can ease wounded feelings.

Scientists say that such beliefs are just superstition dressed up with a little scientific jargon.

But that hasn't stopped crystals from becoming a booming business. There are books about crystals, and even crystal therapists who teach people how to use their rocks. Shops that sell crystals and crystal jewelry have popped up everywhere, charging prices that range from $2 to $150,000 for their wares.

Mood rings, which first came on the scene in the 1970's, have become popular again. They contain liquid crystals, but they aren't believed to have special powers. They are, however, supposed to reflect the state of your emotions. But what they actually reflect is a change in your body temperature. When the temperature in your finger gets warmer, for example, the stone turns dark blue—which is said to mean you are happy. When the temperature turns colder, the stone turns black, which means you are stressed. In-between temperatures will turn the stone blue (you are calm), blue-green (somewhat relaxed), green (average emotions), amber (somewhat troubled), and gray (pretty nervous).

Of course, not everyone who buys these items believes that crystals can cure illness, solve problems, or reflect your mood. Crystals are beautiful to look at—and that may be their greatest benefit.

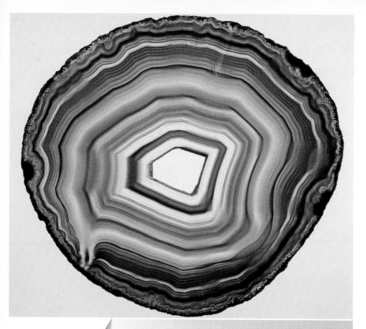

Agate, often used in jewelry, is usually recognized by its bands of color. People who believe in the mystical power of gems say that agate brings happiness.

Emerald, a rich green crystal, is cut to make valuable gems. Some people believe that wearing an emerald can fight depression and sleeplessness.

Rose Quartz is a transparent crystal named for its rosy-pink color. Some people say that rose quartz can heal the pain caused by losing someone you love.

meets freezing air temperatures high in the atmosphere. Salt crystals form through the evaporation of seawater, which contains dissolved salt. But most crystals form underground, from molten rock deep inside the earth or from rock that's placed under heat and pressure by forces in Earth's crust.

As beautiful as they are, crystals that form in nature are rarely perfect—most contain flaws in their structure and have rough or pitted faces. But scientists have also learned to grow crystals in the laboratory, and even in space, and these synthetic crystals usually have fewer flaws. Using a variety of techniques, scientists have created synthetic rubies, silicon and germanium crystals for use in solar cells and transistors, and crystals of many other materials for a wide range of uses. But of all crystals, quartz crystals—either natural or artificial—are the most widely used today.

QUARTZ CRYSTALS

Most people think of quartz as a clear, glasslike stone. But quartz actually occurs in a wide variety of colors and textures. Pure quartz, sometimes called rock crystal, consists of molecules of silicon dioxide. It's colorless and transparent—the crystals look like long six-sided blocks of ice with a pointed tip. Colored quartz crystals form when tiny amounts of impurities such as iron, manganese, and aluminum are mixed with the silicon dioxide. Examples include rose quartz (pink) and smoky quartz (cloudy brown or black). Semiprecious gemstones such as amethyst (purple) and citrine (yellow) are also forms of quartz. In all of these, the six-sided crystal shape is easily visible. Some other kinds of quartz have very fine crystals that can only be seen under a microscope. These include agate, flint, bloodstone, carnelian, and jasper. All these colorful stones

Amethyst is a transparent purple variety of quartz. It was once believed that amethyst could protect soldiers. Some people say it calms nerves.

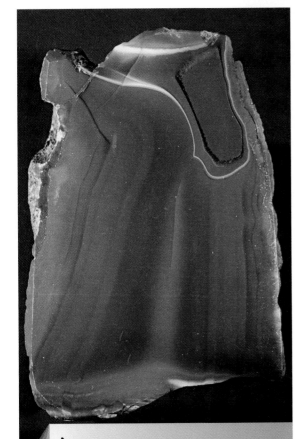

Jasper is a dark red form of quartz that contains large amounts of iron oxide. People in ancient times believed that jasper could cure snakebites.

Topaz, which comes in many colors, is often used as a gemstone. Some people believe that topaz fights high blood pressure and helps people sleep well.

Making Crystal Candy

It's easy to watch crystals form, and to end up with something good to eat. Sugar is an organic substance—that is, one produced by living things (in this case, plants). But like quartz and other inorganic substances, sugar forms crystals. Here's how to make an old-fashioned treat called rock candy, which consists of large sugar crystals.

Gather the following supplies:
2 cups of powdered or granulated sugar
1 cup of water
a large glass or wide-mouthed jar
a saucepan
a pencil
clean cotton string
2 or 3 paper clips

1. Heat the water in the saucepan. When the water begins to boil, gradually add the sugar. Stir well until all the sugar dissolves. Remove the saucepan from the heat, and let the mixture cool for about 15 minutes.

2. Meanwhile, cut two or three pieces of cotton string and tie them to the pencil, as shown in the diagram. Attach a paper clip to the bottom of each piece of string so that it hangs downward.

3. When the mixture has cooled, pour it into the glass or jar. Lay the pencil across the rim of the container, with the strings hanging down into the mixture. Place the container in a spot where it won't be disturbed.

4. Within a few hours, sugar crystals will begin to form on the string. Over a period of several days, as more and more water evaporates, the crystals will get larger and larger. (If sugar crystals also form on the surface of the water, carefully remove them, so that the water can continue to evaporate.)

5. When the crystals are nice and big, remove the strings from the water. Your crystal candy is ready to be eaten!

contain impurities. For example, jasper—which may be red, brown, yellow, or black—contains iron compounds.

People have long fashioned beautiful jewelry and other objects from quartz crystals. And throughout history, many people have believed that quartz has special, even magical, properties. In the Middle Ages, knights rode off to the Crusades wearing quartz amulets. It was thought that fortune tellers could see into the future by gazing into the mysterious depths of a crystal ball—a lump of clear rock crystal, smoothed and polished into a globe. Desert travelers held pieces of agate in their mouths, believing that it would ease their thirst. And amethyst was believed to protect soldiers, help hunters track game, and guard against disease and drunkenness.

It wasn't until the late 1800's that scientists learned that quartz crystals really do have remarkable—although not magical—properties. In 1880, two French scientists, the brothers Jacques and Pierre Curie, discovered an odd phenomenon. They attached electrodes to two sides of a slab of quartz, and then piled weights on the slab. As the pressure of the weights increased, the electrodes detected electrical charges on the surface of the quartz. The charges were positive on one side of the quartz and negative on the other.

Today this phenomenon is known as the piezoelectric effect (*piezo* comes from a Greek word that means "to press"). It has another aspect as well. Quartz and crystals with similar structures not only produce surface electrical charges under pressure. They also oscillate, or vibrate, when alternating electrical charges are applied to them. What's more, the oscillations occur at a precise, regular frequency, or rate of speed, that depends on the thickness of the crystal—the thinner the crystal, the higher the frequency.

Together, these two aspects of the piezoelectric effect have led to hundreds of uses for quartz and similar crystals. In fact, crystals that oscillate, called crystal oscillators, are at the heart of our modern high-tech society. They are highly accurate frequency-control and timing devices, and new applications for them continue to be found.

Perhaps the most important uses of crystals are in the field of electronics, and many of these uses have grown out of the ability of crystals to vibrate in response to alternating

electrical charges. Because they vibrate at constant frequencies, quartz crystals can be used to regulate broadcast waves and time-keeping devices. For example, quartz crystals allow radio stations to broadcast at set frequencies. Wafer-thin quartz disks, vibrating at extremely high frequencies, allow quartz clocks and watches to keep time. Quartz crystals in your television help decode color signals that arrive over the airwaves.

Crystals are also used in personal computers and in microprocessors, the tiny computers that today help operate automobiles, dishwashers, and many other machines. And they help keep your telephone conversations from mixing with hundreds of other conversations that are traveling through the same channels.

Science has learned a great deal about crystals, and industry has found many uses for them. In the future, crystals may be even more widely used than they are today. They are already an important part of computer voice-recognition systems, which one day may allow people to control computers by speaking. Crystals may even be used to generate electrical power.

But even as more uses are found for these fascinating objects, it's likely that crystals will never lose the sense of beauty and mystery that surrounds them.

This man-made crystal, shaped like a tuning fork, is an example of a piezoelectric crystal. When exposed to an alternating current, it vibrates rapidly at a specific frequency. Such crystals are used as timers in quartz watches.

Three space shuttle missions were successfully completed in 2006. During the *Atlantis* mission in September, two huge solar wings were attached to the *International Space Station* (above).

SPACE BRIEFS

The adventures of astronauts, cosmonauts, and even a space tourist highlighted the 2006 year in space. Other exciting developments occurred as scientists here on Earth changed the status of Pluto, examined comet dust, and studied information gathered by spacecraft exploring distant planets and moons.

PEOPLE IN SPACE

The United States conducted three space-shuttle missions during 2006. The primary objective of the missions was to resume construction of the *International Space Station* (*ISS*), a giant structure that orbits 240 miles (386 kilometers) above Earth. Construction began in 1998. But it was halted when the space shuttle fleet was grounded after the accident that destroyed the shuttle *Columbia* in 2003.

In July, the 13-day mission of the space shuttle *Discovery* included three spacewalks, during which astronauts made repairs to the half-finished *ISS* structure. They also fixed a rail-mounted car on the outside of the *ISS* that was used to carry construction equipment. And they tested new repair technologies planned for future missions.

The space shuttle *Atlantis* traveled to the *ISS* in September on a 12-day mission. It carried an enormous 17.5-ton truss with two attached solar wings. Astronauts used the shuttle's robotic arm to remove the structure from the shuttle's cargo bay. Then, during three spacewalks, they attached it to the *ISS*.

Finally, the panels on the solar wings, which will provide 25 percent of the space station's power, were unfurled.

With the electricity-generating solar wings in place, the next step came in December, when *Discovery* returned to the *ISS*. In one of the most complex missions ever, astronauts rewired the *ISS*—which had been running on a temporary electrical system since 1998.

The *ISS* is continually staffed by the United States and Russia, who send crews back and forth aboard Russian *Soyuz* craft or U.S. space shuttles. Each of the three crews aboard the *ISS* in 2006 included a U.S. astronaut and a Russian cosmonaut. The Expedition 12 crew, which arrived at the *ISS* in October 2005, remained there until April 2006. It was replaced by the Expedition 13 crew, which remained until September, when it was replaced by the Expedition 14 crew. In addition, German astronaut Thomas Reiter, who arrived aboard *Discovery* in July, joined the *ISS* crew. He remained on the space station until December, when he was succeeded by America's Sunita L. Williams, who arrived on *Discovery*.

The Expedition 13 crew was accompanied by Brazil's first man in space, astronaut Marcos Pontes, who spent nine days at the *ISS* before returning to Earth with the previous *ISS* crew. Also visiting the space station for several days was Anousheh Ansari, an Iranian-American businesswoman who paid about $20 million for the opportunity. And the *Discovery* crew that arrrived in December included Sweden's first man in space, astronaut Christer Fuglesang.

PLUTO BECOMES A DWARF PLANET

Is it or isn't it a planet? This question about Pluto—a far-off icy ball of rock—has bothered scientists for years. It became a controversial issue following the discovery of Xena, an icy ball of rock that orbits the sun far beyond Pluto, has a moon, and is bigger than Pluto. Both Pluto and Xena belong to the Kuiper (KY-per) belt, a ring of icy debris beyond Neptune. There are thousands of Kuiper-belt objects, with more being found all the time.

The International Astronomical Union (IAU) tackled the question of what makes a

Anousheh Ansari: Space Tourist

When Anousheh Ansari was a young girl in Iran, she dreamed of going into space. Years later, after moving to the United States and becoming a wealthy business-woman, her dream came true. On September 18, she became the world's first paying female space tourist.

Ansari, 40, and two astronauts blasted off aboard a Russian *Soyuz* spacecraft. Two days later they arrived at the *International Space Station,* where the astronauts would remain for about six months. Ansari was there for eight days. During this time she conducted several experiments. She studied anemia, how changes in muscles influence lower-back pain, and how space radiation affects *ISS* crew members. She also became the first person to publish a blog from outer space.

"I am having a wonderful time here," she told reporters. "It's been more than what I expected, and I am enjoying every single second of it."

planet. They debated whether any large body orbiting a star gets into the planet club. Or, they asked, does an object need certain qualities to be called a planet?

In August, the IAU demoted Pluto. It declared that bodies in our solar system, except moons, fall into three distinct categories. A planet was defined as an object that orbits the sun, has a nearly round shape, and has enough gravity to clear its neighborhood of continent-size rocks and other objects. Pluto and Xena don't meet the third criterion. They aren't massive enough to dominate other bodies in their neighborhood; their gravity isn't strong enough to either add the other bodies to their own mass or to knock them away.

So Pluto and Xena fell into a new IAU category, called "dwarf planets." These bodies orbit the sun, have a nearly round shape, do not orbit other objects, and haven't cleared the neighborhood around their orbit. All other objects, except moons, that orbit the sun, fall into the third category, called "small solar system bodies."

The demotion angered fans of Pluto, who were unhappy that there are now only eight official planets. But most astronomers agreed with the new categories. They said the decision looks not to the past but to the future, when more bodies will be discovered in the outskirts of the solar system.

A drawing of *New Horizons* on its way to the dwarf planet Pluto. Inset: The piano-sized spacecraft was loaded with scientific instruments before it was launched.

New Horizons. Distant Pluto has not yet been viewed close-up by a spacecraft. But in January, 2006, the National Aeronautics and Space Administration (NASA) launched a robot spacecraft named *New Horizons* to the faraway world. It traveled faster than any craft before, so fast that it reached our moon in only nine hours!

On its way to Pluto, *New Horizons* will swing past Jupiter in 2007. That giant planet's gravity will act like a slingshot, hurling the spacecraft to the edge of the solar system. In all, *New Horizons* will travel 3 billion miles (4.8 billion kilometers).

New Horizons, about the size of a piano, carries seven scientific instruments. When it reaches Pluto in 2015, the instruments will gather data about the dwarf planet and its atmosphere. The spacecraft will also check out Pluto's moon Charon, which is almost half as big as Pluto. It will also look at two tiny moons orbiting Pluto, which were discovered by the Hubble Space Telescope in 2005. These moons have been named Nix and Hydra.

The mission will continue on past Pluto, visiting other objects in the Kuiper belt. Scientists hope that the data gathered by *New Horizons* will not only increase our knowledge of Pluto but will also provide clues to how the sun and planets formed.

VISITORS TO OTHER PLANETS

Mars. The spacecraft *Mars Reconnaissance Orbiter,* launched by the United States in August 2005, reached Mars on March 10, 2006, joining three other spacecraft that were circling the Red Planet. Gradually, the *Orbiter* inched closer and closer to the Red Planet, until it was orbiting less than 200 miles (322 kilometers) above the planet's surface.

The *Orbiter*'s main job was to learn more about water on Mars. Expectations of success increased when photographs from an older U.S. space probe provided strong evidence in December that water still flows occasionally on the planet's surface. Liquid water, as opposed to

The *Mars Reconnaissance Orbiter* reached the Red Planet on March 10 and provided new details of Martian craters and valleys. And the two little robot rovers launched in 2004 continued to explore sites on the planet.

the water ice and water vapor known to exist on Mars, is considered necessary for life.

Meanwhile, two hardy little robot rovers that landed on Mars in January 2004 continued to explore sites on opposite sides of the planet. *Mars Reconnaissance Orbiter* photographed one of the rovers, *Opportunity*, as it explored layered rocks in cliffs that ring the massive Victoria crater. Details in the photos from the high-resolution camera on *Orbiter* helped scientists guide the rover's exploration of Victoria—rather like an aerial map might help a hiker decide which way to walk around a mountain, or where to head for the best views.

Venus. *Venus Express,* an unmanned space-craft launched by the European Space Agency (ESA) in November 2005, reached Venus on April 11, 2006. Its objective was a detailed study of the planet's dense atmosphere and clouds. Scientists want to find out how its atmosphere works and how it formed. What causes Venus's strong winds and spiraling polar clouds? What accounts for the chemical makeup of the atmosphere? And scientists were hoping to learn if a "greenhouse effect" played a role in creating Venus's broiling climate. The greenhouse effect occurs when certain gases in the air, such as carbon dioxide, trap heat at the planet's surface. This effect has been blamed for a global warming trend now taking place on Earth.

Venus Express reached Venus in April on its mission to study the planet's dense atmosphere and clouds. Its infrared camera immediately took pictures of a dramatic cloud pattern known as a "double-eye" vortex (inset).

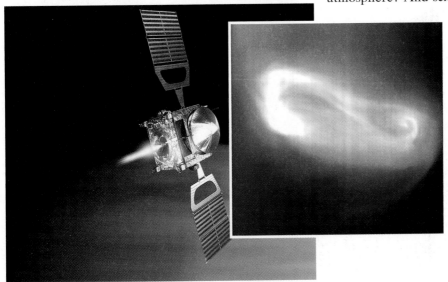

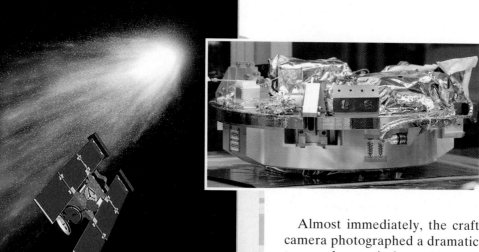

Stardust's Precious Cargo

On January 15, 2006, the spacecraft called *Stardust* completed an amazing seven-year journey. It was launched in 1999 on a mission to Comet Wild-2. It traveled billions of miles through space to catch up with the comet (above). Then it scooped up samples of tiny dust particles from the comet and became the first spacecraft to bring material from a comet back to Earth.

Comets travel around the sun in wildly uneven orbits. They are close to the sun at some points and far out in the dark reaches of space at others. When a comet nears the sun, the sun's heat causes some of the comet's ice to vaporize, or turn to gas. As this gas forms a cloud around the comet, it takes some of the comet's dust with it.

When *Stardust* met up with Comet Wild-2, it flipped out its cosmic dust collector. The collector gathered dust from the comet's cloud. Then the spacecraft folded the dust collector into a return capsule and headed home. The return capsule was released and parachuted to a safe landing in the Utah desert.

Scientists were thrilled when they opened the canister containing the comet dust (inset above). There were tens of thousands of particles. Most were too small to see without a microscope, but some were as thick as a human hair and could be seen with the naked eye. One scientist called the samples "an ancient cosmic treasure from the very edge of the solar system." Some of the particles are thought to be older than the sun. Scientists hope the dust will help unlock the secrets of how our solar system took shape.

Almost immediately, the craft's infrared camera photographed a dramatic cloud pattern—a huge spiral over Venus's south pole known as a "double-eye" vortex. The vortex, never clearly seen before, was similar to one present at the planet's north pole. Scientists couldn't immediately explain why double and not single vortexes form at the poles, or why there's a collar of cold air around each vortex structure.

Venus Express also carried instruments to investigate stripe-like structures in the atmosphere. The nature of these interesting structures is still unexplained. However, some scientists believe they may be due to the presence of dust and aerosols in the atmosphere.

Cassini has been orbiting Saturn since 2004. In 2006, the spacecraft sent back photos of the planet's bright-white moon Enceladus (opposite page). Fountains of icy water appear to be shooting up from its surface (the inset shows a color-enhanced image of the spewing water).

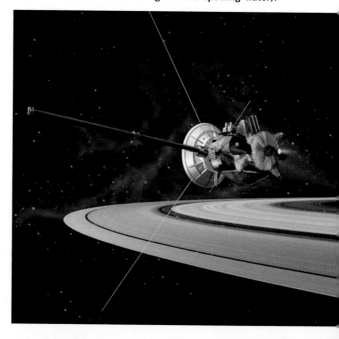

Hubble Keeps Making Discoveries

Since it was launched in 1990, the Hubble Space Telescope has revolutionized our understanding of the universe. Recently, it provided the strongest evidence yet of the existence of a Jupiter-sized planet orbiting the sunlike star Epsilon Eridani. Only 10.5 light-years away, this is the nearest-known extrasolar planet to our solar system. Hubble and other telescopes haven't been able to snap pictures of the giant gas planet. However, this may change in 2007 when the planet's orbit is closest to Epsilon Eridani.

Meanwhile, Hubble has produced an ever-growing scrapbook of star images from far beyond the solar system. One of the most dramatic is this sharp image of the majestic spiral galaxy M51—nicknamed the Whirlpool Galaxy because of its swirling structure. The two curving arms are actually long lanes of stars and gas laced with dust.

It's here that young stars reside, while the galaxy's yellowish core is home to older stars.

Hubble has been among the most valuable spacecraft ever launched. To extend its life, NASA plans to launch a repair mission in 2008. Astronauts aboard a space shuttle will make a "house call" to fix or replace old equipment and add some new instruments.

Saturn. *Cassini,* a U.S. spacecraft that went into orbit around Saturn in 2004, continued to study the giant planet's rings and some of its moons. Now scientists are wondering if there is—or if there ever has been—life on Enceladus, a small, icy moon that's only

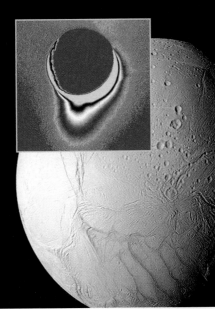

300 miles (483 kilometers) wide. In 2006, *Cassini* spotted what appeared to be plumes of icy crystals shooting up from the moon's surface. Scientists think the plumes are geysers, like the famous Old Faithful geyser in Yellowstone National Park, but much colder. This suggests that there are reservoirs of liquid water just beneath Enceladus's surface.

In addition to water vapor, *Cassini* flybys of Enceladus found hints of carbon-based molecules, including carbon dioxide and methane. Thus the moon seems to possess the three basic ingredients for life: water, carbon-based molecules, and heat.

Meanwhile, new images from *Cassini* of the moon Titan—Saturn's largest moon—revealed a landscape not unlike some seen on Earth, with mountains, dunes, and lakes. It was the first time that evidence of standing bodies of liquids was found on Titan. Now scientists must determine whether the lakes do hold liquid, and what that liquid might be.

MAKE & DO☆

Happy Birthday!

It's fun to use stickers to create unique works of art, such as these nifty notecards. To make a notecard, take a sheet of colored paper and fold it in half; then fold it in half again. Decorate the front with your favorite stickers, or create designs with sticker hearts, dots, and stars. Add scenery, a border, or a message such as "Happy Birthday" using paints and felt-tip pens. Then open the card and write a note to one of your favorite people!

Come to My Picnic

From shoveling snow to baking cookies, you can find many ways to make $$$!

WE'RE IN THE MONEY!

One thing just about everyone can use more of is money. And that probably includes you. Many young people are discovering that there are lots of ways to earn money. One of the best ways is to start your own business.

"But what should I do?" you ask. The answer is simple: Provide people with anything they need. . .or want. Some kids have a snow-shoveling or lawn-mowing service. Some bake cookies to sell at local fairs. Others help vacationing neighbors by feeding pets, watering plants, and bringing in mail and newspapers. Here are some guidelines that may help you decide what kind of business would be best for you.

1. What can you do well? A business will be successful only if the product or service you sell is of good quality. Make a list of the things that you do well. Do you have a green thumb? Then raise and sell houseplants. Do you speak fluent Spanish or excel in math? Begin a tutoring service.

2. What do you like to do? A business is generally more successful if it revolves around something you enjoy doing. Do you like young children? Open a babysitting service. Do you love parties? How about starting a party business—help people create party themes, and then set up and serve at the parties.

3. Do your neighbors need any special service that you might be able to provide? The best way to learn your neighbors' needs is to ask them. For instance, if you have elderly neighbors who don't get out much, ask if they're interested in a grocery shopping service.

4. How will competition affect you? Even if you're providing a desired service or product, your chances of having a successful business will improve if you don't have a lot of competition. Consider, for example, a business involving crafts. Many people make and sell such items as bookmarks, wreaths, placemats, and potholders. Therefore, you should try to create products that are unique—maybe personalized T-shirts.

5. How much money do you need to spend to get started? Most businesses require some start-up money. For example, if you are going to create posters for people, you'll need to buy posterboard, construction paper, and paints

A business is usually more successful if you enjoy the work. Mowing lawns is a great job for someone who likes being outdoors. If you enjoy being around children, a baby-sitting service is a terrific opportunity.

and brushes. If you're planning to create T-shirts, you'll have to buy T-shirts and paints.

Once you've decided what type of business you'll have, you must figure out what to charge for your work. One way to do this is to find out what other people are charging for the same service or product and perhaps price your work slightly lower. But remember: If you want to make a profit, you have to charge more than what it costs you to make and sell your product.

Sometimes, instead of charging less than your competition, you may want to give your customers something extra. If you have a lawn-service business, give people a coupon each time you mow their lawn. Tell them that you'll provide a free plant trimming when they've collected ten coupons.

Now it's time to let people know about your business. Advertise! Make lively announcements that can be hung in local stores (be sure to first get the store manager's permission). Distribute flyers in your neighborhood. Make sure that each flyer lists your name and telephone number and clearly indicates the service you provide.

For some businesses, you may want to make appointments with potential customers. Dress neatly. People are more likely to listen to you—and buy your product—if you look professional. Smile when you introduce yourself, and shake hands. Explain why you're there. If the person isn't interested, keep smiling! Offer one of your flyers and say something like, "Please call me if you need this work done in the future."

Many people will say "no" to you. But some will say "yes." And if you do a good job, they'll become satisfied customers. They'll call on you again, and they'll recommend you to their friends. That's the way a business—any business—grows and becomes successful.

Let's take a closer look at three areas in which you might start a business.

A PASSION FOR PETS

If you like animals and if there are lots of animal owners in your community, start a business that involves caring for pets. A dog-walking service is a good way to begin.

You don't need any money to start a dog-walking service. You do, however, have to be very responsible. Dog owners will probably want you to walk their dogs on a regular schedule. Be sure to stick to the schedule, and always arrive on time.

You can build a business by finding out what people need. Grocery shopping might provide a welcome service for elderly neighbors.

If you're an animal lover, you can earn money by caring for pets. Begin with a dog-walking service, then perhaps expand to include dog grooming.

Agree ahead of time on how long you are to walk the dog. Try to be exact about this. If you bring the dog back early, customers may feel they aren't getting what they're paying for. If you keep the dog out longer, customers may worry that there was an accident. Remember, too, that there's value in offering a little extra—an occasional bonus walk or a free brushing.

Sometimes you may not be able to get to your job, perhaps because you're sick or out of town. Try to have someone else available to walk the dog when you can't. It's a good idea to introduce this person to your customers and their pets ahead of time. Go over the route you follow, point out do's and don't's (such as areas where it's illegal to walk dogs), and in general familiarize the person with your routine—and your professional standards.

After a while, you may wish to expand the services you provide. Let customers know that

you will groom dogs or take care of them for extended periods of time, such as when owners are on vacation.

You can even sell items related to your service. Pet identification tags, collars, toys, and pet placemats are popular. You can make these yourself. Or you can sell them for a friend who makes them—and collect a commission (a percentage of the sale) on every item you sell.

THE CLEAN SCENE

Cleaning may not be your favorite activity, but it can be the basis of a very profitable business—simply because many people hate to clean. They dislike cleaning windows and garages and cars and floors and yards. So offer to do it for them!

In planning your business, decide who will provide the cleaning supplies. If you provide them, you can charge more but you'll have to spend money in advance. If the customers provide the cleaning supplies, you don't have to spend money and you'll know that you'll be using the products they prefer.

Have a Tag Sale

Do you have video games you no longer play with? Clothing that no longer fits? Comic books you no longer want? Do you have other items that are gathering dust in drawers and closets? If so, why not hold a tag sale. You can sell these items to people who want them—and make some money along the way.

First, gather everything you want to sell. Clean all the items so they look as good as possible. Then organize them—all the books in one box, all the clothes in another, and so on.

Ask your parents if they have anything they could donate to your tag sale. Invite friends to set up tables with their own tag-sale items. Generally, the larger the sale, the more buyers it will attract.

Mark the price of each item on a tag or easily removable sticker. People like to feel they're getting a bargain, so don't price things too high. But don't ask too little, either.

Hold your sale on a Saturday or Sunday. Make signs announcing the sale, and ask local stores to display them.

Good luck!

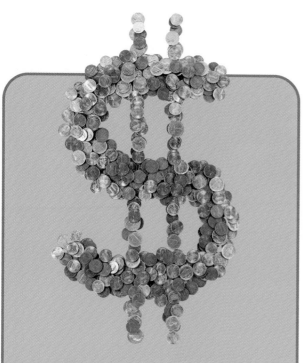

Business Basics

It's fun to enjoy the business that you start—but the basic objective is to make money! Before you can do that, however, there are some business basics you need to learn.

For example, if you're selling a product, you need to know how much to charge for it. One factor that goes into that decision is how much your competitors are charging. You also need to know how much it will cost you to make and sell your product, in order to make a profit. You need to know how to efficiently control your inventory, so you don't waste money. And you need to know how to produce a quality product— and know how to maintain that quality—so you get (and keep) customers.

To try your hand at running a small business, go to *http://www.coolmath-games.com/lemonade/*, where you'll learn that running a lemonade stand requires more than just cutting up a few lemons and adding water, sugar, and ice.

The business basics you'll learn from this enjoyable game can be applied to many other types of businesses.

Before offering to clean something, be sure you know how to do it. Cleaning a window is different from cleaning a floor. And cleaning a boat is different from cleaning a car. Your best bet is to learn the job by helping someone who already knows how to do it. If you want to learn to clean cars, for example, learn from people who keep their own cars shining.

A successful car-washing service can bring in steady money. Try to line up customers by leaving flyers under windshield wipers of cars. Once you have your customers, you can keep them by doing a better job than the local car wash. Scrub the tires and shine the chrome.

Start small and with a service that you can do really well. Then expand. You might consider offering to clean the interior for an additional fee. (You should vacuum the inside, empty ashtrays, dust the dash, and wash the windows.) Then add a waxing service to your car-wash business!

COMPUTER SERVICES

If you enjoy using computers, there are many ways in which you can turn this talent

Left: You can have a successful car-washing service if your customers see that you do a better job than the local car wash. Above: If you're a computer whiz, you can use your talents to start a business at home. Your services might include editing digital videos for customers.

into money-making opportunities. For example, many people want to learn how to use a computer or specific computer programs. You can earn money simply by teaching them. Or if you've designed your own Internet Web site, offer your expertise to others.

If your computer has a word-processing or desktop publishing program, you may want to become a publisher. You could publish a neighborhood paper, with stories about the people who live and work in your area. Include information on local events, such as soccer games, art shows, and public meetings. Sell the newspaper door-to-door. After you've published several issues and people are familiar with the paper, try to get subscriptions. Ask local store owners if they would like to advertise in the paper. Neighbors who are planning tag sales may wish to place ads. So may friends who offer baby-sitting, lawn-cutting, and other services.

With a desktop publishing program, you can create business cards, letterhead stationery, and other printed matter for par-

ents, friends, teachers, and store owners. Make sure to get feedback from them: Would they prefer different styles of type? A border or other graphic design? A slogan? It's important to create a card that matches people's specific needs and preferences. For large orders, you'll probably want to take the design to a professional printer; that would be quicker and easier than using your own printer. You then bill the cost— plus your design fee—to the clients.

Perhaps someone you know needs a birthday card for her father, or wants to send congratulations to a friend who just won her first tennis tournament. If you have an artistic flair—plus a color printer and a desktop publishing program—you can offer to create personalized, one-of-a-kind greeting cards.

With hard work and a little luck, you may soon find that your part-time business has grown too big for you to handle by yourself. Then it's time to look for assistants. You won't have to look far, because there are lots of kids out there looking for ways to earn some extra money!

147

A LEGENDARY HEROINE

Clara Barton is best remembered as the founder of the American Red Cross. And in 2006, that organization celebrated its 125th anniversary.

But Barton first gained fame during the Civil War (1861–65), when she helped care for wounded soldiers. Medical care during the Civil War was very limited. There were few doctors or hospitals, no antibiotics, and none of the high-tech medical tools common today.

Soldiers whose pains were eased and lives were saved by Barton were extremely grateful. In recognition of her efforts, they gave her a nickname. To learn this name, you need a pencil and a sheet of paper. Carefully follow the directions given below. (Hint: It will be easier if you rewrite the complete words at each step.)

1. Print the words CLARA BARTON. Leave the words separated as you continue to work.

2. Add two L's to the end of the second word.

3. Move the O to the end of the first word.

4. Remove the first consonant of the first word.

5. Change every R to an E.

6. Insert F–I–E between the two L's.

7. Find the first vowel from the left. Replace it with G–N.

8. Replace the fifth letter of the second word with a T.

9. After the O, add the letter that comes before G in the alphabet.

10. Insert the word THE between the first and second words.

11. Find the first vowel from the left. Move it between the L–G combination.

12. Attach a D to the end of the third word.

13. Put a space between A and O, to separate the first word into two words.

14. Find the second vowel in the last word. Move it between the L–F combination.

15. Reverse the order of the letters of the first word.

After the Civil War was over, Barton headed a group that searched for missing soldiers.

ANSWER: Angel of the Battlefield

ARE LOW OWLS SHREWD LATE HOOTERS?

Look at the words "low" and "owl." What do they have in common? They are anagrams. In an anagram, the letters of one word are re-arranged to make another word. For example, the letters in "low" can be rearranged to spell "owl." Groups of words can also form anagrams, and the anagrams can even relate to one another. For example, "shrewd late hooters" spells "the short-eared owls." Can you solve the anagrams in the sentences below? (Hint: One word in each pair of anagrams is an animal.)

1. A __ __ __ __ __ galloped along the sandy __ __ __ __ __.

2. A nasty __ __ __ __ stung the puppy on its __ __ __ __.

3. The __ __ __ sat in the sun and got a __ __ __.

4. You'll never see a __ __ __ shoot a __ __ __ .

5. And you'll never see a billy __ __ __ __ wear a
__ __ __ __.

6. The grizzly __ __ __ __ lost all his fur and now he's
__ __ __ __.

7. A poisonous __ __ __ doesn't feed on tree __ __ __.

8. The gray __ __ __ got stuck in sticky black __ __ __.

9. Tarzan's favorite __ __ __ sat in the jungle and ate a small green __ __ __.

10. Always remain __ __ __ __ when you eat a __ __ __ __
on the half shell.

11. The entire __ __ __ __ of this famous musical is dressed up as furry, whiskered __ __ __ __.

12. Can you __ __ __ __ a __ __ __ __ calling to its mate?

13. A __ __ __ __ __ __ __ __ __ __ __ __ itself on building a beautiful web.

14. Before it bites your dog, a __ __ __ __ might take a nap
on a __ __ __ __.

15. As the big bad __ __ __ __ swam through the raging river, he said, "You have to go with the __ __ __ __!"

ANSWERS: 1. horse, shore; 2. wasp, paws; 3. ant, tan; 4. gnu, gun; 5. goat, toga; 6. bear, bare; 7. asp, sap; 8. rat, tar; 9. ape, pea; 10. calm, clam; 11. cast, cats; 12. hear, hare; 13. spider, prides; 14. flea, leaf; 15. wolf, flow.

You don't need a knowledge of math to do a sudoku number puzzle.
You just have to have time and patience—and think logically.

HOOKED ON SUDOKU!

At airports and coffee shops, in classrooms and around kitchen tables, pencils were scribbling and minds were working overtime in 2006. People everywhere were caught up in a new puzzle craze—sudoku! These number puzzles were turning up in newspapers, on the Internet, in bookstores, and even in classrooms. What was the attraction? Sudoku puzzles are challenging—and addictive!

A NOT-SO-SIMPLE GRID

At first glance, sudoku puzzles look easy. A basic sudoku has a grid of nine squares, called regions. Each region is divided into nine cells, for a total of 81 cells. Numbers appear in some of the cells. These are "givens." To solve the puzzle, your job is to put numbers in the other squares. The rules are simple. Each row and column must contain the numbers 1 through 9. Each region must also contain numbers 1 through 9. The numbers can be in any order, but each can appear just once in each row, column, and region.

Solving sudoku isn't as easy as it looks. You don't have to know math or any other subject—but you do have to think. That's why sudoku puzzles are turning up in classrooms. Teachers are using sudoku as a way to teach logical thinking.

People use different methods to solve sudoku. One way is to lightly pencil possible numbers in the blank squares. For example, if the numeral 1 is given, you know that 1 can't appear in a blank cell in that row, column, or region. But numbers 2 through 9 can appear. As you work, gradually cross off penciled numbers until only one is left in each square.

The fewer "givens" a puzzle contains, the greater the challenge. The challenge also increases with the number of squares and cells in the puzzle. For beginners, there are simple grids of four squares, each with four cells. And for expert sudoku solvers who find the nine-square grid too easy, there are complicated versions with as many as 25 squares. And letters, shapes, or symbols can be used instead of numbers. Puzzle makers have even come up with circular sudoku in addition to other variations.

THE SUDOKU CRAZE

Although the sudoku craze is new, these puzzles have been around for many years. The first one, called Number Place, appeared in a U.S. magazine in 1979. It was inspired by the Latin square, a pattern developed by the Swiss mathematician Leonhard Euler in the 1780's. In a

A game company set up these giant sudoku puzzles in New York City, challenging passersby to complete each one in less than eight minutes.

Latin square, symbols are arranged in a grid so that each appears once and only once in every row and in every column.

Number Place puzzles didn't really catch on in the United States at first. But in the mid-1980's these number-grid puzzles were introduced in Japan, where they became hugely popular. It was there that they picked up the name sudoku. The name, which comes from words that mean "single number," refers to the fact that numbers are used once.

Sudoku didn't take off worldwide until Wayne Gould, a retired judge and puzzle fan from New Zealand, developed a computer program to create the puzzles quickly and easily. Gould began to sell his puzzles to the British newspaper *The Times* in late 2004. Sudoku turned out to be an instant hit with the British, who already loved crosswords and other puzzles. Within months, other British newspapers had started to print sudoku of their own as a way to attract and keep readers.

In 2005, sudoku hopped the Atlantic Ocean and returned to the United States. Before long the puzzles were everywhere. In 2006, 50 percent of U.S. newspapers fea-

tured daily sudoku. Books of sudoku were on the best-seller lists, with millions of copies in print. There were versions for computers and hand-held devices, too. Nearly all the puzzles are generated by computer programs today.

People have compared the sudoku craze to the mania for crossword puzzles that swept the United States in the mid-1920's. Sudoku has also been compared to Rubik's Cube, a hugely popular mechanical puzzle of the 1980's. This cube was made up of 26 smaller cubes with different colored faces. The object was to twist and turn the puzzle so that the small cubes matched, making each side of the large cube a solid color.

The Rubik's Cube mania faded, but crossword puzzles are still popular. No one can say if the sudoku craze will last. But fans don't need to worry that they'll run out of new sudoku to solve. The basic nine-square grid can be filled in more than 6 sextillion different ways!

If you haven't tested your wits with sudoku yet, try it! Solving these puzzles takes time and patience. But chances are that you, too, will soon be hooked.

STAMP COLLECTING

From Wonder Woman to natural wonders, from endangered animals to elegant costumes, stamps showcased a huge range of subjects in 2006. Here are a few highlights.

U.S. STAMPS

Ten comic-book superheroes were saluted on U.S. commemorative stamps in 2006. All characters from DC Comics, they were Aquaman, Batman, The Flash, Green Arrow, Green Lantern, Hawkman, Plastic Man, Supergirl, Superman, and Wonder Woman. The special pane of 20 stamps had two designs for each—one showing a classic comic-book cover, and the other depicting a scene from the character's adventures.

Real-life marvels appeared on a pane of 40 stamps. Wonders of America: Land of Superlatives depicted American places, plants, animals, and structures that were all at the top of their class. They ranged from the largest reptile (American alligator) and the tallest cactus (saguaro) to the deepest lake (Crater Lake) and the longest span (Verrazano-Narrows Bridge, in New York City).

A set of five 39-cent stamps featured a bountiful harvest of American crops—squashes, a sunflower and seeds, ears of corn, chili peppers, and beans—in colorful illustrations. And a set of four stamps showed classic American motorcycles. The featured bikes were a 1918 Cleveland, a 1940 Indian Four, a 1965 Harley Davidson Electra-Glide, and a 1970 "chopper," a customized bike with a stretched-out frame and raised handlebars.

New stamps in the American Treasures series displayed ten quilts made in the tiny community of Gee's Bend, Alabama. The African-American women there traditionally have made beautiful quilts from whatever fabric they had at hand. The stamps honored their artistry and ingenuity.

2006 STAMPS FROM AROUND THE WORLD

A new stamp in the Black Heritage series honored Hattie McDaniel, the first African American to win an Academy Award. McDaniel won as Best Supporting Actress for her role in the 1939 film *Gone With the Wind*. She worked behind the scenes to change the negative way that Hollywood often portrayed African Americans.

A set of four stamps titled Sluggers depicted baseball greats Roy Campanella, Hank Greenberg, Mickey Mantle, and Mel Ott—all powerful hitters who helped lead their teams to victory. Other notable Americans honored on stamps included Sugar Ray Robinson, boxing champion in the 1940's and 1950's; and actress and singer Judy Garland.

Animal characters from favorite children's books frolicked across a pane of eight stamps. Among them were Eric Carle's *The Very Hungry Caterpillar*, Dr. Seuss's *Fox in Socks*, Ian Falconer's *Olivia*, Lucy Cousins' *Maisy*, Leo Lionni's *Frederick*, and Margret and H. A. Rey's *Curious George*. Rounding out the group were a creature from Maurice Sendak's *Where the Wild Things Are* and illustrator Garth Williams' depiction of Wilbur the pig, from E. B. White's book *Charlotte's Web*.

The United States and Canada honored the French explorer Samuel de Champlain in a joint issue. It marked the 400th anniversary of Champlain's 1606 voyage, in which he explored the North American coast from Nova Scotia, Canada, to Cape Cod, Massachusetts. The 39-cent U.S. and 51-cent Canadian stamps showed his ship, and souvenir sheets from both countries showed a map of the voyage.

STAMPS AROUND THE WORLD

Canada and the United States were among the many countries that issued stamps saluting the 2006 Winter Olympic Games, which were held in February in Turin, Italy. Canada's stamps illustrated two sports—skeleton and team-pursuit speed skating—with the figures of the athletes slightly blurred to show their speed.

As always, the natural world was a popular theme for stamps. Two stamps from Morocco depicted flowers, the delicate narcissus and the peony. A pair from Japan showed a silver-eye bird and beautiful cherry blossoms. The Cayman Islands featured animals of tropical coral reefs on its Underwater Treasures stamps, including a diamond blenny, a spotted drum, a hawksbill turtle, and a queen angelfish. Taiwan showed fireflies on a set of four stamps.

Romania issued a group of six stamps showing different cat breeds. A cat was also featured on a stamp from the Netherlands. Montserrat depicted dog breeds, including the corgi. Since it was the Year of the Dog in the Chinese lunar calendar, many other countries also issued stamps depicting dogs.

Canada showcased four native land animals on a group of Endangered Species stamps. They were the blotched tiger salamander, the blue racer snake, the swift fox, and the Newfoundland marten. Meanwhile, the United Nations continued its Endangered Species series with stamps featuring threatened frogs, chameleons, and snakes.

The United Nations also released new stamps in its Indigenous Art series. The 2006 additions showed different traditional musical instruments of Africa, including some shaped like people. Like all U.N. stamps, these were issued in three denominations—dollars, euros, and Swiss francs—for use at different U.N. locations.

Member nations of PostEurop (the Association of European Public Postal Operators) issued stamps on the theme of integration as viewed through the eyes of young people. Sweden's version featured artwork by children. Several countries also issued stamps honoring the 250th anniversary of the birth of the composer Wolfgang Amadeus Mozart. France showed elegant costumes from six Mozart operas on its stamps, including *Cosi fan tutte*.

Austria came out with one of the year's more unusual stamps. Its design showed a meteor

A TOPICAL COLLECTION OF DISNEY STAMPS

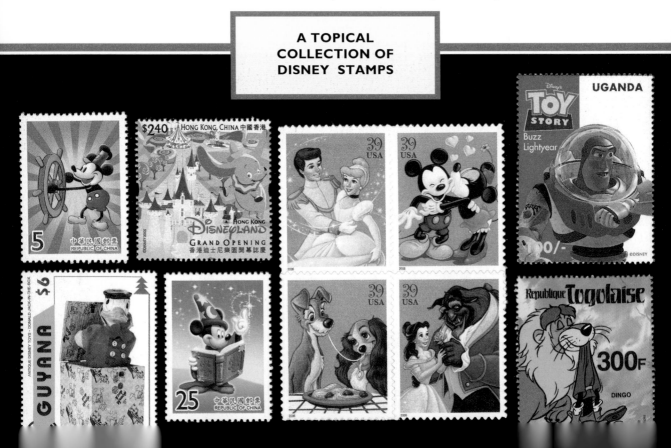

approaching Earth, and each stamp carried a bit of actual meteor dust. The Netherlands issued a stamp showing Elvis Presley singing "Heartbreak Hotel"—his first number-one hit in Europe, back in 1956. The subject was one of several chosen by popular vote.

China, Hong Kong, and Macao produced a joint issue on the theme of Chinese lanterns. Each of the four stamps in the set showed a different paper lantern, including one shaped like a fish.

Many countries issued stamps to mark holidays, including Christmas and Easter. A colorful chicken sat atop a decorated egg on an Easter stamp from the Czech Republic. Colorful balloons—symbols of celebration—bounced across a birthday stamp from Canada. Canada also released a set of four stamps honoring two of its tasty food products, wine and cheese.

With an eye to upcoming postal-rate increases, Canada introduced "Permanent" stamps in the fall. These stamps carried the letter P in place of a denomination. They sold for 51 cents, the current letter rate, and would remain valid even when the rate went to 52 cents in January 2007.

A TOPICAL COLLECTION

Stamps featuring Disney characters have been issued by many countries since 1970, when the first such stamp appeared. These stamps make a great subject for a topical collection—a collection built around a single theme.

You might begin your collection with some U.S. stamps. Since 2004 the U.S. Postal Service has issued three different panes of stamps in its Art of Disney series. For 2006, the theme was romance. The four stamps in the pane showed Mickey Mouse and Minnie Mouse, Cinderella and Prince Charming, Beauty and the Beast, and Lady and the Tramp.

But why stop at the U.S. border? From Hong Kong in Asia, to Uganda in Africa, to the Caribbean nation of Dominica, you can travel the world in the company of your favorite Disney characters.

WHAT'S MY LINE?

Mention the name J. K. Rowling, and people immediately know you are talking about the author of the Harry Potter series. Mention the name Tiger Woods, and just about everyone knows you mean the champion golfer.

Every profession has its leaders—people who have made important contributions to the field. The names of 26 such leaders are listed below (in the left column). Match them up with their professions (in the right column).

1.	Lance Armstrong	**a.**	actor
2.	Clara Barton	**b.**	anthropologist
3.	Jimmy Carter	**c.**	architect
4.	Eileen Collins	**d.**	artist
5.	Jacques Cousteau	**e.**	astronaut
6.	Marie Curie	**f.**	author/illustrator
7.	Johnny Depp	**g.**	aviator
8.	Emily Dickinson	**h.**	baseball player
9.	Amelia Earhart	**i.**	business leader
10.	Albert Einstein	**j.**	chemist/physicist
11.	Bill Gates	**k.**	civil-rights leader
12.	Tommy Hilfiger	**l.**	comedian
13.	Edmund Hillary	**m.**	cyclist
14.	Martin Luther King, Jr.	**n.**	fashion designer
15.	Michelle Kwan	**o.**	ice skater
16.	David Letterman	**p.**	jazz musician
17.	Wynton Marsalis	**q.**	marine explorer
18.	Steve Martin	**r.**	mountain climber
19.	Margaret Mead	**s.**	moviemaker
20.	Pablo Picasso	**t.**	nurse
21.	Babe Ruth	**u.**	physicist
22.	William Shakespeare	**v.**	playwright
23.	Steven Spielberg	**w.**	poet
24.	Chris Van Allsburg	**x.**	tennis player
25.	Serena Williams	**y.**	TV host
26.	Frank Lloyd Wright	**z.**	U.S. president

ANSWERS:

1.m; 2.t; 3.z; 4.e; 5.q; 6.j; 7.a; 8.w; 9.g; 10.u; 11.i; 12.n; 13.r; 14.k; 15.o; 16.y; 17.p; 18.l; 19.b; 20.d; 21.h; 22.v; 23.s; 24.f; 25.x; 26.c.

Next, go on a hunt. The last names of all 26 people are hidden in this word-search puzzle. Try to find them. Cover the puzzle with a sheet of tracing paper. Read forward, backward, up, down, and diagonally. Then draw a neat line through each name as you find it.

C	U	R	I	E	Z	O	R	E	T	R	A	C	A
R	O	N	G	I	H	I	L	F	I	G	E	R	S
U	S	U	N	R	Y	W	H	A	S	H	M	N	P
T	H	Y	S	A	E	N	I	E	T	S	N	I	E
H	A	R	K	T	U	B	T	L	T	D	C	T	E
N	K	A	I	S	E	A	L	R	L	A	M	R	D
O	E	L	N	I	G	A	O	E	S	I	E	A	E
S	S	L	G	L	N	N	U	S	I	K	A	M	P
N	P	I	V	A	G	N	O	R	F	P	D	M	P
I	E	H	W	S	C	O	L	L	I	N	S	O	S
K	A	K	E	R	I	T	A	W	R	I	G	H	T
C	R	I	N	A	M	R	E	T	T	E	L	C	B
I	E	P	O	M	E	A	R	H	A	R	T	I	O
D	E	N	G	R	U	B	S	L	L	A	N	A	V

RIBBON-AND-LACE HEART

Ribbons and lace are always fun to work with. Use them to make this pretty heart wreath.

You'll need a 10-inch (25-centimeter) foam heart form, 6 yards (5.5 meters) each of print and lace ribbon, 8 yards (7.3 meters) of velvet tube ribbon, 4 yards (3.7 meters) of a solid color ribbon, 1¼ yards (1.2 meters) of gathered lace, and a spray of seed pearls. You'll also need scissors, straight pins, craft glue, and a glue gun.

First, wrap the solid color ribbon around the foam heart form. Slightly overlap the edges of the ribbon, so that the heart is completely covered. Use a pin to hold the ribbon in place.

Cut the print and lace ribbons into 4-inch (10-centimeter) lengths. To make the loops, roll each length into a tube; overlap the ends, glue them together, and allow to dry. For each tube, dip a pin into craft glue and place it through the tube's seam and into the heart. Alternate print and lace tubes until the heart is completely covered.

Now cut 3½ yards (3.2 meters) of the velvet tube ribbon into 6-inch (15-centimeter) lengths. Roll each length into a loop, and use the glue gun to glue the ends together. Place 15 of the loops around the outer edge of the heart, evenly spaced. Pinch each remaining loop in the center and glue, forming a figure 8. Place a pin through the center of the "8" and attach it to the heart form, in between the ribbon loops.

Glue the gathered lace around the back of the heart, so it peeps out beyond the loops. Use some of the remaining velvet tubing to make a large bow. Attach it and the pearl spray to one side of the heart. Glue the ends of the remaining piece of velvet tubing to the top back of the heart, to form a loop for hanging.

Your ribbon-and-lace heart will add a soft touch to any room.

FROM THE HEART!

Crafting is a great way to spend your leisure time. But sometimes you may wonder: "What should I make?" How about making a heart! Almost every craft technique lends itself to hearts, and hearts are happy gifts for friends and family and for yourself.

Before you begin a project, gather all the supplies, and find a clean, dry surface on which to work. Follow the directions exactly, or change them to create something that's uniquely your own.

PAINTED HEARTS

Here's a cool way to send someone a pin that you've made: Attach it to a notecard so that it shows through a window you have cut in the front of the card.

Make the notecard from a sheet of construction paper or other sturdy paper. You will also need two small wood hearts, two pin backs, white eyelet lace, red satin ribbon to insert through the lace, narrow satin ribbon for a bow, red and white acrylic paint, a paintbrush, and craft glue.

Cover the wood hearts with two coats of red paint. When they are dry, use the white paint to add tiny designs to the hearts. After the white paint has dried, glue on the pin backs. Insert the ribbon through the lace, and glue the lace across the front of the card, between the bottom edge and the window. Paint red hearts on the card, add a tiny red bow, and pin the wood hearts onto the card.

Mail this card to someone you care about. It's a great way to say, "I like you!"

POTPOURRI HEARTS

Want to send hearts and flowers to your Mom? It's easy with the sweet-smelling potpourri hearts shown on the following page.

You'll need potpourri such as dried rosebuds, lavender, and leaves; a heart-shaped metal cookie cutter; and decorations such as ribbons, pearls, and silk flowers. You'll also need an old bowl that can be thrown away afterward, cooking spray, craft glue, waxed paper, a popsicle stick, a foam cup, and a pencil.

Fill the foam cup with potpourri and empty it into the bowl. Fill the cup ⅓ full of glue and empty it into the bowl. Use the popsicle stick to mix the potpourri and glue together. If it's too hard to mix, add more glue. Mix well—the glue must be distributed evenly throughout the potpourri. (The glue will dry clear.)

Lightly spray the inside of the cookie cutter with cooking spray. Also spray the top of the waxed paper. Place the cookie cutter on the waxed paper.

Fill the cookie cutter with the potpourri mixture. Use your fingers and the popsicle stick to spread the mixture evenly. Let the mixture sit for 15 minutes. (Timing is important—if you wait any longer, the potpourri might stick to the cookie cutter.) Then carefully remove the heart from the cookie cutter and place the heart on the waxed paper. If you

Painted hearts

DECOUPAGE HEART

Decorating a box by gluing on pieces of paper is a popular craft technique called decoupage. Almost any kind of paper will do—even paper napkins!

To make the box shown on the opposite page, you will need a heart-shaped wood box, pretty paper napkins, dimensional paints, gloss sealer, a sponge brush, a paintbrush, craft glue, and scissors. Also have two food cans handy.

Use the sponge brush to coat the outside top and sides of the lid with gloss sealer. While the gloss sealer is still damp, place a napkin on top of the lid. Smooth it down flat and over the sides, so that there are no bumps. Cut off any pieces of napkin that hang over the edges. Place the lid over a food can to dry.

Follow the same steps to cover the outside of the bottom part of the box. If you use more than one napkin, be sure to slightly overlap adjoining pieces.

When the surface is dry, use dimensional paints to enhance the design. Here's an opportunity to use your imagination as you outline flowers, add leaves, or create a border. You can also paint the inside of the box with regular acrylic paints.

Stash your treasures in this special heart box.

HARVEST HEART

The wreath of wheat shown on the opposite page may take extra time and care to make, but you'll be happy with the results.

To make the wreath, you'll need 80 wheat straws; beige carpet thread; a large tub; gold ribbon; and decorations such as dried roses, ferns, and silk. You'll also need scissors, a ruler, and craft glue.

Remove the outer leaf from each wheat sheaf. Cut each stem to a 10-inch (25-centimeter) length. Then fill the tub with cold water, and soak the wheat for at least 30 minutes.

Use the carpet thread to tie together eight stems of wheat just

plan to add a ribbon loop for hanging, use the pencil to poke a hole through the upper part of the heart, right below the V.

Let the heart dry for at least 24 hours. During this time, turn it over several times so that it dries evenly. When the heart is dry, glue on flowers, ribbon, and other decorations.

These wonderful potpourri "cookies" aren't for eating!

To form the heart, place the wheat on a flat surface. Separate the bundles to form a V, with the wheat heads downward. Bend the stem ends of the two bundles toward each other at the top center of the heart. Tie the ends together just below the heads. Trim the stems so they are about 1 inch (2.5 centimeters) long.

Place the wreath on a flat surface to dry. Then decorate it and glue a loop of ribbon to the back for hanging.

This delicate hand-crafted heart is so lovely that you just may want to keep it for yourself!

below the heads. Make a double knot but don't cut the thread. This will eventually be the bottom point of the heart. Separate the stems into two bundles of four stems each. You'll work with one bundle first, then the other.

Wrap thread around the stems of one bundle for ½ inch (1.2 centimeters). Add four more stems to the bundle, with heads facing in the same direction. Starting just below the heads of the new stems, continue to wrap the stems for ½ inch. Add four stems every ½ inch until you have added 36 stems. Tie the stems together just below the last bunch of wheat heads. Now repeat this process with the other bundle.

Harvest heart

161

COIN COLLECTING

More U.S. state quarter coins, a square coin, a crystal-studded coin, and coins with holograms were among the interesting and unusual new coins released in 2006.

U.S. COINS

As it has been doing since 1999, the U.S. Mint released five new state quarters in 2006. First up was Nevada. Its quarter showed wild stallions galloping in front of snow-capped

The Mint also launched two new commemorative sets. The first celebrated the 300th anniversary of Benjamin Franklin's birth. Two Franklin silver dollars were released. One, called "Scientist," showed Franklin flying a kite in a famous experiment with electricity. The coin's reverse showed his political cartoon promoting the unity of the colonies. The second silver dollar, "Founding Father," showed Franklin in his later years. The coin's reverse depicted

U.S. state quarters representing Nevada, Nebraska, Colorado, North Dakota, and South Dakota.

mountains, along with the state nickname—the Silver State. Nevada was home to the famous 1859 silver strike at the Comstock Lode in Virginia City.

Nebraska's quarter featured a scene from pioneer days. Oxen pulled a covered wagon on the Oregon Trail, past Nebraska's picturesque Chimney Rock. Colorado showed a sweeping view of the Rocky Mountains. On North Dakota's quarter, two bison grazed before a backdrop of the rugged buttes and canyons in the state's Badlands. And South Dakota showed the state bird, a Chinese ring-necked pheasant, soaring over the Mount Rushmore National Memorial.

U.S. $5 gold coin honoring the San Francisco Old Mint (also called the Granite Lady).

a 1776 Continental Currency dollar, which carried Franklin's saying "Mind Your Business."

The San Francisco Old Mint, also called the Granite Lady, was honored on a silver dollar and a $5 gold coin. The Granite Lady, which opened in 1874 and produced gold, silver, and copper coins until 1937, is to be turned into a museum. It was one of the few public buildings to survive the 1906 San Francisco earthquake. Both coins showed views of the building on the obverse and, on the reverse, designs from old U.S. coins struck there.

For 2006, the U.S. nickel showed a new portrait of Thomas Jefferson—for the first time, facing forward rather than in profile. The reverse of the nickel again displayed Jefferson's Virginia home, Monticello. Monticello was removed from the nickel in 2004 and 2005 in favor of designs commemorating the Louisiana Purchase and the Lewis and Clark Expedition.

The famous Buffalo nickel design, used on the U.S. five-cent piece from 1913 through 1938, reappeared in 2006 on the American Buffalo gold coin. The coin had a face value of

Canada's unusual square $3 silver coin depicting a beaver.

$50 and showed a Native American on the front and a bison on the back.

CANADIAN COINS

Canada issued its first square coin. The unusual $3 silver coin depicted a beaver. The design of the coin was based on tokens used as money in Canada's fur trade during the 17th and 18th centuries. The fur trade—especially trade for beaver pelts—played a huge role in the beginning of the nation.

Winter in Canada means snow, and a blue snowflake graced a special holiday silver dollar sold in a set with a CD of favorite carols. Another snowflake was featured on a limited-edition $300 gold coin that was set with six glittering crystals. Only 1,000 of these special coins were minted.

Animals were featured on other precious-metal coins. Among the issues were a silver $5 coin showing a peregrine falcon, and another showing a wild horse and foal on Sable Island, off Nova Scotia. The coins were included in sets with stamps on the same themes. A dog-sled team mushed across the Canadian Arctic on $30 silver and $250 gold coins. And a cowboy rode a bucking bronco on a 50-cent gold coin, the world's smallest pure-gold coin.

The Royal Canadian Mint marked the tenth anniversary of one of its most popular coins— the $2 polar-bear coin. The special 2006 anniversary issue featured an update of the original design, which shows a polar bear on a snow pack. A very different sort of bear—a teddy bear—appeared on a silver coin that was part of the Lullaby Loon dollar set. The set included a CD with lullabies by famous composers.

Canada also released two more coins in its Butterfly series. The first of the 50-cent silver coins showed the short-tailed swallowtail, and the second the silvery blue butterfly. A hologram depicted the shifting colors of the silvery blue's wings. The country also used a hologram for the image on a $150 gold coin honoring the Year of the Dog in the Chinese lunar calendar.

ANIMALS ON WORLD COINS

Animals were popular themes for coins from around the world. A number of countries issued Year of the Dog coins. But cats weren't left out. Each year the Isle of Man (home of the Manx cat) issues a copper-nickel 1-crown coin honoring a different breed of cat. The 2006 release showed three exotic shorthair kittens.

Clockwise from top: Canada's holographic coin celebrating the Year of the Dog; the Isle of Man's coin showing exotic kittens; Australia's coin featuring a cockatoo; the British Virgin Islands' coin showing frolicking dolphins.

Two dolphins swam on copper-nickel, silver, and gold coins from the British Virgin Islands. And one of Australia's rarest birds, the southeastern red-tailed black cockatoo, was featured on new $150 and $200 gold coins from that country.

Dinosaurs disappeared 160 million years ago, but they were back in 2006—on coins from Sierra Leone. Four $1 and $10 coins showed the *Tyrannosaurus rex,* the *Brontosaurus,* the *Stegosaurus,* and the *Triceratops.*

ROBERT VAN RYZIN
Editor, *Coins* magazine

SPORTS

Shaun White, the "Flying Tomato," is the world's best—and best-known—snowboarder and the winner of the gold medal in the half-pipe at the 2006 Winter Olympics in Turin, Italy. Here, he shows his stuff by soaring high above the rim of the near-vertical wall of the half-pipe. The half-pipe, with its grabs, twists, flips, and spins, is one of the most exciting winter sports to watch.

THE 2006 WINTER OLYMPIC GAMES

Italy was the host of the 20th Winter Olympic Games, which lasted from February 10 through February 26, 2006. It was the first time in 50 years that the Winter Games were held in Italy. The official site of the Games was Turin (Torino), a city set at the base of the Italian Alps, with world-famous resorts nearby. Ceremonies marking the opening and closing of the Games were held there, as were numerous sporting events. Other competitions took place at sites near the city.

THE OPENING CEREMONIES

Song, dance, and spectacle kicked off the Winter Games on February 10. Some 35,000 people packed the Olympic Stadium to see the opening ceremonies, and 2 billion more worldwide watched on television. The three-hour event showcased Italian culture as well as sports.

The 20th Winter Olympic Games were held in Turin, Italy, in February. The spectacular opening ceremonies featured giant glowing Olympic rings and the lighting of the Olympic flame.

The "Sparks of Passion"—in-line skaters in red body suits—whizzed around the stage as flames shot out of their helmets. Clowns, acrobats, and dancers performed in fantastic costumes. In one segment, dancers wore silver suits with big white bubbles on their heads. They were supposed to be snowballs.

In a highlight of the show, five giant rings were raised from the stage floor to form the Olympic symbol. Aerial acrobats rode up on the rings. They dropped back to the stage on wires as colorful fireworks exploded around the rings.

Then the parade of Olympic athletes began. Team by team, some 2,600 athletes marched into the stadium to the beat of disco music. More than 200 U.S. athletes were there, wearing white coats and blue and

The Olympic Torch Relay

The city of Turin is about 435 miles (700 kilometers) from Rome, Italy's capital. You can make the trip in about six hours by train or one hour by air. But that's not how the Olympic flame went from Rome to Turin for the Winter Games. It traveled more than 7,000 miles (11,265 kilometers) in 64 days.

The Olympic Torch Relay began in Rome on December 8, 2005. There, Italian President Carlo Azeglio Ciampi lit a torch from a flame that had been flown to Rome from Greece, which was the site of the ancient Olympic Games. He passed the torch to Olympic marathon champion Stefano Baldini, the first torchbearer.

Over the next two months, torchbearers carried the flame all over Italy and to a few neighboring countries. A Ferrari sports car carried the flame in the town of Maranello. A gondola carried it through the canals of Venice. It was even carried up Monte Bianco in the Italian Alps. In all, 10,001 torchbearers helped carry the flame. They included all of Italy's living Olympic champions, as well as celebrities and others. Each bearer lit his or her torch from the bearer before.

The relay ended in Turin on February 10. In a highlight of the opening ceremonies, the final torchbearer lit the Olympic flame that burned throughout the Games.

Left: A torchbearer carries the flame in a gondola, as it makes its way through the canals of Venice. Below: Another torchbearer carries the flame past Rome's famous Colosseum.

red hats. Greece, as the birthplace of the Olympics, led the parade, and Italy, as the host country, brought up the rear.

With the athletes gathered in the stadium, a relay of past Italian medal winners brought in the Olympic torch. Stefania Belmondo, who had won a gold and a silver medal in cross-country skiing at the 2002 Winter Games, was the last torchbearer. She touched the flame to a wire, lighting the Olympic cauldron and setting off a sensational fireworks display.

The ceremonies closed with famed Italian tenor Luciano Pavarotti singing the beautiful aria "Nessun Dorma" ("Let No One Sleep"), from Puccini's opera *Turandot*.

THE CHAMPIONS

Athletes from 80 different countries and territories competed in 84 events. Germany won the most medals, 29, and the most gold medals, 11. The United States was right behind, with 25 medals, 9 of them gold. Canada was third, with 24 medals, 7 of them gold; Austria was fourth, with 23 medals, 9 of them gold; and Russia was fifth, with 22 medals, 8 of them gold.

Beauty on Ice. Figure skating is the showcase event of the Winter Olympics. Fans love the grace, harmony, and teamwork of the pairs and ice-dance skaters. But they most enjoy the jumps, spins, and other acrobatic movements—as well as the elegance—of singles skating.

Michelle Kwan, a nine-time U.S. and five-time world figure-skating champion, was hoping to win her first Olympic gold medal at Turin. After she pulled out of the Games because of an injury, most people thought that American Sasha Cohen, 21, or Russian Irina Slutskaya, 27, would win the championship. However, it was Shizuka Arakawa of

Medals and Mascots

In the ancient Games, the winners were crowned with olive wreaths. Winners at the modern Olympics get medals—gold, silver, and bronze. The design of the medals is chosen by the host city. Turin chose a unique design: The medals had holes in the center. The hole represented the open space of the piazzas, or squares, in Italian cities.

Olympic mascots are also selected by the host city. Turin chose two cartoon characters as mascots. Neve was a gentle, feminine snowball. Gliz was a lively, masculine ice cube. The mascots represented the spirit of the Games and the young athletes competing in Turin.

NEVE   GLIZ

Golden figure skaters: Shizuka Arakawa of Japan and Yevgeny Plushenko of Russia.

Japan who skated elegantly and brilliantly to the gold. It was Japan's first-ever gold in figure skating and the country's only medal of the Turin Games. Cohen won the silver medal, and Slutskaya won the bronze.

Arakawa, 25, began skating when she was 5 years old—and she landed her first triple jump when she was only 8. At Turin, she became the second-oldest woman to win the Olympic figure-skating gold. After the Olympics, she announced her retirement.

Russian figure-skater Yevgeny Plushenko, 23, the winner of three world championships and the silver medal at the 2002 Winter Olympics, was the favorite in the men's event. He didn't disappoint his fans, winning the gold medal at Turin with a magnificent routine that included a quadruple and triple toe loop, as well as a double loop combination.

Plushenko began figure skating when he was 4. He was doing triple jumps by the time he was 11. Today, he is considered to be the best male figure skater in the world, and in Russia he's as popular as a rock star.

This was the fifth Olympic win in a row for Russian or Soviet male figure skaters. The silver medalist was Stephane Lambiel of Switzerland. Jeffrey Buttle of Canada won the bronze.

Russian skaters Tatiana Totmianina, 24, and Maxim Marinin, 28, won the gold medal in pairs figure skating. Russian and Soviet skaters have long dominated pairs figure skating, winning every Olympic gold medal in the sport since 1964.

Tatiana Navka, 30, and Roman Kostomarov, 29, won the gold medal in ice dancing for Russia. U.S. skaters Tanith Belbin, 21, and Ben Agosta, 24, won the silver medal. This was the first time U.S. skaters won any Olympic medal in dance since 1976.

Long-Track Speed Skating. U.S. men and Canadian women excelled in the long-track speed-skating events, winning five of the

Cindy Klassen: Woman of the Games

International Olympic Committee president Jacques Rogge called her the "Woman of the Games." That woman was 26-year-old Canadian speed-skater Cindy Klassen, of Winnipeg, Manitoba. She won five medals at the Turin Games—more than any other Canadian has won in a single Winter Olympics. Klassen also won a bronze medal at the 2002 Winter Olympics in Salt Lake City, Utah. Now she has six Olympic medals. That's more than any other Canadian Olympian—Summer or Winter!

Klassen won the gold medal in the 1,500-meter race, silver in the 1,000-meter, and bronzes in the 3,000 and 5,000 meters. And as part of the Canadian team, she won silver in the women's team pursuit.

In 2003, Klassen won a gold medal at the World Cup Championships—and she became the first Canadian in 27 years to win the overall title at the World Speed Skating Championships. In 2005, she won gold medals in the 1,500-meter and 3,000-meter races at the World Cup Championships. Klassen was named The Canadian Press female athlete of the year in 2005.

Joey Cheek: Fastest Man on Ice

Joey Cheek, of Greensboro, North Carolina, won the gold medal in the 500-meter speed-skating race, and the silver in the 1,000-meter race. At the 2002 Winter Olympics, he had won the bronze medal in the 1,000-meter race.

In the 500-meter race, skaters actually skate two races. Cheek finished in 34.82 seconds in the first race and in 34.94 seconds in the second race. He was the only skater to break 35 seconds—and he did it in both races.

Cheek, 26, was a Junior National Champion inline skater. He turned to speed skating in 1995. Just three years later, he became the U.S. Junior Speed-Skating Champion. In January 2006, he won the World Sprint Speed-Skating Championship.

Like all other medalists, Cheek received bonus checks from the U.S. Olympic Committee for winning the gold and silver medals. He donated this money—$40,000—to refugee children from the war-torn region of Darfur, in the African country of Sudan.

"For me to walk away with a gold medal is amazing," Cheek said. "And the best way to say thanks that I can think of is to help somebody else."

Antoine Deneriaz: Fastest Man on Skis

In January 2005, French skier Antoine Deneriaz was hoping to win the Alpine downhill World Cup. But during training, he crashed and tore a ligament in his knee; he could barely walk. "I told my coach," Deneriaz said, "that since I would not be the world champion, I would be the Olympic champion!"

Deneriaz was true to his word. Over 13 months, he steadily regained his strength and form. And at the Turin Games, the 29-year-old skier won the gold medal in the downhill event.

The downhill is perhaps the most dramatic of the Alpine events. The course is the longest, and the speeds the highest. The skier must race over ice and through dangerous, challenging turns.

Deneriaz raced down the slope at the dizzying speed of 70 miles (113 kilometers) an hour, finishing in 1 minute, 48.8 seconds. He beat Austrian Michael Walchhofer, the reigning World Cup champion, by 0.72 seconds, to capture his first victory in more than two years and the first major title of his career.

"I had the race of my life today," Deneriaz said. "I was in another world, like nothing could happen to me."

Janica Kostelic: Alpine Skiing Record Breaker

At the 2002 Winter Olympics in Salt Lake City, Utah, Janica Kostelic of Croatia won four Alpine skiing medals—three golds and one silver. In the 2006 Games in Turin, she won another gold and a silver. This made her the first woman ever to win four Olympic golds in Alpine skiing. And it made her the only woman in the history of the Olympic Games to win six medals overall in Alpine skiing.

Kostelic's gold medal was in the combined (downhill racing and slalom). The silver was in the Super-G. In the combined, her time was 2 minutes, 51.08 seconds. The 24-year-old super skier has had 11 knee operations. And she has suffered from other ailments. That makes her successes on the slopes even more astonishing.

Kostelic is very popular in her homeland. The Croatian government put a picture of her on a postage stamp in 2001. And she's not the only Kostelic to win an Olympic medal. At Turin, her brother Ivica won a silver medal in the men's combined. Janica and Ivica became the first sister and brother to win Alpine skiing medals in the same Winter Games since 1980.

"I'm more happy for my brother than for my own medal," she said. "It means so much to him."

twelve gold medals. American Joey Cheek won the gold in the 500-meter race—and the silver in the 1,000-meter race. Shani Davis won the gold medal in the 1,000-meter race. He was the first African American ever to win an individual gold medal in a Winter Olympics. He also won the silver medal in the 1,500-meter race. The third American gold-medal winner was Chad Hedrick, in the 5,000-meter race.

Cindy Klassen was Canada's shining light at Turin. She won five speed-skating medals: gold in the 1,500-meter race, silver in the 1,000-meter, bronzes in the 3,000- and 5,000-meters, and a silver as part of the Canadian team in the women's team pursuit. Clara Hughes won Canada's second gold medal, in the 5,000-meter race.

The Netherlands also did well, winning three gold speed-skating medals—Bob de Jong, in the men's 10,000-meter; Marianne Timmer, in the women's 1,000-meter; and Ireen Wust, in the women's 3,000-meter.

The two other individual gold-medal winners were Italy's Enrico Fabris, in the men's 1,500-meter; and Russia's Svetlana Zhurova, in the women's 500-meter.

Short-Track Speed Skating. Short-track speed-skating races are head-to-head events that require strategy as well as speed. The races are held on an oval track that's about the same size as a hockey rink. There's plenty of action around the tight curves, and painful collisions are common.

At Turin, the South Korean short-track speed skaters let the world know that they were the best at this relatively new Winter Olympic sport. They won gold medals in six of the eight short-track events—plus three silvers and a bronze. Ten of their 11 medals were in this sport. Their other medal, a bronze, was in long-track speed skating.

The star among the South Korean men was Ahn Hyun-Soo. A four-time world champion, he holds the world record for the 1,500-

The South Korean short-track speed skaters won gold medals in six of the eight events. The star among the men was Ahn Hyun-Soo (below), who skated to three golds.

Flying High on the Half-Pipe

Snowboarding consists of three events: the parallel slalom, the snowboard cross, and the half-pipe. The parallel slalom and the snowboard cross involve head-to-head competitions. The half-pipe doesn't—yet it's the most popular and exciting event. That's because the riders perform fantastic aerials. In the half-pipe, which had its origins in skateboarding, competitors take off from a near-vertical 16-foot-high (5 meters) wall to perform their aerial tricks.

the women's event, Hannah Teter of Belmont, Vermont, won the gold medal; and Gretchen Bleiler of Aspen, Colorado, won the silver.

Shaun White. In Shaun White's gold-medal-winning performance, his first jump took him an amazing 25 feet (7.6 meters) above the edge of the half-pipe. Also amazing were his seemingly effortless 900- and 1,080-degree spins.

With his flowing red hair, the 19-year-old was known as the Flying Tomato. He began

Shaun White (left and center) and Hannah Teter (right) took home the half-pipe golds.

Starting at the top of the half-pipe, riders snowboard down one wall, pick up speed, and make their way up the opposite wall to perform the first maneuver. They then make their way down the half-pipe, crossing from side to side and performing aerials each time they hit the top of a wall. Twists, spins, flips, and grabs are among the spectacular maneuvers performed by these daredevil athletes. Some top competitors can soar more than 20 feet (6 meters) above the top of the walls!

Snowboarding was invented in the United States, and Americans have done well in the sport—especially in the half-pipe. At the 2006 Winter Games, Shaun White of Carlsbad, California, won the men's gold medal; and Daniel Kass of Portland, Maine, won the silver. In

snowboarding when he was 6 years old and turned pro at 13. His ability to put together a series of exciting consecutive maneuvers made him an instant star. Even before winning the gold medal, White was the best-known snowboarder in the world.

Hannah Teter. Nineteen-year-old Hannah Teter won the women's gold medal in the half-pipe. Her 900-degree spin in midair, while grabbing her snowboard in the process, thrilled audiences.

Teter began snowboarding when she was 8 years old. She learned with a hand-me-down skateboard from her four older brothers. Two of them are also ace snowboarders. Teter won a spot on the U.S. Olympic team at the age of 16. She captured gold medals at the 2004 Winter X Games and the 2004 Grand Prix.

meter and 3,000-meter races. At Turin, Ahn won four medals. He finished first in the men's 1,000-meter and 1,500-meter races. He won another gold as a member of the men's 5,000-meter relay team. And he won a bronze in the 500-meter race. Ahn's time in the 1,000-meter race—1 minute, 26.739 seconds—set a new world record.

The star among the South Korean women was Jin Sun-Yu. She had won two medals at the World Championships in late 2005, and was the overall champion. At Turin, she won gold medals in the 1,000- and 1,500-meter races. She added a third gold medal as a member of the women's 3,000-meter relay team.

Ahn and Jin were the first South Korean athletes ever to win three gold medals in a single Olympics. The only non-Korean woman to win a gold in Turin was Wang Meng of China, in the 500-meter; the only non-Korean man to win was Apolo Anton Ohno of the United States, in the 500-meter. Ohno had won the 1,500-meter race in the 2002 Winter Games.

Skiing. Once again, the U.S. Alpine skiing team did poorly against the European skiers. The only American medalists were Ted Ligety, who won the gold medal in the men's combined; and Julia Mancuso, who won gold in the women's giant slalom. The European Alpine stars included Austrian Benjamin Raich, who won gold medals in the men's slalom and the men's giant slalom. Michaela Dorfmeister of Austria also won two golds, in the women's downhill and the Super-G. And Janica Kostelic, the "Croatian Sensation" who won three golds and one silver at the 2002 Winter Games, added two more in 2006: a gold in the women's combined and a silver in the women's Super-G.

In cross-country skiing, Sweden and Estonia each won three gold medals, and Italy and Russia each won two golds. Canada's Chandra Crawford won gold in the women's sprint.

In the biathlon, which combines cross-country skiing and shooting, Germany took four of the five gold medals in the men's events, and one in the women's events.

In ski jumping, Lars Bystoel of Norway won the gold medal in the 90-meter event, and Thomas Morgenstern of Austria won the 120-meter event. Austria won the team gold.

In freestyle skiing, Americans won only one medal—the bronze, by Toby Dawson in the men's moguls. Canada did better, with Jennifer Heil winning the women's moguls. Dale Begg-Smith of Australia won the men's moguls, Evelyne Leu of Switzerland won the women's aerials, and Han Xiaopeng of China won the men's aerials.

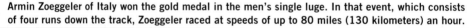

Armin Zoeggeler of Italy won the gold medal in the men's single luge. In that event, which consists of four runs down the track, Zoeggeler raced at speeds of up to 80 miles (130 kilometers) an hour.

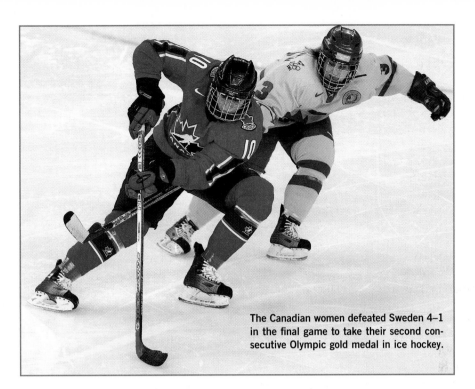

The Canadian women defeated Sweden 4–1 in the final game to take their second consecutive Olympic gold medal in ice hockey.

Snowboarding. Americans once again excelled in the snowboarding events, winning three of the six gold medals and seven of the 18 medals overall. The golds went to Shaun White in the men's half-pipe, Seth Wescott in the men's snowboard cross, and Hannah Teter in the women's half-pipe. Silver medals went to Danny Kass in the men's half-pipe, Gretchen Bleiler in the women's half-pipe, and Lindsey Jacobellis in the women's snowboard cross.

Shooting the Chute. In bobsledding, Germany dominated the field, winning gold medals in all three events—the two-man, the four-man, and the two-woman. But the United States and Canada picked up silver medals, the United States in the two-woman and Canada in the two-man.

Canada did even better in the skeleton events. Duff Gibson won the men's gold, and Jeff Pain won the silver. Maya Pedersen of Switzerland won the women's event.

In the men's singles luge, Armin Zoeggeler of Italy won the gold medal. He had won the same event at the 2002 Winter Games. This was the Olympic host country's first gold medal of the Turin Games.

Ice Hockey. Hockey is Canada's national sport, and Canadian hockey players had shown their excellence at the 2002 Winter Games, when both the men's and women's teams won gold medals. In 2006, the men's team finished without a medal, but the women defeated Sweden 4–1 to take their second consecutive Olympic gold medal.

Hayley Wickenheiser, the Canadian team's captain and star forward, was named the Most Valuable Player of the tournament. With 5 goals and 12 assists, she had more points than any other player. Wickenheiser had also been named MVP at the 2002 Winter Games.

The U.S. men's and women's hockey teams had won silver medals at the 2002 Winter Games. But in 2006, the women's team could only salvage a bronze medal, defeating Finland 4–0. The men's team didn't make it to the medal round.

THE CLOSING CEREMONIES

The 2006 Winter Olympic Games ended on February 26. Carnival, a festival celebrated across Italy at that time of year, was the theme for the closing ceremonies.

More than 2,000 acrobats, dancers, and other performers took part. A stilt walker jumped rope, and a parade of clowns zoomed around the stadium in Italian motor scooters and mini cars.

Fireworks exploded over the Olympic Stadium as the spectacular Turin Winter Olympics came to an end.

The Olympic athletes marched into the stadium as Italian pop songs played. A flag-bearer led each country's athletes. Joey Cheek, a gold-medal winner in speed skating, led the U.S. athletes; and gold-medal-winning speed-skater Cindy Klassen carried the Canadian flag.

All the athletes had ringside seats for a breathtaking aerial display. Performers dressed in white costumes with flowing wing-like sleeves were lifted from the ground by blasts of forced air. One by one, they floated above the stage and glided gracefully back to earth.

Onward to the Next Olympic Games. As the show came to an end, an Olympic flag was handed to Sam Sullivan, the mayor of Vancouver, Canada. Vancouver will host the next Winter Olympic Games, in 2010. But before that, sports lovers will be able to watch the next Summer Olympic Games in 2008 in Beijing, the capital of China.

FINAL MEDAL STANDINGS

Country	Gold	Silver	Bronze	Total
Germany	11	12	6	29
United States	9	9	7	25
Canada	7	10	7	24
Austria	9	7	7	23
Russia	8	6	8	22
Norway	2	8	9	19
Sweden	7	2	5	14
Switzerland	5	4	5	14
South Korea	6	3	2	11
Italy	5	0	6	11
China	2	4	5	11
France	3	2	4	9
Netherlands	3	2	4	9
Finland	0	6	3	9
Czech Republic	1	2	1	4
Estonia	3	0	0	3
Croatia	1	2	0	3
Australia	1	0	1	2
Poland	0	1	1	2
Ukraine	0	0	2	2
Japan	1	0	0	1
Belarus	0	1	0	1
Great Britain	0	1	0	1
Bulgaria	0	1	0	1
Slovakia	0	1	0	1
Latvia	0	0	1	1

GOLD MEDAL WINNERS

BIATHLON
Men
10-km Sprint: Sven Fischer, Germany
12.5-km Pursuit: Vincent Defrasne, France
20-km Individual: Michael Greis, Germany
15-km Mass Start: Michael Greis, Germany
30-km Relay: Germany
Women
7.5-km Sprint: Florence Baverel-Robert, France
10-km Pursuit: Kati Wilhelm, Germany
15-km Individual: Svetlana Ishmouratova, Russia
12.5-km Mass Start: Anna Carin Olofsson, Sweden
24-km Relay: Russia

BOBSLEDDING
Two-man: Kevin Kuske/Andre Lange, Germany
Four-man: Germany
Two-woman: Sandra Kiriasis/Anja Schneiderheinze, Germany

CURLING
Men: Canada
Women: Sweden

FIGURE SKATING
Men's Singles: Yevgeny Plushenko, Russia
Women's Singles: Shizuka Arakawa, Japan
Pairs: Tatiana Totmianina/Maxim Marinin, Russia
Dance: Tatiana Navka/Roman Kostomarov, Russia

ICE HOCKEY
Men: Sweden
Women: Canada

LUGE
Men's Singles: Armin Zoeggeler, Italy
Women's Singles: Sylke Otto, Germany
Doubles: Andreas Linger/Wolfgang Linger, Austria

SKELETON
Men: Duff Gibson, Canada
Women: Maya Pedersen, Switzerland

SKIING, ALPINE
Men
Downhill: Antoine Deneriaz, France
Slalom: Benjamin Raich, Austria
Giant Slalom: Benjamin Raich, Austria
Combined: Ted Ligety, United States
Super-G: Kjetil Andre Aamodt, Norway
Women
Downhill: Michaela Dorfmeister, Austria
Slalom: Anja Paerson, Sweden
Giant Slalom: Julia Mancuso, United States
Combined: Janica Kostelic, Croatia
Super-G: Michaela Dorfmeister, Austria

SKIING, CROSS COUNTRY
Men
15-km Classic: Andrus Veerpalu, Estonia
30-km Pursuit: Eugeni Dementiev, Russia
50-km Freestyle Mass Start: Giorgio di Centa, Italy
Sprint: Bjoern Lind, Sweden
Team Sprint: Thobias Fredriksson/Bjoern Lind, Sweden
40-km Relay: Italy

Women
10-km Classic: Kristina Smigun, Estonia
15-km Pursuit: Kristina Smigun, Estonia
30-km Freestyle Mass Start: Katerina Neumannova, Czech Republic
Sprint: Chandra Crawford, Canada
Team Sprint: Anna Dahlberg/Lina Andersson, Sweden
20-km Relay: Russia

SKIING, FREESTYLE
Men's Aerials: Han Xiaopeng, China
Women's Aerials, Evelyne Leu, Switzerland
Men's Moguls: Dale Begg-Smith, Australia
Women's Moguls: Jennifer Heil, Canada

SKIING, NORDIC COMBINED
15-km: Georg Hettich, Germany
7.5-km Sprint: Felix Gottwald, Austria
20-km Relay: Austria

SKI JUMPING
90-m: Lars Bystoel, Norway
120-m: Thomas Morgenstern, Austria
20-km Team: Austria

SNOWBOARDING
Men
Half-pipe: Shaun White, United States
Giant Slalom: Philipp Schoch, Switzerland
Snowboard Cross: Seth Wescott, United States
Women
Half-pipe: Hannah Teter, United States
Giant Slalom: Daniela Meuli, Switzerland
Snowboard Cross: Tanja Frieden, Switzerland

SPEED SKATING, LONG TRACK
Men
500-m: Joey Cheek, United States
1,000-m: Shani Davis, United States
1,500-m: Enrico Fabris, Italy
5,000-m: Chad Hedrick, United States
10,000-m: Bob de Jong, Netherlands
Men's Team Pursuit: Italy
Women
500-m: Svetlana Zhurova, Russia
1,000-m: Marianne Timmer, Netherlands
1,500-m: Cindy Klassen, Canada
3,000-m: Ireen Wust, Netherlands
5,000-m: Clara Hughes, Canada
Women's Team Pursuit: Germany

SPEED SKATING, SHORT TRACK
Men
500-m: Apolo Anton Ohno, United States
1,000-m: Ahn Hyun-Soo, South Korea
1,500-m: Ahn Hyun-Soo, South Korea
5,000-m Relay: South Korea
Women
500-m: Wang Meng, China
1,000-m: Jin Sun-Yu, South Korea
1,500-m: Jin Sun-Yu, South Korea
3,000-m Relay: South Korea

St. Louis shortstop David Eckstein completes a double play in the second inning of Game 2 in the World Series. The Cardinals beat the Detroit Tigers, four games to one, to win the Series. Eckstein was named Series MVP.

BASEBALL

The St. Louis Cardinals entered the 2006 playoffs with the poorest record of any team qualifying for postseason competition. But the Redbirds soared high after that. They outplayed each opponent and dominated the Detroit Tigers in the World Series, winning four games to one. Their victory in the Fall Classic was the Cards' first since 1982 and their tenth overall.

Under manager Tony La Russa, St. Louis finished first in the regular season in the National League (NL) Central Division. Joining them in the NL playoffs were the East Division-champion New York Mets; the West Division-leading San Diego Padres; and the Los Angeles Dodgers, the wild-card winners.

The Cardinals eliminated the Padres in the best-of-five Division Series in four games, while the Mets swept the Dodgers in three.

New York then extended St. Louis to the full seven games in the National League Championship Series (NLCS), but the Cards prevailed to win the NL pennant.

In the American League (AL), Detroit was the wild-card team, finishing behind the Minnesota Twins in the Central. The Oakland A's topped the West, and the New York Yankees ran away with the East.

2006 WORLD SERIES RESULTS

		R	H	E	Winning/Losing Pitcher
1	St. Louis	7	8	2	Anthony Reyes (W)
	Detroit	2	4	3	Justin Verlander (L)
2	St. Louis	1	4	1	Jeff Weaver (L)
	Detroit	3	10	1	Kenny Rogers (W)
3	Detroit	0	3	1	Nate Robertson (L)
	St. Louis	5	7	0	Chris Carpenter (W)
4	Detroit	4	10	1	Joel Zumaya (L)
	St. Louis	5	9	0	Adam Wainwright (W)
5	Detroit	2	5	2	Justin Verlander (L)
	St. Louis	4	8	1	Jeff Weaver (W)

Visiting team listed first, home team second.

The Tigers took down the Yankees in four games in the Division Series, while the A's toppled the Twins in three straight. In the ALCS, Detroit swept Oakland in four.

The Fall Classic began on October 21 in Detroit. The Tigers scored a run in the first inning and collected another in the ninth. But in between, the Redbirds piled up seven runs to win, 7–2. Detroit won Game 2 by the score of 3–1, as Tiger pitcher Kenny Rogers handcuffed St. Louis for eight frames. The Tigers' last game at home, it would be their only victory.

Cardinal hurlers Chris Carpenter and Braden Looper combined to shut out Detroit, 5–0, in Game 3. St. Louis shortstop David Eckstein, hitless in Games 1 and 2, poked two singles to lead his team. Eckstein rapped four hits in Game 4, including three doubles, as the Cards won, 5–4, and took a lead of three games to one.

Eckstein wasn't through. In Game 5, the St. Louis sparkplug smashed two more hits in the Cardinals' 4–2 triumph. The season was over, the Redbirds rejoiced, and Eckstein was named the Most Valuable Player (MVP) of the World Series. He had batted .364 in the five contests.

Tony La Russa became only the second manager in baseball history, after George "Sparky" Anderson, to pilot a World Series champion in both the NL and the AL.

The Philadelphia Phillies' Ryan Howard was named MVP of the NL regular season; the first baseman smacked 58 home runs and drove in 149 runs. AL MVP was Minnesota first baseman Justin Morneau, a .321 hitter with 34 homers and 130 runs batted in.

Minnesota's Johan Santana took the Cy Young Award as the AL's top pitcher; the lefthander posted a 19–6 won-lost record, a 2.77 earned run average (ERA), and 245 strikeouts. Arizona Diamondback righty Brandon Webb captured the NL Cy Young; he won 16 games and recorded a 3.10 ERA.

Rookie-of-the-Year Awards went, in the AL, to Detroit pitcher Justin Verlander, a 17-game winner. In the NL, it went to Florida Marlin shortstop Hanley Ramirez, who batted .292 and stole 51 bases.

The team from Japan is jubilant after defeating Cuba in the World Baseball Classic championship game.

The World Baseball Classic

For the first time in professional baseball history, a *real* World Series was held in 2006. Called the World Baseball Classic (WBC), this March tournament featured teams from Australia, Canada, China, Cuba, the Dominican Republic, Italy, Japan, Korea, Mexico, the Netherlands, Panama, Puerto Rico, South Africa, the United States, and Venezuela. Japan won the WBC title, defeating Cuba in the championship game.

About 180 Major League Baseball players took part in the WBC, and many of them—like New York Yankee Bernie Williams (Puerto Rico)—played for their homelands. The games were played in stadiums in Japan, Puerto Rico, and the United States. (The U.S. team didn't make it to the semifinal round of the tournament.)

At the hard-fought title game, held in San Diego, California, Japan downed Cuba 10–6. Much of the credit went to pitcher Daisuke Matsuzaka. With a record of 3–0 and an ERA of 1.38 in the tournament, he was named WBC Most Valuable Player. (In December, Matsuzaka was signed to a six-year, $52 million contract with the Boston Red Sox.)

2006 MAJOR LEAGUE BASEBALL FINAL STANDINGS

AMERICAN LEAGUE

Eastern Division

	W	L	Pct.	GB
New York	97	65	.599	—
Toronto	87	75	.537	10
Boston	86	76	.531	11
Baltimore	70	92	.432	27
Tampa Bay	61	101	.377	36

Central Division

	W	L	Pct.	GB
Minnesota	96	66	.593	—
*Detroit	95	67	.586	1
Chicago	90	72	.556	6
Cleveland	78	84	.481	18
Kansas City	62	100	.383	34

Western Division

	W	L	Pct.	GB
Oakland	93	69	.574	—
Los Angeles	89	73	.549	4
Texas	80	82	.494	13
Seattle	78	84	.481	15

NATIONAL LEAGUE

Eastern Division

	W	L	Pct.	GB
New York	97	65	.599	—
Philadelphia	85	77	.525	12
Atlanta	79	83	.488	18
Florida	78	84	.481	19
Washington	71	91	.438	26

Central Division

	W	L	Pct.	GB
*St. Louis	83	78	.516	—
Houston	82	80	.506	1.5
Cincinnati	80	82	.494	3.5
Milwaukee	75	87	.463	8.5
Pittsburgh	67	95	.414	16.5
Chicago	66	96	.407	17.5

Western Division

	W	L	Pct.	GB
San Diego	88	74	.543	—
Los Angeles	88	74	.543	—
San Francisco	76	85	.472	11.5
Arizona	76	86	.469	12
Colorado	76	86	.469	12

*League Championship Series winners

MAJOR LEAGUE LEADERS

AMERICAN LEAGUE

Batting
(top 10 qualifiers)

	AB	H	Avg.
J. Mauer, Minnesota	521	181	.347
D. Jeter, New York	623	214	.343
R. Canó, New York	482	165	.342
M. Tejada, Baltimore	648	214	.330
V. Guerrero, Los Angeles	607	200	.329
I. Suzuki, Seattle	695	224	.322
J. Morneau, Minnesota	592	190	.321
M. Ramirez, Boston	449	144	.321
C. Guillén, Detroit	543	174	320
R. Johnson, Toronto	461	147	.319

Home Runs

	HR
D. Ortiz, Boston	54
J. Dye, Chicago	44
T. Hafner, Cleveland	42
J. Thome, Chicago	42
F. Thomas, Oakland	39

Pitching
(top qualifiers, based on number of wins)

	W	L	ERA
J. Santana, Minnesota	19	6	2.77
C.-M. Wang, New York	19	6	3.63
J. Garland, Chicago	18	7	4.51
K. Rogers, Detroit	17	8	3.84
J. Verlander, Detroit	17	9	3.63
F. Garcia, Chicago	17	9	4.53
R. Johnson, New York	17	11	5.00

NATIONAL LEAGUE

Batting
(top 10 qualifiers)

	AB	H	Avg.
F. Sánchez, Pittsburgh	582	200	.344
M. Cabrera, Florida	576	195	.339
A. Pujols, St. Louis	535	177	.331
G. Atkins, Colorado	602	198	.329
M. Holliday, Colorado	602	196	.326
P. Lo Duca, New York	512	163	.318
L. Berkman, Houston	536	169	.315
R. Howard, Philadelphia	581	182	.313
D. Wright, New York	582	181	.311
C. Utley, Philadelphia	658	203	.309

Home Runs

	HR
R. Howard, Philadelphia	58
A. Pujols, St. Louis	49
A. Soriano, Washington	46
L. Berkman, Houston	45
A. Jones, Atlanta	41
C. Beltran, New York	41

Pitching
(top qualifiers, based on number of wins)

	W	L	ERA
C. Zambrano, Chicago	16	7	3.41
B. Webb, Arizona	16	8	3.10
D. Lowe, Los Angeles	16	8	3.63
J. Smoltz, Atlanta	16	9	3.49
B. Penny, Los Angeles	16	9	4.33
A. Harang, Cincinnati	16	11	3.76

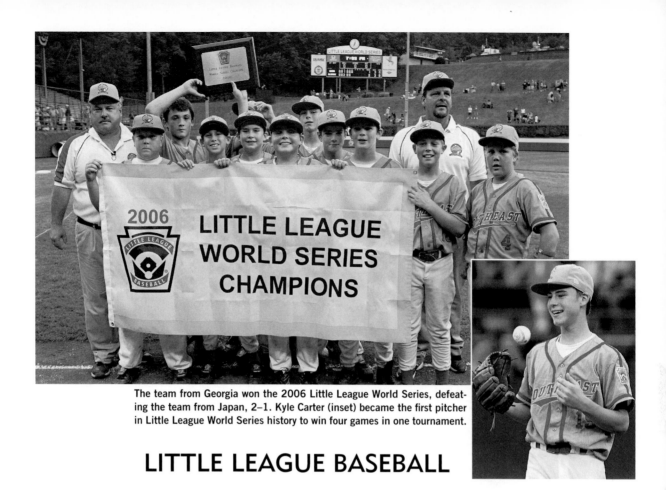

The team from Georgia won the 2006 Little League World Series, defeating the team from Japan, 2–1. Kyle Carter (inset) became the first pitcher in Little League World Series history to win four games in one tournament.

LITTLE LEAGUE BASEBALL

On August 30, 1905, Ty Cobb—"The Georgia Peach"—played his first major-league baseball game. The future Hall-of-Famer was only 18 years old.

Almost 101 years later—on August 28, 2006—a group of youngsters also from Georgia made their own baseball history: A team from the city of Columbus won the Little League World Series. As U.S. champions, they defeated the International champs, from Kawaguchi City, Japan, in the final game by the score of 2–1.

Georgia's victory was the second in a row for a U.S. squad. In 2005, the Little League champs hailed from Hawaii. The last time two U.S. teams had won the Series in consecutive years was 1982–1983.

Pitching dominated the final game in 2006. Georgia's Kyle Carter, a 12-year-old left-hander, struck out 11 batters, relying on a tough curveball. Thirteen-year-old Go Matsumoto of Japan, meanwhile, fanned nine Georgians in the six-inning affair. Georgia's two tallies scored on Cody Walker's third-inning home run. With Josh Lester on base, the righty batter blasted a Matsumoto pitch over the right-field fence.

With the victory, Kyle Carter became the first hurler in the annals of the Little League World Series to win four games.

Each August, 16 teams travel to Williamsport, Pennsylvania, to compete in the Little League World Series. Eight are from the United States, and eight are International. The U.S. teams battle one another for the chance to play the final game against the winner of the International bracket of the tournament.

The other U.S. teams represented Beaverton, Oregon; Columbia, Missouri; Lake Charles, Louisiana; Lemont, Illinois; Phoenix, Arizona; Portsmouth, New Hampshire; and Staten Island, New York.

Besides Japan, the International teams were from Barquisimeto, Venezuela; Dhahran, Saudi Arabia; Matamoros, Mexico; Moscow, Russia; Saipan, Pacific Region; Surrey, British Columbia, Canada; and Willemstad, Curaçao.

Led by Dwyane Wade, the Miami Heat beat the Dallas Mavericks for their first-ever NBA championship. Wade was named MVP of the playoffs.

BASKETBALL

The Miami Heat captured their first National Basketball Association (NBA) title in 2006. In the playoff finals against the Dallas Mavericks, the Heat lost the first two games but rebounded to win four straight.

Igniting the Heat throughout the long schedule was 24-year-old guard Dwyane Wade, who led the team in regular-season scoring (27.2 points per game) and assists (6.7 per game). Dominating the middle for Miami was the formidable 7-foot-1-inch center Shaquille ("Shaq") O'Neal, who averaged 20.0 points and 9.2 rebounds per game.

Pat Riley coached the Heat. In addition to Wade and Shaq, Riley relied on guards Gary Payton and Jason Williams, forwards Udonis Haslem and Antoine Walker, and the veteran Alonzo Mourning, who backed up Shaq at center.

During the regular season, Miami finished first in the Southeast Division. The other playoff qualifiers from the NBA's Eastern Conference were the Detroit Pistons, who topped the Central Division; the New Jersey Nets, the Atlantic Division champs; the Cleveland Cavaliers; the Indiana Pacers; the Chicago Bulls; the Milwaukee Bucks; and the Washington Wizards.

For the second consecutive year, Steve Nash, the point guard of the Phoenix Suns, won the MVP award for the NBA's regular season.

2006 NBA FINAL STANDINGS

EASTERN CONFERENCE
Atlantic Division

	W	L	Pct.
New Jersey	49	33	.598
Philadelphia	38	44	.463
Boston	33	49	.402
Toronto	27	55	.329
New York	23	59	.280

Central Division

	W	L	Pct.
Detroit	64	18	.780
Cleveland	50	32	.610
Chicago	41	41	.500
Indiana	41	41	.500
Milwaukee	40	42	.488

Southeast Division

	W	L	Pct.
Miami	52	30	.634
Washington	42	40	.512
Orlando	36	46	.439
Atlanta	26	56	.317
Charlotte	26	56	.317

WESTERN CONFERENCE
Northwest Division

	W	L	Pct.
Denver	44	38	.537
Utah	41	41	.500
Seattle	35	47	.427
Minnesota	33	49	.402
Portland	21	61	.256

Pacific Division

	W	L	Pct.
Phoenix	54	28	.659
L.A. Clippers	47	35	.573
L.A. Lakers	45	37	.549
Sacramento	44	38	.537
Golden State	34	48	.415

Southwest Division

	W	L	Pct.
San Antonio	63	19	.768
Dallas	60	22	.732
Memphis	49	33	.598
New Orleans/Oklahoma City	38	44	.463
Houston	34	48	.415

NBA Championship: Miami Heat

COLLEGE BASKETBALL

Conference	Winner
Atlantic Coast	Duke (regular season and tournament)
Atlantic 10	George Washington (regular season) Xavier (tournament)
Big East	Connecticut and Villanova (tied, regular season) Syracuse (tournament)
Big Ten	Ohio State (regular season) Iowa (tournament)
Big 12	Kansas and Texas (tied, regular season) Kansas (tournament)
Big West	Pacific (regular season and tournament)
Ivy League	Pennsylvania
Missouri Valley	Wichita State (regular season) Southern Illinois (tournament)
Pacific-10	UCLA (regular season and tournament)
Southeastern	Eastern: Tennessee Western: LSU (regular season) Florida (tournament)
Southwestern Athletic	Southern (regular season and tournament)
Western Athletic	Nevada (regular season and tournament)

NCAA, men: Florida
women: Maryland

NIT: South Carolina

The Heat gored the Bulls, four games to two, in the first round of the playoffs. They knocked off the Nets, four games to one, in round two. Miami then downed Detroit in six games in the Eastern Conference finals.

Dallas, under NBA Coach of the Year Avery Johnson, placed second in the South-west Division of the Western Conference. Power forward Dirk Nowitzki led the Mavericks in scoring and rebounds. Point guard Jason Terry was tops in assists.

The other Western Conference teams qualifying for postseason play were the San Antonio Spurs, champs of the Southwest Division; the Denver Nuggets, best in the Northwest Division; the Pacific Division title-winning Phoenix Suns; the Memphis Grizzlies; the Los Angeles Clippers; the Los Angeles Lakers; and the Sacramento Kings.

In the first round of the playoffs, Dallas swept Memphis, four games to none. The Mavs then stopped the Spurs in seven games in round two. In the Western Conference finals, Dallas eliminated Phoenix, four games to two.

The NBA finals began on June 8 in Dallas. The Mavs took Game 1, 90–80, behind Jason

Led by Deanna Nolan, the Detroit Shock defeated the Sacramento Monarchs to win the WNBA playoffs. Nolan took the MVP award for the playoff finals.

Game 5 went to overtime, but the result was again a Miami triumph, 101–100. Wade went wild: 43 points!

The rivals returned to Dallas for Game 6. Wade's 36 points raised the Heat to a 95–92 win and the NBA championship.

Wade—his nickname is "Flash"—was the finals' most valuable player (MVP). The Heat's first NBA crown was the fourth for Shaquille O'Neal; he had collected the others with the Lakers in 2000, 2001, and 2002. It was Riley's fifth title as a coach.

For the second year in a row, guard Steve Nash of Phoenix was the regular-season MVP. Point guard Chris Paul of the New Orleans Hornets was named Rookie of the Year. And the Lakers' Kobe Bryant led all scorers with 35.4 points per game.

WNBA. The Detroit Shock defeated the Sacramento Monarchs, three games to two, in the finals of the Women's National Basketball Association playoffs, which were contested in the summer. Detroit's Deanna "Tweety" Nolan was named MVP of the finals. Center Lisa Leslie of the Los Angeles Sparks collected her third regular-season MVP award; she averaged 20.0 points and 3.2 assists per game.

College Play. The University of Florida, coached by Billy Donovan, won the men's National Collegiate Athletic Association (NCAA) championship. The Gators upended UCLA, 73–57, in the final game of the NCAA tournament. Power forward Joakim Noah, son of former French tennis star Yannick Noah, served as the Gators' ace, registering 16 points, 9 rebounds, and 6 blocked shots. The sophomore was named the Final Four's most outstanding player.

Brenda Frese coached the University of Maryland to the NCAA women's title. In the final game of the tournament, the Terrapins defeated Duke, 78–75, in overtime. Maryland's Laura Harper collected 16 points and took home the outstanding-player honors.

Terry's 32 points. In Game 2, Dirk Nowitzki fired up 26 points as Dallas won, 99–85.

The shellshocked Heat returned to Miami. And everything changed. In Game 3, though down by 13 points midway through the fourth quarter, the Heat surged to a 98–96 victory. Playing on a sore knee, Dwyane Wade poured in 42 points.

In Game 4, Wade erupted for 36 points, and Shaq added 17, plus 13 rebounds. The final score was 98–74, and the series was tied.

Running back LaDainian Tomlinson scored a single-season record-breaking 31 touchdowns and led the San Diego Chargers to a spot in the 2006–07 playoffs.

FOOTBALL

The Pittsburgh Steelers, a franchise with a strong history in the National Football League (NFL), won their fifth Super Bowl in 2006. In the Canadian Football League (CFL), the B.C. (British Columbia) Lions locked up the Grey Cup. And the Florida Gators and the Ohio State Buckeyes ended the year as the two top teams among U.S. colleges.

THE NFL PLAYOFFS AND SUPER BOWL XL

Coach Bill Cowher's Steelers qualified for the 2005–06 playoffs as an American Conference (AFC) wild-card team. The AFC division champs were the Cincinnati Bengals, the New England Patriots, the Indianapolis Colts, and the Denver Broncos. The other wild card went to the Jacksonville Jaguars.

To reach the Super Bowl, Pittsburgh had to win three road games—no easy task. The Steelers stomped the Bengals, 31–17, in the first week of postseason play (January 2006), while the Patriots pummeled the Jaguars, 28–3. A week later, Pittsburgh upset Indianapolis, 21–18; and Denver dropped New England, the 2005 Super Bowl champs, by 27–13.

Facing the Broncos in the AFC title game, Steeler quarterback Ben Roethlisberger connected on 21 of 29 passes for 275 yards and two touchdowns, sparking Pittsburgh to a 34–17 victory and a trip to the Super Bowl—the team's first since 1996, when they lost to the Dallas Cowboys.

Over in the National Conference (NFC), the 2005–06 division titles went to the Seattle Seahawks, the Tampa Bay Buccaneers, the Chicago Bears, and the New York Giants. The Washington Redskins and the Carolina Panthers picked up the wild cards.

Seattle, sporting the best regular-season record in the NFC, together with Chicago, earned "byes" and sat out week one of the playoffs. Carolina shut out New York, 23–0, and Washington edged Tampa Bay, 17–10. In week two, the Seahawks stopped the Redskins, 20–10, while the Panthers beat the Bears, 29–21.

In the NFC title game, Seattle swamped Carolina, 34–14. Seahawk Shaun Alexander, who led the NFL in rushing in 2005–06, ran for 132 yards and two touchdowns. Seattle, coached by Mike Holmgren, was on its way to its first Super Bowl.

The big game, Super Bowl XL, took place at Ford Field in Detroit, Michigan, on February 5, 2006. Seattle went up, 3–0, at the end of the first quarter. But with two minutes left in the half, Steeler Roethlisberger took a snap on the Seahawks' 1-yard line and scampered into the end zone. Jeff Reed kicked the extra point to make the score 7–3, Pittsburgh.

The second half had barely begun when the Steelers lengthened their lead to 14–3 on Willie Parker's 75-yard touchdown dash, an all-time Super Bowl record for the longest scoring run from scrimmage.

Later in the third quarter, Seattle closed to within 14–10. But Pittsburgh settled matters in the fourth period on a flashy play. Wide receiver Antwaan Randle El, who had been a quarterback in college, became a passer once again. He took a handoff from Parker, ran to

Quarterback Drew Brees's 26 touchdown passes helped the New Orleans Saints capture the NFC South division.

his right, and tossed a strike to Hines Ward for a 43-yard touchdown. The final score was 21–10.

Ward, who caught five passes for 123 yards, was named Most Valuable Player (MVP) of the Steelers' first Super Bowl victory since they captured four between 1975 and 1980. Only two other teams—the San Francisco 49ers and the Dallas Cowboys—have won five.

Pittsburgh became the first team to win three road playoff contests and then the Super Bowl. Super Bowl XL was also the final game for Steeler running back Jerome ("The Bus") Bettis, the NFL's fifth-leading career rusher with 13,662 yards.

THE 2006-07 REGULAR SEASON

Pittsburgh faltered in 2006–07. The AFC playoff teams were division champs New England, Indianapolis, the Baltimore Ravens, and the San Diego Chargers; plus the wild cards, the New York Jets and the Kansas City Chiefs. The NFC qualifiers were division winners Seattle, Chicago, the Philadelphia Eagles, and the New Orleans Saints; and the wild cards, Dallas and the New York Giants.

THE CANADIAN FOOTBALL LEAGUE (CFL)

The B.C. Lions secured the 2006 CFL title by defeating the Montreal Alouettes, 25–14, in the Grey Cup game, played in Winnipeg, Manitoba, on November 19. Lion quarterback Dave Dickenson earned the MVP award; he completed 18 passes for 184 yards, and rushed for another 53 yards. B.C. placekicker Paul McCallum tied a Grey Cup record by booting six field goals.

COLLEGE PLAY

Ranked numbers one and two at the end of the regular season, Ohio State's Buckeyes and Florida's Gators prepared to meet in the national championship game on January 8, 2007. USC overwhelmed Michigan in the Rose Bowl; LSU downed Notre Dame in the Sugar Bowl; Boise State outscored Oklahoma in the Fiesta Bowl; Louisville beat Wake Forest in the Orange Bowl; and Auburn defeated Nebraska in the Cotton Bowl.

The Heisman Trophy went to Buckeye quarterback Troy Smith in a runaway vote. The senior passed for 2,507 yards and 30 touchdowns in the regular season.

Ohio State quarterback Troy Smith won the 2006 Heisman Trophy as the best college player.

COLLEGE FOOTBALL

Conference	Winner
Atlantic Coast	Wake Forest
Big Ten	Ohio State
Big 12	Oklahoma
Pacific-10	California, USC (tied)
Southeastern	Florida
Western Athletic	Boise State

Cotton Bowl: Auburn 17, Nebraska 14
Fiesta Bowl: Boise State 43, Oklahoma 42
Gator Bowl: West Virginia 38, Georgia Tech 35
Orange Bowl: Louisville 24, Wake Forest 13
Rose Bowl: USC 32, Michigan 18
Sugar Bowl: LSU 41, Notre Dame 14

Heisman Trophy: Troy Smith, Ohio State

2006–07 NFL FINAL STANDINGS

AMERICAN CONFERENCE

East

	W	L	T	Pct.	PF	PA
New England	12	4	0	.750	385	237
N.Y. Jets	10	6	0	.625	316	295
Buffalo	7	9	0	.438	300	311
Miami	6	10	0	.375	260	283

North

	W	L	T	Pct.	PF	PA
Baltimore	13	3	0	.813	353	201
Cincinnati	8	8	0	.500	373	331
Pittsburgh	8	8	0	.500	353	315
Cleveland	4	12	0	.250	238	356

South

	W	L	T	Pct.	PF	PA
Indianapolis	12	4	0	.750	427	360
Tennessee	8	8	0	.500	324	400
Jacksonville	8	8	0	.500	371	274
Houston	6	10	0	.375	267	366

West

	W	L	T	Pct.	PF	PA
San Diego	14	2	0	.875	492	303
Kansas City	9	7	0	.563	331	315
Denver	9	7	0	.563	319	305
Oakland	2	14	0	.125	168	332

NATIONAL CONFERENCE

East

	W	L	T	Pct.	PF	PA
Philadelphia	10	6	0	.625	398	328
Dallas	9	7	0	.563	425	350
N.Y. Giants	8	8	0	.500	355	362
Washington	5	11	0	.313	307	376

North

	W	L	T	Pct.	PF	PA
Chicago	13	3	0	.813	427	255
Green Bay	8	8	0	.500	301	366
Minnesota	6	10	0	.375	282	327
Detroit	3	13	0	.188	305	398

South

	W	L	T	Pct.	PF	PA
New Orleans	10	6	0	.625	413	322
Carolina	8	8	0	.500	270	305
Atlanta	7	9	0	.438	292	328
Tampa Bay	4	12	0	.250	211	353

West

	W	L	T	Pct.	PF	PA
Seattle	9	7	0	.563	335	341
St. Louis	8	8	0	.500	367	381
San Francisco	7	9	0	.438	298	412
Arizona	5	11	0	.313	314	389

TIGER! TIGER! BURNING BRIGHT!

Tiger Woods developed a burning passion to play golf when he was only a child. He won his first championship when he was 8. And he won the U.S. Junior Amateur Championship and the U.S. Amateur Championship three times each before turning professional in 1996, at the age of 20.

In 2006, at age 30, Woods celebrated his tenth anniversary as a professional golfer. And—already considered the best golfer in the world—he had another terrific year!

Woods played in 13 Professional Golf Association (PGA) tournaments and won seven of them—an incredible 54 percent win rate. Between July 20 and October 1, he won six in a row. And two of them—the British Open and the PGA Championship—were major, or Grand Slam, events.

Where did this outstanding performance put Woods on the roster of great golfers? Overall, he has won 54 times on the PGA Tour, placing him fifth on the list of Tour win leaders. Only Sam Snead, Jack Nicklaus, Ben Hogan, and Arnold Palmer have had more wins.

And Woods's victories at the 2006 British Open and PGA Championship were his 11th and 12th career majors. He has now won the U.S. Open twice, the British Open three times, the PGA Championship three times, and the Masters four times. Only the great Jack Nicklaus has had more wins—18—in the major championships.

GOLF

PROFESSIONAL		AMATEUR	
	Individual		**Individual**
Masters	Phil Mickelson	U.S. Amateur	Richie Ramsay
U.S. Open	Geoff Ogilvy	U.S. Women's Amateur	Kimberly Kim
Canadian Open	Jim Furyk	British Amateur	Julien Guerrier
British Open	Tiger Woods	British Ladies Amateur	Belen Mozo
PGA	Tiger Woods	Canadian Amateur	Richard Scott
U.S. Women's Open	Annika Sorenstam	Canadian Ladies Amateur	Jessica Potter
Ladies PGA	Se Ri Pak		
	Team		**Team**
Ryder Cup	Europe	Curtis Cup	United States

The Carolina Hurricanes defeated the Edmonton Oilers, four games to three, for their first Stanley Cup. Carolina goalie Cam Ward (left) was named Most Valuable Player of the playoffs.

HOCKEY

An exciting season in 2006 was exactly what the National Hockey League (NHL) needed. The year before, a lockout shut down the NHL, and the season was canceled. Competition resumed in 2005–06, and the Carolina Hurricanes stormed to their first title: They defeated the Edmonton Oilers in the Stanley Cup finals by four games to three.

Carolina's roster included veterans such as 38-year-old right wing Mark Recchi; defenseman Glen Wesley, 37; and center Rod Brind'Amour, 35. Coach Peter Laviolette also relied on some younger players. Twenty-two-year-old goalie Cam Ward excelled in the playoffs. And center Eric Staal, 21, led the team in scoring in the regular season, amassing 100 points on 45 goals and 55 assists. Among the other Hurricane players were goalie Martin Gerber; defensemen Aaron Ward, Bret Hedican, and Frantisek Kaberle; wings Ray Whit-

ney, Cory Stillman, and Justin Williams; and center Doug Weight.

Carolina finished atop the Southeast Division in the regular season, compiling the second best record in the Eastern Conference: 52 wins, 22 losses, and 8 overtime losses, for a total of 112 points. The other Eastern Conference squads making the playoffs were the New Jersey Devils, who led the Atlantic Division; the Philadelphia Flyers; the New York Rangers; the Ottawa Senators, champs of the Northeast Division; the Buffalo Sabres; the Montreal Canadiens; and the Tampa Bay Lightning.

In the first round of the playoffs, Carolina eliminated Montreal, four games to two. In the second round, the conference semifinals, the Hurricanes ousted the Devils in a quick five games. Carolina then needed the full seven contests to outduel the Sabres in the Eastern Conference finals.

Edmonton's journey through the regular season was shaky. The Oilers finished third in the Northwest Division and were the last team in the Western Conference to qualify for the playoffs. Ahead of them in the Northwest Division were the Calgary Flames and the Colorado Avalanche. The other Western Conference playoff teams were the Central Division champion Detroit Red Wings, who topped the NHL with 58 victories and 124 points; the Nashville Predators; the Dallas Stars, who took the Pacific Division title; the San Jose Sharks; and the Anaheim Mighty Ducks.

In the playoffs, Edmonton dropped Detroit, four games to two, in round one; and stopped the Sharks in six games in round two. And in the Western Conference finals, the Oilers felled the Mighty Ducks in five games.

The Stanley Cup finals began in Raleigh, North Carolina, on June 5. Carolina's regular goalie, Martin Gerber, who struggled early in the playoffs, was replaced by rookie Cam Ward.

Game 1 went to the Hurricanes, 5–4. Ray Whitney and Rod Brind'Amour each collected two goals; Brind'Amour's second goal came with less than 32 seconds left on the clock. In Game 2, also played in Raleigh, Cam Ward stopped 25 shots as Carolina shut out Edmonton, 5–0. Up two games to none, the Hurricanes looked unbeatable. But the Oilers, back at home, won Game 3. The final tally was 2–1.

Game 4, also in Canada, went to the Hurricanes, 2–1, on goals by Cory Stillman and Mark Recchi. Ward registered 20 saves. By now, hockey fans were marveling at the rookie net minder's confidence, poise, and positioning. Their backs to the wall, the Oilers wouldn't quit, winning Game 5 in overtime, in North Carolina, 4–3. They also won Game 6, in Edmonton, 4–0.

But back home, Carolina took Game 7, 3–1, and the Hurricanes celebrated their first Stanley Cup. They had joined the NHL as the Hartford (Connecticut) Whalers in 1979, and had moved to North Carolina in 1997. Cam Ward racked up 22 saves and won the Conn Smythe Trophy as the Most Valuable Player (MVP) of the playoffs.

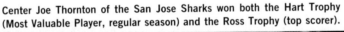

Center Joe Thornton of the San Jose Sharks won both the Hart Trophy (Most Valuable Player, regular season) and the Ross Trophy (top scorer).

2006 NHL FINAL STANDINGS

EASTERN CONFERENCE

Atlantic Division

	W	L	OL	SL	Pts.
New Jersey	46	27	5	4	101
Philadelphia	45	26	5	6	101
N.Y. Rangers	44	26	8	4	100
N.Y. Islanders	36	40	3	3	78
Pittsburgh	22	46	8	6	58

Northeast Division

	W	L	OL	SL	Pts.
Ottawa	52	21	3	6	113
Buffalo	52	24	1	5	110
Montreal	42	31	6	3	93
Toronto	41	33	1	7	90
Boston	29	37	8	8	74

Southeast Division

	W	L	OL	SL	Pts.
Carolina	52	22	6	2	112
Tampa Bay	43	33	2	4	92
Atlanta	41	33	3	5	90
Florida	37	34	6	5	85
Washington	29	41	6	6	70

WESTERN CONFERENCE

Central Division

	W	L	OL	SL	Pts.
Detroit	58	16	5	3	124
Nashville	49	25	5	3	106
Columbus	35	43	1	3	74
Chicago	26	43	7	6	65
St. Louis	21	46	7	8	57

Northwest Division

	W	L	OL	SL	Pts.
Calgary	46	25	4	7	103
Colorado	43	30	3	6	95
Edmonton	41	28	4	9	95
Vancouver	42	32	4	4	92
Minnesota	38	36	5	3	84

Pacific Division

	W	L	OL	SL	Pts.
Dallas	53	23	5	1	112
San Jose	44	27	4	7	99
Anaheim	43	27	5	7	98
Los Angeles	42	35	4	1	89
Phoenix	38	39	2	3	81

Stanley Cup: Carolina Hurricanes

OUTSTANDING PLAYERS

Hart Trophy (most valuable player)	Joe Thornton, San Jose
Ross Trophy (scorer)	Joe Thornton, San Jose
Vezina Trophy (goalie)	Miikka Kiprusoff, Calgary
Norris Trophy (defenseman)	Nicklas Lidstrom, Detroit
Selke Trophy (defensive forward)	Rod Brind'Amour, Carolina
Calder Trophy (rookie)	Alex Ovechkin, Washington
Lady Byng Trophy (sportsmanship)	Pavel Datsyuk, Detroit
Conn Smythe Trophy (Stanley Cup play)	Cam Ward, Carolina

For the regular season, San Jose center Joe Thornton collected the Hart Trophy as MVP; he also won the Art Ross Trophy as scoring leader (125 points on 29 goals and a league-leading 96 assists). Thornton's San Jose line mate Jonathan Cheechoo took the Maurice Richard Trophy as he led the NHL with 56 goals.

Detroit's Nicklas Lidstrom captured the Norris Trophy—his fourth—as the league's best defenseman. Named best goaltender (Vezina Trophy) was Miikka Kiprusoff of Calgary. The top rookie (Calder Trophy) was 20-year-old Alex Ovechkin, left wing for the Washington Capitals, who tallied 106 points (52 goals, 54 assists). Lindy Ruff of the Buffalo Sabres won the Jack Adams Award as coach of the year. Ruff edged out Carolina's coach Peter Laviolette.

College Play. For the first time in the history of National Collegiate Athletic Association (NCAA) hockey, the women's and men's national champions represented the same school. In March, the University of Wisconsin took the women's title. The Badgers shut out Minnesota, 3–0, in the final game of the "Frozen Four." Freshman goalie Jessie Vetter was named the tournament's Most Outstanding Player.

In April, the Wisconsin men beat Boston College, 2–1, for their championship. Robbie Earl, who notched the Badgers' first goal, was named Most Outstanding Player.

Defenseman Matt Carle, a junior at the University of Denver who had begun playing for the San Jose Sharks, was honored with the Hobey Baker Award as the top men's player in NCAA Division I.

Sasha Cohen. American figure-skater Sasha Cohen won four silver medals at the U.S. Figure Skating Championships—from 2002 to 2005. In 2006, the graceful, athletic skater struck gold. Cohen performed seven triple jumps, four of them in combination. And her spins and spirals brought cheers from the audience. "When she spins, she looks like that ballerina in the music box," said one sportswriter.

Stephane Lambiel. For the second year in a row, Swiss figure-skater Stephane Lambiel won the men's title at the World Figure Skating Championships. This superstar on ice has also won six Swiss national championships. And he won the silver medal at the 2006 Winter Olympics in Turin, Italy.

ICE SKATING

FIGURE SKATING

World Championships

Men	Stephane Lambiel, Switzerland
Women	Kimmie Meissner, U.S.
Pairs	Qing Pang/Jian Tong, China
Dance	Albena Denkova/Maxim Staviski, Bulgaria

United States Championships

Men	Johnny Weir
Women	Sasha Cohen
Pairs	Rena Inoue/John Baldwin
Dance	Tanith Belbin/Benjamin Agosto

SPEED SKATING

World Championships

Men	Shani Davis, U.S.
Women	Cindy Klassen, Canada

SKIING

WORLD CUP CHAMPIONSHIPS

Men	Benjamin Raich, Austria
Women	Janica Kostelic, Croatia

U. S. ALPINE CHAMPIONSHIPS

Men

Downhill	Bode Miller
Slalom	Ted Ligety
Giant Slalom	Bode Miller
Super Giant Slalom	Daron Rahlves
Combined	Ted Ligety

Women

Downhill	Kirsten Clark
Slalom	Kaylin Richardson
Giant Slalom	Caitlin Ciccone
Super Giant Slalom	Stacey Cook
Combined	Julia Mancuso

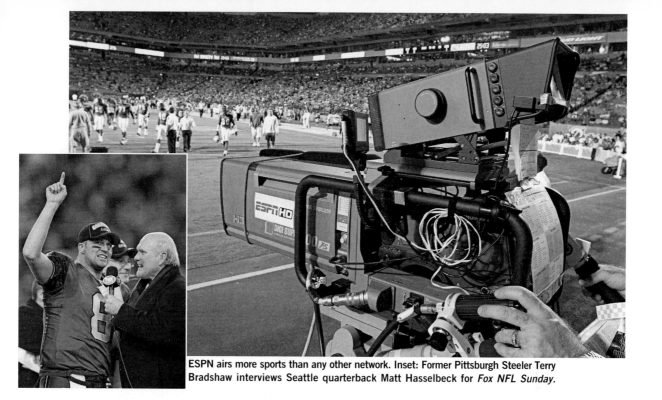

ESPN airs more sports than any other network. Inset: Former Pittsburgh Steeler Terry Bradshaw interviews Seattle quarterback Matt Hasselbeck for *Fox NFL Sunday*.

TV SPORTS—ALL THE TIME

On May 17, 1939, an Ivy League baseball game between Columbia and Princeton became the first sporting event ever to be televised. It was seen by only a few thousand people, mainly visitors to the RCA Pavilion at the New York World's Fair in Flushing, New York. Since that historic telecast, televised sports have come a long way!

In 2006, millions of sports fans could turn on the TV at any hour of the day and find a selection of sports shows. An audience of 140 million watched pro football's Super Bowl, which remained one of the most popular programs on TV. On the first five nights of the Winter Olympics, seven of ten U.S. homes tuned in the Games. More than one billion people in 215 countries watched National Basketball Association (NBA) programming. And soccer's World Cup tournament attracted a record U.S. television audience.

Who supplies all this sports programming? The major television networks—ABC, CBS, NBC, and Fox—have separate sports divisions and compete for the rights to televise the big sporting events. In addition, there are a number of cable stations devoted solely to sports.

Entertainment and Sports Programming Network (ESPN), which was founded in 1979, was the first cable network offering 24 hours of sports programming daily. By 2006, the company was worldwide and included seven networks. The Turner Networks feature TBS Superstation Sports and TNT Sports. The Golf Channel has delighted golf fans since 1995. The NFL Network, which began in 2003, offers football programming 24 hours a day. CSTV, a digital sports-media company owned by CBS, covers more than 35 men's and women's college sports.

Both ESPN and Fox Sports Net now broadcast high-school football games. And there are many stations that specialize in regional sports coverage.

Television has had a tremendous effect on the popularity of sports. For example, figure skating has become one of the most watched sports on TV. Television coverage has also led to an increased American interest in gymnastics. And viewers can not only watch every pitch of baseball's World Series but even follow the latest in beach volleyball and women's softball. In addition, the many retired stars who have become TV sports announcers have added insight and color to television coverage.

TENNIS

Roger Federer's legend grew in 2006. The young Swiss star continued his dominance of men's tennis, winning three of the four Grand Slam events. But he didn't go unchallenged. An even younger Rafael Nadal, of Spain, was the only man to beat Federer in a "major."

The women's game was highly competitive, as three different athletes collected the major titles. Like Federer on the men's side, Justine Henin-Hardenne of Belgium was a four-time Grand Slam finalist. But unlike Federer, she won only once.

At the **Australian Open** in January, the first major of the year, the 24-year-old Federer outmatched Marcos Baghdatis in the men's final, 5-7, 7–5, 6–0, 6–2. Baghdatis, from Cyprus, had been ranked 54th in the world, but he later jumped to the top ten. Federer's victory was the seventh Grand Slam title of his career.

Amelie Mauresmo of France took the women's crown in Australia—her first Grand Slam championship. In the final, the 26-year-old won the first set over Henin-Hardenne by 6–1. With Mauresmo leading 2–0 in the second set, Henin-Hardenne withdrew because of stomach problems.

France's Amelie Mauresmo won her first Grand Slam titles in 2006: the Australian Open and Wimbledon.

TOURNAMENT TENNIS

	Australian Open	French Open	Wimbledon	U.S. Open
Men's Singles	Roger Federer, Switzerland	Rafael Nadal, Spain	Roger Federer, Switzerland	Roger Federer, Switzerland
Women's Singles	Amelie Mauresmo, France	Justine Henin-Hardenne, Belgium	Amelie Mauresmo, France	Maria Sharapova, Russia
Men's Doubles	Bob Bryan, United States/ Mike Bryan, United States	Jonas Bjorkman, Sweden/ Max Mirnyi, Belarus	Bob Bryan, United States/ Mike Bryan, United States	Martin Damm, Czech Republic/ Leander Paes, India
Women's Doubles	Zi Yan, China/ Jie Zheng, China	Lisa Raymond, United States/ Samantha Stosur, Australia	Zi Yan, China/ Jie Zheng, China	Nathalie Dechy, France/ Vera Zvonareva, Russia

Davis Cup Winner: Russia

Henin-Hardenne, 24, had better luck at the **French Open** final in June. She topped Russia's Svetlana Kuznetsova, 6–4, 6–4. Henin-Hardenne thus captured her third French title in four years, and the fifth Grand Slam event of her career.

Rafael Nadal, a 20-year-old lefthander, outfought Federer in the French men's final, 1–6, 6–1, 6–4, 7–6 (4). Nadal had also won the event in 2005.

At **Wimbledon** in July, Federer got revenge, downing Nadal in the final by 6–0, 7–6 (5), 6–7 (2), 6–3. For the champion, it was his fourth consecutive Wimbledon win.

Mauresmo scored her second Grand Slam title of 2006—and of her career—at Wimbledon. She needed all three sets to defeat Henin-Hardenne: 2–6, 6–3, 6–4.

Maria Sharapova took her second major at the **U.S. Open** in September, played in Flushing Meadows, New York. Sharapova employed a slugging forehand to beat Henin-Hardenne, 6–4, 6–4. The 19-year-old Russian-born champion had also won at Wimbledon in 2004.

Andy Roddick of the United States fell victim to Roger Federer in the men's U.S. final, by scores of 6–2, 4–6, 7–5, 6–1. Federer's ninth Grand Slam singles crown—achieved at the age of 25—put him on track to challenge the all-time record of 14, owned by Pete Sampras.

Also at the U.S. Open, Andre Agassi and Martina Navratilova—both all-time greats—competed in their last tournaments. Agassi was eliminated in the third round by Benjamin Becker. The 49-year-old Navratilova—already a member of the International Tennis Hall of Fame—ended her career by teaming with Bob Bryan to win the mixed-doubles event. It was her 59th Grand Slam title—singles, doubles, and mixed doubles combined.

As the year ended, the top-three-ranked men were Federer, Nadal, and Russia's Nikolay Davydenko. Henin-Hardenne, Mauresmo, and Sharapova led the women.

Farewell, Andre Agassi

"The scoreboard said I lost today, but what the scoreboard doesn't say is what it is I have found. . . . I have found loyalty," tennis star Andre Agassi told 24,000 adoring fans.

Agassi had just lost his third-round match at the 2006 U.S. Open in New York City. And as his loyal fans knew, that tournament was his last. Extreme back pain had forced him to end his remarkable 21-year career. But he left behind a legacy of tennis greatness.

From the time he was a flamboyant teenage tennis wonder, to the time he was a husband (to tennis star Steffi Graf) and father, Agassi was a class act. He won 60 titles during his career, including eight Grand Slam events: the Australian Open four times, the U.S. Open twice, and the French Open and Wimbledon once each.

Agassi earned millions of dollars on the tennis court and with product endorsements. He used much of this money to set up charitable foundations. His 1995 Arthur Ashe Humanitarian Award, given by the Association of Tennis Professionals, is probably as valuable to him as his tennis trophies.

The Italian team celebrates its victory over the French in the 2006 World Cup. Inset: Fabio Grosso scores Italy's fifth and final penalty shot in the tension-filled shootout.

SOCCER: THE 2006 WORLD CUP

Soccer is the most popular sport in the world. And the World Cup soccer tournament is the world's most watched sporting event. In 2006, the tournament was held in Germany, in 12 different cities. The tournament began on June 9 and ran through July 9. Italy took home the World Cup for the fourth time.

There were 64 matches involving teams from 32 countries. Italy emerged as champion by defeating France 5–3 in a penalty-kick shootout. After 120 minutes of regular time and overtime play, the two teams were still tied at 1–1, forcing the shootout.

The World Cup is played every four years. From 1930 to 2006, only seven nations won the tournament—all of them from South America or Europe. Brazil won it five times; Italy four times; (West) Germany three times; Argentina and Uruguay twice each; and England and France once each.

THE SEMIFINALS

The two semifinal matches in the 2006 World Cup pitted France against Portugal, and Germany against Italy. To reach the semifinals, France had beaten Spain in the Round of 16 and Brazil in the quarterfinals.

Portugal had beaten the Netherlands and England. But the Portuguese were no match for the French, who beat them 1–0 on a penalty kick by French captain Zinedine Zidane. In the other semifinal match, Italy stunned Germany by scoring two goals in the last two minutes of extra time.

ITALY TAKES ON FRANCE

On July 9, more than 75,000 spectators crammed into the Olympic Stadium in Berlin, Germany, to watch the championship match between Italy and France. Among the spectators were former U.S. President Bill Clinton and U.N. Secretary General Kofi Annan. Hundreds of millions of other people around the world watched the World Cup on television. The biggest asset for France was Zinedine Zidane, the legendary player who had scored two goals in the 1998 World Cup to give France its only World Cup victory.

In 2006, Zidane was decisive in getting France to the final match against Italy. In the Round of 16 match against Spain, he set up a teammate for France's second goal, and scored its third goal, giving France a 3–1 win. And in the quarterfinal match against Brazil, his free kick led to another French goal and a 1–0 victory.

In the final match against Italy, Zidane scored again—in the 7th minute of play. But 12 minutes later, Italy tied the score on a header by defender Marco Materazzi. And that's how the score stayed through the remainder of regular time and two 15-minute periods of extra time.

It was at the end of that second period of extra time that Zidane, apparently provoked by something said by Materazzi, head-butted the Italian in the chest. Zidane was expelled from the game—before the crucial penalty-kick shootout.

In the penalty-kick shootout, all five Italians scored, while the French scored only three times. This was only the second time in World Cup history that the winner was decided by penalty kicks. And despite the controversial head-butt, Zidane was named Most Outstanding Player of the tournament.

ONWARD TO THE 19TH WORLD CUP

The 18 World Cups have been held in Europe 10 times, Latin America 6 times, Asia once, and the United States once. The 19th World Cup, in 2010, will be held in Africa—a first for that continent.

The host country will be South Africa, located at the southern tip of the continent. The tournament will take place in 10 stadiums in 9 different cities. Four of the stadiums will be built or rebuilt for the World Cup, which will be the largest sporting event ever held in Africa.

Prince Poldi: World Cup's Best Young Player

Germany didn't win the 2006 World Cup, but it did walk away with third-place honors by defeating Portugal 3–1 the day before the final match between Italy and France. And one of the German players, 21-year-old Lukas Podolski—nicknamed Prince Poldi—walked away with the first-ever Gillette Best Player Award.

The award was given to "the player born on or after January 1, 1985, who makes the biggest impression at the FIFA World Cup, with the criteria for the award including style, charisma, fair play and appetite for the game, as well as pure technical skill."

"I'm very honored," Podolski said. "Of course this is a big motivation for myself to keep on improving in my career and to play an even better World Cup in four years' time. . ."

Podolski was born in Poland, where his father was a professional soccer player. But Prince Poldi has lived in Germany

since childhood. He began playing in international matches when he was 19, and is already considered one of the best soccer players in Germany.

Entered according to act of Congress in the year 1876 by Currier & Ives, in the Office of the

THOMAS JEFFERSON.   ROGER SHERMAN.   BENJAMIN FRANKLIN.

THE DECLARATION CO

THOMAS JEFFERSON, of Virginia, JOHN ADAMS, of Massachusetts, BENJAMIN FRANKLIN, of Pensylva
were appointed June 11th 1776 a Committee to draw up a Declaration in accordance with the resolution o
(who being suddenly called to the bedside of his sick wife, was unable to serve personally upon the Co
Thomas Jefferson, and with few alterations reported by the Committee to the Congress July 1

orarian of Congress at Washington.   125 NASSAU ST. NE

ROBERT R. LIVINGSTON.   JOHN ADAMS.

OMMITTEE.

a, ROGER SHERMAN, of Connecticut, ROBERT R. LIVINGSTON, of New York,
ered in Congress, June 7th 1776, by Richard Henry Lee, of Virginia,
mittee,) the Declaration was prepared by the Chairman,
and at mid-day July 4th 1776, the Thirteen Colonies were declared,

LIVING HISTORY

This picture shows Benjamin Franklin (standing, center) with the other members of the committee that drafted the Declaration of Independence in 1776. Franklin played an important role in the founding of the United States. But that was just one of the remarkable things he accomplished during his life. In 2006, the 300th anniversary of Franklin's birth, Americans honored him as a great patriot, a scientist, an inventor, a writer, a businessman, and much more.

Benjamin Franklin was a statesman. . .a postmaster. . .a scientist. . .an inventor. . . a writer. Franklin had many interests and talents; he did just about everything! In 2006 the 300th anniversary of the birth of this remarkable man was celebrated.

BENJAMIN FRANKLIN: THE MAN WHO COULD DO ANYTHING

Benjamin Franklin wrote, "Never leave that till tomorrow which you can do today." He must have taken his own advice to heart, because he accomplished an amazing amount in his life. Franklin is best remembered today as a great patriot and one of the founders of the United States. But he was also a scientist, an inventor, a writer, a businessman, and much more.

In 2006, Americans celebrated the 300th anniversary of Benjamin Franklin's birth. It was a good time to look back at his remarkable life and accomplishments.

EARLY LIFE

Franklin was born on January 17, 1706, in Boston, the capital of Britain's Massachusetts Bay Colony. He was the 15th of 17 children in a poor family. And like most kids in colonial days, he didn't spend much time in school. But he learned to read, and he read everything he could get his hands on. He went to work for his father, Josiah, a candlemaker, when he was just 10 years old. Then, at the age of 12, he went to work for his brother James, a printer who also published a newspaper, the *New England Courant*.

As an apprentice to James, Ben learned the printing trade. Not content to simply set type and deliver newspapers, he also wrote for the *New England Courant*—but not under his own name. Using the pen name Mrs. Silence Dogood, he wrote a series of letters filled with amusing and satirical comments on life in Boston. Silence Dogood was supposedly the widow of a country parson, and she had plenty to say about Boston society. Ben slipped the letters under the door of the print shop at night, and James published them without knowing that they were the work of his young brother.

James was a hard boss who abused and sometimes beat his young brother. Ben was eager to be on his own. When he was 17, he ran away. He made his way to Philadelphia, Pennsylvania, where he found work as a printer.

PRINTER AND CIVIC LEADER

Franklin was a hard worker, and by the time he was 22 he was able to open his own printing shop. He put in long hours, six and sometimes seven days a week, to make his business a success. He started his own newspaper, the *Pennsylvania Gazette*. And in 1732 he began to publish his own almanac.

People in colonial times relied on almanacs for basic information—the dates of holidays and important annual events, the phases of the moon, the tides, and so on. Franklin called his *Poor Richard's Almanack,* and he filled it with clever sayings and advice. The book was supposed to be the work of an astrologer named Richard Saunders, but Franklin wrote it himself. It became a best-seller throughout the colonies.

Advice from Poor Richard

From 1732 to 1758, Benjamin Franklin published a sort of yearbook, *Poor Richard's Almanack,* stuffed with little sayings and pieces of advice. Many people think Franklin wrote all the sayings, but many were taken from other sources and reworked in his style. People still use lots of these "Sayings of Poor Richard." Here are a few:

✦ Early to bed and early to rise, makes a man healthy, wealthy, and wise.

✦ A penny saved is a penny earned.

✦ Fish and visitors smell after three days.

✦ Eat to live, and not live to eat.

✦ The doors of wisdom are never shut.

✦ Hunger never saw bad bread.

✦ One today is worth two tomorrows.

✦ Well done is better than well said.

✦ Lost time is never found again.

✦ Haste makes waste.

✦ There are lazy minds as well as lazy bodies.

Above: Ben Franklin in his printing shop. Left: The title page of the first edition of *Poor Richard's Almanack.*

A Shocking Story: Franklin and Electricity

Electricity was little understood in Franklin's day, but there was great curiosity about it nevertheless. To learn more, Franklin acquired a Leyden jar, a device that scientists of the time used to build and store electric energy. He used this and other equipment in a series of experiments that revealed a great deal about the nature of electricity. He showed, for example, that electric sparks are drawn to sharp points rather than flat surfaces. And he developed the theory of positive and negative electricity.

In his most famous experiment, in 1752, Franklin flew a kite high in the air during a thunderstorm. Electricity from a bolt of lightning traveled down the wet kite string to a metal key he had tied near the end of the string. The experiment was very dangerous—the electricity could have killed him. But it showed that lightning was electricity, as Franklin had theorized.

Franklin developed a practical use for this knowledge: the lightning rod. These metal rods draw lightning down to the ground during storms, protecting buildings from damage.

As his business grew, Franklin established partnerships with printers in other colonies. He also ran a bookshop in Philadelphia; served as postmaster of Philadelphia; and became clerk of the colony's legislature, the Pennsylvania Assembly.

Meanwhile, he worked to improve life in Philadelphia in different ways. He helped start the first lending library in America, Philadelphia's first fire company and street-cleaning department, an insurance company, and a city hospital. He also helped found the American Philosophical Society and an academy that later grew to become the University of Pennsylvania. He organized many of these civic efforts through the Junto, a club that he helped found in 1727.

Franklin's successful business made him wealthy. At the age of 42 he was able to turn the day-to-day running of the business over to a partner and retire. He turned his attention to other interests—and he had lots of other interests!

SCIENTIST AND INVENTOR

Franklin was endlessly curious about the world. He was especially interested in electricity. But there was hardly any aspect of science that didn't interest him, and he carried out many scientific experiments and observations. For example, he studied the tracks of fast-moving storms by racing after them on horseback. He discovered that dark colors absorb more heat than light colors by laying swatches of different-colored cloth on snow in sunlight. The snow melted most under black cloth and least under white, telling him that black absorbed heat while white reflected it.

Sailing across the Atlantic Ocean to and from Europe, a trip he made eight times in his life, gave Franklin a chance to study ocean currents, navigation, and shipbuilding. He was one of the first people to chart the Gulf Stream, one of the North Atlantic's major currents, and measure its temperature. The British Royal Society and the French Academy of Science made him an honorary member, acknowledging his achievements.

Franklin loved to tinker, too. He invented the Franklin stove, which gave out more heat than open fireplaces. He boasted that it made his living room "twice as warm as it used to be with a quarter of the wood I formerly consumed." He also invented bifocal eyeglasses, a combination writing desk and chair, an odometer for wagons, a mechanical hand for getting books off high shelves, and other useful items. But he never made money from his inventions. He thought they should be used to help everyone.

Franklin's Musical Glass Armonica

Music was one of Franklin's great enjoyments. He played several musical instruments and even invented one of his own: the glass armonica (right), in which spinning glass bowls create sounds.

Franklin got the idea for this instrument after watching a performance on musical glasses in England. The performer set up a group of glasses on a table, put water in them, and produced notes by passing wet fingers around their brims. Because each glass held a different amount of water, each produced a different tone.

Franklin loved the sound, and he figured out how to produce it in a more convenient way. He used a series of glass bowls of different sizes. Each bowl was sized to make a different tone, so there was no need to fill them with water. The bowls were nested sideways on a spindle. To play the instrument, a musician would use a foot pedal to turn the spindle and touch the edges of the spinning bowls with dampened fingers.

Franklin named the instrument the "armonica," after the Italian word for harmony. He often played it at parties in London. It quickly became popular in Europe and America, and composers wrote music especially for it. The most famous composers to write for the armonica were Wolfgang Amadeus Mozart and Ludwig van Beethoven.

The armonica went out of fashion in the early 1800's. One reason was a false rumor that listening to armonica music would drive people insane. Another reason was a change in musical tastes. People were starting to go to big concert halls to hear symphony orchestras perform. The delicate sounds of the armonica were drowned out in these settings.

Franklin and the Mail

In Franklin's time, a letter often took two weeks to go from Philadelphia to New York. Franklin did a lot to change that.

After serving as postmaster in Philadelphia, he became joint deputy postmaster general for the northern British colonies in 1753. In that role he toured the colonies to inspect postal operations and figure out how to improve them. He had routes surveyed to find the best and most direct ways between the colonies, and he had milestones placed on main roads. He also published the first postal-rate chart, with standardized rates based on weight and distance. And he halved the delivery time between Philadelphia and New York by having mail wagons travel both day and night.

The British government fired Franklin as deputy postmaster in 1774 for his sympathy to the colonial cause. The next year, the Continental Congress appointed him the

first postmaster of what would become the United States. He held that post until November 1776.

In 2006, the U.S. Postal Service marked Franklin's 300th anniversary by issuing a set of four stamps in his honor (above). The stamps show him in four roles: printer, postmaster, statesman, and scientist.

STATESMAN AND DIPLOMAT

Franklin's life entered a new phase in 1751. He was elected to the Pennsylvania Assembly, the colonial legislature. Before long he took on additional duties. In 1754 the Assembly sent him to Albany, New York, to represent Pennsylvania at a colonial conference on defense against the Indians. At the conference he proposed the first plan for a union of the colonies. His Albany Plan wasn't adopted, but it laid the groundwork for the union that would come later.

The Pennsylvania Assembly also sent Franklin to Britain as its agent, and he was there from 1757 to 1762 and again from 1764 to 1775. Relations between Britain and the colonies were souring at the time. At first, Franklin didn't think that the colonies should break away. He presented the American viewpoint to the British government and hoped that the disagreements would be worked out. But he had little success. By the time he returned to Philadelphia in 1775, he had come to support independence.

Franklin was 70 in 1775, past the age when many people retire. But the years of the Revolutionary War were some of the busiest of his life. He served in the Second Continental Congress. He traveled to Montreal in the hope of getting Canadians to join the rebellion. He helped draw up articles of confederation for the new union, based on his Albany Plan. He also helped draft the Declaration of Independence and was among its signers.

Late in 1776 he crossed the Atlantic again. This time he went to France, as a representative of the new United States. Wearing plain clothes and a fur hat, he charmed the French court by presenting himself as a simple back-

Whose picture can appear on U.S. money? Only someone who's done something great for the country—like Benjamin Franklin. That's why his picture is on the $100 bill.

woods philosopher—which, of course, he wasn't. More importantly, he helped win French support for the revolution. That support was important in helping Americans win the war and become independent.

Franklin also helped work out the peace treaty that ended the war. Then he went home to Philadelphia—but his work wasn't done. He served as governor of Pennsylvania. In 1787 he helped draw up a new Constitution for the United States. And he worked on his autobiography. He died in 1790, one of the most loved and honored people in the country.

REMEMBERING FRANKLIN

Among the many events celebrating the 300th anniversary of Franklin's birth were two exciting exhibits. "Benjamin Franklin: In Search of a Better World" was at the National Constitution Center in Philadelphia, Pennsylvania. It then went on the road, with scheduled stops in St. Louis, Missouri; Houston, Texas; Denver, Colorado; Atlanta, Georgia; and, in December 2007, Paris, France.

The exhibit featured more than 250 items related to Franklin, including the only surviving copy of his first *Poor Richard's Almanack* and early versions of the Declaration of Independence and the Constitution. The exhibit also featured a number of Franklin's inventions, including his glass armonica. Interactive displays let visitors test their knowledge of "Sayings of Poor Richard" and play with number puzzles that Franklin enjoyed.

Another exhibit, "Benjamin Franklin: In His Own Words," was at the Library of Congress in Washington, D.C. It featured letters, documents, prints, and other items by and about Franklin and his world. Among the items were Franklin's own designs for bifocal glasses and his writings on electricity, fire prevention, and cures for the common cold. Engravings, cartoons, and maps completed the picture of Franklin's era.

The two largest malls in the world are in China. The Golden Resources Mall in Beijing (above) has been dubbed the "Great Mall of China." The beautiful South China Mall in Dongguan (right) is surrounded by an artificial river.

IT'S A MALL WORLD!

The first fully enclosed shopping mall, South-dale Center in Edina, Minnesota, opened in 1956. In 2006, the 50th anniversary of that opening, there was hardly a place in the United States that didn't have a local or regional mall. The mall is where you can meet your friends on a Saturday afternoon, have a quick dinner out with your family, shop for a new pair of sneakers, and maybe take in a movie—all under one roof. Malls are part of everyday life in the United States and Canada.

Now malls are catching on around the world. From Madrid, Spain, to Mumbai, India, to Manila, in the Philippines, shoppers are flocking to malls. And many of today's largest malls offer much more than shopping. They are entertainment centers, with a huge range of attractions. Some even have their own hotels. That way, people can spend days at the mall.

ONE-STOP SHOPPING

Shopping malls—clusters of stores linked by walkways—began in North America. In the early 20th century two trends helped bring them into being. One was the growing importance of the automobile, and the other was the growth of suburbs. When people first began to move from cities to suburbs, shopping was inconvenient. If you had several items to buy, you had to drive from store to store, and sometimes from town to town, to find them all. Retailers quickly realized that they could increase their sales by making shopping easier for suburbanites. They hit on the idea of the shopping center, where people could park their cars and make all their purchases with one stop.

Shopping centers began to spread across the United States after World War II, when the economy was booming and droves of

The West Edmonton Mall in Alberta, Canada, contains an ocean-wave swimming pool.

people were moving to the suburbs. Most were strip centers, with a single row of stores facing a parking lot. Then developers began to build double rows of stores with a mall—an open area for pedestrians—between them. The shopping mall was born.

In areas with cold winters or hot summers, however, the shopping mall had a drawback. It was no fun walking from store to store in bad weather. Developers soon hit on the solution: an enclosed mall with its own heating and cooling system, for perfect weather all year.

MALL MANIA

A typical mall is "anchored" by two or more major department stores, with long rows of smaller shops in between. The idea is that people will be drawn to the mall by the major stores and will walk past the small shops (and perhaps stop and buy) on the way from one major store to the next. Grouping stores this way increases sales—a shopper goes to the mall for a pair of shoes, sees a nice sweater in another shop, and buys that too.

Teens often meet at the mall to shop, hang out, gossip, and maybe grab a bite at a fast-food restaurant.

The owners of malls (usually insurance and investment firms) lease space to stores. They strive for a good mix of tenants, with everything from clothing shops to restaurants to movie theaters, because that gives people more reasons to go to the mall. To attract even more shoppers, malls schedule special events—auto shows, fashion shows, antique shows, and so on—in the open areas between the stores.

But people like to go to malls even when they have nothing in particular to buy and no special events are scheduled. For some, a mall is a place to forget about the cares of life—a sort of fantasy world, with a perfect cli-

Indoor Shopping the Old-Fashioned Way

While modern enclosed shopping malls have been around for just half a century, the idea of indoor shopping goes back much further. In Iran, Turkey, and several Arab countries, there are covered markets (called bazaars and souks) that date back to the Middle Ages. Some of these markets are almost cities within cities. The Grand Bazaar (below) in Istanbul, Turkey, is a warren of streets with more than 4,000 shops and stalls selling carpets, jewelry, pottery, leather goods, spices, and more.

An enclosed shopping gallery, the Burlington Arcade, opened in London in 1819. It had more than 70 shops lining a walkway covered by a glass ceiling. The Burlington Arcade inspired similar galleries in other countries, including the United States. Among them were the Providence Arcade in Rhode Island, built in 1828; and the Cleveland Arcade in Ohio, built in 1890. Both these arcades still stand, the oldest indoor shopping malls in the United States.

The word "mall" itself comes from the old English game of pall-mall, or "ball and mallet." This 16th-century game was something like croquet. Players used a mallet to drive a wood ball through an iron ring suspended at the end of an alley. The alley became known as a mall. Later, the word mall was used for other walkways.

mate and windows filled with merchandise. And in many towns and cities in the United States and Canada, the local mall has become the new Main Street. It's a place to meet friends, socialize, and watch the world go by.

A trip to the mall is a common Saturday outing for families. Friends meet for lunch or dinner at the mall. Teenagers gather at the mall to hang out, gossip, and check out kids from other schools. Senior citizens stroll the walkways or relax on benches.

Stores are still the main focus of any shopping mall. But since so many people spend so much time in malls, other facilities have multiplied. And malls have grown bigger and bigger as they compete to offer more.

MEGAMALLS

In recent years, giant malls in the United States and Canada have been matched and surpassed by malls in other countries. You might be surprised to learn that China claims to have the world's two largest malls, the South China Mall in Dongguan and the Golden Resources Mall in Beijing. And China is building even bigger malls.

Here's what you'll find at some of the world's largest megamalls.

The Mall of America in Bloomington, Minnesota (left), has an amusement park complete with a roller coaster. In the United Arab Emirates, the Mall of the Emirates (above) boasts the first indoor ski resort in the Middle East.

■ The South China Mall in Dongguan sprawls over 150 acres (60 hectares) and is surrounded by an artificial river. Its 6.5 million square feet (604,000 square meters) of floor space contain shopping plazas, hotels, fountains, bridges, and much more. The complex is as much a theme park as a shopping mall. It has replicas of streets in Hollywood, Paris, and Amsterdam—even a replica of the famous Arc de Triomphe in Paris. The mall opened in 2005, and some sections were still under construction in 2006.

■ The Golden Resources Mall in Beijing opened in October 2004. It has 6 million square feet (557,000 square meters) of floor space, only a bit less than the South China Mall. A total of 230 escalators move shoppers around this six-story mall. There are more than 1,000 shops, restaurants, and a skating rink inside. The mall has 20,000 employees. On slow days, they outnumber the shoppers.

■ The West Edmonton Mall, in Alberta, Canada, is the largest in North America. With 5.2 million square feet (483,000 square meters) of floor space, it was the world's largest mall from its opening in 1985 until 2004. It has about 800 stores, a hotel, an amusement park, an ocean-wave swimming pool, a skating rink, an aquarium, and a miniature golf course. Four submarines (more than in the Canadian Navy) are on display.

■ The Mall of America, in Bloomington, Minnesota, is the biggest in the United States, with more than 4 million square feet (372,000 square meters) of floor space. It opened in 1992. Along with about 520 stores, the mall has restaurants, movie theaters, nightclubs, and an amusement park with a roller coaster and other rides. More than 40 million shoppers visit the mall each year.

■ The Mall of the Emirates is the newest of several megamalls in Dubai, in the United Arab Emirates. With more than 2.4 million square feet (223,000 square meters) of space, it has plenty of room for shops, restaurants, two hotels, an art center, and a multiplex movie theater. But the mall's big attraction is the first indoor ski resort in the Middle East. Called Ski Dubai, it has five slopes, a snowboard pipe, and a snow park where kids can throw snowballs and build snowmen. Machines make fresh snow daily, and giant air-conditioners keep the temperature below freezing.

Of course, few people in this hot desert country can ski. But the ski resort is another great reason to head to the mall!

211

PEOPLE WORDS

John Montagu, Earl of Sandwich, was playing cards with friends one night when he grew hungry. Perhaps he was having a run of good luck; but for whatever reason, he was unwilling to leave the card table for a meal. Instead, he asked his servant to bring him a slice of meat between two pieces of bread.

The earl, who headed the British Admiralty from 1748 to 1751 and again from 1771 to 1782, probably expected to be remembered for his work in public service. He doubtless had no idea that he would achieve immortality in quite another way—by giving his name to the **sandwich**, one of the most popular foods of our time. The Earl of Sandwich became an *eponym*—a person for whom something is named. Many common English words began this way. We use these "people words" without thinking about how they began, and often the people themselves are forgotten.

- The sandwich is just one of many foods that are named for people. **Graham crackers** are named for Sylvester Graham (1794–1851), an American minister who favored a vegetable-and-grain diet. The Australian

SANDWICH

LEOTARD

opera star Nellie Melba (1861–1931) gave her name to **melba toast** and also to **peach melba**, the luscious dessert made from peaches, ice cream, and raspberry sauce. And François-René de Chateaubriand (1768–1848), a French count who was known for throwing lavish banquets, is remembered in the name of a tender cut of beefsteak, **chateaubriand**.

● Clothing is another route to immortality. Back in 1859, for example, a daredevil performer thrilled audiences at the Cirque Napoleon in Paris by soaring through the air on the first flying trapeze. This daring young man's name lives on today—but not for his brave act. The man was Jules Léotard, and he's remembered for his tight-fitting costume. If you've ever taken a dancing or an exercise class, you have probably worn a **leotard**.

You may find other famous people in your closet, too. Maybe you have a **cardigan sweater**—which is named for the collarless jacket worn by the British Army officer Lord Cardigan, who led the ill-fated Charge of the Light Brigade in 1854, during the Crimean War. And in stormy weather, you may put on your **mackintosh**, named for Charles Macintosh, a Scot who developed a waterproof cloth in the early 1800's.

● Style-setters of all kinds can win lasting fame, it seems. For example, Ambrose Everett Burnside, a dashing Union Army officer during the U.S. Civil War, is remembered not for his bravery but for his whiskers. Burnside's military career wasn't distinguished; in fact, he was relieved of his command after a few costly defeats. But that did nothing to dampen his ambition. After the war he was elected governor of Rhode Island and, later, a U.S. senator. Burnside was at his best in Washington's social circles. His conversation was witty and his appearance was striking—with luxuriant whiskers that swept from his ears to his clean-shaven chin. But some people thought that Burnside was a vain, conceited dandy. Many cartoonists seized on his whiskers and made them famous—as **sideburns**.

● Madame de Pompadour was a favorite of King Louis XV of France, and she wore her hair swept up from the forehead. That style, which we call a **pompadour**, has been popular several times since her day, in the mid-1700's. But Madame de Pompadour was much more than a fashion trendsetter. She advised the king and played an active role in governing France.

One of the people she worked closely with was Étienne de Silhouette, the finance minister. Silhouette established so many new taxes that he angered rich and poor alike. People complained that so much was being taken from them that nothing would be left— they would be mere outlines or shadows, like the little shadow portraits that were popular at the time. Today we call these portraits **silhouettes**.

CHAUVINISM

● Some people reach eponym status because they are mocked. That was the case with Nicolas Chauvin, a French soldier utterly devoted to the French Revolution and Napoleon, the leader who followed it. Chauvin was wounded seventeen times. In recognition of his service, Napoleon gave him a sword, a red ribbon, and a pension. Chauvin was unbearable after that. Even when Napoleon fell from power, Chauvin continued to praise him and to brag about his own patriotism. **Chauvinism** came to mean extreme patriotism and, eventually, blind and illogical attachment to any group.

● Sometimes words develop from names through very twisted logic. John Duns Scotus is a case in point. He was a Scottish philosopher of the 1200's, known far and wide for his keen reasoning. How, then, did his name give rise to the word **dunce**? The blame goes to his followers, called Scotists. They had closed minds about philosophy and shouted down anyone who disagreed with them. Pretty soon, any bad-mannered blockhead was called a dunce.

● Franz Anton Mesmer, an 18th-century doctor, claimed he could heal people by

MESMERISM

● Less than thirty years after Silhouette's time, the French monarchy was swept away by revolution. Aristocrats—and before long anyone who was thought to stand in the way of the French Revolution—were sentenced to death. So many were killed that a newly elected legislator, Dr. Joseph Ignace Guillotin, suggested that the government needed a more efficient way of executing people: a machine that would chop off heads with one quick blow. The first such machine was set up in Paris in 1792. It was called a Louisette, after Antoine Louis, an official who had worked out the design specifications. But Louis himself was soon condemned. He was beheaded by his own machine, which became famous as the **guillotine**, after the man who had first proposed it.

touching them or rubbing them with magnets. However, it's believed that what he actually did was to stare deep into his patients' eyes until they entered a trancelike state and agreed that they felt better. Authorities in Austria and then France disapproved of Mesmer. He ended his days in Switzerland, practicing conventional medicine. But years later, doctors found uses for a trancelike state like the one Mesmer may have induced. Today **mesmerism**, or hypnotism, is used mainly by psychologists. And the word mesmerizing is used to describe anything that is spellbinding.

● Metathesis is a speech condition in which the speaker mixes up the beginning sounds of words. For example, "conquering kings" might come out "kinkering congs." The best-known victim of this disorder was William Archibald Spooner, a dean at Oxford University in England during the 1800's. Students loved Spooner's lectures—they were hilarious. "A crushing blow" was transformed into "a blushing crow." "A half-formed wish" became "a half-warmed fish." And "our dear old queen" became "our queer old dean." Spooner is said to have dismissed one student by saying, "You have deliberately tasted two worms and you can leave Oxford by the town drain." Today, any similar example of misspeech is called a **spoonerism**.

● Another form of misspeech is the use of one word in place of another that sounds similar. A character in *The Rivals* (1775), a play by English dramatist Richard Brinsley Sheridan, has long made audiences roar by doing this. The character, Mrs. Malaprop, says, for example, "He is the very pineapple [pinnacle] of politeness." She also refers to "contagious" countries (meaning contiguous) and uses "dissolve" when she means "resolve." Such slips of the tongue have become known as **malapropisms**.

● The names of many other characters in plays and stories have become words, too. The 16th-century French writer François Rabelais created the giant named Gargantua to poke fun at the greedy nobles of his day. Gargantua was so huge that it took 17,913 cows to provide him with milk as a baby. When he was full-grown, it took 1,100 hides to make one pair of his shoes, and the horse he rode was as big as six elephants. Today the word **gargantuan** is used to describe something that is truly enormous.

The list of people words is very long. Dozens of scientists and inventors have given their names to processes and materials that they discovered. Gabriel Fahrenheit, Georg Simon Ohm, Louis Pasteur, Adolphe Sax, Allesandro Volta, James Watt, and Count Ferdinand von Zeppelin all had something named for them. And as new ideas and styles and inventions appear, the list will grow longer still.

Perhaps someday, if you do something utterly startling or remarkable, you too may become an eponym!

GARGANTUAN

President James Garfield (inset) was assassinated by Charles Guiteau on July 2, 1881, at a railroad station in Washington, D.C.

ASSASSINATION!

Since its founding, the United States has had 43 presidents—and four of them have been assassinated. James A. Garfield, the 20th president of the United States, was the second. On the morning of July 2, 1881, Garfield walked into the Baltimore and Potomac railroad station in Washington, D.C. There, Charles J. Guiteau stepped up behind him and shot him in the back. Garfield died 2½ months later, on September 19. The 125th anniversary of that assassination was marked in 2006.

A DISTINGUISHED CAREER

James Garfield had a long and distinguished history of public service. He was an Ohio state senator from 1859 to 1861, and a U.S. congressman from 1863 to 1880. And in the years between, he served gallantly with the Union forces in the Civil War, rising to the rank of major general.

At the Republican National Convention in 1880, Civil War hero and former U.S. President (1869–77) Ulysses S. Grant battled Senator James G. Blaine of Maine for the presidential nomination. Garfield was a staunch Grant supporter. But when the Republican Convention became deadlocked, delegates started casting their votes for Garfield. To his amazement, he was nominated on the 36th ballot.

In the 1880 presidential election, Garfield went on to defeat Democrat Winfield S. Hancock, another Civil War hero.

Garfield was inaugurated on March 4, 1881. But just four months later, before he could accomplish anything, he was shot by Charles Guiteau.

THE ASSASSINATION

Guiteau was a failed lawyer and an unhappy office seeker with a history of mental illness. He believed he deserved a great deal of credit for Garfield's victory—which wasn't the case. Nevertheless, Guiteau insisted on being named U.S. ambassador to Austria or France. Garfield's Secretary of State, James Blaine, personally told Guiteau to stay away from the White House.

Guiteau then bought a gun. He practiced shooting, and he stalked President Garfield. Finally, on July 2, as Garfield entered the train station, Guiteau shot him twice from behind. The first bullet grazed Garfield's arm; the second lodged in his back. Had Garfield lived today, his life would probably have been saved. But in the late 1800's, there were no X-rays that could detect the bullet, and no antibiotics that could fight infections.

Garfield was treated first at the White House and then at a summer resort cottage at Elberon, New Jersey, where his family was staying. To try to find the bullet, Garfield's doctors poked around the bullet hole—without washing their hands. Alexander Graham Bell even built a crude metal detector to try to find the bullet, but to no avail.

Garfield developed blood poisoning, and he died eleven weeks after being shot.

DEATH BY HANGING

Meanwhile, Guiteau surrendered to the Washington police. He had a note stating, "I have just shot the President. I shot him several times, as I wished him to go as easily as possible. His death was a political necessity."

Guiteau was charged with murder and put on trial in November 1881. His was probably the first trial in the United States to deal with the question of insanity. In the courtroom, his behavior was certainly bizarre. He fashioned his testimony into poems. He criticized his defense team, which included his brother-in-law. And he made plans to run for the presidency in 1884!

In the end, Guiteau was sentenced to death by hanging. "I am going to the Lordy," said Guiteau, while standing on the scaffold. It was part of a poem he had written for the occasion.

Other Assassinations of Presidents

Three other U.S. presidents have been assassinated:

Abraham Lincoln, the 16th president, was shot by John Wilkes Booth on April 14, 1865. Booth, a famous actor who had supported the Confederacy in the Civil War, shot Lincoln during a performance at Ford's Theatre in Washington, D.C. Booth then jumped onto the stage and shouted, "The South is avenged!" Lincoln died the following day. Booth fled but was shot to death by soldiers in a barn near Port Royal, Virginia, on April 26. Eight conspirators were tried and sentenced for the assassination. Four were hanged and four were sent to prison.

William McKinley, the 25th president, was shot by Leon F. Czolgosz on September 6, 1901. The shooting took place at the Pan-American Exposition in Buffalo, New York. Czolgosz, an anarchist—a person who rebels against governmental authority—shot McKinley twice at point-blank range. The president died on September 14. Czolgosz was tried, convicted, and sentenced to death in a trial that lasted only 8½ hours. He was electrocuted in the prison at Auburn, New York, on October 29. His last words were: "I am not sorry for my crime."

John F. Kennedy, the 35th president, was assassinated by Lee Harvey Oswald in Dallas, Texas, on November 22, 1963. He was shot while riding in an open car in a motorcade that was going past the Texas School Book Depository, where Oswald worked. Two days after police arrested Oswald, a known Communist who had lived in the Soviet Union, Oswald himself was killed while being transferred to the county jail. His killer was Jack Ruby, a Dallas nightclub owner. The entire episode was captured live on television.

The Warren Commission, which investigated the president's assassination, declared that Oswald was the lone assassin. But some reports cast doubts on that conclusion, calling the assassination the result of a conspiracy. The issue remains controversial to this day.

The life of the great Italian Renaissance artist and scientist Leonardo da Vinci has been endlessly fascinating. He sketched this realistic self-portrait about 1512, when he was 60 years old.

Leonardo was famous during his lifetime, and his fame has never faded. During 2006, however, his name was in the news—thanks to a popular film, *The Da Vinci Code*, based on a best-selling novel of the same title. The suspenseful plot of *The Da Vinci Code* presents the idea that Leonardo's paintings are full of mysterious symbols, and decoding the symbols can reveal deep secrets.

That idea is pure fiction. But Leonardo's real life and achievements are just as fascinating.

EARLY TALENT

Leonardo was born on April 15, 1452, near the small town of Vinci, not far from the city of Florence. (His name means "Leonardo of Vinci.") As a boy he developed a great love of nature. He also showed artistic talent, so his father sent him to be an apprentice in the workshop of the well-known painter and sculptor Andrea del Verrocchio in Florence.

In Florence, Leonardo quickly showed his abilities. In his seven years as an apprentice, he learned about perspective (the method artists use to create the illusion of depth) and other techniques of painting and sculpture. He also studied architecture, anatomy, and the natural sciences. These studies fed his natural ability to see the world and to represent it in his art.

Leonardo opened his own studio in Florence in 1478. He worked on several important commissions, including an altarpiece, *The Adoration of the Kings*, that helped establish his reputation as a painter. Then, in 1482, he moved to Milan to take a position in the court of Duke Lodovico Sforza. There he became a court painter, and he served the duke in many ways. He designed sets, costumes, and stage machinery for court pageants. He also

LEONARDO DA VINCI: TURNING DREAMS INTO REALITY

Leonardo da Vinci was one of the greatest painters, sculptors, and inventors in the world. He lived most of his life in Italy, during the 15th and 16th centuries. This was the period of remarkable European creativity known as the Renaissance, when new ideas flooded art, science, and civic life. People believed that human beings could accomplish almost anything. And no one represented that idea better than Leonardo.

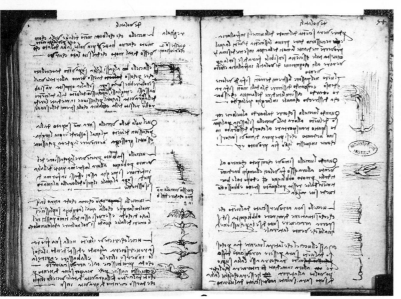

Leonardo filled notebooks with detailed records and drawings of his studies, experiments, and ideas. He was interested in just about everything. He sketched the anatomy of animals (left) and dreamed up countless inventions (above).

designed catapults and other machines of war. He even installed central heating in the duke's palace.

While he was in Milan, Leonardo created one of his most famous paintings, *The Last Supper*, on a wall in the church of Santa Maria delle Grazie. He used an experimental technique, painting in oil on a damp wall. The experiment didn't work, and the paint soon began to fade and peel. Although the painting is badly damaged today, it is still a remarkable work of art.

LEONARDO'S NOTEBOOKS

Leonardo also continued his studies of anatomy in Milan. He became fascinated with the inner structure of the human body, and he dissected corpses to see how it was put together. His studies of the heart were especially advanced for the day. He also studied the anatomy of animals and the structure of plants. He filled notebooks with detailed drawings and records of his studies, experiments, and ideas. The notes are written backwards, from right to left, so people have to hold the pages up to a mirror to read them. It's not clear why Leo-nardo used mirror writing. He was left-handed, so writing this way may have been easier for him. Or he may have wanted to keep other people from reading his notes.

Leonardo kept up the practice of making notes throughout his life. The notes show that he had an amazing range of interests—biology, architecture, urban planning, mapmaking, military engineering, mathematics, optics, geology, and more. There was nothing, it seems, that he didn't want to understand.

He also put his ideas to use, dreaming up countless inventions. Most of these devices were never actually built, and not all would have worked. But many of them seem to foreshadow inventions of modern times. More than 400 years before the first airplane flight, for example, Leonardo designed hang gliders, parachutes, and an "air screw" that was like a helicopter of today. He based his designs on detailed studies of bats and birds. He also drew designs for a

This 24-foot-tall bronze statue of a horse was based on sketches that Leonardo did 500 years ago! In 1999, the statue was presented as a gift from the American people to the Italian people.

Leonardo's *Mona Lisa* is one of the world's most famous paintings. The mysterious smile in this portrait of an Italian lady has fascinated people for generations.

robot. Dressed as a knight in medieval armor, it could sit up, wave its arms, move its head, and open and close its jaw.

There are plans for churches, palaces, cathedral domes, and an entire city with a sanitary sewer system in Leonardo's notebooks. He drew a life preserver, a webbed swim fin, a diving bell, and shoes that were supposed to let a person walk on the surface of the water. He dreamed up devices to heat bathwater and cool rooms. He designed a reading lamp that used lenses to focus light.

He even came up with a recipe for a material that was a lot like plastic, which no one had dreamed of at the time. And he invented all kinds of automated machines—a cooking spit, a forge, a saw, various hoists, and more. These devices operated with the help of gears, pulleys, levers, weights, springs, and steam or waterpower. Many of Leonardo's inventions were designed for use by the military. Among them were movable bridges that soldiers could build and take down quickly, so that armies could cross rivers freely.

One of Leonardo's most ambitious designs was for a permanent bridge that would have spanned the Golden Horn in Istanbul, Turkey. (The Golden Horn is an inlet of the Bosporus, a strait that links the Black Sea to the Sea of Marmara. The land to the east of the strait is part of Asia, and the land to the west is part of Europe.) A graceful stone arch, it was to be 720 feet (219 meters) long, the longest in the world at that time. The Turkish sultan didn't think the bridge could be built, and he vetoed the plan. But when a sketch of the bridge turned up in modern times, engineers were certain that the design was sound. A small version of Leonardo's bridge was constructed as a footbridge in southern Norway in 2001.

Another of Leonardo's designs that took shape in modern times was a huge bronze statue of a horse, originally planned as part of a monument to Duke Sforza's father. A 24-foot-tall (7 meters) version of the horse, based on Leonardo's sketches, was presented as a gift from the American people to the Italian people in 1999.

Leonardo himself got as far as completing a full-size clay model of the horse. But then, in 1499, French troops invaded Milan. They destroyed the model, using it as a target for crossbow practice. That was the end of the project. It was also the end of Leonardo's time in Milan. He fled to Venice. The following year, he returned to Florence.

Leonardo painted *The Last Supper* in oil on a damp wall in a church in Milan. His experimental technique didn't work, and the paint soon began to fade and peel. A 20-year restoration of the remarkable mural was completed in 1999.

Leonardo: Man, Inventor, Genius

Leonardo's genius as an inventor was on display in a special exhibit at the Museum of Science and Industry in Chicago during 2006. "Leonardo da Vinci: Man, Inventor, Genius" featured more than 100 of Leonardo's sketches brought to life through computer animation, along with some 60 models of his inventions and designs.

Among the models was a 7-foot-long (2 meters) catapult, which visitors could use to hurl foam "boulders." They could try their hands at constructing one of Leonardo's portable bridges. And they could see models of his robot, dressed like a knight, and of his tank. The tank was a turtle-shaped invention, with an armor-plated roof to protect soldiers inside as they fired cannons out the sides. Also on display were models of Leonardo's hang glider, parachute, air screw, paddle-boat, gearshift, and several machines.

The final section of the exhibit highlighted works and ideas by 40 contemporary inventors and artists. Some of their concepts—such as a space elevator designed to take people and supplies to an orbiting satellite—seemed far out. But, then, so must Leonardo's inventive ideas have seemed to people in his day!

The large interactive exhibit featured Leonardo's sketches and models of his inventions and designs.

LATER YEARS

Back in Florence, Leonardo painted some of his best-known works. These included an altarpiece, *The Virgin and Child with Saint Anne;* and the *Mona Lisa*, the most famous of all his artworks. A portrait of a Florentine lady, the *Mona Lisa* was painted around 1503 and is considered a masterpiece of Renaissance art.

Leonardo later returned to Milan as an adviser to the city's new French governor. He also spent several years in Rome at the invitation of Giuliano de' Medici, a brother of Pope Leo X. In 1516 he left Italy for France, where he was named chief painter and engineer to King Francis I. The king gave Leonardo a chateau near Amboise, where he continued his studies. He also received many visitors who came to hear his ideas about science and art. He died there on May 2, 1519.

Leonardo didn't complete a great many paintings during his life, but those he did firmly established his reputation as one of the world's greatest artists. Many artists of his own time and later centuries were influenced by the way he depicted the human form and the effects of light and shadow in his paintings.

And people are still amazed by the brilliance revealed in Leonardo's notebooks, which were left to his assistant at his death. Their pages—more than 4,000 in all—wound up scattered among libraries across Europe. They reveal the full breadth of his achievements as an artist, scientist, engineer, inventor, and genius.

The Empire State Building, New York City's tallest building, dominates the midtown Manhattan skyline. The skyscraper celebrated its 75th birthday in 2006.

CELEBRATING THE EMPIRE STATE BUILDING

New York City is famous for its skyscrapers—and, at 1,250 feet (381 meters), the Empire State Building is the tallest skyscraper in the city. On May 1, 2006, this landmark building, located on Fifth Avenue, turned 75 years old, and fans of the building celebrated the birthday.

BUILDINGS SOAR HIGHER AND HIGHER

The idea for the Empire State Building was born in the boom years of the 1920's. New York City was growing, especially the borough of Manhattan. There wasn't enough land for new offices and apartments, so the answer was to build taller buildings.

Two men competed to build the tallest tower. One was Walter Chrysler, founder of the Chrysler Corporation. The other was John Jakob Raskob, a financier. In 1929 the Chrysler Building was completed; and at 1,048 feet (319 meters), it took the title of "world's tallest building." But Raskob was already planning an even taller skyscraper—the Empire State Building. It was named after New York State's nickname—The Empire State.

William Lamb, the architect of the Empire State Building, based his design on a pencil. The main tower rises straight up, like a pencil, to the 80th floor. Then the building tapers at the top. The final floors make up a slender spire.

The Empire State Building went up amazingly fast—just one year and 45 days from start to finish. At the peak of activity, more than 3,000 men, mostly European immigrants, worked on the building at the same time. They included 674 brick workers, 294 elevator installers, 285 ironworkers, 194 heating and ventilating workers, 192 plumbers, 107 derrick workers, and 105 electricians.

Among the workers was a group of fearless men called the "sky boys." They were Mohawk Indians, Irish Americans, immigrants from Scandinavia and Newfoundland, and others who specialized in structural ironwork. It was their job to raise the building's steel frame. During construction, they could be seen balancing hundreds of feet in the air while they joined columns and beams a floor at a time. As the steel frame grew, other workers added stone

The fearless "sky boys" built the steel frame of the Empire State Building—floor by floor. Right: a group of sky boys takes a lunch break high above the city streets. Below: Back to work—one of them hitches a ride on a derrick's lifting hook. (The ghostly shape of the Chrysler Building appears in the background.)

and metal strips for the outer walls. Windows were popped into place. And inside, workers installed the plumbing, electrical wires, and other necessities.

THE WORLD'S TALLEST BUILDING

All 102 floors were ready by opening day: May 1, 1931. At 11:30 A.M., in Washington, D.C., President Herbert Hoover hit a switch that turned on the lights in the Empire State Building. The Empire State Building was now officially the "world's tallest building."

From the day that it opened until the 1940's, the Empire State Building had few tenants. This was primarily because the Great Depression, which started in 1929, was in full swing. That earned the building the nickname the "Empty State Building." But with the entry of the United States into World War II (1939–45) in December 1941, the economy improved, and tenants began to move into the building.

President Franklin D. Roosevelt led the country during almost all of the war years. Sadly, he didn't live to see Victory in Europe Day, May 8, 1945—the defeat of the Nazi Germans and the end of World War II in Europe. Nor did he see a strange and tragic event at the Empire State Building almost three months later, on July 28. Just before 10 A.M. on that foggy morning, a B-25 bomber accidentally crashed into the north side of the skyscraper, between the 79th and 80th floors. It created a huge hole in the building, killing 11 office workers and the 3 crew members. The building was quickly repaired.

The Empire State Building ranked as the world's tallest skyscraper until 1972, when the twin towers of the World Trade Center were built in New York City. However, on September 11, 2001, terrorists flew two hijacked planes into the twin towers, and both towers collapsed. The Empire State Building once again became the tallest building in the city. However, it isn't the tallest building in the United States or in the world. The Sears Tower in Chicago is taller. And Taipei 101, in Taiwan, became the world's tallest building when it opened in 2004.

But the Empire State Building remains one of the most famous buildings in the world. In 1981, the New York City Landmarks Preservation Commission declared the building a landmark. And in 1986, the National Park Service recognized the skyscraper as a National Historic Landmark.

By the Numbers

The Empire State Building's statistics are amazing. Here are some of the numbers:

■ The Empire State Building measures 1,250 feet (381 meters), from base to roof. A lightning rod extends the total height to 1,454 feet (443 meters).

■ The total weight is 365,000 tons.

■ The base covers about 2 acres (0.8 hectare).

■ The foundation reaches 55 feet (17 meters) below ground.

■ There are 1,860 steps from street level to the 102nd floor.

■ The Empire State Building has 10 million bricks, 2.5 million feet (762,000 meters) of electrical wires, 6,500 windows, 250 staff members, 73 elevators, 70 miles (113 kilometers) of water pipes, 8 high-speed escalators, and 5 entrances.

■ The building produces 100 tons of garbage every month.

■ Some 4 million people visit the 86th-floor observatory every year to view New York City.

■ Lightning strikes the Empire State Building about 100 times a year.

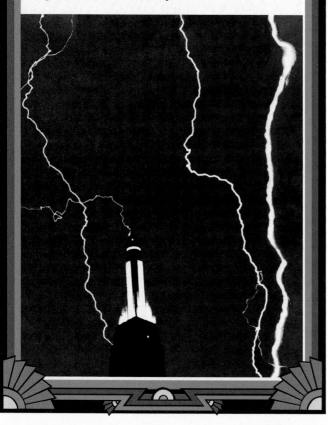

The Empire State Building shows some of its true colors: red, white, and blue to celebrate the 4th of July; and royal purple and gold to honor Great Britain's Queen Elizabeth II.

ALL LIT UP!

Each year, millions of tourists visit the Empire State Building to take in the 360-degree panoramic view of New York City from the tower's observatory. Celebrities—including Great Britain's Queen Elizabeth II, Ronald McDonald, and Lassie—have come for the view, too. You can see the view online, through the Empire State Building "towercams" at *www.esbnyc.com.*

However, the Empire State Building isn't just a place to look down from; it's also a place to look up at—especially since colored lighting was introduced in 1976. That was the year of the United States' Bicentennial, and the top of the building was bathed in red, white, and blue lights.

What started in 1976 has turned into a year-round spectacle of colored lights. Throughout the year, floodlights illuminate the top of the building to mark holidays and other events. Depending on the event being celebrated, the building has been lit with either one or three

of these 12 different colors: black, blue, gold, green, purple, orange, pink, red, teal, yellow, lavender, and white.

In late 2006, for example, these events were celebrated with differing bands of colors: Veterans Day (red/white/blue), fall foliage (red/yellow/red), the March of Dimes (blue/pink/blue), and Christmas (red/green/green). Also, when New York sports teams play at home, the building is lit with the colors of those teams.

Others that have been honored with a light display include: Oscar Week (gold), St. Patrick's Day (green), St. Valentine's Day (red), Easter (yellow/yellow/white), and Mardi Gras (purple/green/gold). And in 2002, during her Golden Jubilee, Great Britain's Queen Elizabeth II was honored with a display of purple and gold, her royal colors—to thank her for British support in the dark days after the terrorist attacks of September 11.

Its lights, its height, its amazing construction, its art-deco beauty—these are among the reasons the American Society of Civil Engineers declared the Empire State Building one of the Seven Wonders of the Modern World!

Starring the Empire State Building!

The Empire State Building isn't just a skyscraper. It's a movie star! Over the years, the famous tower has appeared in more than 90 films. The best known of these movies is probably *King Kong* (below). When this story about a giant ape was first filmed, in 1933, the Empire State Building was still new. In the movie's climax, the ape scales the skyscraper, carrying the heroine. New versions of *King Kong* were made in 1976 and 2005.

In *An Affair to Remember* (1957), another famous movie, Cary Grant and Deborah Kerr play a man and woman who fall in love and agree to meet in six months on the Empire State Building's observation deck.

Here are ten more movies in which the Empire State Building appears. If you watch them, look for the building.

- *Easter Parade* (1948)
- *On the Town* (1949)
- *Daddy Long Legs* (1955)
- *Auntie Mame* (1958)
- *The World of Henry Orient* (1964)
- *Coogan's Bluff* (1968)
- *Superman II* (1980)
- *When Harry Met Sally* (1989)
- *The Last Action Hero* (1993)
- *Sleepless in Seattle* (1993)

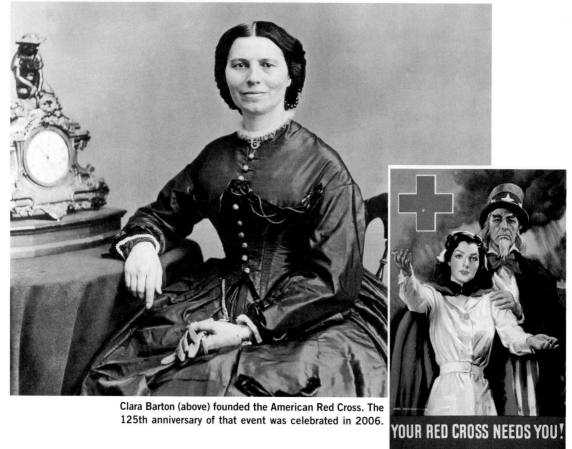

Clara Barton (above) founded the American Red Cross. The 125th anniversary of that event was celebrated in 2006.

YOUR RED CROSS NEEDS YOU!

CLARA BARTON: Founder of the American Red Cross

While in her forties, Clara Barton put her own life in danger by venturing onto the bloody battlefields of the Civil War (1861–65) to nurse and care for wounded soldiers. Because of this, she became known as the "Angel of the Battlefield."

That courageous work alone would have earned Barton a place in American history. But her lasting fame stems from something she did long after the Civil War: In 1881, she organized the American Red Cross. In 2006, Americans marked the 125th anniversary of that event, as well as the 185th anniversary of Barton's birth.

A LIFE OF GIVING

Clarissa Harlowe Barton was born on December 25, 1821. She grew up on a farm in Massachusetts, the youngest of five children. At age 15, she began to teach school, and she kept teaching until 1854. Then a

throat ailment forced her to give up her career. She moved to Washington, D.C., to work as a clerk in the U.S. Patent Office. That's what she was doing in 1861 when the Civil War broke out. Before long, Washington was filled with Union soldiers. Regiments assembled there, and hospitals were set up to care for the wounded.

The battles of the Civil War were the bloodiest Americans had seen. And medicine was crude. Modern painkillers, blood transfusions, antibiotics to fight infections, and other lifesaving medical tools weren't available then.

Many wounded soldiers died on the battlefields or later, in hospitals, when their wounds became infected. Often the only way to save a life was to amputate a wounded leg or arm, before infections spread too far. Barton's heart went out to the wounded soldiers. She worried that they lacked supplies and "comforts," and she became determined to provide them.

She wasn't a trained nurse, but in those days, few people were. Nursing was done by family members, and Barton knew as much about it as anyone. She began to collect food and supplies for the wounded, and she asked for permission to go to the front lines as a nurse.

The authorities refused at first. The sound and smoke of gunfire, the cries of the wounded—the battlefields of the Civil War were no place for women! At least, that's what people of that time believed. But Clara Barton insisted. Finally, they allowed her to drive medical supply wagons. And before long she was nursing soldiers on the battlefields—and cooking pies, puddings, and other treats for them, too. She had some close calls. At the Battle of Antietam, a bullet passed through her sleeve. At the Battle of Fredericksburg, a piece of shrapnel tore through her coat and dress. But she was unharmed. By the end of the war she was an army superintendent of nurses.

When the war ended, Barton began a new job: gathering records on thousands of missing soldiers. She helped identify many of the war's casualties. She also gave lectures, and she became well known. But in 1869 she fell ill and went to Switzerland to rest.

THE BIRTH OF THE AMERICAN RED CROSS

Barton hadn't been in Switzerland long before she heard of the International Red Cross. This organization had been founded five years earlier in Geneva, Switzerland, to help soldiers and civilians in wartime—work that was very like her efforts during the Civil War. Barton volunteered to help victims of the Franco-Prussian War (1870–71), and she stayed abroad working with the Red Cross until 1873.

During the bloody battles of the Civil War (1861–65), Clara Barton went to the front lines to nurse wounded soldiers.

One of the original first-aid kits is displayed at the Clara Barton Birthplace Museum in North Oxford, Massachusetts.

After she returned to Washington, International Red Cross officials asked her to found an American society linked to their group. It took some time, but in 1881 she organized the American Association of the Red Cross. The following year the U.S. Senate approved the Geneva Convention, an international agreement that allows Red Cross groups to provide relief to all sides during war.

As the first president of the American Red Cross, Barton expanded the group's work to help victims of natural disasters, such as floods and hurricanes. She organized fund-raising drives. And she personally led many relief expeditions. At 77, she was still going strong, helping American soldiers in the Spanish-American War (1898). Her assertive leadership was sometimes criticized. But she remained this famous relief organization's respected president for 22 years.

Clara Barton retired in 1904, at the age of 83. She died eight years later, on April 12, 1912, at Glen Echo, Maryland. She had devoted her life to helping others, and her accomplishments live on through the work of the American Red Cross.

227

"The Star-Spangled Banner" celebrated its 75th anniversary as America's national anthem in 2006.

"THE STAR-SPANGLED BANNER": AMERICA'S NATIONAL ANTHEM

*"O say, can you see,
by the dawn's early light. . ."*

You hear those familiar words sung at ceremonies, sports events, and anywhere the American flag is raised. They begin "The Star-Spangled Banner." This patriotic song was written almost 200 years ago. And 2006 marked the 75th year in which it was the official national anthem of the United States.

The anthem's anniversary brought new attention to the song—and to the story of how it came to be written. Patriotic songs are often written during times of crisis. That was the case with "The Star-Spangled Banner." It was written during the War of 1812, between Great Britain and the United States.

THE ROCKETS' RED GLARE

In September 1814, a British fleet sailed to attack Baltimore, Maryland. The British had already raided Washington, D.C., the nation's capital, and set fire to the White House and the Capitol. Now their fleet anchored off Fort McHenry, which defended Baltimore's port, and prepared to shell it.

While the ships were at anchor, two Americans boarded a flag-of-truce ship (a ship used for negotiations) and sailed out to them. The Americans were Francis Scott Key, a Maryland lawyer, and Colonel John Skinner, the U.S. exchange agent for prisoners of war. They went to plead for the release of William Beanes, a friend of Key's who had been taken captive after the attack on Washington. Beanes was now being held on one of the British ships.

The British agreed to release Beanes, but by then the attack on Fort McHenry was under way. The British held all three men overnight—the night of September 13 —as they bombarded the fort. All night long Key could see the "rockets' red glare" and the "bombs bursting in air" over the fort. From time to time he caught sight of the American flag that fluttered over the fort. As long as he could see the Stars and Stripes, he knew the fort hadn't fallen to the British.

At dawn on September 14, thick fog and smoke blocked his view. But when the misty curtain parted, he saw that the flag still flew! Tradition has it that Key was so moved that he pulled an envelope from his pocket and began to scribble some verses on the back.

Later that day, the British let the three Americans return to shore. Key polished up his verses, and they were published under the title "The Defense of Fort McHenry." The poem was widely distributed in Baltimore, and it wasn't long before the words were being sung to the melody of a popular English drinking tune, "To Anacreon in Heaven." This tune, written around 1780 by John Stafford Smith, had already been adapted for several popular songs. As "The Star-Spangled Banner," the combination of Key's words and Smith's melody made a great patriotic song.

OH SAY, CAN YOU SING?

"The Star-Spangled Banner" quickly became popular, spreading through the country state by state. But it would be many years before the song would become the official U.S. national anthem.

By the end of the 19th century, soldiers and sailors had begun to sing "The Star-Spangled Banner" at the raising and lowering of the flag. In 1916, the year before the United States entered into World War I, President Woodrow Wilson ordered it to be

Francis Scott Key, aboard a British ship in 1814, gazes at the American flag flying over Fort McHenry in Baltimore harbor.

played as the official anthem at military services. The song gained popularity during the war years, especially after it was sung at baseball games during the 1917 World Series. Congress finally made it the national anthem on March 3, 1931, more than 116 years after it was written.

Over the years, different printers have made small changes to Key's original text, especially in spelling and punctuation. Thus you'll see slightly different versions. Most Americans wouldn't notice these differences. In fact, a poll taken in 2004 showed that two out of three Americans didn't know all the words to the song. Many didn't even know all the words to the first of its four verses!

Hoping to change that, a national organization of music teachers sent the anthem on a road tour in 2006. The group said that

Francis Scott Key: Lawyer and Songwriter

Francis Scott Key is best known as the author of "The Star-Spangled Banner," but he was a lawyer by training. Key was born on August 1, 1779, in Frederick (now Carroll) County, Maryland, where his family had an estate. He graduated from St. John's College in Annapolis, studied law, and practiced law for a while in Frederick, Maryland. In 1802 he moved to Georgetown, in the District of Columbia. As a lawyer there, he argued cases before the U.S. Supreme Court.

Key was deeply religious and was opposed to war. But during the War of 1812 he served for a brief time in the military. After the war he returned to his law practice. Eventually he became U.S. attorney for the District of Columbia. In 1833, President Andrew Jackson sent him to settle a dispute over Indian lands in Alabama.

Key also opposed slavery. He helped found the American Colonization Society, which hoped to return slaves to Africa. And he continued to write poems and verses, including lyrics for hymns. Some of his poems were published in a collection after his death on January 11, 1843. But only his words for "The Star-Spangled Banner" are famous today.

THE
STAR SPANGLED BANNER

A PARIOTIC SONG.

Baltimore. Printed and Sold at CARRS Music Store 36 Baltimore Street.
Air. Anacreon in Heaven.

The first page of the first printed sheet music of Francis Scott Key's "The Star-Spangled Banner." (Note the misprint in the subtitle.)

budget cuts to school music programs in recent years have led to dwindling opportunities for students to learn about the national anthem and other patriotic songs. The tour was organized to help solve the problem. It stopped at schools, sports events, and other locations from Florida to Alaska during the anthem's 75th anniversary year. At each stop, people had a chance to learn about—and learn to sing—"The Star-Spangled Banner."

"The Star-Spangled Banner" isn't the easiest song to sing. It has a big range, with low notes followed by some high notes that are especially hard to reach. But Americans love their national anthem. Few can hear it without feeling a patriotic thrill.

The national anthem is often sung by celebrities at sports events. Here, Mariah Carey sings the national anthem at the start of the prestigious Daytona 500 auto race.

Sing It!

Do you know the words to "The Star-Spangled Banner"? Many Americans know only the first verse. But the song actually has four verses.

The third verse expresses anger toward the British. That's not surprising—the British were attacking America when the song was written. Now, however, the United States and Great Britain are friends. So on the rare occasion that more than the first verse is sung, the third verse is usually skipped.

Here are the complete lyrics.

O say, can you see, by the dawn's early light,
What so proudly we hailed at the twilight's last gleaming?
Whose broad stripes and bright stars, through the perilous fight,
O'er the ramparts we watch'd, were so gallantly streaming?
And the rockets' red glare, the bombs bursting in air,
Gave proof through the night that our flag was still there.
O say, does that star-spangled banner yet wave
O'er the land of the free and the home of the brave?

On the shore dimly seen, through the mists of the deep,
Where the foe's haughty host in dread silence reposes,
What is that which the breeze, o'er the towering steep,
As it fitfully blows, half conceals, half discloses?
Now it catches the gleam of the morning's first beam,
In full glory reflected, now shines on the stream;
'Tis the star-spangled banner, O, long may it wave
O'er the land of the free and the home of the brave!

And where is that band who so vauntingly swore
That the havoc of war and the battle's confusion
A home and a country should leave us no more?
Their blood has wash'd out their foul footstep's pollution.
No refuge could save the hireling and slave
From the terror of flight or the gloom of the grave,
And the star-spangled banner in triumph doth wave
O'er the land of the free and the home of the brave.

O! thus be it ever when free men shall stand,
Between their loved homes and the war's desolation,
Blest with vict'ry and peace, may the heav'n-rescued land
Praise the Pow'r that has made and preserved us a nation!
Then conquer we must, when our cause it is just,
And this be our motto: "In God is our trust,"
And the star-spangled banner in triumph shall wave
O'er the land of the free and the home of the brave!

Seven-year-old Braxton Bilbrey made it into the record books on May 22, 2006. The second-grader swam 1.4 miles (2.3 kilometers) from Alcatraz Island in San Francisco Bay to the city of San Francisco. He's believed to be the youngest person ever to make the crossing. Braxton's swim coach and two other adults swam next to him. Inset: Braxton, of Glendale, Arizona, gets a hug from his parents after his feat.

The fashion industry is glamorous, frenzied, and competitive—it's one of the most challenging industries around. And there are hundreds of job opportunities.

CAREERS IN FASHION

The fashion industry: Outsiders see it as a world of glamour, talent, and constant change—a world that thrives on new ideas and creativity. It is all these things. . .and more. It's also an unpredictable world, with crazy schedules, frenzied activity, and intense competition. In short, it's one of the most exciting and challenging industries around.

The most glamorous fashion careers—the ones that most people think of right away—are designing and modeling clothes. Each of these careers includes many specialties, and

each requires certain talents and skills. But there are hundreds of different kinds of jobs in fashion, each with its own responsibilities and educational requirements. That's because fashion is such a broad field—it includes everything from designing fabrics to selling clothes in stores.

FIRST COME THE FABRICS

There are two basic elements in any item of clothing: the fabric and the design. Fabrics, or textiles, are a very important part of the world of fashion. The kinds of fabrics available help determine the kinds of clothes that designers will create—and, therefore, the kinds of clothes that you will find in stores in the coming season.

In textile companies, the people responsible for creating fabric designs include stylists, designers, and colorists. They have a technical knowledge of fibers and dyes and a good sense of color. Most of them attended college or technical school, where they studied art and textiles. They usually began their careers as apprentices to more experienced people.

In the world of fashion, the two basic elements in any item of clothing are the fabric and the design.

These people are always on the lookout for ideas—when reading books, going to museums, watching movies, even lying on the beach watching bathers walk past. And they pay great attention to what's happening in the world—to important news events, economic trends, fads among teenagers, and changing styles of music. All these may be sources of ideas. Equally important, all may affect what consumers want to buy.

Stylists oversee the design department, coordinating the work of fabric designers and colorists. In addition to having a good knowledge of design and textiles, they have a knowledge of marketing—they understand what will sell. This is extremely important. You can create the most beautiful fabric or the most stunning garment, but that doesn't mean much if no one buys it.

Stylists play a major role in deciding what designs and colors will be used in the fabrics made by their company. They have to be able to convince the company's management that what they have chosen is what the clothing designers will want to buy—and, eventually, what people will want to wear. Thus, they also need good writing and speaking skills. And later, after the fabrics have been manufactured, stylists often help to promote and advertise the fabrics, too.

Fabric designers are artists who draw the designs that will be printed on the fabrics. In addition to their artistic talents, they must have a strong knowledge of colors and fabrics. They work within guidelines established by the stylist, and they must often draw designs over and over until they produce exactly what the company wants.

Colorists use paints or dyes to color in the designs created by the fabric designers. They may also help forecast colors—that is, help decide what colors will appeal to customers. This isn't as simple as it sounds: Textile manufacturers usually make such decisions two years before garments incorporating the fabrics actually reach the stores!

Stylists help decide what designs and colors will be used in fabrics. They often help to promote their company's fabrics, too.

235

Colorists generally work under the direction of a fabric designer or a stylist. The job is often a stepping stone to becoming a designer and, eventually, a stylist.

CLOTHING DESIGNERS

Clothing designers have many of the same skills as textile designers. They are creative people with artistic talent and a good knowledge of colors and fabrics. They are always studying trends and looking for ideas. They have good communication skills and often spend a lot of time in meetings with their bosses, deciding what the company's new line of clothing will consist of. They must also be able to explain their ideas to pattern-makers, models, and others with whom they work.

Clothing designers also need to understand consumers. They have to create clothes that people want to buy, at prices they can afford. They must always consider the use and cost of the items they create. On a very simple level, this means that a good designer won't use cheap fabric for an expensive evening gown, or put diamond buttons on an inexpensive everyday dress.

Once a designer gets an idea for a garment, he or she makes a sketch—and another, and another. Dozens, perhaps hundreds, of sketches may be made before the garment is completed. The first sketches are rough. Gradually, details are added—a collar, cuffs, buttons, stitching. There's a lot of experimentation, a lot of trial and error. A collar may be drawn and redrawn many times until the designer decides it's right. Pleats may be added, then removed, then added again. And all the time, the designer keeps asking a very unartistic question: Can this garment be manufactured and priced to make a profit?

Clothing designers are talented and artistic, and they must be able to create clothes that people want to buy and can afford.

Designers often make dozens of sketches until they are satisfied with their creations.

Many designers specialize. Some create only sportswear, some only coats and suits, and some only junior clothing. Others work on expensive clothes sold only in exclusive stores. Still others create clothes for the mass market. Each of these markets has different requirements: Business executives and movie stars have different clothing needs; so do lawyers and farmers, or teenagers and senior citizens.

Some people have careers as **accessories designers**. They design shoes, belts, scarves, gloves, hats, and jewelry. Sometimes they work closely with clothing designers to create and coordinate fashions.

Many successful designers followed a liberal arts or business program in college. Most also had specialized training in design, either at a design school or while working in the clothing industry. It's important for a designer to understand fabrics and to know all the steps in the

Many designers specialize. Some have careers as accessories designers, perhaps designing only jewelry.

Michael Kors: Fashion Star

Fashion designer Michael Kors has made his mark with stylish sportswear for men and women. His interest in fashion dates to childhood, when his mother took him on shopping trips to New York City. At age 10, he was designing and selling kids' clothes from his home.

Born in 1959 on Long Island, New York, Kors studied design at the Fashion Institute of Technology in New York City. He gained practical experience at Lothar, a chic New York boutique where he worked on everything from clothing design to window displays. The success of his styles for Lothar prompted him to start his own fashion label in 1981. His line of sportswear for women—featuring simple lines, luxury fabrics like silk and cashmere, and perfect tailoring—was launched at top stores. Two years later, Kors won the American Original Award, the first of many fashion prizes he has won.

Since that start, Kors has built on his reputation and expanded his range. He now heads a fashion empire, producing sportswear for men as well as women; shoes, belts, and other accessories; fragrances; and other fashion items carried in hundreds of high-end stores. His company also has exclusive boutiques in New York, California, Hong Kong, and Dubai.

The entertainment world has gone for the Michael Kors look in a big way. Among those who have worn his clothes are Jennifer Lopez, Charlize Theron, Catherine Zeta-Jones, Pierce Brosnan, Sharon Stone, Madonna, Barbra Streisand, Gwyneth Paltrow, Sigourney Weaver, Usher, Liv Tyler, and Jessica Simpson. As a star of the fashion world, Kors himself has moved into entertainment, serving as a judge on the reality show *Project Runway*.

Project Runway

A feature spread in a top fashion magazine, $100,000 in "seed money" to start a new fashion label, personal guidance from some of the top people in the industry—what young designer wouldn't jump at the chance to win prizes like those? That's the idea behind *Project Runway*. This television reality show, hosted by supermodel Heidi Klum, first aired on the Bravo cable network in 2004. It finished its second season in March 2006 and returned for a third season later that year.

The contestants on *Project Runway* are hopeful designers—unknowns seeking success in the fashion world. Each week they compete in a different design challenge at Parsons: The New School for Design in New York City, designing everything from uniforms to wedding gowns. And each week, some of the contestants are eliminated. The pool shrinks until just three contestants remain. They face off in the final episode, each presenting a line of clothing. Aspiring models also compete on the show, for a chance to be featured in a fashion magazine.

The first season's winning designer was Jay McCarroll, 29, from Pennsylvania. He has since moved to New York City to create and market his first clothing line. The second season's winner was Chloe Dao, 33, from Texas. Dao, a Vietnamese American, came to the United States from Laos with her family in 1979. She has been hooked on fashion since age 10. She studied at the Fashion Institute of Technology and worked for several design houses before returning to Texas in 2000 to open her own boutique, Lot 8, in Houston. Jeffrey Sebelia, 36, captured the top prize in the show's third season. This Los Angeles designer has his own label, called Cosa Nostra.

Project Runway can't guarantee success for these young designers. But it certainly puts a spotlight on their work.

Chloe Dao, *Project Runway*'s second-season winner, is shown here with one of her winning creations.

Some accessories designers specialize in the creation of shoes with hand-painted designs.

manufacturing process. An accessories designer must be familiar with all the materials used in accessories, from leather to metals to gems.

MANY TYPES OF MODELS

When people hear the word "model," they often think of a tall, thin, beautiful woman. But one need not have these attributes to be a fashion model. And even men, children, and senior citizens can have successful modeling careers.

Clothing models work side-by-side with designers. After a designer has completed drawings for a garment, a sample is made, and the clothing model tries it on. The designer sees how the garment looks, and the model tells how it feels—whether it's comfortable and easy to move in. Many changes may have to be made in the design before it's satisfactory. To be a successful clothing model, a person must have a good figure.

Runway models take part in the most important events in the fashion industry—fashion shows, at which the designers' latest lines of clothing are introduced to the public. At the shows, models walk, twirl, and dance down long runways. With the poise and drama of actors and actresses, they show off the new clothes, making each garment seem more glamorous than the last.

Runway models don't have to be physically perfect. But they must be graceful, with an excellent sense of how to move. They must be able to make clothes look attractive, exciting, and desirable.

The best-known and often best-paid models are **photographic models**. They appear on the covers of magazines, in catalogs, even on billboards. These people are tall, slim, and attractive. But that's not enough. They are also photogenic—that is, they photograph well. Some photographic models have looks that consumers think of as "nice" or "average." Such models can be convincing whether they are modeling tennis clothes or business suits or prom dresses.

Open almost any newspaper or fashion magazine and you'll see sketches of models wearing the latest fashions offered by a designer or a store. The models who posed for the artists who drew the sketches are called **illustration models**. Here again, the models' looks aren't particularly important. But they must have excellent figures, so that they make the clothes look terrific.

There are other kinds of models, too. Some designers specialize in creating clothes for people who are larger than average. **Plus-size models** are needed to show off these clothes. Successful plus-size models must be photogenic and well proportioned. **Foot and leg models** are needed to advertise socks, shoes, and pantyhose. These people have well-shaped feet and legs. **Hand models** are needed to hold pocketbooks and display rings and bracelets. They have attractive hands, with long, slender fingers and beautifully groomed nails.

All models have certain characteristics in common, however. They take good care of their hair and skin. They eat good, balanced diets and exercise regularly. And they know how to use makeup. This is true for male models as well as female models.

There are many types of fashion models—from runway models who introduce designers' latest lines of clothing to hand models who display rings and bracelets.

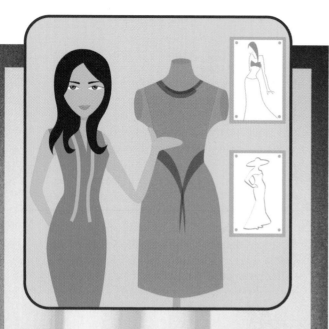

Getting Started

If you want a career in the fashion industry, be prepared to start in low-level, low-paying jobs. People who want to be designers usually begin as trainees and apprentices. Those who want to be models may start by volunteering to take part in fashion shows put on by charitable organizations.

Discuss the subject with school guidance counselors, and read books about it. You can also obtain information from professional organizations and from colleges and universities that offer design, textile, and art programs.

Here are a few organizations that can supply you with career information:

- **American Apparel & Footwear Association**—1601 North Kent Street, Suite 1200, Arlington, VA 22209 (*www.apparelandfootwear.org*)
- **Canadian Apparel Federation**—124 O'Connor Street, Suite 504, Ottawa, Ontario K1P 5M9 (*www.apparel.ca*)
- **Canadian Textiles Institute**—222 Somerset Street West, Suite 500, Ottawa, Ontario K2P 2G3 (*www.textiles.ca*)
- **The Clothing Model** (*www.clothingmodel.com*)
- **Fashion Group International**—8 West 40th Street, New York, NY 10018 (*www.fgi.org*)
- **Fashion Design Council of Canada**—15 Saskatchewan Road, Muzik Building, Toronto, Ontario M6K 3C3 (*www.fdcc.ca*)
- **National Council of Textile Organizations**—910 17th Street NW, Suite 1020, Washington, D.C. 20006 (*www.ncto.org*)

The retail end of the fashion industry: Buyers select the merchandise that will be sold in their stores.

Modeling is a very competitive field. If you wish to become a model, it's important to analyze your features. This will help you determine which type of modeling you're best suited for. If you're very short, you probably would have difficulty getting work as a photographic model. But you might be able to work as a foot or hand model. If you don't photograph well but have a great figure, you might try to get a job as a clothing model or an illustrator's model.

WHOLESALE AND RETAIL

The fashion industry is roughly divided into two branches: the **wholesale industry**, which makes the clothes; and the **retail industry**, which buys the clothes from manufacturers and sells them to the public. Most people who enter retailing begin by selling in a store. In this way, they learn what customers are looking for when they shop.

The wholesale end of the fashion industry: Skilled sewers put the fabric pieces together to produce the garment.

A salesclerk may go on to become a **buyer,** who selects the merchandise that will be sold. A large store may also have a **fashion director,** who is responsible for coordinating the fashions sold in different departments. Buyers and fashion directors need a keen fashion sense, so they can judge which styles will be popular with the customers who shop in their stores. They also need good business sense, so the store can make a profit when it resells the clothes they buy to customers. Many people in retailing study general business courses in college or attend schools that specialize in fashion merchandising.

Clothing manufacturers have salespeople and fashion directors, too—they present the clothes to the store buyers. But there are specialized careers in the wholesale industry. And some of these require special skills.

Pattern-makers, for example, take apart the sample garments made by the designer and use the pieces to make paper patterns. Each piece must be scaled, or graded, to the different sizes that will be produced in the factory. **Cutters** take the patterns and use them to cut out fabric for the garment. **Sewers** put the pieces together. These skills are generally learned at specialized fashion schools or through apprenticeships with experts in the business.

Manufacturers also have **production managers,** who coordinate the various steps in the manufacturing process. **Costing clerks** are responsible for figuring out how much it will cost to produce each garment—an important consideration if the manufacturer is to make a profit. These people generally have business backgrounds.

One group of fashion specialists—**fashion publicists, photographers, writers,** and **illustrators**—may work in both the retail and wholesale fields. They may be involved in advertising for a store or a manufacturer, or in reporting on the latest styles to the public. These people have the skills and talents needed for their specialties plus a knowledge of fashion that comes from years of watching trends.

The 2006 Kids' Choice Awards screamfest was held in Los Angeles, California. Jack Black was the host—but that didn't prevent him, along with Robin Williams, from receiving a superstar sliming!

2006 KIDS' CHOICE AWARDS

What do actress Lindsay Lohan, cycling champ Lance Armstrong, and the cartoon *SpongeBob SquarePants* have in common? They all won Blimps on April 1, 2006–April Fools' Day! That's when Nickelodeon, the children's network, presented its 19th annual Kids' Choice Awards.

The winners were selected by a record 25 million kids who voted online and on their cell phones (via text messaging). The awards were presented in Los Angeles, in a star-studded ceremony that was telecast live. The show was seen in more than 200 million households in the United States, Europe, Asia, Latin America, Australia, and Israel.

As always, the show was part spoof and part audience screamfest. Winners in 16 categories—movie stars, music stars, TV stars, and more—received orange trophies called Blimps—and the lucky ones went home covered in green slime! In fact, slime

Lindsay Lohan *(Herbie: Fully Loaded)* accepts the Blimp for Favorite Movie Actress.

flew in all directions during the event. Actor and comedian Robin Williams was doused in a spectacular superstar sliming. Show host Jack Black got the green goo, too, as did Olympic freestyle aerial skier Ryan St. Onge, who performed a breathtaking stunt that ended with a plunge into a giant tank of green slime.

Celebrity burping reached new heights in "Burping with the Stars," hosted by Tom Bergeron of the television show *Dancing with the Stars*. Two top belchers from past years, Hugh Jackman and Justin Timberlake, faced off in a burp-off. Justin Timberlake got the award—and Hugh Jackman got a pie in the face.

Actor and comedian Chris Rock won the "Wannabe Award" as the celebrity role model kids most "want to be." He also took home his fifth Blimp, for favorite voice in an animated movie *(Madagascar)*.

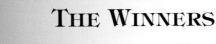

THE WINNERS

Category	Winner
Favorite Movie	*Harry Potter and the Goblet of Fire*
Favorite Movie Actress	Lindsay Lohan *(Herbie: Fully Loaded)*
Favorite Movie Actor	Will Smith *(Hitch)*
Favorite Voice from an Animated Movie	Chris Rock *(Madagascar)*
Favorite Music Group	Green Day
Favorite Female Singer	Kelly Clarkson
Favorite Male Singer	Jesse McCartney
Favorite Song	"Wake Me Up When September Ends" (Green Day)
Favorite TV Show	*Drake & Josh*
Favorite TV Actress	Jamie Lynn Spears *(Zoey 101)*
Favorite TV Actor	Drake Bell *(Drake & Josh)*
Favorite Cartoon	*SpongeBob SquarePants*
Favorite Athlete	Lance Armstrong
Favorite Video Game	"Madagascar: Operation Penguin"
Favorite Book	*Harry Potter* series by J. K. Rowling

KID STUFF

High-school senior **Michael Sessions** had more on his mind than graduation and prom night in spring 2006. Michael was the mayor of Hillsdale, Michigan!

Michael was elected mayor of his hometown in November 2005, just weeks after turning 18. He defeated the incumbent mayor by just two votes. And he did it as a write-in candidate. He couldn't get his name on the official ballot because he was only 17—too young—when the deadline for that passed. So he went door to door, asking people to write his name in. He used $700 saved from a summer job to fund his campaign.

Serving as the nation's youngest mayor while finishing high school meant that Michael had to lead a double life. He was up at 7 A.M. for a full day at Hillsdale High. After school, he took up his duties as mayor. The mayor's job is part-time in Hillsdale. Even so, Michael's day often didn't end until after midnight. He had to run city council meetings, meet with voters and business owners, give speeches, take part in conferences, and deal with the media.

In the fall, Michael enrolled at Hillsdale College. He selected that school because it was in town, so he could continue to serve as mayor. Will he make politics his career? "We'll have to wait and see," he says.

ASBURY PARK PRESS/
HOME NEWS TRIBUNE

As soon as 13-year-old **Katharine Close** heard the final word in the 2006 Scripps National Spelling Bee, her face lit up. The word was "ursprache" (meaning parent language), and she had studied it. Spelling the word correctly made Kerry, as everyone calls her, the winner of the competition, which was held in June in Washington, D.C. This eighth-grader from Spring Lake, New Jersey, was the first girl since 1999 to win the bee.

The 2006 bee was the largest ever. Kerry outspelled 274 other contestants, all winners of regional spelling bees. She took home $42,000 in prizes, including a college scholarship. It was also the first time that the final round was aired on prime-time network television. Several recent movies and a popular Broadway musical have helped build interest in the bee.

This was Kerry's fifth year in the bee. Her strong spelling skills will come in handy in the journalism career she hopes to have. But words aren't her only interest. She's also a competitive sailor and a varsity soccer player.

In the blink of an eye, a student separates stacks of plastic cups and sets them up in pyramids. She's so fast you can barely see her hands move. Just as fast, she takes apart the pyramids and restacks the cups. The student isn't fooling around in the cafeteria. She's competing in a sport that was sweeping the nation in 2006—**sport stacking.** Participants in this sport race the clock as they stack and unstack plastic cups in set patterns.

Sport stacking started in the early 1980's in southern California and spread slowly to other parts of the country. In 2006 more than 11,000 schools had sport-stacking programs. Teachers and kids who take part say there are lots of benefits. Stacking helps build concentration, quick reaction times, and motor skills such as eye-hand coordination. All these skills carry over into other sports and activities.

A group called the World Sport Stacking Association (WSSA) promotes the sport and sets rules. There's even a World Sport Stacking Championship tournament. Nearly 1,100 competitors from across the United States and around the world turned out to compete in the 2006 event, held in April in Denver, Colorado.

Life was looking fabulous for **Emma Roberts** in 2006. This 15-year-old actress was winning raves as the star of the hit Nickelodeon television series *Unfabulous.* She had recently released her first album. And she also co-starred in *Aquamarine,* a movie released in April. She played one of two friends who discover a mermaid in a hotel swimming pool. (At left, she's shown in a scene from the film.)

Emma is the niece of one of the top stars in Hollywood, Julia Roberts, and she shares her famous aunt's brilliant smile. As a tot, she had a chance to visit film sets where her aunt was working. She decided on an acting career at age 5. She landed her first movie role at 9, in the 2001 film *Blow.* In 2004 she was picked to play Addie Singer, a 13-year-old whose life is filled with comic misadventures, on *Unfabulous.* More movie roles are in store for this up-and-coming young star.

Tyler James Williams, 13, starred in one of the top new TV comedies of 2006, *Everybody Hates Chris* (above). This sitcom was based on the childhood of actor and comedian Chris Rock, who narrated each episode. Tyler played Rock at 13, dealing with siblings, a new neighborhood, and a new school. Tyler is an experienced actor—he started his career at age 4 on *Sesame Street.*

Shannon Babb, 18, of Highland, Utah, won the top award in the 2006 Intel Science Talent Search (STS). STS is considered the top high-school science contest in the United States. It's sometimes called the "junior Nobel Prize." Shannon's first-place award, announced in March, brought her a $100,000 scholarship.

Shannon, 18, investigated pollution in the Spanish Fork River near her home. For six months, she got up at dawn to take samples of river water before going to school. She tested the samples for oxygen, chemicals, acidity, and clarity. She also studied the water flow and the plants growing around the river. And she caught water bugs. Some water bugs, such as mayflies, thrive in clean water. Others, such as sow bugs, can live in polluted streams. Shannon found lots of sow bugs, and her tests showed that the river was very polluted. People are responsible for the pollution, she says, because fertilizers and other chemicals wash into the river. Her work has helped start a campaign to clean up the water.

Shannon has been studying pollution in local lakes and streams since eighth grade, carrying out a research project each year. She graduated first in her class from American Fork High School in spring 2006 and then enrolled at Utah State University to study environmental science. Her hobbies include piano playing and fantasy writing. She's also a spelunker—she likes to explore caves.

BONNY JAIN
ILLINOIS

Do you know where the Cambrian Mountains are? **Bonny Jain** did. When this 12-year-old eighth-grader from Moline, Illinois, answered "Wales," he became the winner of the 2006 National Geographic Bee—and a $25,000 scholarship. Bonny's interest in geography started when he was 5. He finished fourth in the 2005 Geo Bee.

The Geo Bee, sponsored by the National Geographic Society, is open to students in grades 4 to 8. In 2006 more than 5 million students from 15,000 schools were involved. After many contests and special tests, the contestants were narrowed down to 55 finalists. They competed in May in Washington, D.C. Alex Trebek, the host of the popular quiz show *Jeopardy!*, moderated the final round.

Seeing double? No, you're just looking at twin stars **Cole and Dylan Sprouse.** Just 13 in 2006, Cole and Dylan have a long list of acting credits and hordes of young fans. They've been on camera ever since they were six months old, when they landed a role on the TV sitcom *Grace Under Fire.* The twins look so much alike that it's impossible to tell which one is on screen, and most of their roles have been shared. But in their hit sitcom *The Suite Life of Zack & Cody,* they were cast in separate roles—as twins.

WWW.COOLSITES

Use your math skills to play Snakes and Ladders, go on a dinosaur dig, or help Professor Wigglesworth find worms. Get advice on how to deal with changing emotions and your changing body. Plunge into the sea and discover how flashlight fish use "blink and run" to escape predators. Obtain your Super Sleuth Pass and use a code breaker to decipher mysteries. You can do all these things on the Internet's World Wide Web—one of the coolest places to be these days. If your computer is connected to an online service, visit the four Web sites described on these pages. Each site has an address that begins with the letters http. Type in the address exactly as shown, and in seconds you'll be at the site.

Count On
http://www.mathsyear2000.org

Count on having fun as you solve puzzles; wander through a curious math-and-art gallery; and learn all sorts of numerical facts, such as how math is used to create cell-phone ringtones. Each day there's a new Sudoku puzzle to challenge you or to e-mail to a friend. You can also send messages on cards featuring fractals, optical illusions, and other colorful images. In Numberland, you'll find answers to such questions as: whose brain weighs 50 ounces, and which game consists of 28 playing pieces. For more curiosities and games and activities, check out the monthly MathZine.

KidsHealth
http://kidshealth.org/kid

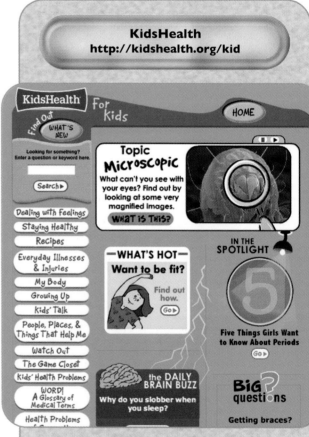

Everyone faces health issues, from illnesses to dealing with emotions such as stress and self-esteem. This useful site covers a wide range of topics, including your changing body; dealing with family and school problems; and going to a therapist or other specialist. Enter the Game Closet for experiments and a quiz that tells you how organized you are—or aren't! Link to TeensHealth for even more information.

The Living Oceans
http://www.ology.amnh.org/marinebiology/index.html

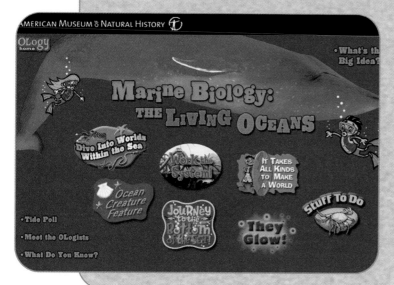

Dive in and explore the most diverse habitat on Earth! Journey to the bottom of the sea and discover the special features that enable ocean creatures to breathe, eat, communicate, and move in their watery world. Scientists from the American Museum of Natural History describe how they study the wide variety of marine habitats. They also explain why fish can breathe underwater but we can't. There are games to play, too. You'll even learn how to make rubber blubber gloves!

History Detectives
http://www.pbs.org/opb/historydetectives

Would you make a good history detective? Explore the complexities of historical research on this site. It offers highlights from the PBS television series *History Detectives*, and includes an archive of case files. Study techniques used by professional investigators and learn how to conduct your own investigations. Test your sleuthing skills as you examine a house or a time capsule and try to find out which year it dates from. And do *you* have a family legend, weird object, or bit of local folklore that's mysterious? Submit it to the history detectives: They are always looking for new mysteries to investigate!

CREATIVITY

High School Musical, *a movie made for cable TV, was a huge hit with kids in 2006. Romance and rivalry drove the plot of this lighthearted film. The cast, made up mostly of unknowns, featured (front, from left) Ashley Tisdale, Zac Efron, Vanessa Anne Hudgens, and Lucas Grabeel. The movie first aired in January. By May, after several reruns, more than 36 million people had seen it! And the soundtrack album climbed to the top of the pop charts.*

Wolfgang Amadeus Mozart was a musical genius who composed his first work when he was just 5 years old! The world celebrated the 250th anniversary of his birth in 2006.

MOZART—THAT MARVELOUS BOY

He composed his first piece of music by the time he was 5 years old. At the age of 8 he wrote his first symphony, and at the age of 12 his first opera. He grew up to become one of the greatest—some people would say *the* greatest—of the world's composers. When he died in 1791, at the young age of 35, he left behind hundreds of works, many of which are still widely performed and loved today.

The name of this musical genius was Wolfgang Amadeus Mozart, and 2006 marked the 250th anniversary of his birth. In honor of the anniversary, festivals and special performances of Mozart's works were held around the world.

A CHILD PRODIGY

Mozart was born in Salzburg, Austria, on January 27, 1756. He was christened Johannes Chrysostomus Wolfgangus Theophilus Mozart. But he was always called Wolfgang by his family, and he usually signed his music Wolfgang Amadeus (the Latin form of Theophilus, which means "beloved of God" in Greek). That is how he is known today.

Mozart's father, Leopold, was a violinist, a composer, and an assistant *kapellmeister*, or conductor, of the court orchestra of the archbishop of Salzburg. He and his wife, Anna Maria, had seven children. But only two of the children—Wolfgang and his older sister, Maria Anna (nicknamed Nannerl)—survived.

When Nannerl was 8 her father began to give her music lessons on the harpsichord, a keyboard instrument resembling the piano. Wolfgang was 3 at the time, and he listened intently to his sister's lessons. Afterward, he

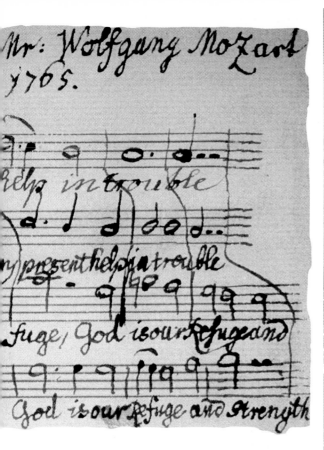

The musical Mozarts: Leopold on the violin, Wolfgang at the keyboard, and Nannerl singing.

would pick out chords on the keyboard. Leopold noticed his son's interest and decided to give him music lessons, too.

The boy learned quickly, throwing himself into the music with great seriousness. His father gave him increasingly difficult pieces to learn, and by the time he was 5 years old he was writing minuets (music based on dance rhythms that were popular at the time). Meanwhile, Nannerl had developed into an excellent musician.

Leopold Mozart decided that he had two exceptional children. In the 1700's, child prodigies—children with extraordinary talent—attracted a great deal of attention. Leopold knew that if Wolfgang and Nannerl performed before royalty and nobility, they could expect to receive money and gifts. Thus he decided that it was time to show his children's brilliance to the world.

In 1762, when Wolfgang was 6 and Nannerl was 11, their father took them to Munich, the capital of Bavaria. There they performed before the Elector, or ruler, of Bavaria, who called Wolfgang a "marvelous boy." From Munich the Mozarts traveled to Vienna, the capital of Austria, where they performed for and delighted the Empress Maria Theresa at the Schönbrunn Palace.

Apart from his genius in music, Mozart at this time was more or less a typical boy. He was healthy, intelligent, and highly spirited, and he had a mischievous sense of fun—characteristics that would stay with him for the rest of his life. When he was introduced to the Austrian empress in Vienna, for example, he jumped into her lap, threw his arms around her, and kissed her. He also proposed marriage to the empress's 6-year-old daughter, Marie Antoinette, who would one day be the queen of France. Both incidents caused much amusement at the court.

The short tour was so successful that the following year Leopold Mozart decided to take the whole family on a much longer one

Mozart performed for the Empress Maria Theresa in Vienna when he was 6 years old. After the performance the boy jumped into her lap and kissed her, delighting the empress with his high-spiritedness.

emperor would commission his son to write an opera, which was then considered the highest form of musical art. (At about this time, Wolfgang contracted smallpox. He survived this often-fatal disease, but it left his face pockmarked for life.) But the emperor didn't commission the opera—because, Leopold was convinced, his court musicians were jealous of Wolfgang's talent.

Wolfgang wrote the opera anyway, in 1768, and called it *The Make-believe Simpleton*. A year later, the family returned to Salzburg again, and the opera was performed at the archbishop's palace. As a reward, the archbishop gave Mozart the honorary title of concertmaster. But this position carried no salary, so Leopold and Wolfgang set out on a tour of Italy. Nannerl stayed home; she was now 18 and could no longer be considered a child prodigy. And at that time, it wasn't expected that a woman would have a career as a musician.

The trip to Italy was one of several that they would make in the next few years. Italy was then the musical center of Europe. Leopold felt that if his son was successful there, his future would be assured. The trip also provided a chance for Wolfgang to polish his skill at writing opera—Italy was the birthplace of opera, and nearly all operas were sung in Italian.

Italy received the boy well. He was applauded and honored. The pope awarded him the Order of the Golden Spur. The philharmonic society of the city of Bologna made him a member—even though he was just 14 and the minimum age for membership was supposed to be 20. In Rome, Wolfgang amazed everyone by writing down from memory the score of a difficult choral piece after hearing it performed just once, in the Sistine Chapel. And he was given commissions for two operas and several other works.

Leopold and Wolfgang returned to Salzburg in 1771. Wolfgang was 15, and his life as a mature composer and performer was beginning. Other musicians looked on him not as a child prodigy but as a potential rival.

IN SEARCH OF SUCCESS

Wolfgang Mozart now drew a small salary in his position as concertmaster at the archbishop's court in Salzburg. He continued to

through Germany, France, England, and the Netherlands. The tour lasted three years and made the young Mozart the talk of Europe. He was called a "little magician." In his performances, he was constantly put to the test. He had to play with the keyboard covered with a cloth, and to play music at sight without having seen it before. These were things that an experienced musician might have trouble doing, but the boy still played perfectly.

Besides performing on the harpsichord and the piano, he also performed on the organ and the violin. And he continued to compose. One day in London, he sat down and composed his first symphony. The year was 1764, and he was 8 years old. He would write two more symphonies within the next year.

The Mozarts returned home in 1766. The tour hadn't brought as much money as they had hoped, and Leopold's salary from the archbishop was small. Thus they soon set out again for Vienna. Leopold hoped that the Austrian

compose new musical pieces, including his first piano concerto. But after so many tours and court performances, he hoped for a better position.

In 1777, he left the archbishop's service and set out on another tour, this time accompanied by his mother. They visited Mannheim, then one of the most important musical centers of Europe, and Paris. Mozart found his reception in Paris colder on this trip. Although he composed several new works that were well received, he didn't find the position he had hoped for. Then, in 1778, his mother fell ill and died suddenly in Paris.

Mozart returned to Salzburg, where he once again worked for the archbishop. His skills as a composer continued to grow. In 1781 he completed the opera *Idomeneo*, considered by some to be his first truly great opera. But he was increasingly unhappy. The archbishop considered him a servant and treated him like one, and he often refused to let Mozart earn extra money by giving concerts for others. In 1781, Mozart left the archbishop's service once again.

Mozart planned to make his living independently in Vienna by performing, selling his compositions, and teaching. This was highly unusual; at that time, musicians were generally employed by a court or by some wealthy patron. Still, Mozart was confident that he would succeed. And despite his unclear future, in 1782 he married. His bride was 19-year-old Constanze Weber, the daughter of a musical family with whom Mozart boarded in Vienna. (They would have six children; only two sons would survive.)

Gradually, students began to come to Mozart. He sold several new compositions, and people flocked to his concerts. The Mozarts lived well in Vienna. They had a spacious apartment, dressed expensively, often entertained their friends, and kept their own carriage. Mozart also enjoyed gambling at billiards and cards. All this cost money, and he was often short of it. To earn more, Mozart kept up a busy schedule, giving concerts, teaching, and producing new compositions.

These years saw some of his greatest works, including the operas *The Marriage of Figaro* and *Don Giovanni* and the serenade *A Little*

When Mozart was 25 years old, he moved from Salzburg to Vienna and lived in this house.

Night Music. And in 1787, Mozart finally received an appointment at the Viennese court, as a composer of chamber music. The salary was small, but it was steady.

All the same, the Mozarts fell deeply in debt and had trouble making ends meet. To make matters worse, both Wolfgang and Constanze fell ill. But Mozart continued to turn out new works at a furious pace. Among them was the comic opera *Cosi fan tutte* ("Women Are Like That"), which was a great hit in Vienna. In 1791, he produced what would be one of his last works and also one of his most famous, the comic opera *The Magic Flute,* which contained some of the composer's most tuneful music. At the same time, he was working on a mysterious commission for a Requiem Mass (church music that would be performed as a memorial to someone who had died).

According to the story, a stranger came to Mozart and offered him a large sum of money to write this work anonymously, on the condition that he wouldn't ask the name of the patron who wanted it. The patron was actu-

Whiz Kids

Wolfgang Amadeus Mozart was writing music by the time he was 5 years old. He was a "whiz kid"—a child prodigy. A prodigy is a person under the age of 10 or 11 who has mastered a skill that's usually mastered only by adults. The child's extraordinary intelligence or talent is usually displayed in a single field—including chess, math, computer science, and music.

What makes a child prodigy? Researchers say there are two important factors, in addition to exceptional ability. Children who become prodigies pursue their interests intently, even single-mindedly. And prodigies generally come from families who encourage their talents and who value hard work and discipline.

Many child prodigies begin with promise but fade in their teens or early 20's. This may happen because they are pushed too far too fast—they are asked to take on the responsibilities of an adult career while they are still children, and they miss too many childhood activities. But there have been many child prodigies who have gained worldwide fame, including those noted below.

❖ Economist and philosopher **John Stuart Mill** (1806–73) was known for his writings on logic and political philosophy. He began to study the Greek language at 3, and Latin at 7. By the time he was 12, he had read the best books available in both of those languages.

❖ Physicist **Murray Gell-Mann** (born 1929) taught himself calculus at the age of 7 and entered Yale University when he was 15. In 1969, he won the 1969 Nobel Prize for Physics for his research on elementary particles.

❖ **Pablo Picasso** (1881–1973) was the most famous artist of the 20th century. Born in Spain, he attended the Barcelona Academy of Fine Arts when he was 15. But he began painting long before that. He completed his first painting, *Picador,* when he was 8.

❖ **Steve Wozniak** (born 1950), is known as Woz or The Wizard of Woz. He, along with Steve Jobs, founded Apple Computers. While still in elementary school, Wozniak developed computer-like machines—and a machine that could play tic-tac-toe.

ally a Viennese nobleman who liked to commission works from composers and pass them off as his own. He wanted the Mass to honor his wife, who had recently died. But Mozart, overworked and in declining health, became convinced that the Mass would mark his own death. "One cannot change one's own destiny," he wrote in a letter. "Here is my death song."

By the late fall of 1791, Mozart was experiencing high fevers and severe stomach pains. Researchers today believe that he was suffering from kidney disease, but doctors at the time didn't know what was wrong. Mozart himself was convinced that his rivals were trying to poison him. In his last days, he worked frantically to complete the Requiem Mass. But the Mass was still unfinished when he died, in Constanze's arms, at one o'clock in the morning on December 5, 1791. He was just 35 years old.

After a simple funeral, the composer was buried in an unmarked pauper's grave outside Vienna. Although it has long been thought that he was buried this way because he had little money, some researchers believe differently. They say the real reason was that elaborate religious funerals had been banned by the Austrian emperor. Whatever the reason, however, to this day no one knows the exact site of Mozart's grave.

MOZART'S LEGACY

The story of Mozart's life has captured many people's imaginations. For example, Mozart's belief that he was poisoned gave rise to rumors after his death that he had in fact been murdered by a rival, possibly the Viennese court composer Antonio Salieri. These rumors were the basis for the Broadway play *Amadeus* and the award-winning 1984 film of the same title. But historians agree that Mozart died a natural death.

Although Mozart died poor, he left a great legacy to the world—his music. His works include serious pieces that are considered among the greatest examples of classical music. They also include light, cheerful pieces that reflect his own sense of humor and fun. If all the major and minor pieces that are known today are counted, there are more than 800 works by this prolific composer. Many of Mozart's works are as popular today as when they were first written, if not more so. And in 2006, the 250th anniversary of his birth, they were presented in special performances all over the world.

In Salzburg, where the composer was born and where he is honored each year with a major music festival, dozens of concerts and special events were staged. And Vienna, where he died, staged new productions of *Idomeneo* and *The Magic Flute,* as well as a performance of his Coronation Mass. Orchestra halls and opera houses around the world joined in the Mozart celebration. In Europe, Mozart's works were performed in Moscow, Russia; Prague, the Czech Republic; Paris, France; London, England; and elsewhere. Mexico City and other Latin American capitals also hosted Mozart events, as did Tokyo, Japan; and Beijing, China.

To celebrate Mozart's birthday in 2006, kids and adults in Vienna dressed up in clothes from his time and danced a minuet.

Mozart festivals were also held in the United States. An ambitious program was assembled by New York City's Lincoln Center, which has held a Mostly Mozart Festival for many years. For the combined 40th anniversary of this event and the 250th anniversary of Mozart's birth, Lincoln Center hosted a month-long summer Mozart festival. It included newly commissioned works—dance, opera, music, and even a digital art installation—that were designed to provide an understanding of Mozart's music within the context of today's world.

And everywhere there were dozens of new recordings of Mozart's works, books about him, television specials, and even Mozart T-shirts, dolls, and coffee mugs. Some people wondered if all this attention would be too much—if people would grow tired of Mozart and his works. But others dismissed that idea. As the Lincoln Center artistic director put it, "Two hundred and fifty years after the occasion of his birth, we wish to reveal that the meaning, resonance, and transcendence of his musical creations are truly timeless and as inspiring to the artists and audiences of today as when they were first created."

2006

Thandie Newton and Matt Dillon
in *Crash* (best motion picture).

ACADEMY AWARDS

CATEGORY	WINNER
Motion Picture	*Crash*
Actor	Philip Seymour Hoffman (*Capote*)
Actress	Reese Witherspoon (*Walk the Line*)
Supporting Actor	George Clooney (*Syriana*)
Supporting Actress	Rachel Weisz (*The Constant Gardener*)
Director	Ang Lee (*Brokeback Mountain*)
Cinematography	*Memoirs of a Geisha*
Visual Effects	*King Kong*
Costume Design	*Memoirs of a Geisha*
Animated Feature Film	*Wallace & Gromit: The Curse of the Were-Rabbit*
Foreign–Language Film	*Tsotsi* (South Africa)
Documentary Feature	*March of the Penguins*
Documentary Short	*A Note of Triumph: The Golden Age of Norman Corwin*

Left: Philip Seymour Hoffman (best actor) and Catherine Keener in *Capote*. Above: Reese Witherspoon (best actress) and Joaquin Phoenix in *Walk the Line*. Below: George Clooney (best supporting actor) in *Syriana*.

Johnny Depp returned as Captain Jack Sparrow in the 2006 hit motion picture, *Pirates of the Caribbean: Dead Man's Chest.*

IT'S MOVIE TIME

Fantasy, comedy, romance, drama, and adventure—there were movies to please every taste in 2006. Animated and live-action films told stories about superheroes and real-life heroes, both human and animal. And several popular books came to life on the screen.

FANTASY ADVENTURE

Larger-than-life adventure tales were big hits in summer 2006. Leading the list was *Pirates of the Caribbean: Dead Man's Chest.* In this sequel to the 2003 *Pirates of the Caribbean: The Curse of the Black Pearl,* Johnny Depp returned as Captain Jack Sparrow, the most colorful pirate ever to sail the silver screen. And once again Keira Knightley and Orlando Bloom played sweethearts Elizabeth Swann and Will Turner.

The bad guy of this fantasy-adventure is the legendary Davy Jones (played by Bill Nighy), a scary character with the face of an octopus. Supposedly dead—but still walking around—Davy Jones is the owner of the "dead man's chest." It holds his beating heart, and whoever controls it will control the sea. Packed with special effects, *Dead Man's Chest* was two-and-a-half hours long. But fans loved every minute.

Superman Returns brought another fantasy-adventure hero back to movie theaters. Newcomer Brandon Routh took over the title role, last played by Christopher Reeve. He brought new seriousness to the part, but there was plenty of action. In this film, Superman returns to Earth after five years traveling through space to visit the remains of his home planet. He finds that the woman he loves—Lois Lane (Kate Bosworth)—has a son and is engaged to marry someone else. But there are still plenty of people to rescue and villains to fight. In particular, there's Lex Luthor (Kevin Spacey), who's plotting to control the world.

X-Men: The Last Stand featured another set of superheroes and super villains from comic books. It was the third recent film featuring the X-Men, mutants with special powers that some use for good and some for evil. This time good mutants, including Storm

(Halle Berry) and Wolverine (Hugh Jackman), battled bad mutants led by Magneto (Ian McKellen).

ANIMATED ANTICS

Automobiles were the stars of *Cars*, one of the year's top animated features. In fact, all the characters in this movie were cars and trucks, magically brought to life with computer animation. The story focuses on Lightning McQueen (voiced by Owen Wilson), an up-and-coming young racecar set on winning fame and fortune in the Piston Cup Championship. He takes a wrong turn on his way to the big race and is stranded in the tiny desert town of Radiator Springs. Forced to cool his tires there for a while, he learns the value of life in the slow lane. His teachers are the town's four-wheeled residents, including Doc Hudson (Paul Newman), a 1951 Hudson Hornet; Sally (Bonnie Hunt), a Porsche; and Tow Mater (Larry the Cable Guy).

Over the Hedge was a lighthearted look at what happens when wild creatures encounter expanding suburbs. This animated tale was about a group of animals whose woodland home has been cut in two by a hedge and, on the other side, a new planned community. A clever raccoon named RJ (Bruce Willis) knows what can be found there—chips, doughnuts, and other junk-food goodies. He tempts the animals to go over the hedge and steal the food.

Interactions between animals and people were also the theme of *The Ant Bully*. Young Lucas Nickle (Zach Tyler Eisen) is picked on by the neighborhood bully, and he takes out his frustration by harassing the ant colony on his lawn at home. Then, in a bit of magic, he wakes up one morning to find that he has shrunk to ant size and is a prisoner in the colony. The ants he meets (voiced by Julia Roberts, Nicolas Cage, Meryl Streep, and others) don't mean to do him harm. They just want to teach him a lesson about the use and abuse of power.

Animated animals starred in several other popular films. *Ice Age: The Meltdown* was a sequel to the 2002 hit *Ice Age*. *Flushed Away* was about a pet mouse named Roddy (Hugh Jackman) who discovers a new and strange world in the sewers of London. And *Happy Feet* featured chorus lines of adorable penguins. Set in Antarctica, it was about an emperor penguin named Mumble (Elijah Wood) who is shunned by his flock because he can't sing. He joins a flock of smaller Adelie penguins who appreciate his real talent—tap-dancing.

There's nothing new about haunted houses. But in *Monster House,* the house

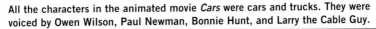

All the characters in the animated movie *Cars* were cars and trucks. They were voiced by Owen Wilson, Paul Newman, Bonnie Hunt, and Larry the Cable Guy.

wasn't just haunted—it was the villain. A creepy old mansion on a suburban block, this house snatches toys and even eats people, although it eventually belches them up. Three brave kids enter the mysterious house and discover its secret. This film used a computer technique called motion capture, in which the movements of real actors are the basis for animated images.

FROM THE PRINTED PAGE

Several popular books for young readers came to the screen in 2006. One was Carl Hiaasen's 2002 novel *Hoot.* Logan Lerman starred as Roy Eberhart, the new kid in the town of Coconut Cove, Florida. He teams up with a school soccer star (Brie Larson) and a mysterious boy (Cody Linley) who seems to be living on his own in the woods. The three friends discover that a new building project is threatening the habitat of some endangered owls, and they set out to stop it.

The film *Nanny McPhee* was loosely based on a series of books by Christianna Brand. Set in Victorian England, the movie starred Emma Thompson as Nanny McPhee, a caretaker whose stern demeanor belies a kindly heart. She is called in by Mr. Brown (Colin Firth),

a widower whose obnoxious children have driven 17 nannies out of the house. They are no match for Nanny McPhee, who uses a bit of magic to keep her young charges in line.

New movies of two classic animal stories also arrived in theaters. *Lassie* was based on Eric Knight's *Lassie Come-Home,* first published in 1940. This was the twelfth film about the brave and loyal collie of the title (the first was made in 1943), and it was a faithful adaptation of the original story. Sold to a wealthy duke (Peter O'Toole) and taken from her home in northern England to Scotland, Lassie escapes and travels hundreds of miles to rejoin her family and the young boy, Joe (Jonathan Mason), whom she loves.

Flicka was an updated version of Mary O'Hara's 1941 novel *My Friend Flicka.* The 2006 version was about a girl, Katy McLaughlin (Alison Lohman), who adopts a wild mustang as a way to show her father (Tim McGraw) that she's capable of one day taking over the family ranch. When her father sells Flicka, Katy tries to win her back by entering a dangerous horse race. The peaks of the Rocky Mountains were a spectacular backdrop for the story.

COMEDY AND ROMANCE

What's it like to work at a top women's fashion magazine? Andy Sachs (Anne Hathaway) finds out in *The Devil Wears Prada,* one of the year's sharpest comedies. Andy gets a job as a personal assistant to Miranda Priestly (Meryl Streep), the editor of prestigious *Runway* magazine. But her dream job turns into a nightmare—Miranda is the world's worst boss. The story, based on a novel by Lauren Weisberger, focused mainly on Andy's trials and tribulations. But Streep's portrayal of the cold and endlessly demanding Miranda stole the show.

American Dreamz mocked politics along with prime-time television. In this satire, a U.S. president (Dennis Quaid) who

Hoot starred Logan Lerman as a teenager who tries to save a group of endangered owls from corrupt land developers in Florida.

With her portrayal as the cold, arrogant editor of a prestigious fashion magazine, Meryl Streep stole the show in *The Devil Wears Prada*.

How to Eat Fried Worms

That's the challenge faced by the 11-year-old hero of *How to Eat Fried Worms*, a movie based on Thomas Rockwell's popular children's story.

Billy (Luke Benward) is the new kid in town. The school bully, Joe (Adam Hicks), and the other boys in his 5th-grade class naturally pick on him. They even put worms into his lunchbox thermos. He's horrified. But Billy stands up to the bullies. He takes their challenge

and proves he can eat ten worms in one day. Over the course of a grim Saturday, he downs the worms—fried, microwaved, pureed, and more—one by one.

Luke Benward and the other young actors in this movie didn't have to take the challenge. Luckily for them, the worms used in the filming were fake!

is involved in an unpopular war decides to appear as a guest judge on the nation's most popular television show. The show, *American Dreamz,* is a thinly disguised spoof of *American Idol.* Its slick host is Martin Tweed (Hugh Grant), and the contestants include a girl from the Midwest (Mandy Moore) who yearns for fame and a man from the Middle East (Sam Golzari) who is a would-be terrorist.

Breaking up is hard to do—but the movie *The Break-Up* showed that it can be funny, too. Gary (Vince Vaughn) and Brooke (Jennifer Aniston) are an unhappy couple who decide to call it quits after years of squabbling. But neither wants to leave the Chicago condo they share. Thus they continue to live together, going out of their way to annoy each other.

A family road trip was the spark for another comedy, *RV.* When an overworked executive named Bob Munro (Robin Williams) is sent to Colorado to finalize a deal, he decides to take his family along in a rickety RV and pretend that the trip is a vacation. Pesky raccoons and roadside weirdos are just a few of the troubles they face.

The Break-Up, a romantic comedy, starred Vince Vaughn and Jennifer Aniston as a bickering couple.

Eight Below

At the start of the Antarctic winter, an emergency forces a team of Antarctic scientists and their guide to evacuate. There's no room on the plane for their eight sled dogs, but the guide vows to come back for them. Then a huge storm hits, and the plane can't return. The dogs are stranded and must fight to stay alive through the brutal winter.

That's the situation in Eight Below, a 2006 movie based on an actual event. The film, shot in Canada, moved back and forth between the abandoned dogs and the humans trying to get back to them. The dogs emerged as the true characters, from the brave pack leader Maya to the rebellious Shorty. The realistic film pulled no punches about the dangers that the dogs faced, and it was a moving portrayal of their grit and determination to survive.

FICTION AND FACT

The Da Vinci Code, by Dan Brown, was one of the top-selling novels of recent years. And in 2006 this complicated suspense tale was brought to the screen. Tom Hanks starred as Robert Langdon, a professor of religious symbology. In Paris to deliver a lecture, he is caught up in a murder investigation and stumbles onto a secret that could shake the foundations of Christianity.

Tom Hanks and Audrey Tautou had the lead roles in the complex thriller The Da Vinci Code, based on the best-selling novel by Dan Brown.

The 21st Bond movie, this was the story of Bond's first mission as British secret agent 007.

Some of the year's most interesting dramas stayed close to real life. *Invincible* was the true and uplifting story of Vince Papale (Mark Wahlberg), a substitute teacher who was signed to play for the Philadelphia Eagles football team in 1972. In an acclaimed performance, Helen Mirren starred as Queen Elizabeth II in *The Queen,* a fictionalized account of events surrounding the 1997 death of Diana, Princess of Wales. And Kirsten Dunst had the title role in *Marie Antoinette,* a lavishly produced historical drama about the infamous 18th-century French queen.

Poseidon was a remake of a 1972 movie, *The Poseidon Adventure.* The new version featured high-tech special effects that added a new layer to the drama, but the plot was unchanged. A giant wave capsizes a luxury ocean liner, trapping passengers in the overturned hull. Some set out through the ship, hoping to find a way out before it goes down. In another action-packed drama, actor Tom Cruise returned as agent Ethan Hunt in *Mission: Impossible III,* the latest in this blockbuster series. Once again, he battled evil-doers with amazing stunts and lots of explosions. In Ian Fleming's *Casino Royale,* Daniel Craig became the latest actor to play James Bond.

Two fact-based dramas focused on the events of September 11, 2001, when terrorists attacked the United States. *United 93* was the heroic story of the passengers on one of the four planes hijacked by terrorists that day. The passengers valiantly fought back, forcing the plane down and preventing the terrorists from completing their deadly mission. *World Trade Center* was the moving story of two men who rushed to the scene when terrorists flew hijacked planes into the twin towers of the World Trade Center in New York City. John McLoughlin (Nicolas Cage) and Will Jimeno (Michael Peña) were trapped when the buildings collapsed around them. The movie switched back and forth between the two men, the rescuers trying to reach them, and their grief-stricken families.

Kirsten Dunst (shown here with Jason Schwartzman) had the title role in *Marie Antoinette,* about the 18th-century French queen who was executed during the French Revolution.

A straight documentary also pulled audiences into theaters. In *An Inconvenient Truth,* former U.S. Vice President Al Gore presented the facts about global warming. The film showed how worldwide climate change, brought on largely by the use of coal, oil, and other fossil fuels, is likely to cause havoc everywhere—a prospect as alarming as any fictional thriller.

The French painter Paul Cézanne holds a special place in the history of art. By emphasizing flat planes and simple shapes in works such as this still life, Cézanne helped lay the foundation for abstract art and other important modern-art movements.

PAUL CÉZANNE: INSPIRED BY NATURE

When did modern art begin? There is no easy answer to that question. No single moment marks the start of modern art, and no single artist started it. But most people agree that the painter Paul Cézanne played an important role in the shift from traditional styles.

Cézanne lived and worked in France during the second half of the 19th century. At the time, France was the center of the art world. Cézanne absorbed the traditions of the great European painters of the past. He also soaked up new ideas about art that were circulating at the time. In his work, he took these ideas a step further. Like many artists of his day, he painted the natural world around him. But in his paintings, color and shape dominate the subjects. In this way, he laid the groundwork for abstract art, cubism, and other modern art trends.

Cézanne died in 1906, and 2006 marked the 100th anniversary of his death. It was an occasion for several exhibits of his work. Among them was a major exhibit called "Cézanne in Provence." It was on view at the National Gallery of Art in Washington, D.C., and then moved to Paris, France.

Provence, in the south of France, was Cézanne's birthplace and the place where he did most of his work. Its rocky landscapes and brilliant sunlight inspired him. "There are treasures to be taken away from this country, which has not yet found an interpreter worthy of the riches it offers," he wrote of his homeland.

EARLY YEARS

Cézanne was born in the city of Aix-en-Provence on January 19, 1839. His father was a successful businessman and banker. But he was a stern man, and Paul always had to worry about displeasing him.

Paul was shy and didn't make friends easily. But at high school in Aix, he began what would be a long friendship with Émile Zola, who later became a celebrated novelist. The two friends dreamed of going to Paris to write and paint. But Paul's father wanted him to stay in Aix and go into business. At his father's insistence, Paul began to study law at the University of Aix in 1859. However, at night he studied art. Finally, in 1861, his father reluctantly allowed him to go to Paris. For the next few years he lived alternately in Aix and Paris.

In Paris, Cézanne often spent afternoons at the galleries at the Louvre, where he studied and copied the works of the masters. In the mornings, he painted at the Académie Suisse, a studio that provided models for aspiring artists. There he met Camille Pissarro, a painter who was part of a new art movement that would eventually become known as Impressionism.

This self-portrait (right) shows Cézanne at midlife. He did most of his work in Provence, his birthplace in the south of France. Scenes such as the view of the sea at the village of L'Estaque (below) inspired him.

Much of Cézanne's work focused on a handful of basic subjects. Besides still lifes, he painted many studies of bathers, including the one at left. In a series of paintings of a rock quarry near his home in Provence (below), he portrayed rocks as rectangles and captured the way light struck their flat surfaces.

WITH THE IMPRESSIONISTS

Pissarro, who was ten years older, took Cézanne under his wing and introduced him to other Impressionist artists, including Claude Monet and Auguste Renoir. These artists were creating works that were unlike most paintings of the time. They sought to capture the changing effects of light on the world around them, using dabs of pure color. And they chose informal subjects, often painting outdoors to capture the light.

Cézanne took to the new style. His early paintings had been dark and moody, and they had often depicted scenes of violence. But by the early 1870's he was choosing sunnier colors. He often painted outdoors, sometimes alongside Pissarro. Landscapes, still lifes, and portraits became his main subjects. His favorite model was Hortense Fiquet, whom he met in 1869 and married many years later.

The Impressionist painters held their first major exhibition in Paris in 1874. Critics ridiculed the new style. Cézanne's only entry in the show, a picture called *The House of the Hanged Man*, came in for special attack. These and later criticisms hurt Cézanne deeply, but he kept painting. By the late 1870's he had started to work on a series of studies of bathers, a subject that he would return to throughout his life. He also began to spend more time in Provence, in Aix or the nearby seaside village of L'Estaque.

Cézanne always thought of himself as an Impressionist painter. But his work gradually took new directions. He favored more formal compositions, in which the basic shapes of objects—their planes (flat surfaces) and their relation to one another—were increasingly important. He applied pigments in parallel brushstrokes, using blocks of color to create a sense of shape and mass. His goal, he said, was "to make out of Impressionism something solid like the art of the museums." He wanted to "not copy nature but represent it."

Although Cézanne painted and exhibited with the Impressionists, he was never fully at ease in their social circle. He was known for his hot temper, frequent bad moods, sloppy dress, and appalling table manners. His one close friend over the years was Zola. But eventually even that friendship came to an end.

Cézanne painted many views of Mont Sainte-Victoire, which he could see from his studio. This one was painted in 1906, the last year of his life. It shows how he eventually simplified nature by reducing objects to the most basic shapes. The cubist and abstract artists who followed him were inspired by his work.

ALONE IN PROVENCE

The cause of the rift between Cézanne and Zola was a novel, *L'Oeuvre* (*The Work*), that Zola published in 1886. Its main character was a failed artist, and Cézanne was certain that the character had been based on him. Deeply insulted, he broke off contact with Zola and never forgave him.

The year 1886 was important for Cézanne in other ways. His father died and left him a fortune, so he no longer had to worry about making a living. He married Hortense Fiquet, with whom he had a son. And he moved back to Aix full time. In the years that followed, he cut off most social contacts and devoted himself to his art.

Cézanne concentrated on a few basic subjects—still lifes of fruit and other objects, his studies of bathers, and scenes of the Provence countryside. Mont Sainte-Victoire, which he could see from his studio, was a favorite subject. He was also fascinated by the way light struck the stones of a nearby rock quarry. He worked and reworked his pictures, never satisfied with the results. His paintings became more and more simplified as he sought to reduce objects to their simplest forms. "Treat nature by the cylinder, the sphere, the cone," he wrote.

Toward the end of Cézanne's life, he began to win recognition. He was invited to show paintings in several important exhibits, and he had his first one-man show in 1895. Young painters began to visit him for advice. "Perhaps I was born too early," he told one of these visitors. "I was more the painter of your generation than of mine."

CÉZANNE'S LEGACY

Cézanne was right about that. But his full influence wasn't felt until after his death, in 1906. The next year, a memorial exhibition of his work was held in Paris. Among those who saw it were two young painters, Georges Braque and Pablo Picasso.

Cézanne's use of simple shapes inspired them to develop a new style, cubism, which was one of the most important in modern art. Like Cézanne, the cubists reduced objects to basic forms and planes. But instead of showing only the visible side, they tried to show all the sides at once—as if they had opened the object up and flattened it out.

Through its emphasis on flat planes and simple shapes, Cézanne's work also laid the foundation for abstract art and other modern-art trends. It is for that reason that he is sometimes called the "father of modern art."

Kiefer Sutherland (best actor, drama series) in *24* (best drama series).

2006

EMMY AWARDS

CATEGORY	WINNER
Comedy Series	*The Office*
Actor—Comedy Series	Tony Shalhoub, *Monk*
Actress—Comedy Series	Julia Louis-Dreyfus, *The New Adventures of Old Christine*
Supporting Actor—Comedy Series	Jeremy Piven, *Entourage*
Supporting Actress—Comedy Series	Megan Mullally, *Will & Grace*
Drama Series	*24*
Actor—Drama Series	Kiefer Sutherland, *24*
Actress—Drama Series	Mariska Hargitay, *Law and Order: Special Victims Unit*
Supporting Actor—Drama Series	Alan Alda, *The West Wing*
Supporting Actress—Drama Series	Blythe Danner, *Huff*
Miniseries	*Elizabeth I*
Variety, Music, or Comedy Series	*The Daily Show With Jon Stewart*
Reality-Competition Program	*The Amazing Race*

Left: Julia Louis-Dreyfus (best actress, comedy series) in *The New Adventures of Old Christine.* Above: Christopher Meloni and Mariska Hargitay (best actress, drama series) in *Law and Order: Special Victims Unit.* Below: The cast of *The Office* (best comedy series): (back) Rainn Wilson, Jenna Fischer, John Krasinski, B.J. Novak; (front) Steve Carell.

One of the year's hot new groups was Panic! At the Disco. Their first album, *A Fever You Can't Sweat Out*, hit the top of the charts.

THE MUSIC SCENE

Digital recording and computer technology are changing the music industry, and signs of that change were all around in 2006. On the Internet, musicians can put their work before the world without waiting for a major record company to produce and distribute their recordings. They can post their music on their own Web sites or on the band sections of sites like *MySpace.com* and *Purevolume.com*. And a CD-burner is all that's needed to produce a record.

The musicians who have benefited most from the change are "indies," bands and solo performers whose recordings are self-produced or produced by independent labels—small companies not affiliated with the major recording labels. In 2006 a growing number of indie bands were on the music scene. Their fresh sounds joined new recordings by established stars in every musical style, from rock to hip-hop to country.

NEW VOICES

Panic! At the Disco was one of the year's hot new bands. This group, whose young members are from Las Vegas, Nevada, made its mark with a platinum-selling debut album, *A Fever You Can't Sweat Out*. Panic! also picked up the MTV Video of the Year award for the video of their hit single "I Write Sins Not Tragedies."

Another Las Vegas group, The Killers, scored with their second album, *Sam's Town*, which included the hit single "When We Were Young." And the All-American Rejects, a young band from Oklahoma, had a huge hit with "Dirty Little Secret," off their gold-selling second album *Move Along*. The Rejects also collected the MTV Best Group Video award for the video version of the album's title track.

An indie band from Britain was also getting lots of buzz in 2006. Four friends from Sheffield, England, formed the group, the Arctic Monkeys, in 2002, after two members got guitars for Christmas. They started to tour, burn their own CDs, and upload their songs to the Internet. Before long, they were playing to sellout crowds—and record companies became interested. The Arctic Monkeys signed with Domino, an independent label, and released their first album, *Whatever People Say I Am*,

That's What I'm Not, in January 2006. The fastest-selling debut album in British pop history, it included the hit track "I Bet You Look Good on the Dancefloor." U.S. release quickly followed.

Teen pop found a new star in Cheyenne Kimball, who turned 16 in July 2006. This young singer-songwriter released a pop-rock debut album, *The Day Has Come,* and starred in her own show, *Cheyenne,* on MTV. But she was already used to being in the spotlight—she had won the NBC reality show *America's Most Talented Kid* at age 13.

STILL ROCKIN'

There were new sounds from familiar voices, too. The Red Hot Chili Peppers, in their 23rd year as standard-bearers of California rock, brought out a 28-song double CD, *Stadium Arcadium.* The Chili Peppers' biggest album ever, it went straight to the top of the charts. Another new release came from Pearl Jam, the classic grunge-rock group of the 1990's. Their comeback album, titled simply *Pearl Jam,* featured an antiwar anthem, "World Wide Suicide."

The Strokes released their third album, *First Impressions of Earth,* with catchy tracks like "Juicebox" and "You Only Live Once." Beck blended genres on his 2006 album *The Information,* drawing on rock, hip-hop, country, and more. And the multi-talented singer, songwriter, and musician Jack White took a break from his work with the White Stripes to record with a new four-man group, The Raconteurs. Their first album, *Broken Boy Soldiers,* was an inventive mixture of keyboard-heavy rock and pop sounds. It included the tuneful single "Steady, As She Goes."

INXS released *Switch,* its first studio album since the death of lead singer Michael Hutchence in 1997. The album featured the pop-rock band's new front man, J. D. Fortune, who beat out rivals on the reality television show *Rock Star* to win the job.

Kelly Clarkson: From Wannabe to Winner

In 2002, Kelly Clarkson was an unknown contestant on the talent-search television show *American Idol.* In 2006, she took home the Grammys for Best Pop Vocal Album (for *Breakaway*) and Best Female Vocal Performance (for her song "Since U Been Gone").

Clarkson, 24, grew up in Burleson, Texas. Teachers there recognized her vocal talent, and she sang in the school choir. After high school she headed to Hollywood, hoping to launch her career. But she had no luck and returned home disappointed.

Clarkson was working as a waitress in Burleson when she heard about the *American Idol* contest. It was the show's first season. She decided to audition—as did about 10,000 other people. With her exceptional voice and sunny personality, she made the cut. Then, in the show's weekly episodes, she edged out her competitors. Clarkson was the show's first-season winner, and her prize was a $1 million recording contract.

Thankful, Clarkson's first album, came out the next year and shot straight to the top of the pop charts. She also made a movie,

From Justin to Kelly, in which she co-starred with Justin Guarini, the 2002 *American Idol* runner-up. *Breakaway,* her second album, followed in 2004, and it included her rock-flavored single "Since U Been Gone." Clarkson had gone from wannabe to winner in just a few short years.

The Arctic Monkeys, an indie band from Britain, played to sellout crowds and released their debut album, *Whatever People Say I Am, That's What I'm Not.*

Stars from earlier eras were on the rock scene, too. Tom Petty marked the 30th anniversary of his debut with the Heartbreakers by releasing a solo album, *Highway Companion.* The Who came out with *Endless Wire,* the group's first full album since 1982. Paul Simon, whose career spans more than 40 years, showed his creativity and staying power in *Surprise,* his first album since 2000. And Neil Young recorded *Living with War,* a protest against the Iraq war. Fans could hear the complete album free on Young's Web site.

THE POP SCENE

On his 2006 album *Continuum,* singer-songwriter John Mayer also included an antiwar song, "Waiting for the World to Change." Listeners who favored the mellow pop sounds that have made Mayer popular had many other choices, too. James Blunt's "You're Beautiful," from the British singer's album *Back to Bedlam,* flooded the pop airwaves and won MTV's Best Male Video award. Daniel Powter topped the charts with "Bad Day," from his self-titled debut album. Nick Lachey's second album, *What's Left of Me,* also made the charts.

The year also saw new releases from Jessica Simpson (*A Public Affair*), Jewel (*Goodbye Alice in Wonderland*), and a debut effort from Paris Hilton (*Paris*). Pink collected the MTV Best Pop Video award for "Stupid Girls," a song that mocked shallow pop divas. It was from her 2006 album *I'm Not Dead.*

Hip-hop's influence on pop music was clear and strong. Canadian singer-songwriter Nelly Furtado teamed up with hip-hop producer Timbaland for her third album, *Loose,* a collection of danceable tracks. One-time boy-band member Justin Timberlake howled, "I'm bringing sexy back," on his second R&B-flavored solo album, *FutureSex/LoveSounds.*

Christina Aguilera's amazing voice pushed her latest release, *Back to Basics,* into top position. The two-disc album included one disc dedicated to singers who have inspired her, and it featured the hit single "Ain't No Other Man." Janet Jackson featured rap star Nelly on "Call on Me," from her album *20 Y.O.* And Beyoncé had two top-ten singles during the year—"Check on It" (featuring Slim Thug) and "Déjà Vu" (featuring Jay-Z)—and a new solo album, *B'Day.*

HIP-HOP AND R&B

After three years spent producing and collaborating on recordings with other artists, including Beyoncé, Jay-Z brought out a new

New sounds from familiar voices included Beck's 2006 album, *The Information.*

The ever-popular Beyoncé came out with two top-ten singles and a new album, *B'Day.* Later in the year, she starred in the hit film, *Dreamgirls.*

album of his own, *Kingdom Come,* late in 2006. The title track and "Show Me What You Got," another single from the long-awaited release, were circulating on the Internet and getting radio airplay before the album hit the stores.

James Todd Smith is the hip-hop artist better known as LL Cool J. In 2006 he released a new album—his twelfth in a 21-year career—titled *Todd Smith.* (He followed that up later in the year with *Todd Smith Pt. 2: Back to Cool.*) *Todd Smith* included a top-ten single, "Control Myself," featuring Jennifer Lopez. Others who collaborated on LL's new disc included Jamie Foxx and Mary J. Blige, both of whom also had new top-ten albums during the year. Jamie Foxx featured contemporary soul on *Unpredictable.* Mary J. Blige was at the top of her game on *The Breakthrough,* which featured the hit single "Be Without You."

Bounce music—New-Orleans-style hip-hop—is the trademark of Juvenile, and he fea-

iPod Power!

You see them everywhere—the Pod people, with white wires leading from their pockets to their ears. Since its introduction in 2001, the popular iPod has changed the way people buy and listen to music.

With an iPod or a similar MP3 player, you don't have to go to a record store to buy a new CD from your favorite artist. You download the music from the Internet with a click of a mouse. And if you don't want every song on an album, you can buy just the songs you want. Since an iPod holds anywhere from 120 to 15,000 songs, you can carry a whole music library in your pocket.

You can listen to your tunes anywhere through the tiny earbuds. You become a walking music machine, carrying your personal soundtrack wherever you go. You can also download podcasts, multimedia files created by individuals and organizations of all kinds. You may even create your own

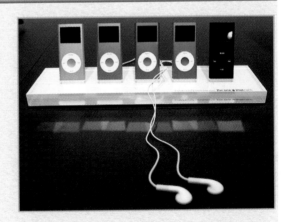

podcasts and post them online for others to download.

There is, however, a downside to the iPod craze. Some people worry that the devices cut off social contact: If you're always listening to your iPod, you can't have a conversation with anyone.

But for now, Pod people rule. Just ask them—though you may have to get them to turn down their iPods first!

Hip-hop artist LL Cool J released his twelfth album, *Todd Smith* (which is his real name). Later in the year, he followed up with *Todd Smith Pt. 2: Back to Cool*.

John Legend was named best new artist at the 2006 Grammy Awards, although this polished R&B singer and pianist was anything but new to music. He had been singing and playing piano since the age of 5 and performing professionally since the 1990's. His first studio album for a major label, *Get Lifted*, included the hit "Ordinary People" and brought him a total of three Grammys in 2006. Late in the year he released his second album, *Once Again*.

More soulful sounds came from singer-songwriter India.Arie, whose third album, *Testimony: Vol. 1, Life & Relationship*, dealt with her struggle to get over a failed relationship. Heather Headley returned with her second album, *In My Mind*. And Prince showed that he was still the king of funk on *3121*, the follow-up to his double-platinum 2004 album *Musicology*.

tured it in his new album *Reality Check*. The artist's growly voice mixed with catchy beats in his first release since Hurricane Katrina destroyed his hometown in 2005. Pharrell, who has produced recordings for Jay-Z, Nelly, and others, made his solo debut with the album *In My Mind*. Ne-Yo had a top-ten hit, "So Sick," off his debut album, *In My Own Words*. Although the album was his first, he had already written songs for stars such as Mary J. Blige and Mario.

The year also brought new albums from Snoop Dogg (*Blue Carpet Treatment*), Ludacris (*Release Therapy*), and Chingy (*Hoodstar*). Atlanta rapper T.I. was on the charts with *King*, his fourth album, and the single "What You Know." Gnarls Barkley—a collaboration between rapper Cee-Lo and producer Danger Mouse—had a hit with the innovative album *St. Elsewhere*. Fergie of the Black Eyed Peas topped the charts with her debut solo single "London Bridge." And Barbados-born teen Rihanna had a danceable hit with "SOS," a track from her second album, *A Girl Like Me*.

COUNTRY

The Dixie Chicks were the top-selling country group of the late 1990's and early 2000's. But after lead singer Natalie Maines criticized U.S. President George W. Bush in 2003, country-music radio stations refused to play their records. In 2006, the Dixie Chicks came out with their first album since that incident. *Taking the Long Way* was also the first album in which group members collaborated in writing all the songs. It had plenty of country flavor, but it aimed at a mainstream pop market—and it shot straight to the top of both the pop and country charts.

Country boy-band Rascal Flatts also reached out to a broader pop audience in 2006, and they had a top-ten album in *Me and My Gang*. But traditional country sounds found favor with fans as well. Alan Jackson drew on the sound of old Appalachian string bands on *Like Red on a Rose*, an album produced by bluegrass star Alison Krauss. Julie Roberts offered sad ballads on *Men & Mascara*, her latest.

The songs on Roseanne Cash's *Black Cadillac* included moving tributes to family members who passed away in recent years—including her father, country great Johnny Cash; and stepmother, June Carter Cash. Songs like

"God Is in the Roses" also showed her coming to terms with her loss. And the voice of Johnny Cash himself was heard in *American V: A Hundred Highways,* an album of songs recorded before his death in 2003.

HALL OF FAME

Four rock groups were inducted into the Rock and Roll Hall of Fame in March 2006. They were the British heavy-metal group Black Sabbath, formed in 1968 by Ozzy Osbourne and others; the 1970's New Wave group Blondie, which featured Deborah Harry as lead singer; the British punk group the Sex Pistols; and Lynyrd Skynyrd, a group whose triple lead guitars popularized Southern rock.

The Hall also inducted one new solo artist, Miles Davis. Davis, one of the greats of jazz, incorporated rock, soul, funk, and hip-hop into his music late in his long career. And Herb Alpert and Jerry Moss received the Hall's Lifetime Achievement Award. In 1962, Alpert and Moss founded A&M Records, which grew into one of the most successful independent record labels in the world.

R&B singer and pianist John Legend captured the 2006 Grammy for Best New Artist.

2006 Grammy Awards

Record of the Year	"Boulevard of Broken Dreams"	Green Day, artists
Album of the Year	*How to Dismantle an Atomic Bomb*	U2, artists
Song of the Year	"Sometimes You Can't Make It on Your Own"	U2, songwriters
New Artist of the Year	John Legend	
Pop Album	*Breakaway*	Kelly Clarkson, artist
Pop Performance, Female	"Since U Been Gone"	Kelly Clarkson, artist
Pop Performance, Male	"From the Bottom of My Heart"	Stevie Wonder, artist
Pop Performance, Group	"This Love"	Maroon5, artists
Rock Album	*How to Dismantle an Atomic Bomb*	U2, artists
Rock Song	"City of Blinding Lights"	U2, artists
Rock Vocal Performance	"Devils & Dust"	Bruce Springsteen, artist
Rock Performance, Group	"Sometimes You Can't Make It on Your Own"	U2, artists
Rhythm and Blues, Album	*Get Lifted*	John Legend, artist
Rhythm and Blues Performance, Female	"We Belong Together"	Mariah Carey, artist
Rhythm and Blues Performance, Male	"Ordinary People"	John Legend, artist
Rhythm and Blues Performance, Group	"So Amazing"	Beyoncé and Stevie Wonder, artists
Rap Album	*Late Registration*	Kanye West, artist
Rap Solo Performance	"Gold Digger"	Kanye West, artist
Rap Performance, Group	"Don't Phunk With My Heart"	Black Eyed Peas, artists
Score for a Motion Picture	*Ray*	Craig Armstrong, composer
Musical Show Album	*Monty Python's Spamalot*	John Du Prez/Eric Idle, producers

PEOPLE, PLACES, EVENTS

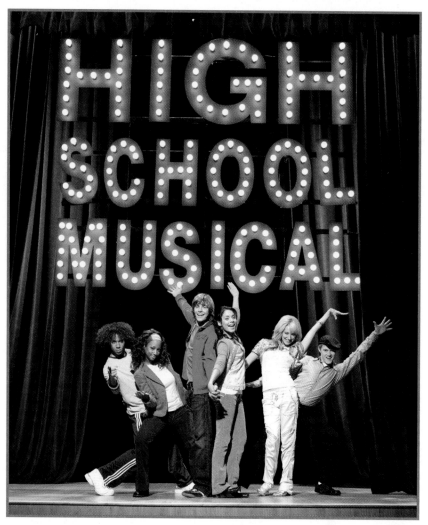

A made-for-TV movie musical was one of the big hits of 2006. **High School Musical** premiered on the Disney Channel on January 20, and kids just couldn't get enough of it.

The film was about a high-school romance between two kids who seem to have nothing in common. Brainy Gabriella Montez (Vanessa Anne Hudgens) and basketball star Troy Bolton (Zac Efron) meet on vacation, when they are picked to sing a karaoke duet. Later, back at East High, Troy discovers that Gabriella is the new girl in his school. The plot gets moving when Troy and Gabriella decide to try out for the school musical. Will their friends understand? Will they get the leading roles? Not if spoiled drama queen Sharpay Evans (Ashley Tisdale) and her brother Ryan (Lucas Grabeel) can stop them!

The movie's cable-television premiere drew 7.7 million viewers! The network followed up with a sing-along version, with on-screen lyrics. Meanwhile, the soundtrack album climbed to the top of the pop charts. (Above, from left: cast members Corbin Bleu, Monique Coleman, Zac Efron, Vanessa Anne Hudgens, Ashley Tisdale, and Lucas Grabeel.)

Long before television crime shows—in fact, long before television—there was **Dick Tracy,** the square-jawed comic-strip detective. The strip, originated by Chester Gould, first appeared in newspapers in 1931; so 2006 marked Tracy's 75th birthday. Over the years, the intrepid lawman put a rogues' gallery of criminals behind bars, using amazing (at the time) technology like two-way wrist radios. And he's still at it, chasing terrorists and corporate crooks across the pages of the comics.

In the world of high fashion, looks are everything. What happens when an ordinary girl—slightly plump and completely unsophisticated—lands a job as assistant to the top editor of a leading fashion magazine? That's the idea behind ***Ugly Betty,*** a new TV sitcom that was a surprise hit in 2006. The show was based on a TV series in Colombia that became an international sensation. The U.S. version starred America Ferrera as Betty Suarez, the clueless assistant. With her braces and loud, ill-fitting clothes, Betty is a fish out of water at *Mode* magazine. But her natural intelligence, sweetness, and willingness to work hard help her navigate in this corporate shark pool.

The year 2006 marked the 400th anniversary of the birth of one of the world's greatest artists—the 17th-century Dutch painter **Rembrandt van Rijn.** Rembrandt (above left, in a self-portrait painted at age 34) is known for his masterful brushwork and his sympathetic portrayals of human nature. A miller's son, he was born in Leiden, Holland, on July 15, 1606, and studied art in Amsterdam. He had a studio in Leiden for several years before returning to Amsterdam, where there were more opportunities for commissions from wealthy clients. Both cities held events celebrating the anniversary in 2006.

Rembrandt is particularly known for his use of chiaroscuro—contrasts of light and dark—especially in his early works. In many of his later paintings, the subjects seem to be bathed in a soft, golden light. The paintings cover a wide range. Rembrandt did portraits of ordinary people as well as of wealthy patrons. He also painted stories from the Bible and group portraits, in which he posed people in dramatic scenes.

Rembrandt married a wealthy woman, Saskia van Uijlenburgh (above right, in a portrait he painted). He enjoyed much success. But he lived extravagantly and, as a result, went bankrupt. He died in 1669, at the age of 63.

Easter Island, far out in the Pacific Ocean, is dotted with hundreds of huge stone statues called **moai,** carved in ancient times. Between 400 and 1,000 years ago, the people of Easter Island went on a statue-carving spree. No one knows why. The moai may have represented the islanders' sacred ancestors. But the statue carvers are long gone. And the statues are keeping their secret.

Over the years, a dozen moai were taken from the island. But in 2006 one of those statues was boxed up (inset) and shipped back to Easter Island. A Chilean artist returned it, to help preserve the island's heritage.

The Phantom of the Opera set a record on January 9, 2006. With its 7,486th performance, this musical by Andrew Lloyd Webber became the longest-running show in Broadway history. *Phantom* opened at New York City's Majestic Theatre on January 26, 1988. The show's music, lush sets, and romantic plot made it an instant hit.

The story is set in Paris during the 1800's. The Phantom of the title is a bitter composer whose face has been terribly disfigured. He lives in the sewers beneath the Paris Opera House, where he terrorizes the opera troupe. When he falls in love with a young opera singer, Christine, he dons a mask and privately tutors her, hoping to make her a star. But when Christine falls in love with someone else, the Phantom's jealousy brings the tale to a climax.

The musical was first staged in London in 1986. It was still running there in 2006, too.

"You ought to be ashamed of yourself!"

The Wonderful Wizard of Oz is one of the most famous children's books of all time. Ever since it appeared in 1900, kids have loved the story of Dorothy, her little dog Toto, and her friends the Tin Man, the Scarecrow, and the Cowardly Lion (above right, in a picture from the first edition). And 2006 marked the 150th birthday of the man who wrote the tale, **L. Frank Baum** (above left).

Baum was born in Chittenango, New York, in 1856. His father, a barrel maker, struck it rich in the oil business, and Baum led a life of privilege. As a young man the theater was his great love. His father bought a string of theaters for him to manage. He also wrote plays and even acted a bit. But in the late 1880's, after his father's death, the family business failed. Baum, his wife, and their four children headed west. In South Dakota and, later, Chicago, he worked as a journalist and in various other jobs.

Baum liked to tell fantasy stories to his children, and he began to jot some of the tales down. In 1897 he published his first children's book, *Mother Goose in Prose*. That was followed by *Father Goose, His Book,* the best-selling children's book of 1899. Then came *The Wonderful Wizard of Oz,* another instant hit. From then on, Baum built on the success of *Oz*. He moved his family to California, to a house he named Ozcot, and wrote more than a dozen *Oz* sequels. He also wrote other children's books under various pen names.

Today, only the first *Oz* book lives on. And many people know the story best not from the book but from the 1939 movie *The Wizard of Oz,* which starred Judy Garland as Dorothy.

Imagine stepping off the rim of the Grand Canyon and looking straight down to the Colorado River, some 4,000 feet (1,220 meters) below. That's the experience in store for tourists at the **Grand Canyon Skywalk,** which was under construction in 2006. The skywalk is on the canyon's West Rim, in the Hualapai Indian Reservation.

The skywalk is a semicircular platform that juts out about 70 feet (21 meters) from the canyon wall. The floor and sides are clear Plexiglas, so nothing blocks the breathtaking view. Although it looks fragile, the platform is said to be strong enough to support the weight of 71 fully loaded jumbo jets. And it's built to withstand major earthquakes and winds of up to 100 miles (160 kilometers) per hour. Tourists may want to keep those statistics in mind as they gaze down at the canyon floor.

Music Television—**MTV**—turned 25 in 2006. Back in 1981, the brand-new cable network had a simple format. It showed music videos all day, and that made it a huge hit with kids. MTV helped build the popularity of some of the biggest stars of the era, including U2, Michael Jackson, and Madonna. In the late 1980's it helped make rap music a mainstream success. The network also began to change its format, producing original game shows and reality shows.

Today, reality shows such as *Parental Control* and *Next* make up much of the schedule. But MTV still shows music videos, and on *Total Request Live* (*TRL*) it highlights performers like Monica (on the set with *TRL*'s VJ Vanessa Minnillo, right).

FUN TO READ

From front cover to back, a good book grabs your attention and keeps you reading. Stories, poems, nonfiction—they're all fun to read! Check out the following pages for some favorite stories and poems. You'll also find lots of information about some of the top books of 2006.

DR. JACKSON'S CROSS-COUNTRY JAUNT

Today, in the early years of the 21st century, automobiles play a major role in the lives of most Americans. More than 136 million cars are registered in the United States. About 80 percent of all American households have one or more cars. And some 17 million new cars are sold every year. To accommodate this love of cars and traveling, there are some 2.6 million miles (4.2 million kilometers) of paved roads in America.

The Age of the Automobile began just over a century ago, in 1895, when Frank Duryea and his brother Charles founded the first American automobile manufacturing company. Just a few years later, a number of U.S. companies were turning out cars. By 1903, production was up to 11,000 a year, and about 31,000 cars were on the roads—such as roads were at the time.

Actually, when it came to automobile driving, the United States was considered a backward nation in the early 1900's. In all of the United States, there were barely 200 miles (320 kilometers) of paved roadways—and these were all in major cities. Only about 10 percent of the total 2 million miles (3.2 million kilometers) of roadways were even "improved," which generally meant they had just a covering of gravel. The rest were dusty trails that became mudholes when it rained or that were streaked with frozen ruts in winter.

Little wonder, then, that by 1903, despite several attempts, no one had been able to drive a car across the country from the Pacific coast to the Atlantic coast. That is, not until a Canadian-born Vermont physician named Horatio Jackson decided he would do just that—drive a newfangled "horseless carriage" from San Francisco, California, to New York City. Having recently given up his medical practice, Jackson was spending some time in San Francisco with his wife when he made a bet with some friends that he could make the transcontinental auto trip in 90 days or less.

Jackson acquired a Winton Motor Carriage, considered one of the best cars of its day. Accompanied by a young mechanic named Sewall Crocker, he set out from San Francisco on May 23, 1903. After 63½ days of travel, marked by a series of adventures and mishaps, Jackson and his traveling companion reached New York City on July 26. They had braved all sorts of hazards—not least of which was the weather.

But despite all the obstacles, Jackson and Crocker made history. What follows is a dramatized account, with some fictionalized events, of that first cross-country automobile trip.

Horatio Jackson, Sewall Crocker, and Bud, during their cross-country trek.

"You're crazy, Jackson—stark, raving mad," the elegantly dressed man in the dark linen suit said forcefully. "You can't drive an automobile from San Francisco to New York. It's impossible!"

Dr. Horatio Nelson Jackson hauled his husky 200-pound frame from the cushioned armchair in San Francisco's plush University Club and straightened himself up to his full six-foot height before replying.

"And I say it *can* be done, and furthermore I can do it," the New England physician-turned-businessman responded, his mustache bristling and his voice rising with each word.

"Look here, Dr. Jackson," said another of the group gathered in the club bar. "If you take the southern route, you'll get bogged down in the desert scrublands—buried in dust, sand, and sagebrush. And if you go north through the Rockies, you'll end up being snowed under in some obscure mountain pass."

"That's right," the first man interrupted with a chuckle. "Why, you'll end up a block of ice. We'll be using little pieces of you to chill our drinks."

The crowd at the club bar broke out into merry laughter.

Dr. Jackson turned red with anger. Dramatically, he pulled out a new $50 bill from his wallet, waved it in front of his companions, and flung out a challenge: "Gentlemen, I will bet this $50 bill that I can drive my automobile across the United States—from coast to coast—in no more than ninety days. I'll be in New York City no later than August 15th!"

"I'll take that bet," the first man responded eagerly. "And I'll wager that long before August 15th, you and your ridiculous auto will have to be hauled back to San Francisco by a team of mules."

When Horatio Nelson Jackson made a bet, he meant it. The 31-year-old hard-headed New Englander would make it to New York in ninety days if he had to carry the car on his back.

Later that balmy spring day, Jackson broke the news to his wife. After four years of marriage, Bertha Jackson knew better than to argue with her adventurous husband when he told her of his intention to become the first man to drive the newfangled automobile across the United States—at a time when there were no highways, and most of the country was a maze of tangled wilderness and mountain trails. She merely suggested that her husband should spend a little more time learning about cars before embarking on such a hazardous journey. "After all, dear," she observed, "you only began driving a few months ago."

Sewall Crocker, a slim 22-year-old mechanic from Washington state who served as Jackson's chauffeur, was less diplomatic. "With all due respect, boss," he sputtered, "you belong in a loony bin if you think you can drive this crate across country. Whattaya gonna do, Doc, fly it over the Rockies?"

"No, Sewall," Jackson replied, a twinkle in his eye, "it will be driven across the continent by you and me."

Realizing that it would be useless to try to change his boss's mind, Crocker instead tried to persuade Dr. Jackson to trade in his steam car for a gas-powered automobile. The Locomobile that Jackson owned, Crocker pointed out, would need vast amounts of water and would surely break down under the stress of rough roads.

Crocker suggested a touring car produced by the Winton Motor Carriage Company of Cleveland, Ohio. Jackson had great respect for Crocker's automobile know-how and mechanical skill, and he readily agreed to the change. "A Winton it shall be, Sewall."

But finding a Winton wasn't easy. The company's California agent didn't have any in stock, and those on the way from the factory were all bought and paid for. Finally, they found a local businessman willing to part with his for $3,000—$500 more than the cost of a *new* Winton. Surveying his newly purchased horseless carriage with its bright red wooden body and laminated fenders, Jackson observed, "No expense will be spared on this expedition, Sewall, my boy. To a man of means like myself, $3,000 is just petty cash."

Crocker's face broke into a catlike grin. "I sure hope you take that attitude when I ask for a raise, Doc."

Like other cars of the period, the Winton #1684 was a clumsy-looking mass of cylinders, pumps, valves, gears, levers, brakes, rods, and bolts. The whole maze of machinery encased in the wooden carriage was plopped onto four wooden-spoked wheels. Propelling the vehicle was a twenty-horsepower, water-cooled, two-cylinder engine, which was mounted under the two leather seats. A pair of levers jutting up from the floorboards provided two forward speeds and reverse. The steering wheel conveniently tilted forward, making it easier for a big man like Jackson to ease into the right-side driver's seat.

Extra equipment was carried behind the seats. Among the carefully chosen items taken along were waterproof sleeping bags; leather coats to protect them from the cold; corduroy suits and canvas coats; a rifle, shotgun, and two pistols—in case they ran into outlaws; canteens; an ax, a shovel, and a full set of tools; fishing rods; spare tires; and a block

and tackle with 150 feet of heavy rope. This last item would turn out to be the most valuable piece of equipment.

Finally, all was in order. Mrs. Jackson boarded a train that would carry her comfortably back East, and her husband and his co-driver were ready to take off on their great adventure. At 1:00 P.M. on Saturday, May 23, 1903—with members of the University Club looking on in shocked silence—Jackson ordered Sewall Crocker, who was in the driver's seat, to start the car.

"Good-bye, gentlemen," Jackson shouted with a haughty wave of his motor cap. "I'll send you all a postcard from New York!"

And with a bouncing, gasping lurch, the Winton was off—leaving a pungent cloud of gas fumes in its wake.

During the first few days, the "Vermont"—as the Winton was dubbed in honor of Jackson's home state—chugged confidently northward through the land of skyscraping redwood trees. Jackson and Crocker took turns at the wheel, while the car bounced over rutted gravel trails and boulder-strewn dirt roads.

In the late morning hours of May 30, near the town of Alturas, California, the trailblazers pulled up in front of their first major obstacle—a winding stream whose gurgling waters seemed to be daring them to find a way across.

"What now?" Crocker asked. "It's a good 30 feet to the other side."

Jackson studied the situation for a moment, peering intently through his driving goggles. "We're certainly not going to let a little body of water like that hold us up," he remarked.

"Okay, Doc," Crocker said resignedly as he pushed the throttle forward and put the car into fast gear. "Hold on."

With a long, loud belch from the exhaust, the Winton lunged forward, picking up momentum as it rolled along the embankment. Down it roared at full speed—twenty miles an hour—until it slammed with a thud into the stream. A great sheet of water cascaded up, drenching the two men as the car plowed its way over the muddy bottom. About halfway across it stopped abruptly, settled back, and sputtered into silence.

Crocker leaned forward, shook the water from his ears, and rested his bony head on his left hand. The unflappable Jackson sat erect and formal, allowing the water to drip from his body.

"Well," Jackson said at last, "I guess I underestimated the situation. Let's get out the block and tackle."

For the next hour, the two men labored furiously. They tied the rope to the rear wheels of the car and then wound the other end around a

tree. When the engine was turned on and the rear axle began to revolve, the effect was like that of a windlass—the apparatus on a ship that's used to raise and lower the anchor. It was backbreaking work, but at last the Winton was hauled onto the opposite bank.

A few hours later, they creaked into Alturas. By now their tires were cut to shreds by the rocky roads. Jackson wired San Francisco for new tires, but after three days none had come. So they decided to make do with what they had. Wrapping thick rope around the rear wheels, they continued their journey.

Navigating mountainous areas, the two adventurers found themselves chugging along on slender trails that narrowed at some points to a mere ten feet. A little too much speed and they might plunge over a precipice. And when meeting horse-drawn wagons along the way, they had to carefully back up to a point wide enough to allow the wagon and the usually frightened horse to pass.

Finally, they arrived in Lakeview, Oregon, where new tires were obtained. Off they went across the barren Oregon scrublands. Here the desertlike terrain presented a new set of problems. There were no roads to follow and no hard surfaces to hold up under the car's wheels. During the day, the blazing sun scorched them. At night, they slept fitfully, alert to the menacing howling of wolves.

The Winton paused briefly at the town of Ontario, where the borders of Oregon and Idaho meet. The travelers picked up another new set of tires there before boarding a ferry that took them across the Snake River.

Turning southeast, they followed the Union Pacific railroad tracks. The roadbeds were being graded by workers using scraper plows hauled by mule teams. One afternoon, Jackson and Crocker collided with a group of these teams, causing a panic. As the Winton roared through the middle of the work gangs, the mules balked and reared, screeching loudly. Workers scattered in all directions, cursing and shaking their fists at the clanking red monster that suddenly loomed in front of them. The two "beelists" —as automobile drivers were then known—laughed heartily, and Crocker gave the workers a "bleep-bleep" on the bulb horn.

A few miles down the road, the situation became more difficult. Torrential rains poured down on them, turning the road into a swamp of thick mud. Like quicksand, the slime had a suctionlike effect on the car, pulling it deeper into the quagmire until the wheels were spinning feverishly but uselessly around.

"It's no use this way," Crocker said, shaking his head so that his sandy hair flopped wetly from side to side. "We'll have to block and tackle from here on."

"Then let's get at it," Jackson replied, his wide jaw set with determination as he jumped down into the ankle-deep mud.

It was hard going for the rest of the day. Sharp winds slashed across their faces. The rain cascaded over them with the force of pressure hoses. Straining every muscle, the two men inched the car forward with the block and tackle, hauling it by hand until the ropes cut deep welts into their shoulders and hands.

"All this for a miserable fifty dollars—you're mad, Doc!" Crocker yelled over the howling wind.

On they went, making slow but steady progress. Finally, on the evening of June 13, the "Vermont"—caked with layers of mud—snorted and bumped into Caldwell, Idaho. It was a magic moment for the townspeople, who had never before seen a real automobile. Within minutes of the first sighting, a horde of cowboys, sheepherders, Indians, and everyone who could hear the car's noisy engine came rushing onto the wagon-rutted main street.

They came trotting up on horses, which reared and plunged at the frightening sound of the Winton's motor. Others circled the car on foot, whooping and hollering and waving their hats. A few got carried away and fired off their rifles.

The dozing Crocker almost jumped out of the car when the first Winchester banged its welcome. "What's happening, Doc," he shouted in panic. "Are we being attacked by Indians?"

"No, cowboys!" Jackson laughed as he steered the car with one hand and waved his cap in triumph at the welcoming committee with the other.

When the dust had settled, Jackson and Crocker were treated royally. Drinks were on the house at every saloon, and local civic groups held a banquet in their honor. But the most important thing that happened in Caldwell was the addition of a third passenger. As they were preparing to leave, the two adventurers noticed a bull terrier sniffing around the Winton's mud-caked tires. After a careful inspection, the cheerfully panting dog bounded into the car and landed on the leather driver's seat.

"Will you look at that," exclaimed Crocker with a laugh. "Maybe he can spell us at the wheel, Doc."

"We could use a mascot, Crocker," said Jackson. With a flourish, he produced a spare set of driver's goggles and placed them on the bewildered pooch's head.

"I hereby christen you 'Bud,'" Jackson continued, "and designate you official mascot of this cross-country adventure."

Bud replied with a few yelps and friendly barks, as if he understood the honor that had just been bestowed on him. From then on he was the expedition's unofficial navigator—giving out with a loud "woof-woof" whenever obstacles loomed on the road.

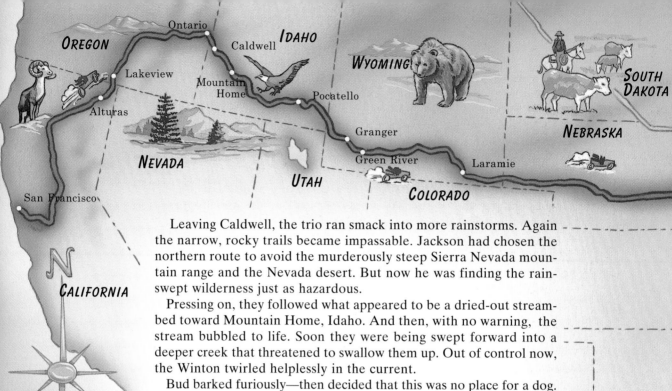

Leaving Caldwell, the trio ran smack into more rainstorms. Again the narrow, rocky trails became impassable. Jackson had chosen the northern route to avoid the murderously steep Sierra Nevada mountain range and the Nevada desert. But now he was finding the rain-swept wilderness just as hazardous.

Pressing on, they followed what appeared to be a dried-out streambed toward Mountain Home, Idaho. And then, with no warning, the stream bubbled to life. Soon they were being swept forward into a deeper creek that threatened to swallow them up. Out of control now, the Winton twirled helplessly in the current.

Bud barked furiously—then decided that this was no place for a dog. Plunging into the water, he paddled to shore. "Man overboard," Jackson bellowed. Bud struggled up the low bank, shaking himself off. Then the pooch sat down on his haunches and began to howl wildly. In the middle of the swirling stream, Jackson and Crocker sat stranded in their now amphibious automobile.

Bud's vocal smoke signals saved the day. The shrill barking attracted the attention of a nearby farmer, who trotted over to the bank.

"What are you fellers doin' out there?" he shouted.

"We're stuck, you fool," Jackson yelled, standing up in the auto, then flopping back down again as the current seized the vehicle and spun it around.

The farmer roared with laughter, slapping his blue-jeaned thighs. Cupping his hands he cried out, "That's the trouble with them horseless carriages. People who drive 'em ain't got no horse sense!"

When he finally tired of poking fun at the stranded travelers, the farmer brought out his team of plow horses and hauled the water-logged Winton onto the bank. An hour later, Jackson, Crocker, and Bud were bumping along the crossties of the Union Pacific railroad tracks toward Pocatello, Idaho, which they reached on June 17.

Worse was still to come. Crossing into Wyoming, they found that recent rainstorms had washed out the roadways, leaving no signposts to guide them. Near Granger they turned north onto a barren stretch of sagebrush country. It was hot and desolate, with scorching daytime temperatures. During the next 36 hours, Jackson and Crocker had their most agonizing experience. They had no idea where they were, and no water was to be found. Then their food gave out.

Parched with thirst and their stomachs rumbling, the two men pushed on doggedly. Each hour brought more suffering. Poor Bud lay stretched out, his tongue lolling. The stinging rays of the sun beat down on them relentlessly. Then it rained, relieving them of the dried-

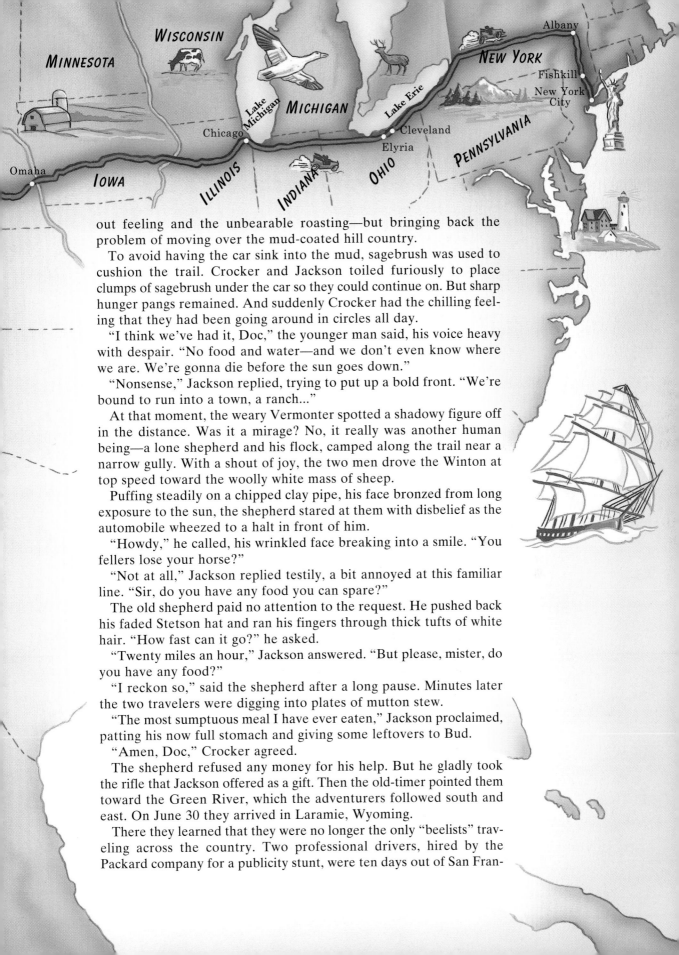

out feeling and the unbearable roasting—but bringing back the problem of moving over the mud-coated hill country.

To avoid having the car sink into the mud, sagebrush was used to cushion the trail. Crocker and Jackson toiled furiously to place clumps of sagebrush under the car so they could continue on. But sharp hunger pangs remained. And suddenly Crocker had the chilling feeling that they had been going around in circles all day.

"I think we've had it, Doc," the younger man said, his voice heavy with despair. "No food and water—and we don't even know where we are. We're gonna die before the sun goes down."

"Nonsense," Jackson replied, trying to put up a bold front. "We're bound to run into a town, a ranch..."

At that moment, the weary Vermonter spotted a shadowy figure off in the distance. Was it a mirage? No, it really was another human being—a lone shepherd and his flock, camped along the trail near a narrow gully. With a shout of joy, the two men drove the Winton at top speed toward the woolly white mass of sheep.

Puffing steadily on a chipped clay pipe, his face bronzed from long exposure to the sun, the shepherd stared at them with disbelief as the automobile wheezed to a halt in front of him.

"Howdy," he called, his wrinkled face breaking into a smile. "You fellers lose your horse?"

"Not at all," Jackson replied testily, a bit annoyed at this familiar line. "Sir, do you have any food you can spare?"

The old shepherd paid no attention to the request. He pushed back his faded Stetson hat and ran his fingers through thick tufts of white hair. "How fast can it go?" he asked.

"Twenty miles an hour," Jackson answered. "But please, mister, do you have any food?"

"I reckon so," said the shepherd after a long pause. Minutes later the two travelers were digging into plates of mutton stew.

"The most sumptuous meal I have ever eaten," Jackson proclaimed, patting his now full stomach and giving some leftovers to Bud.

"Amen, Doc," Crocker agreed.

The shepherd refused any money for his help. But he gladly took the rifle that Jackson offered as a gift. Then the old-timer pointed them toward the Green River, which the adventurers followed south and east. On June 30 they arrived in Laramie, Wyoming.

There they learned that they were no longer the only "beelists" traveling across the country. Two professional drivers, hired by the Packard company for a publicity stunt, were ten days out of San Fran-

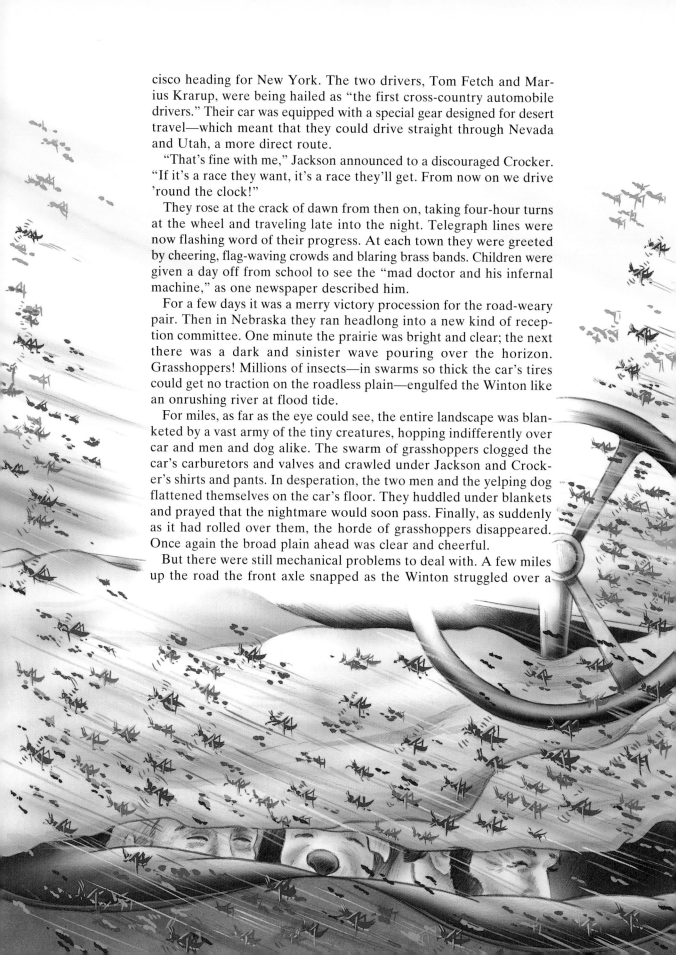

cisco heading for New York. The two drivers, Tom Fetch and Marius Krarup, were being hailed as "the first cross-country automobile drivers." Their car was equipped with a special gear designed for desert travel—which meant that they could drive straight through Nevada and Utah, a more direct route.

"That's fine with me," Jackson announced to a discouraged Crocker. "If it's a race they want, it's a race they'll get. From now on we drive 'round the clock!"

They rose at the crack of dawn from then on, taking four-hour turns at the wheel and traveling late into the night. Telegraph lines were now flashing word of their progress. At each town they were greeted by cheering, flag-waving crowds and blaring brass bands. Children were given a day off from school to see the "mad doctor and his infernal machine," as one newspaper described him.

For a few days it was a merry victory procession for the road-weary pair. Then in Nebraska they ran headlong into a new kind of reception committee. One minute the prairie was bright and clear; the next there was a dark and sinister wave pouring over the horizon. Grasshoppers! Millions of insects—in swarms so thick the car's tires could get no traction on the roadless plain—engulfed the Winton like an onrushing river at flood tide.

For miles, as far as the eye could see, the entire landscape was blanketed by a vast army of the tiny creatures, hopping indifferently over car and men and dog alike. The swarm of grasshoppers clogged the car's carburetors and valves and crawled under Jackson and Crocker's shirts and pants. In desperation, the two men and the yelping dog flattened themselves on the car's floor. They huddled under blankets and prayed that the nightmare would soon pass. Finally, as suddenly as it had rolled over them, the horde of grasshoppers disappeared. Once again the broad plain ahead was clear and cheerful.

But there were still mechanical problems to deal with. A few miles up the road the front axle snapped as the Winton struggled over a boulder-strewn stretch of terrain. It was the worst damage the car had yet suffered, and it threatened to take the "Vermont" out of the cross-continental competition for good.

"Don't panic, Doc. The old buggy isn't dead yet," Crocker said reassuringly. Then he scampered off in the direction of a nearby farmhouse. Twenty minutes later he was back with a length of pipe. As Jackson watched with a look of respectful awe, Crocker skillfully and patiently fitted the broken ends into the piece of pipe.

"Will it work?" Jackson asked skeptically. Crocker smiled and started the engine up. Minutes later they were rolling smoothly again. Actually, this was only one of a dozen ingenious makeshift repairs the younger man had made on the trip. Throughout, Crocker saved the day with his mechanical know-how.

The determined duo had an easy run from Omaha, Nebraska, to Chicago, Illinois—taking only two days to complete this leg of the journey. Newspapers trumpeted their progress with banner headlines proclaiming "FROM OCEAN TO OCEAN IN AN AUTOMOBILE CAR" and "BEELISTS STOP HERE."

On July 20, the pair roared into Elyria, Ohio, the home of the Winton Company, just outside Cleveland. A delegation of Winton executives drove out to meet them—and then escorted them to Cleveland's finest hotel for a full-scale banquet. Recognizing the publicity value of the cross-country jaunt, the Winton Company offered to overhaul the car and foot the bill for further expenses on the final part of the journey. But Jackson flatly refused.

"I don't want people to say this was just a company-backed publicity stunt," he told the Winton people firmly. "We'll keep the mud and the grime and the makeshift repairs and make it the rest of the way on our own."

So off they went on the last leg of their adventure. Seeking to avoid another bout of mountain climbing, the pair chose to skirt the Alleghenies and take a longer route through Pennsylvania and northern New York. Roads were relatively good now, but at one point in western Pennsylvania they decided to take a short cut—and it nearly cost them their lives.

Using a technique they had often employed in the western states, they crawled over a narrow railroad trestle bridge spanning a deep gorge. However, in the East, trains weren't as few and far between as in the West. Midway across the bridge, a sharp whistle suddenly broke the silence in the low hills ahead of them, freezing the pair with terror. Around a sharp bend, a freight train clattered head-on toward them.

"My God, Doc," Crocker shouted hoarsely, the blood draining from his face, "if he makes it onto the bridge before we get off we'll be knocked all the way back to Frisco!"

Acting on sheer instinct alone, his heart pounding, Jackson did the only thing possible. The trestle was only a foot wider than the tracks on each side. Clutching the steering wheel for dear life—and knowing that the slightest movement left or right meant a steep plunge to the rocks below—Jackson accelerated to full speed.

Crocker sat with his eyes closed and his hands covering his face, mumbling a barely audible prayer. The car bounced crazily while the chugging of the oncoming train grew louder and louder. The Winton and the train reached the edge of the cliff only seconds apart. Fortunately, it was the car that made it first—as the hulking engine swept around the bend, a mere thirty feet ahead. The doctor swerved into a tangled hedgerow, avoiding a collision with the train by a few yards.

"Well, Sewall, the gods are certainly with us," Jackson exclaimed with relief, the throbbing in his chest gradually tapering off. Speechless, Crocker could only sigh heavily, while Bud gave out a few cheerful yelps.

From there on it was smooth sailing. On July 23, the Winton arrived in Rochester, New York. Next came a fast run to Albany, and then down along the Hudson River toward New York City. On Saturday, July 25, they stopped briefly at Fishkill, where Jackson had a short but happy reunion with his wife, who had come down from Vermont. Leaving Mrs. Jackson to join them later, the two automobilists continued on toward New York City.

On Sunday, July 26, 1903, at about 4:30 A.M., the Winton passed through Yonkers and then into New York City. It was a humid summer morning, but after all that Jackson and Crocker had experienced, New York's sultry weather seemed like paradise. At a casual speed they rolled down Broadway, then east to Fifth Avenue. A few pedes-

trians gaped in amazement at the battered Winton. Its wheels were solid disks of hard-packed mud, and its passengers were covered from head to foot with oil and grime.

"Where in the world have you fellows been?" a brass-buttoned policeman shouted at them, pushing back his cork helmet and staring in wonderment.

"Why, we've been out for a little country jaunt," Jackson replied with a wink. Then he and Crocker exploded in laughter as the Winton rattled and rumbled past the elegant town houses on smoothly paved Fifth Avenue.

The first cross-country automobile trip had come to an end.

HENRY I. KURTZ; Author, *The Art of the Toy Soldier*

⌒EPILOGUE⌒

Crocker and Jackson became overnight celebrities. Everywhere, people were awed by the story of their ordeal—and the fantastic journey that had lasted 63 days, 12 hours, and 30 minutes. The two had traveled an estimated 4,500 miles (7,240 kilometers) in their meandering ocean-to-ocean trip. They had done what many believed was impossible.

Controversy over the feat soon arose, however. A month after Jackson had completed his trip, Fetch and Krarup finally made it to New York, insisting that their Packard was the first car to cross the country under its own power. Many newspapers accepted that claim, and one implied that Jackson and Crocker had lied about their feat. "It is well known to men familiar with the western part of the United States," this paper commented, "that for a car to get through certain parts of Oregon and Nebraska without the assistance of a railroad train is an impossibility."

Rallying behind Jackson, the Winton Company offered a reward to anyone who could prove that the doctor and his mechanic sidekick had put their car on a train during the journey. The reward was never claimed. The Smithsonian Institution in Washington, D.C., put the matter to rest in 1944 when it accepted the "Vermont" for its permanent automotive collection. The old Winton, sporting a fresh coat of bright red paint, may now be seen at the Smithsonian's National Museum of American History (shown in the photo below).

Jackson, who later became a newspaper publisher, served as an army officer in World War I, winning several medals. But he never received any medals for his cross-country trip—in fact, he never even collected on that $50 bet! Years afterward, however, it wasn't his war exploits that he delighted in relating. Until the day he died in 1955, at the age of 82, he constantly recalled for all who would listen every detail of those harrowing two months when he and Sewall Crocker had been the first people to drive an automobile from San Francisco to New York.

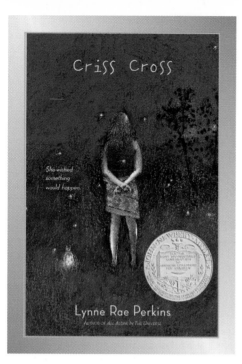

BEST BOOKS, 2006

The John Newbery Medal and the Randolph Caldecott Medal are important children's book awards. They are sometimes considered the "Academy Awards" of U.S. children's book publishing. That is, they are as prestigious as the famous Academy Awards handed out each year by the motion-picture industry.

The American Library Association gives both awards annually. The Newbery Medal is given to the author of the best American literary work for young readers. The Caldecott Medal is given to the illustrator of the best American picture book for children. Here are the 2006 winners.

NEWBERY MEDAL

Criss Cross, by Lynne Rae Perkins, is a novel about teenage friends in a small town. Most of the story is told from the point of view of two 14-year-olds, Debbie and Hector. Each is at a personal crossroads, trying to understand the meaning of life and love. The book follows their thoughts and feelings as they try to decide how to live their lives. Its short chapters are sprinkled with questions, photographs, funny drawings, and snatches of poetry and song lyrics.

Newbery Honor Books. *Hitler Youth: Growing Up in Hitler's Shadow,* by Susan Campbell Bartoletti, tells the story of how Nazi dictator Adolf Hitler used German boys and girls to rise to power and to keep power once he became leader of Germany in 1933. The youngsters were lured into an organization called the Hitler Youth by camping trips and parades and the promise of adventure. By 1939, the Hitler Youth numbered 7 million young people. Bartoletti also tells the stories of some young Germans who resisted the evils of Nazism but paid for it with their lives.

Alan Armstrong's *Whittington* is in part a retelling of *Dick Whittington and His Cat,* an old English folktale. The hero of this modern-day story is a tomcat named Whittington, who says he's descended from Dick Whittington's cat. Upon arriving at a barn owned by kindhearted Bernie, Whittington regales the farm animals—and Bernie's two orphaned grandchildren, Ben and Abby—with tales about his ancestor, Dick Whittington's cat, and about Dick Whittington's rags-to-riches story. And in the telling of this story, young Ben finds his own riches: He overcomes dyslexia and learns to read.

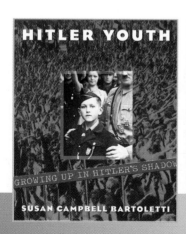

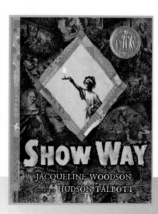
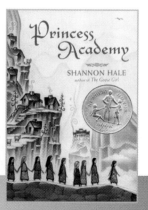

Jacqueline Woodson's story of her family—from slavery, through emancipation, to the present—is told in *Show Way*. It is told in poetry and through the use of magnificent artistic renderings of show ways—beautiful quilts that were actually maps that showed slaves the way to freedom.

The young heroine of *Princess Academy,* a fantasy tale by Shannon Hale, is 14-year-old Miri. The king of her village announces that the prince will soon come to select a wife. In preparation, the village girls must go to a special academy to learn how to be a princess. There, Miri becomes a leader in the girls' fight against the harsh treatment they receive. And she gains the knowledge that will enable her to better the lives of all the villagers.

CALDECOTT MEDAL

The Hello, Goodbye Window, illustrated by Chris Raschka and written by Norton Juster, is about a young girl's visit to her grandparents' house. The window of the title is where they wave hello when she arrives and say goodbye when she leaves. And through the window, she sees all sorts of exciting things—even a dinosaur. Raschka's pictures echo children's drawings and show the warmth of family life.

Caldecott Honor Books. The story of civil-rights activist Rosa Parks is told in *Rosa,* illustrated by Bryan Collier and written by Nikki Giovanni. It was Parks's refusal to give up her seat to a white person on a segregated bus that ushered in the civil-rights movement of the 1950's. For the remainder of her life (she died in 2005), Parks was an icon of the civil-rights movement.

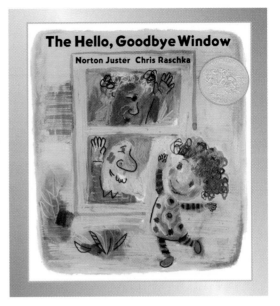

Three Zen stories of love and enlightenment are told in *Zen Shorts,* illustrated and written by Jon J. Muth. The tales are told to three young inquisitive siblings by a giant panda that moves into their neighborhood. Lovely watercolor artwork accompanies the story.

In 1783, two French brothers, Joseph Michel and Jacques Étienne Montgolfier, built a hot-air balloon with a basket underneath that carried a rooster, a duck, and a sheep. This was the first time that live passengers were carried into the air and returned safely. *Hot Air: The (Mostly) True Story of the First Hot-Air Balloon Ride,* illustrated and written by Marjorie Priceman, is a comical version of the historic event.

Song of the Water Boatman and Other Pond Poems, illustrated by Beckie Prange and written by Joyce Sidman, is a collection of eleven poems about turtles, beetles, peepers, and other inhabitants of ponds. Richly colored woodcuts illustrate the poems.

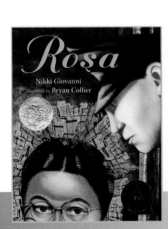

THE PIED PIPER OF HAMELIN

The West German town of Hameln is probably one of the few places on Earth to become famous for its rats. Actually, it wasn't the rats themselves that brought renown to this town on the banks of the Weser River—it was a strange legend that grew up about them in the Middle Ages.

The legend is the story of the Pied Piper of Hamelin (as the town's name was spelled in earlier times), and it has been told in many forms. One of the most famous versions, a poem by Robert Browning, is reproduced here. According to the tale, to get rid of the town's hordes of rats, the town council hired a piper with magical powers. (He was called "pied" because of his multicolored clothes.) When he played his pipe, all the rats came tumbling out and followed him to the river, where they drowned. But the town refused to pay the piper, and he took a terrible revenge. He played his pipe and lured all the town's children away, and they were never seen again.

No one is sure when these events took place. Some town records give 1284 as the year. Browning gives 1376. Most historians say, however, that these events most likely never took place at all. Instead, the story of the rats and the piper probably grew up around some other event that involved the disappearance of many children from a town. Some think the event was a crusade to the Holy Land, although the last children's crusade took place many years earlier.

All the same, the story made Hamelin famous. Today it's a quaint town, with many old buildings. If you visit, you'll see a clock on which figures of the piper, the rats, and the children come out to chime the hour. And during the year, local children re-enact the tale, following a piper who dances through the streets. Of course, when the show is over, the children go home!

Hamelin Town's in Brunswick
By famous Hanover city;
  The river Weser, deep and wide,
  Washes its wall on the southern side;
  A pleasanter spot you never spied;

But, when begins my ditty,
  Almost five hundred years ago,
  To see the townsfolk suffer so
    From vermin was a pity.
                        Rats!

They fought the dogs, and killed the cats,
  And bit the babies in the cradles,
And ate the cheeses out of the vats,
  And licked the soup from the cook's own ladles,
Split open the kegs of salted sprats,
Made nests inside men's Sunday hats,
And even spoiled the women's chats,
  By drowning their speaking
  With shrieking and squeaking
In fifty different sharps and flats.

  At last the people in a body
    To the Town Hall came flocking:
  " 'Tis clear," cried they, "our Mayor's a noddy;
    And as for our Corporation—shocking
  To think that we buy gowns lined with ermine
  For dolts that can't or won't determine
  What's best to rid us of our vermin!
  You hope, because you're old and obese,
  To find in the furry civic robe ease?
  Rouse up, sirs! Give your brain a racking
  To find the remedy we're lacking,
  Or, sure as fate, we'll send you packing!"
At this the Mayor and Corporation
Quaked with a mighty consternation.

  An hour they sat in council,
    At length the Mayor broke silence:
  "For a guilder I'd my ermine gown sell;
    I wish I were a mile hence!
  It's easy to bid one rack one's brain—
  I'm sure my poor head aches again
  I've scratched it so, and all in vain,
    Oh for a trap, a trap, a trap!"
Just as he said this, what should hap
At the chamber door but a gentle tap?
  "Bless us," cried the Mayor, "what's that?"

(With the Corporation as he sat,
Looking little though wondrous fat;
Nor brighter was his eye, nor moister,

Than a too-long-opened oyster,
Save when at noon his paunch grew mutinous
For a plate of turtle green and glutinous),
  "Only a scraping of shoes on the mat?
  Anything like the sound of a rat
  Makes my heart go pit-a-pat!"

  "Come in!"—the Mayor cried, looking bigger:
And in did come the strangest figure.
  His queer long coat from heel to head
  Was half of yellow and half of red;
  And he himself was tall and thin,
  With sharp blue eyes, each like a pin,
  And light loose hair, yet swarthy skin,
  No tuft on cheek nor beard on chin,
  But lips where smiles went out and in—
  There was no guessing his kith and kin!
  And nobody could enough admire
  The tall man and his quaint attire.
  Quoth one: "It's as my great grandsire,
  Starting up at the Trump of Doom's tone,
  Had walked this way from his painted tombstone."

He advanced to the council-table:
And, "Please, your honours," said he, "I'm able,
  By means of a secret charm, to draw
  All creatures living beneath the sun,
  That creep, or swim, or fly, or run,
  After me so as you never saw!
  And I chiefly use my charm
  On creatures that do people harm,
  The mole, and toad, and newt, and viper;
  And people call me the Pied Piper."
(And there they noticed round his neck

303

A scarf of red and yellow stripe,
To match with his coat of the selfsame cheque;
   And at the scarf's end hung a pipe;
And his fingers, they noticed, were ever straying
As if impatient to be playing
Upon this pipe, as low it dangled
Over his vesture so old-fangled.)
   "Yet," said he, "poor piper as I am,
   In Tartary I freed the Cham,
   Last June, from his huge swarms of gnats;
   I eased in Asia the Nizam
   Of a monstrous brood of vampire bats:
   And, as for what your brain bewilders,
   If I can rid your town of rats
   Will you give me a thousand guilders?"
   "One? fifty thousand!"—was the exclamation
Of the astonished Mayor and Corporation.

Into the street the Piper stept,
   Smiling first a little smile,
As if he knew what magic slept
   In his quiet pipe the while;
Then, like a musical adept,
To blow the pipe his lips he wrinkled,
And green and blue his sharp eyes twinkled
Like a candle-flame where salt is sprinkled;
And ere three shrill notes the pipe uttered,
You heard as if an army muttered;
And the muttering grew to a grumbling;
And the grumbling grew to a mighty rumbling;
And out of the house the rats came tumbling.
Great rats, small rats, lean rats, brawny rats,
Brown rats, black rats, gray rats, tawny rats,

Grave old plodders, gay young friskers,
   Fathers, mothers, uncles, cousins,
Cocking tails and pricking whiskers,
   Families by tens and dozens,
Brothers, sisters, husbands, wives—
Followed the Piper for their lives.
From street to street he piped advancing,
And step by step they followed dancing,
Until they came to the river Weser
Wherein all plunged and perished
—Save one, who, stout as Julius Caesar,
Swam across and lived to carry
(As he the manuscript he cherished)
To Rat-land home his commentary,
Which was, "At the first shrill notes of the pipe,
I heard a sound as of scraping tripe,
And putting apples, wondrous ripe,
Into a cider press's gripe;
And a moving away of pickle-tubboards,
And a leaving ajar of conserve cupboards,
And a drawing the corks of train-oil-flasks,
And a breaking the hoops of butter casks;
And it seemed as if a voice
(Sweeter far than by harp or by psaltery
Is breathed) called out, Oh, rats! rejoice!
The world is grown to one vast drysaltery!
To munch on, crunch on, take your nuncheon,
Breakfast, supper, dinner, luncheon!
And just as a bulky sugar puncheon,
All ready staved, like a great sun shone
Glorious scarce an inch before me,
Just as methought it said, come, bore me!
—I found the Weser rolling o'er me."

You should have heard the Hamelin people
Ringing the bells till they rocked the steeple.
    "Go," cried the Mayor, "and get long poles!
    Poke out the nests and block up the holes!
    Consult with carpenters and builders,
    And leave in our town not even a trace
    Of the rats!"—when suddenly up the face
    Of the Piper perked in the market-place,
With a, "First, if you please, my thousand guilders!"

A thousand guilders! The Mayor looked blue;
So did the Corporation too.
For council dinners made rare havoc
With Claret, Moselle, Vin-de-Grave, Hock;
And half the money would replenish
Their cellar's biggest butt with Rhenish.
To pay this sum to a wandering fellow
With a gipsy coat of red and yellow!
    "Beside," quoth the Mayor, with a knowing wink,
    "Our business was done at the river's brink;
    We saw with our eyes the vermin sink,
    And what's dead can't come to life, I think.
    So, friend, we're not the folks to shrink
    From the duty of giving you something to drink,

And a matter of money to put in your poke,
But, as for the guilders, what we spoke
Of them, as you very well know, was in joke.
Besides, our losses have made us thrifty;
A thousand guilders! Come, take fifty!"

The Piper's face fell, and he cried,
"No trifling! I can't wait, beside!
I've promised to visit by dinnertime
Bagdad, and accepted the prime
Of the Head Cook's pottage, all he's rich in,
For having left the Caliph's kitchen,
Of a nest of scorpions no survivor—
With him I proved no bargain-driver,
With you, don't think I'll bate a stiver!
And folks who put me in a passion
May find me pipe to another fashion."
"How?" cried the Mayor, "d'ye think I'll brook
Being worse treated than a Cook?
Insulted by a lazy ribald
With idle pipe and vesture piebald?
You threaten us, fellow? Do your worst,
Blow your pipe there till you burst!"

Once more he stept into the street;
    And to his lips again
Laid his long pipe of smooth straight cane;
    And ere he blew three notes (such sweet
Soft notes as yet musicians cunning
    Never gave the enraptured air),

There was a rustling, that seemed like a bustling
Of merry crowds justling, at pitching and hustling,
Small feet were pattering, wooden shoes clattering,
Little hands clapping, and little tongues chattering,
And, like fowls in a farmyard when barley is scattering,
Out came the children running.
All the little boys and girls,
With rosy cheeks and flaxen curls,
And sparkling eyes and teeth like pearls,
Tripping and skipping, ran merrily after
The wonderful music with shouting and laughter.
The Mayor was dumb, and the Council stood
As if they were changed into blocks of wood,
Unable to move a step, or cry
To the children merrily skipping by—
And could only follow with the eye
That joyous crowd at the Piper's back.
But how the Mayor was on the rack,
And the wretched Council's bosoms beat,
As the Piper turned from the High Street
To where the Weser rolled its waters
Right in the way of their sons and daughters!
However, he turned from South to West,
And to Koppelberg Hill his steps addressed,
And after him the children pressed;
Great was the joy in every breast.
    "He never can cross that mighty top!
    He's forced to let the piping drop,
    And we shall see our children stop!"
When lo! as they reached the mountain's side,
A wondrous portal opened wide,
As if a cavern was suddenly hollowed;
And the Piper advanced and the children followed,

And when all were in to the very last,
The door in the mountain-side shut fast.
Did I say all? No! one was lame,
And could not dance the whole of the way;
And in after years, if you would blame
His sadness, he was used to say:
    "It's dull in our town since my playmates left;
    I can't forget that I'm bereft
    Of all the pleasant sights they see,
    Which the Piper also promised me;
    For he led us, he said, to a joyous land,
    Joining the town and just at hand,
Where waters gushed and fruit trees grew,
And flowers put forth a fairer hue,
And everything was strange and new.
The sparrows were brighter than peacocks here,
And their dogs outran our fallow deer,
And honey-bees had lost their stings;
And horses were born with eagle's wings;
And just as I became assured
My lame foot would be speedily cured,
The music stopped, and I stood still,
And found myself outside the Hill,
Left alone against my will,
To go now limping as before,
And never hear of that country more!"

Alas, alas for Hamelin!
    There came into many a burgher's pate
    A text which says, that Heaven's Gate
    Opes to the Rich at as easy rate
As the needle's eye takes a camel in!

306

The Mayor sent East, West, North and South,
To offer the Piper by word of mouth,
  Wherever it was men's lot to find him,
Silver and gold to his heart's content,
If he'd only return the way he went,
  And bring the children all behind him.
But when they saw 'twas a lost endeavour,
And Piper and dancers were gone forever
They made a decree that lawyers never
  Should think their records dated duly
If, after the day of the month and year,
These words did not as well appear,
  "And so long after what happened here
  On the twenty-second of July,
  Thirteen hundred and seventy-six:"
And the better in memory to fix
The place of the Children's last retreat,
They called it, the Pied Piper's street—
Where any one playing on pipe or tabor,
Was sure for the future to lose his labour.
Nor suffered they hostelry or tavern
  To shock with mirth a street so solemn;
But opposite the place of the cavern
  They wrote the story on a column,

And on the great church window painted
The same, to make the world acquainted
How their children were stolen away;
And there it stands to this very day.
And I must not omit to say
That in Transylvania there's a tribe
Of alien people that ascribe
The outlandish ways and dress,
On which their neighbours lay such stress,
To their fathers and mothers having risen
Out of some subterraneous prison,
Into which they were trepanned
Long time ago in a mighty band
Out of Hamelin town in Brunswick land,
But how or why they don't understand.

So, Willy, let you and me be wipers
Of scores out with all men—especially pipers;
And, whether they pipe us free from rats or from mice,
If we've promised them aught, let us keep our promise.

307

POETRY

STILL NIGHT THOUGHTS

Moonlight in front of my bed—
I took it for frost on the ground!
I lift my eyes to watch the mountain moon,
Lower them and dream of home.

LI PO (8th Century)

VELVET SHOES

Let us walk in the white snow
In a soundless space;
With footsteps quiet and slow,
At a tranquil pace,
Under veils of white lace.

I shall go shod in silk,
And you in wool,
White as a white cow's milk,
More beautiful
Than the breast of a gull.

We shall walk through the still town
In a windless peace;
We shall step upon white down,
Upon silver fleece
Upon softer than these.

We shall walk in velvet shoes:
Wherever we go
Silence will fall like dews
On white silence below.
We shall walk in the snow.

ELINOR WYLIE (1885–1928)

ON STILTS

I mount my stilts from the garden wall,
I have to take care that I don't fall,
But once I'm on them away I stalk
Just as the giants used to walk.

I can step over the roses' heads,
Over 'most of the flower-beds,
And to all sorts of distant places
I can go in a dozen paces.

Seven league boots, the stories say,
Giants wore when they walked away;
I'd like to race a giant or two,
And see what my trusty stilts could do.

Sometimes I wobble when I go slow,
The faster the better on stilts, you know;
But over a smooth and level strip
I can go at a giant's clip.

RUPERT SARGENT HOLLAND (1878–1952)

BEE! I'M EXPECTING YOU!

Bee! I'm expecting you!
Was saying Yesterday
To Somebody you know
That you were due—

The Frogs got Home last Week—
Are settled, and at work—
Birds, mostly back—
The Clover warm and thick—

You'll get my Letter by
The seventeenth; Reply
Or better, be with me—
Yours, Fly.

EMILY DICKINSON (1830–1886)

AN EGG

In marble walls as white as milk,
Lined with a skin as soft as silk,
Within a fountain crystal clear,
A golden apple doth appear,
No doors there are to this stronghold,
Yet thieves break in and steal the gold.

UNKNOWN

THE EAGLE

He clasps the crag with crooked hands;
Close to the sun in lonely lands,
Ringed with the azure world, he stands.

The wrinkled sea beneath him crawls;
He watches from his mountain walls,
And like a thunderbolt he falls.

ALFRED, LORD TENNYSON (1809–1892)

OLD NOAH'S ARK

Old Noah once he built an ark,
And patched it up with hickory bark.
He anchored it to a great big rock,
And then he began to load his stock.
The animals went in one by one,
The elephant chewing a caraway bun.
The animals went in two by two,
The crocodile and the kangaroo.
The animals went in three by three,
The tall giraffe and the tiny flea.
The animals went in four by four,
The hippopotamus stuck in the door.
The animals went in five by five,
The bees mistook the bear for a hive.
The animals went in six by six,
The monkey was up to his usual tricks.
The animals went in seven by seven,
Said the ant to the elephant, "Who're ye shov'n?"
The animals went in eight by eight,
Some were early and some were late.
The animals went in nine by nine,
They all formed fours and marched in a line.
The animals went in ten by ten,
If you want any more, you can read it again.

AMERICAN FOLK RHYME

Twelve Dancing Princesses

Once upon a time there lived a farm boy named Michael, without either father or mother. He was a handsome youth with blue eyes and blond curly hair. And all the village girls liked him. But Michael dreamed of greater things. He imagined he would marry a princess.

One night Michael went to sleep and dreamed that there appeared before him a beautiful lady dressed in a golden robe, who said: "Go to the King's castle and you shall marry a princess."

The following day, to the great astonishment of the whole village, the farm boy quietly announced, "I am going away today." And he said good-bye to his friends and set out to seek his fortune.

It was well known that there lived in the King's castle twelve beautiful princesses. And it was said that they were so very sensitive and of such royal blood that they would have felt a pea in their beds even if five mattresses had been laid over it.

The princesses had twelve beds all in the same room. And it was known that they slept far into the morning, never getting up till midday. But what was extraordinary was the fact that although they were locked in their room at night, every morning their satin shoes were found worn with holes!

When the princesses were asked what they had been doing all night, they always answered that they had been asleep. And, indeed, no noise was ever heard in their room. Yet how did their shoes become so worn? The King was puzzled and worried. So he proclaimed that whoever could discover how his daughters wore out their shoes should choose one of them for his wife.

On hearing the proclamation, fifty princes arrived at the castle to try their luck. They watched all night—but when morning came the princes had all disappeared, and no one could find them!

When Michael reached the King's castle, he went straight to the gardener and offered his services. The gardener immediately agreed to take him on, as he thought that his handsome face and golden curls would please the twelve princesses.

The first thing Michael was told was that when the princesses awoke, he was to present each one with a bouquet of flowers. The following day he went to the princesses' room, with the twelve bouquets in a basket. He gave one to each of the sisters, and they took them without even deigning to look at the lad—except for Lina, the youngest. She fixed her large black eyes on him, and exclaimed, "Oh, how pretty he is, our new flower boy!" The other princesses all burst out laughing, and the eldest pointed out that a princess should never lower herself by looking at a garden boy.

Now Michael had heard what had happened to all the princes. Still, the sweetness of Princess Lina inspired him to try his luck. But he dared not come forward, fearing that he would be turned away.

Then Michael had another dream, and the lady in the golden robe appeared to him once more. In one hand she held two young laurel trees—a cherry laurel and a rose laurel—and in the other hand she held a little golden rake and a little golden bucket. She said to him:

"Plant these two laurels in two large pots, rake them over with the rake, and water them with the bucket. When they have grown tall, say to each of them, 'My beautiful laurel, with the golden rake I have raked you and with the golden bucket I have watered you.' Then ask anything you choose and you will get it." Michael thanked her, and when he awoke he found the two laurel bushes beside him.

The trees grew very fast. When they were several feet tall, he said to the cherry laurel, "My lovely cherry laurel, with the golden rake I have raked you and with the golden bucket I have watered you. Teach me how to become invisible." Instantly there appeared on the laurel a pretty white flower, which Michael stuck into his buttonhole.

That evening, when the princesses went upstairs to bed, the invisible Michael followed them barefoot so that he might make no noise, and he hid himself under one of the twelve beds so that he might not bump into them.

The princesses began to put on the most lovely dresses. They turned all around in front of a mirror to admire their appearance.

Michael could see nothing from his hiding place, but he could hear everything the princesses said. At last the eldest said, "Be quick, my sisters, our partners will become impatient."

At the end of an hour, when Michael heard no more noise, he peeked out and saw the twelve sisters dressed in their splendid garments, with beautiful satin shoes on their feet, and holding the bouquets he had brought them.

"Are you ready?" asked the eldest sister.

"Yes," replied the other eleven.

Then the eldest princess clapped her hands three times, and a trap door opened. All the princesses disappeared down a secret staircase, and Michael hastily followed them.

As he was following immediately behind Princess Lina, he accidentally stepped on her dress.

"There is somebody behind me," cried the princess.

"You foolish thing," said her eldest sister. "You are always afraid of something."

They went down, down, down, till at last they came to a passage with a door at one end. The eldest princess opened it, and they found themselves in a lovely little wood, where the leaves of the trees were spangled with drops of silver. They next crossed another wood where the leaves were sprinkled with gold, and after that another still, where the leaves glittered with diamonds.

At last Michael saw a large lake, and on the shore of the lake twelve little boats with awnings. In the boats were seated twelve princes, who, grasping their oars, awaited the princesses.

Each princess entered one of the boats, and Michael slipped into the one that held the youngest. The boats glided along rapidly, but Lina's, from being heavier, was always behind the rest. "Why are we going so slowly tonight?" asked the princess.

"I don't know," answered the prince. "I assure you I am rowing as hard as I can."

On the other side of the lake Michael saw a beautiful castle splendidly illuminated, from which came the sound of lively music. When the boats reached land, the princes gave their arms to the princesses and led them to the castle.

Michael followed and entered the ballroom. He placed himself out of the way in a corner, and admired the grace and beauty of the princesses. Some were fair and some were dark; some had red hair and some had golden locks. But the one whom the farm boy thought the most beautiful was the little princess with the velvet eyes.

With what eagerness she danced! Leaning on her partner's shoulder, she swept by like a whirlwind. Her cheeks were flushed, and her eyes sparkled. And the poor farm boy envied those handsome young men with whom she danced so gracefully.

Now, these men were really the fifty princes who had tried to learn the princesses' secret. The princesses had made them drink a magic potion, which froze the heart and left nothing but a love of dancing.

They danced on until the shoes of the princesses were worn out with holes. At dawn the music stopped, and a delicious meal was served to all.

Afterward, the dancers all went back to their boats. Again Michael entered the boat of the youngest princess. Again they walked through the wood with the diamond-spangled leaves, the wood with the gold-sprinkled leaves, and the wood whose leaves glittered with drops of silver. As proof of where he had been, the boy broke a small branch from a tree in the last wood. Lina turned as she heard the noise made by the breaking of the branch.

"What was that noise?" she asked.

"It was nothing," replied her eldest sister. "It was only the screech of an owl that roosts in the castle's turrets."

While she was speaking, Michael quickly slipped in front and, running up the hidden staircase, he reached the princesses' room first. He flung open the window, slid down the vine that climbed up the wall, and found himself in the garden just as the sun was beginning to rise. It was time for him to begin work.

That day, when he made up the bouquets, Michael hid the branch with the silver drops in the nosegay for the youngest princess. When Lina discovered it she was much surprised. But she said nothing.

In the evening the twelve sisters again went to the ball, and Michael again followed them. During the ball, the little princess looked everywhere for the gardener's boy, but she never saw him.

As they came back, Michael gathered a branch from the wood with the gold-spangled leaves, and now it was the eldest princess who heard the noise that it made in breaking.

"It is nothing," said Lina, "only the cry of an owl."

As soon as Lina awoke the next morning, she found the branch in her bouquet. When the sisters went down she stayed a little behind and said to the garden boy, "Where does this branch come from?"

"Your Royal Highness knows where it comes from," answered Michael.

"So you have followed us?"

"Yes, Princess."

"How did you manage it? We never saw you."

"I hid myself," replied Michael quietly.

The princess was silent a moment, and then said, "You know our secret. Keep it." And she flung the boy a purse of gold.

"I do not sell my silence," answered Michael, and he went away without picking up the purse.

For three nights Lina neither saw nor heard anything odd. On the fourth night she heard a rustling among the diamond-spangled leaves of the wood. The following morning there was a branch of the tree in her bouquet.

She took the garden boy aside and said to him harshly, "Do you know what my father has promised to pay for learning our secret?"

"I know, Princess," answered Michael.

"Don't you mean to tell him?"

"That is not my intention."

Lina's sisters had seen her talking to the garden boy, and they jeered at her for it.

"What prevents your marrying him?" asked the eldest. "You could become a gardener too. It is a charming profession. You could live in a cottage and help your husband draw water from the well. And when we get up, you could bring us our bouquets."

Princess Lina was very angry. And when the garden boy presented her bouquet, she received it in a disdainful manner.

Michael behaved most respectfully. He never raised his eyes to her, but all day she felt him at her side without ever seeing him.

One day she decided to tell everything to her eldest sister.

"What!" said she. "This rogue knows our secret and you never told me! I must lose no time in getting rid of him."

"But how?"

"Why, by having him taken to the dungeon, of course."

But the youngest sister did not seem to want to harm the garden boy, who, after all, had said nothing to their father about their secret adventures.

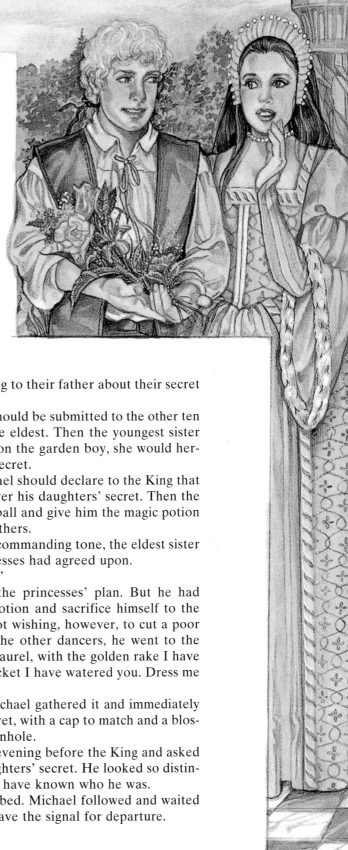

It was agreed that the question should be submitted to the other ten sisters. All were on the side of the eldest. Then the youngest sister declared that if they laid a finger on the garden boy, she would herself go and tell their father their secret.

At last it was decided that Michael should declare to the King that he would like to attempt to discover his daughters' secret. Then the princesses would take him to the ball and give him the magic potion that would enchant him like the others.

They sent for Michael and, in a commanding tone, the eldest sister ordered him to do what the princesses had agreed upon.

He only answered, "I will obey."

Michael had actually guessed the princesses' plan. But he had made up his mind to drink the potion and sacrifice himself to the happiness of his little princess. Not wishing, however, to cut a poor figure at the ball by the side of the other dancers, he went to the laurels and said: "My lovely rose laurel, with the golden rake I have raked you and with the golden bucket I have watered you. Dress me like a prince."

A beautiful flower appeared. Michael gathered it and immediately found himself clothed in black velvet, with a cap to match and a blossom of the rose laurel in his buttonhole.

He next presented himself that evening before the King and asked if he could try to discover his daughters' secret. He looked so distinguished that hardly anyone would have known who he was.

The princesses went upstairs to bed. Michael followed and waited behind the open door until they gave the signal for departure.

At the ball, he danced with each princess, and he was so graceful that everyone was delighted with him. At last the time came for him to dance with the little princess. She found him the best partner in the world, but he did not speak a single word to her.

When he was taking her back to her place she said to him in a mocking voice, "Here you have all you could wish for—you are being treated like a prince."

"Don't be afraid," replied Michael gently. "You shall never be a gardener's wife."

The little princess stared at him with a frightened face, and he left her without waiting for an answer.

When the satin slippers were worn through, the music stopped and the dinner table was set. Michael was fed the most exquisite dishes, and compliments and flattery were heaped on him from every side. But he took care not to be too enthusiastic, either about the food or the compliments.

At last the eldest sister made a sign, and one of the pages brought in a large golden cup.

"The enchanted castle has no more secrets for you," she said to Michael. "Let us drink to your triumph."

He cast a glance at the little princess and lifted the cup.

"Don't drink!" cried the little princess. "I would rather marry a gardener." And she burst into tears.

Michael flung the contents of the cup behind him, leaped over the table, and fell at Lina's feet. The rest of the princes fell likewise at the feet of the other princesses, each of whom chose a husband and raised him to her side. The spell was broken.

The twelve couples embarked in the boats, which crossed back many times in order to carry over the other princes. Then they all went through the three woods, and when they had passed the door of the underground passage a great noise was heard. It sounded as if the enchanted castle were crumbling to the ground.

They went straight to the room of the King, who had just awakened. Michael held in his hand the golden cup, and he revealed the secret of the holes in the shoes.

"Choose, then," said the King, "whichever you prefer."

"My choice is already made," replied the garden boy, and he offered his hand to the youngest princess.

And so the garden boy became a prince. But before the marriage ceremony, the princess insisted that he tell her how he had discovered the secret.

Michael showed her the two laurels that had helped him. And she, being a sensible girl, thought that the laurels would give him too much advantage over his wife. So she cut them off at the root and threw them in the fire!

THE NEW BOOK OF KNOWLEDGE
2007

The following articles are from the 2007 edition of *The New Book of Knowledge*. They are included here to help you keep your encyclopedia up to date. Cross-references appearing in these articles refer to the 2007 edition of the set. Some of the articles referenced may not be found in older editions.

MONTENEGRO

Montenegro is one of the smallest countries in Europe, in population as well as in area. It is situated in southeastern Europe, on the Balkan Peninsula on the coast of the Adriatic Sea. Podgorica is the country's capital and largest city.

People. Ethnically, Montenegrins are mostly South Slavs. Their official language is Serbo-Croatian, specifically a dialect called Ijekavian. Most Montenegrins belong to the Eastern Orthodox Church. There are smaller communities of Muslims (who are mostly ethnic Albanians) and Roman Catholics.

Land. Montenegro is largely mountainous. In fact, its name means "Black Mountain." The ranges are heavily forested, which makes transportation difficult. Bobotov Kuk, the nation's highest peak, rises 8,274 feet (2,522 meters) in the Dinaric Alps. Montenegro's major river, the Morača, flows into Lake Scutari.

Along the Adriatic coast, summers are warm and dry. Winters are mild.

Economy. Services, including those related to tourism, make up the fastest-growing seg-

FACTS and figures

REPUBLIC OF MONTENEGRO is the official name of the country.

LOCATION: Southeastern Europe.

AREA: 5,415 sq mi (14,026 km²).

POPULATION: 631,000 (estimate).

CAPITAL AND LARGEST CITY: Podgorica.

MAJOR LANGUAGE: Serbo-Croatian (Ijekavian dialect official).

MAJOR RELIGIOUS GROUPS: Eastern Orthodox Christian, Muslim.

GOVERNMENT: Republic. **Head of state**—president. **Head of government**—prime minister. **Legislature**—Assembly.

CHIEF PRODUCTS: Agricultural—wheat and other cereal grains, tobacco, potatoes, citrus fruits, grapes, livestock. **Manufactured**—steel, processed foods, consumer goods. **Mineral**—bauxite (aluminum ore).

MONETARY UNIT: Euro (1 euro = 100 cents).

ment of Montenegro's economy. Agriculture is limited due to the scarcity of fertile land. Cereal grains and potatoes are the most important crops. The raising of livestock is a chief economic activity. Kotor and Bar, on the Adriatic coast, are the country's chief ports.

History and Government. Montenegro has historically been allied with Serbia. But when the Serbs fell under Ottoman rule in 1389, the Montenegrins were able to hold off their invasions, due in part to the rugged mountainous landscape. After 1516, Montenegro was ruled by Orthodox bishops, until it became an independent principality in 1878. In 1918, it became part of a Yugoslav kingdom.

A Communist Yugoslavia was created after World War II (1939–45). After 1991, Yugoslavia began to break up, and four of its six republics declared their independence. In 2003, the two remaining republics formed the nation of Serbia and Montenegro. In 2006, Montenegrins voted to separate from Serbia. The current leaders are President Filip Vujanović and Prime Minister Milo Djukanović.

Reviewed by JANUSZ BUGAJSKI
Center for Strategic and International Studies

SERBIA

Serbia is a landlocked nation on the Balkan Peninsula in southeastern Europe. It is bordered on the north by Hungary and Romania, on the east by Bulgaria, on the south by Macedonia and Albania, and on the west by Montenegro, Bosnia and Herzegovina, and Croatia. Serbia has long been one of the most powerful states in the Balkans. In 1918, after World War I, Serbia became part of a larger nation called Yugoslavia. The country did not regain its independence until 2006.

▶ PEOPLE

Serbia is home to nearly 10 million people, most of whom are of South Slavic origin. Serbs make up nearly two-thirds of the total population. The rest is made up of Albanians, Muslim Slavs, Croats, and Macedonians as well as smaller numbers of Magyars (Hungarians), Slovaks, Romanians, and Romanies.

Language. The official language of Serbia is Serbo-Croatian, which belongs to the South Slavic language group. Romanian, Hungarian, Slovak, and Croatian are all official within the autonomous region of Vojvodina; Albanian is official in Kosovo.

Religion. Most Serbs belong to the Eastern Orthodox Church. Croats are mostly Roman Catholics. Muslim Slavs are a legacy of Ottoman rule. Many of the country's ethnic Albanians also are Muslims.

Education. Schools in Serbia are free, and attendance is required for children aged 7 to 14. Universities are located in all the major cities.

Food and Drink. National dishes are served on special occasions. *Čulbastija*, grilled pork or beef, served with slivovitz (a brandy made from plums) is popular. Shashlik—meat (usually lamb) cut into small cubes and broiled on a skewer over an open fire—is a favorite in Muslim areas. In villages and large towns, workers meet at the *kafana* (coffeehouse) to sip strong "Turkish" coffee and talk politics.

▶ LAND

Serbia is situated on the Balkan Peninsula of southeastern Europe. The country includes two autonomous provinces—Kosovo in the south (largely Albanian in population) and Vojvodina in the north.

Left: Grapes and other fruits are grown in Serbia. About half the country's land is used for agriculture. *Below left:* Most Serbs are Eastern Orthodox Christians. *Below:* Belgrade is Serbia's capital and largest city.

Serbia

Land Regions. Serbia has both lowlands and mountains. The lowlands of Vojvodina have the richest agricultural land. Valleys in the northwest have forests and patches of densely cultivated lands, but irrigation is needed to grow the area's main crops. Central and southern Serbia are mountainous. Mount Daravica, which rises 8,714 feet (2,656 meters) near the Montenegro border, is the country's highest peak.

Rivers. The lowlands are watered by the Danube River and its tributaries, the Sava and Tisza rivers. South of the Danube are the Drina, Morava, and Ibar rivers.

Climate. In the lowlands, winters are cold and summers are hot and dry. In the interior highlands, winters are very cold. There are heavy rains in early summer, and summers are generally cool.

Natural Resources. About one-quarter of Serbia is covered with forests, primarily oak and beech trees. The mountains of eastern Serbia contain most of the country's deposits of lignite (brown coal), smaller amounts of bituminous (soft) coal, and copper ore. Other important resources include lead and zinc in Kosovo and oil and natural gas in Vojvodina.

Rivers and hot springs provide thermal and hydroelectric power.

▶ ECONOMY

Services. Service industries, including retail trade and tourism, employ a significant number of workers. Tourism is an important source of foreign currency. Relatives working abroad also send money home.

Agriculture. About half the land is used for farming. The leading food crops are wheat and corn. Sugar beets and other vegetables as well as a variety of fruits are grown. They include olives, cherries, grapes, figs, peaches, pears, and plums. Forestry and livestock raising are also important to the economy.

Manufacturing. Serbia produces a variety of goods. The chief products are agricultural machinery, electrical and communications equipment, paper and pulp, and transportation equipment.

▶ MAJOR CITIES

Belgrade is Serbia's capital and largest city. Strategically located at the joining of the Sava and Danube rivers, it has been called the Key to the Balkans. For more information, see the article on Belgrade in Volume B. Other important cities include Novi Sad, the capital of Vojvodina; Priština, the capital of

FACTS and figures

REPUBLIC OF SERBIA is the official name of the country.

LOCATION: Southeastern Europe.

AREA: 34,116 sq mi (88,361 km²).

POPULATION: 9,400,000 (estimate).

CAPITAL AND LARGEST CITY: Belgrade.

MAJOR LANGUAGES: Serbo-Croatian (official), Romanian, Hungarian, Slovak, Croatian (official in Vojvodina), Albanian (official in Kosovo).

MAJOR RELIGIOUS GROUPS: Eastern Orthodox Christian, Muslim, Roman Catholic.

GOVERNMENT: Republic. Head of state—president. Head of government—prime minister. Legislature—National Assembly.

CHIEF PRODUCTS: Agricultural—wheat, corn, sugar beets, sunflowers, beef, pork, milk. Manufactured—agricultural machinery, electrical and communications equipment, paper and pulp, transportation equipment. Mineral—lignite (brown coal), nonferrous ores (copper, lead, and zinc), iron ore, limestone.

MONETARY UNIT: Dinar (1 dinar = 100 paras).

Ferries on the Danube River pass through the Iron Gate, a gorge that separates Serbia and Romania.

Kosovo; and **Subotica**, a largely Magyar city near the Hungarian border.

▶ GOVERNMENT

The government of Serbia is transitioning to a new constitution. Meantime, it is based on a constitutional charter ratified in 2003. The charter provides for a president, who is elected to a 5-year term. Members of the one-house legislature, the National Assembly, are elected to 4-year terms. The Assembly elects a prime minister to serve as head of government. A group called the Federal Ministries acts as an advisory board in the areas of foreign affairs, defense, international economic relations, internal economic relations, and human and minority rights.

▶ HISTORY

The region containing Serbia was originally known as Illyria. It was long a part of the Roman Empire. The South Slavs, who settled there in the A.D. 600's, came under the political and cultural influence of the Byzantine Empire. In the late 1100's, Stephen Nemanja founded the first independent Serbian state. He became its first king.

Serbia reached the height of its power during the 1300's, under King Stephen Dushan. But in 1389 the Ottoman Turks defeated Ser-

A shepherd tends her animals. Livestock raising, particularly in the mountainous regions, is important to Serbia's economy.

bia and its allies at the historic Battle of Kosovo Polje. Thus began a period of Ottoman rule that lasted nearly 500 years.

The Formation of Yugoslavia. Serbia won its independence from the Ottoman Empire in 1878. It quickly began to gather all inhabited Serbian lands into a single state. Therefore, the Serbs bitterly resented Austria-Hungary's annexation of Bosnia and Herzegovina in 1908. Then in 1914, a Serbian nationalist assassinated the Austrian archduke Francis Ferdinand, heir to the throne. This single event triggered the outbreak of World War I. When the war ended in 1918, Serbia led the movement to form the Kingdom of Serbs, Croats, and Slovenes under the Serbian royal dynasty. The new country, which also included Montenegro, was renamed the Kingdom of Yugoslavia in 1929.

Yugoslavia was occupied by Nazi Germany in 1941 during World War II. Afterward, it became a battleground between two rival guerrilla groups, the Serbian Chetniks and the Partisans. The Partisans were led by the Communist leader Tito (Josip Broz). At the war's end in 1945, Serbia became one of the republics of the new Socialist Federal Republic of Yugoslavia under Tito's command. (For more information, see the biography of Tito in Volume T.)

The Breakup of Yugoslavia. By the late 1980's, Yugoslavia's economic system was on the verge of total collapse. Caught up in the

In 1998, the Serbs began an aggressive civil war against ethnic Albanians in Kosovo. Hundreds of thousands of refugees fled across the border to Albania and Macedonia.

revolutionary political and economic changes that shattered the Soviet Union and transformed Communist Eastern Europe, the country began to break apart. Croatia and Slovenia demanded that Yugoslavia be made a loose confederation of states. But Serbia refused. There was also disagreement over the replacement of the nation's Communist system with a democratic government and free-market economy. Serbia also claimed that the boundaries between the republics established by Tito were unfair to Serbs and tried to redraw them.

The crisis came to a head in 1991. On May 15, a Croat took over the presidency, as required by the constitution. But Serbia rejected his succession. On June 25, Croatia and Slovenia proclaimed their independence. Macedonia, another of Yugolslavia's republics, did the same later in the year. The result was a civil war.

In April 1992, the republics of Serbia and Montenegro together proclaimed themselves the Federal Republic of Yugoslavia (FRY), the successor to the former Yugoslav state. For more information, see the article YUGO-SLAVIA in Volume WXYZ.

The Federal Republic.   Slobodan Milošević, who had been president of Serbia since 1989, assumed control over the new Yugoslav republic. A Communist nationalist who had opposed the breakup, Milošević backed Serb attacks on Croatia and Bosnia and Herzego-vina after they declared their independence. In the fall of 1992, in an effort to end Serbian aggression against the Croats and Bosnians, the United Nations imposed economic sanctions on Yugoslavia. A peace accord signed in Dayton, Ohio, ended the conflict in 1995.

Milošević became president of Yugoslavia in July 1997. The following year, civil war broke out between the Serbs and the ethnic Albanians in Kosovo. News of Serbian atrocities prompted the North Atlantic Treaty Organization (NATO), led by the United States, to threaten force against the Serbs. Peace talks held in early 1999 failed to settle the dispute. NATO then authorized air strikes against Serbian military targets. After the Yugoslav army withdrew from Kosovo, NATO ceased its offensive. It installed peacekeeping forces to safely resettle the refugees.

In 2000, a revolt swept through Yugoslavia when Milošević refused to acknowledge losing the presidential election to opposition candidate Vojislav Koštunica. Milošević finally stepped down when it became clear he had lost the support of the military. Koštunica assumed the presidency on October 5. In 2001, Milošević became the first former national leader brought to trial for war crimes by the International Court in The Hague.

In 2002, in response to a growing independence movement in Montenegro, the two republics agreed to a new federation pact so that each might assume semi-independence. A new constitution was approved in 2003, and Yugoslavia was officially renamed Serbia and Montenegro. As part of the agreement, the charter offered each state the right to hold a referendum in 2006 to decide if the union should continue or be split into two independent states.

An Independent Serbia.   On May 21, 2006, Montenegrins voted to end their union with Serbia. Montenegro's parliament formally declared independence on June 3. On June 6, Serbia declared itself the legal successor to the union and inherited Serbia and Montenegro's seat in the United Nations. Boris Tadić and Vojislav Koštunica, leaders of the Serbian republic, became president and prime minister respectively.

Reviewed by JANUSZ BUGAJSKI
Director, Eastern European Project
Center for Strategic and International Studies

See also BALKANS; YUGOSLAVIA.

GAMBLING

Gambling is wagering money or other valuables on the outcome of a game or other event. It has existed since ancient times.

Gambling in the United States. Horse racing was popular in colonial America. In the mid-1800's, professional card players plied their trade in the gambling halls of the West and on steamships traveling the Mississippi River. In 1887 the invention of the slot machine revolutionized gambling. Players deposited coins in the machine and pulled a handle to set it in motion. With slot machines, people could wager without having the skills needed to succeed at playing cards or betting on horses. But gambling was considered a vice by many, especially religious groups. So it was made illegal in every state by 1910.

In 1931, in response to revenue shortages during the Great Depression, Nevada became the first state to legalize casino gambling. Several states had approved horse racing by 1935. In 1941 the first "modern" casino opened in the town of Las Vegas, Nevada. Called El Rancho Las Vegas, it was located on a highway now famous as "The Strip." El Rancho Las Vegas offered slot machines, gaming tables, rooms to rent, dining, and entertainment. This is basically the same mix offered by today's casinos.

In 1963, New Hampshire established the first legal state lottery in 70 years. State lotteries eventually spread throughout most of the country. In 1976, New Jersey emerged as the second state to permit casino gambling, which became centered in Atlantic City. The next major stage in casino gambling occurred in 1988, when American Indian casinos became legal. In the 1990's some states also began authorizing casino gambling on riverboats along the Mississippi River.

Most legal gambling operations in the United States are run for profit by corporations or state governments. But there is also charitable gambling, such as that used by churches to raise money for good causes.

Online Gambling. Yet another type of gambling took hold in the 1990's and 2000's. The first online casino began operating in August 1995. By 2003 more than 300 companies around the world were operating over 2,000 Web sites. The sites offer wagering on sports, casino games, lotteries, and bingo.

Gamblers at this Las Vegas casino are trying their luck at the slot machines. Each year Las Vegas draws close to 40 million visitors.

Growth of Gambling. Gambling in the United States has grown largely because many Americans have come to accept it as a legitimate way to have fun and be entertained. Some form of legalized gambling is now available in the District of Columbia and all U.S. states except Hawaii and Utah. In most states, the minimum legal age for gambling is 21. But in some states it is 18. Las Vegas, Nevada, is the world's most important gaming center.

Political and Social Issues. In 1999 a national commission found problem gambling to be one of the most important negative aspects of the spread of gambling. Problem gamblers tend to need to bet more money more frequently and find it difficult to stop.

Of particular concern to lawmakers is gambling by young people. This is because they are even more likely than adults to become problem gamblers. Some 600,000 young people aged 14 to 22 are reported to gamble online each week. In 2006, the U.S. government intensified its efforts to prohibit online gambling, including preventing online gamblers from using credit cards.

BILL EADINGTON
Director, Institute for the Study of Gambling and Commercial Gaming, University of Nevada

UNIVERSE

When astronomers speak of the universe, or cosmos, they are referring to space and everything in it. Our planet, Earth, is one of a small group of planets that orbit a star we call the sun. These planets and the sun form a solar system, which also includes asteroids and comets. Our sun is one of billions of other stars that have been drawn together by gravity to form a galaxy, which we call the Milky Way. The Milky Way is just one of billions and billions of other galaxies scattered throughout the vast expanse of space we call the universe. The study of the structure, composition, and evolution of the universe is called **cosmology**.

The universe is about 13.7 billion years old. It began with a violent explosion called the Big Bang. This explosion released all the matter and all the energy that exists anywhere. Gas and dust eventually condensed to form stars, planets, and then galaxies.

The universe is so big that it is difficult to explain its size in conventional measurements. Therefore the vast distances in the universe are measured in light-years. A light-year is the distance light travels in a year, which is 6 trillion miles (10 trillion kilometers). If you could travel at the speed of light, it would take you more than 4 years to reach the star nearest the Earth (other than the sun). On the other hand, if you traveled at the same speed to the most distant objects known (quasars), it would take you about 12 billion years. And the universe is even bigger than that. In fact, it is still expanding from the Big Bang, growing larger and larger every day.

▶ EARLY THEORIES ABOUT THE UNIVERSE

The origin and nature of the universe have been subjects of speculation from the earliest times. Ancient myths were the first attempts to explain the universe's existence. These tales were common among cultures through-

out the world. According to Norse mythology, for example, the universe was created when a giant was killed by three gods. The giant's body became the Earth, his blood the seas, and his skull the holder of the heavens.

As far back as 4000 B.C., the Earth was seen as the center of the entire universe. The sun, the other planets, and all the stars revolved around it. This is called a **geocentric world system**. During the 300's B.C., the Greek scholar Eudoxus proposed that the sun, moon, and planets revolved around the Earth on transparent, or crystal, spheres. About A.D. 150, the astronomer Ptolemy of Alexandria refined this concept to better account for the motions of celestial objects. For the next 1,400 years, the **Ptolemaic system** was the accepted model of the universe.

▶ DEVELOPMENT OF MODERN COSMOLOGY

Beginning in the 1500's, more accurate observations were made by astronomers such as Nicolaus Copernicus, Tycho Brahe, Johannes

The universe is a vast expanse of space that contains a dazzling array of celestial objects. *Left to right:* Dust and gas stream away from a comet as it approaches the sun. The Crab Nebula is formed from the remains of an exploded star. Black holes are extremely dense objects whose gravity is so strong that not even light can escape them. There are billions of galaxies in the universe, each containing billions of stars.

Kepler, and Galileo Galilei. From these observations, it was determined that the Earth and all the other planets revolved around the sun. This concept was very controversial. In time, however, this accurate view of the solar system became widely accepted.

With the sun established as the center of the solar system, it was also thought to be the center of the universe. This theory remained popular until the 1920's. That was when the astronomer Edwin Hubble discovered that many of the small, fuzzy patches of light in the sky were in fact other galaxies outside our own. These galaxies were filled with billions of other suns. And they were located at

325

Space-based telescopes can be used to observe the most distant galaxies. Many deep-space views have been collected by the Hubble Space Telescope.

if they are in nearby galaxies. Otherwise, they are not bright enough to be seen. Type Ia supernovas are much brighter and can be used with more distant galaxies. However, supernova explosions are not predictable, and they do not stay at peak brightness for long. (See the articles PULSARS in Volume P and STARS in Volume S.)

For distant galaxies that lack supernovas, scientists measure overall brightness and then compare that to the brightness and apparent size of similar galaxies whose distances are known. However, the space between galaxies may contain dust that absorbs light energy and makes stars appear dimmer (and thus farther away) than they actually are.

Scientists also estimate how quickly distances are changing. They do this by measuring the **red shift**. This is the degree to which wavelengths of light are "stretched" by the expansion of the universe. In the visible spectrum, red light has the longest wavelength. If light from an object were to shift toward the red end of the spectrum, it would mean that the distance between the object and Earth was growing.

When scientists analyze the light of galaxies, they observe a red shift. In the late 1920's, Edwin Hubble compared red shift data to distances calculated from Cepheid variable measurements. He found that the farther away a galaxy is, the greater its red shift.

Because of this relationship between red shift and distance, red shifts are sometimes used to estimate distances to galaxies. However, this method may give inaccurate results. Over large distances, red shifts can reflect expansion rate changes that have occurred over the history of the universe. Still, red shifts are sometimes used in large-scale galaxy surveys. And red shifts are useful for finding distances to nearby galaxies.

▶ GALACTIC CLUES TO COSMIC MYSTERIES

When scientists study galaxies, they often learn more about the universe. When Hubble discovered that increasingly distant galaxies had increasingly large red shifts, scientists realized that the universe had to be expanding. And when they traced this expansion backward in time, they realized it was consistent with the idea of the Big Bang. (See the article UNIVERSE in Volume UV.)

Scientists who catalogue the contents of galaxies realize they cannot account for all the mass that galaxies must contain. These scientists believe some "missing" or invisible mass must be present. Otherwise, they cannot explain how galaxies are held together by gravity. One theory is that the source of this missing mass is an unusual substance called **dark matter**. It seems to make its presence known only through its gravitational effects.

Estimates for the amount of dark matter relate to basic questions about the universe. With enough dark matter, gravitational attraction could slow or even reverse the expansion of the universe. However, it appears that this expansion is speeding up, or accelerating. This finding is based on distance estimates for supernovas.

Most scientists believe the supernova data shows that the expansion of the universe began accelerating about 5 billion years ago. To explain this acceleration, scientists have proposed several theories. According to the most popular theory, the acceleration is due to **dark energy**. This is a kind of reverse gravity that seems to be a fundamental property of space itself. Many scientists believe that billions of years from now, dark energy will be expanding the universe at such a rate that distant galaxies will become invisible to each other. Light will not travel fast enough to cross the growing distance between them.

WILLIAM A. GUTSCH, JR.
President, The Challenger Center
for Space Science Education

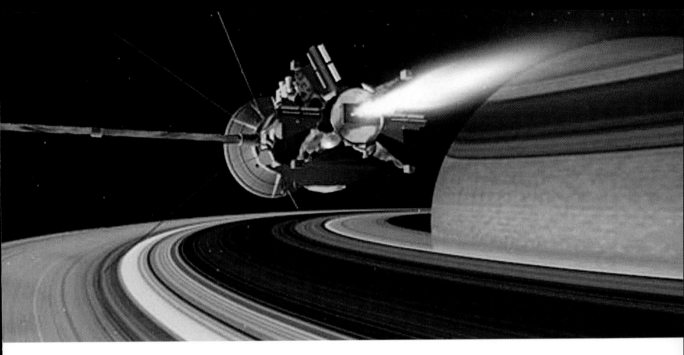

SPACE PROBES

Most spacecraft are sent into space without astronauts or scientists on board. These spacecraft are called space probes. They are sent beyond the orbit of the Earth to explore and study the sun, the other planets and their moons, and other objects in our solar system. Onboard instruments such as cameras, radar, and other sensors send valuable information back to astronomers on Earth.

▶ EARLY SPACE PROBES

Sputnik I, launched by the former Soviet Union on October 4, 1957, is usually considered a space probe even though it only orbited the Earth. No other object made by human beings had ever ventured into space. *Sputnik I* was the first to "probe" the unknown environment around the Earth.

During the 1950's and 1960's, the Earth's moon was a frequent target of space probes. Some, like the *Ranger* probes launched by the United States, carried cameras that sent back pictures to Earth before smashing into the moon's surface. Others orbited the moon and mapped

Above: In 2004, the *Cassini* space probe became the first to orbit the planet Saturn. *Right: Sputnik I*, the first space probe, was launched in 1957.

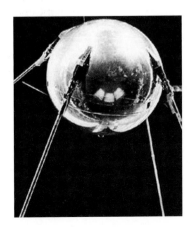

its surface. By the mid-1960's, space probes had landed successfully on the moon.

▶ EXPLORING VENUS

The first attempts to send a probe to Venus were not successful. But in 1962, the United States successfully launched *Mariner 2*, which became the first probe to fly past another planet. It discovered that Venus had a surface temperature of more than 750°F (400°C) and an atmosphere dense with clouds. In 1970, the former Soviet Union's *Venera 7* became the first vehicle to land on Venus and to send back data. Some probes to Venus sent back color photographs and radar maps of the planet's surface. The European Space Agency's first mission to the planet was the *Venus Express*. The probe reached Venus in 2006 and began a detailed study of the atmosphere.

▶ EXPLORING MARS

The first attempts to explore Mars were also failures. But the United States was again the first to succeed when *Mariner 4* flew by the planet in 1965. *Mariner 4* had a simple camera that could take only 22 black-and-white pictures. The images showed many craters and dry plains. Later *Mariners* were better equipped. They photographed more of the planet's surface and detected

333

IMPORTANT SPACE PROBES

*The former Soviet Union
**European Space Agency

Craft	Sponsor	Launched	Flight Information
Sputnik 1	U.S.S.R.*	Oct. 4, 1957	First artificial satellite.
Luna 3	U.S.S.R.*	Oct. 4, 1959	First photographs of the far side of the moon.
Mariner 2	U.S.A.	Aug. 27, 1962	First planetary flyby (Venus).
Ranger 7	U.S.A.	July 28, 1964	First close-up images of the moon's surface.
Mariner 4	U.S.A.	Nov. 28, 1964	First photographs of the surface of Mars.
Luna 9	U.S.S.R.*	Jan. 31, 1966	First soft landing on the moon.
Surveyor 1	U.S.A.	May 30, 1966	Moon lander analyzed soil; sent back 11,000 photographs of the surface that were used to select landing sites for Apollo moon landings.
Venera 7	U.S.S.R.*	Aug. 17, 1970	First probe to successfully land on another planet, Venus; sent back data.
Luna 17	U.S.S.R.*	Nov. 10, 1970	Landed automated vehicle on the moon, which made studies of its surface.
Mars 2	U.S.S.R.*	May 19, 1971	Lander became first human-built craft to reach surface of Mars.
Mariner 9	U.S.A.	May 30, 1971	First probe to orbit a planet other than the Earth, Mars; sent back images of craters, canyons, and volcanoes on Martian surface.
Pioneer 10	U.S.A.	March 2, 1972	First close-up probe of Jupiter; sent back photographs of the planet; provided information about Jupiter's atmosphere and its structure. In June 1983, *Pioneer 10* became the first artificial object to leave the solar system.
Pioneer 11	U.S.A.	April 5, 1973	Flybys of Jupiter (Dec. 1974) and Saturn (Sept. 1979); detected a polar icecap on one of Jupiter's satellites; discovered one more ring around Saturn and possibly more satellites.
Mariner 10	U.S.A.	Nov. 3, 1973	First good pictures of Venus' clouds; first close-up photographs of Mercury.
Venera 9	U.S.S.R.*	June 8, 1975	Transmitted first images from surface of Venus.
Viking 1/2	U.S.A.	Aug. 20, 1975/ Sept. 9, 1975	Deployed landers on Mars; photographed entire planet; analyzed the planet's soil and atmosphere; measured temperature on Martian surface.
Voyager 2	U.S.A.	Aug. 20, 1977	Flybys of Jupiter (July 1979), Saturn (Aug. 1981), Uranus (Jan. 1986), and Neptune (Aug. 1989). Discovered volcanic activity on Jupiter's moon, Io; provided close-up photographs of the rings and satellites of Jupiter, Saturn, Uranus, and Neptune.

Luna 3

Far side of the moon

Uranus' moon Miranda

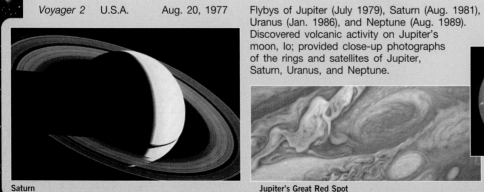

Saturn

Jupiter's Great Red Spot

Neptune

IMPORTANT SPACE PROBES

Craft	Sponsor	Launched	Flight Information
Voyager 1	U.S.A.	Sept. 5, 1977	Flybys of Jupiter (March 1979) and Saturn (Nov. 1980). Found new moons around both planets, and a new ring around Saturn.
Giotto	ESA**	July 2, 1985	Flew to within 367 miles of Halley's comet; took detailed images of its nucleus.
Galileo	U.S.A.	Oct. 18, 1989	Orbited Jupiter; released separate probe into the planet's atmosphere; found evidence of liquid salt water on three of the large moons; first probe to fly by an asteroid.
Ulysses	U.S.A./ ESA**	Oct. 6, 1990	First probe to study polar regions of the sun.
NEAR (*Near Earth Asteroid Rendezvous*) *Shoemaker*	U.S.A.	Feb. 17, 1996	First probe to land on an asteroid (Eros); analyzed its geology, mass, and other properties.
Mars Global Surveyor	U.S.A.	Nov. 7, 1996	Orbited Mars to take pictures and conduct detailed surface mapping.
Mars Pathfinder	U.S.A.	Dec. 4, 1996	Landed on Mars; delivered first surface rover, *Sojourner*; analyzed atmosphere, weather, and geology.
Cassini	U.S.A./ ESA**	Oct. 15, 1997	First probe to orbit Saturn; studied its rings and moons; deployed *Huygens* probe, which landed on Titan.
Stardust	U.S.A.	Feb. 7, 1999	Rendezvoused with comet Wild-2 and collected samples of dust from its coma; returned samples to Earth in 2006.
Genesis	U.S.A.	Aug. 8, 2001	Collected samples from the sun's solar wind and returned them to Earth.
Hayabusa	Japan/ U.S.A.	May 9, 2003	Collected samples from an asteroid and will eventually return them to Earth.
Spirit/ Opportunity	U.S.A.	June 10, 2003/ July 7, 2003	Twin surface rovers deployed on Mars; found evidence of liquid water in planet's past.
Deep Impact	U.S.A.	Jan.12, 2005	Deployed device that collided with comet Tempel 1; studied results of impact.
New Horizons	U.S.A.	Jan. 19, 2006	Sent to rendezvous with Pluto and its moons to photograph them, analyze their compositions, and map their surfaces.

Nucleus of Halley's comet

Jupiter's moon Io

Asteroid Eros

Saturn's moon Titan from *Huygens*

Saturn's moon Enceladus

Rover *Spirit* on surface of Mars

a thin atmosphere with little oxygen and temperatures far below zero.

When *Mariner 9* reached Mars in 1971, it was the first probe to orbit a planet other than the Earth. The probe found giant volcanoes as well as countless channels that seemed to have been formed by flowing water. These discoveries suggested that Mars may have had a more Earthlike past. It may have even supported life. To learn more, a probe would have to land on Mars.

Landing on Mars. The former Soviet Union's *Mars 2* and *Mars 3* space probes both reached the planet within a few weeks of *Mariner 9*. *Mars 2* ejected a small capsule containing a Soviet flag. It became the first human-built craft to reach the surface.

In 1976 the U.S. *Viking 1* and *Viking 2* space probes entered orbit around Mars. *Viking 1* sent its lander to the surface, where it took photographs and studied soil samples for signs of life. *Viking 2*'s lander later provided more data.

In 1997 the American spacecraft *Mars Pathfinder* and its robotic rover, *Sojourner*, landed on July 4 to investigate Martian surface and atmospheric features. On September 12, the *Mars Global Surveyor* eased into orbit around Mars to conduct a two-year mapping and data-collecting mission.

In 2004 the twin Mars Exploration Rovers *Spirit* and *Opportunity* touched down on opposite sides of the planet. They began to analyze Martian rock and soil for evidence of water. The rovers discovered compelling— but not conclusive—evidence for the past presence of liquid water. They also provided vast amounts of information about the planet's geology. In 2006 the *Mars Reconnaissance Orbiter* arrived in orbit around the planet to learn if water had ever existed on the surface long enough to give rise to life.

▶ EXPLORING MERCURY

The U.S. *Mariner 10* was the first probe to use the gravity of a planet to help propel it to another planet, Mercury. This process is called **gravity assist**. It has been used by other probes to alter their direction and increase their speed.

In 1974, *Mariner 10* reached Venus and passed just 3,580 miles (5,764 kilometers) above the planet's clouds. The images transmitted from the probe's cameras were the first good pictures of the planet's clouds. Cameras sensitive to ultraviolet light revealed details not easily seen in normal light. These images helped astronomers better understand the planet's atmosphere.

With a gravity assist from Venus, *Mariner 10* then flew to Mercury. There it took thousands of pictures of the heavily cratered planet. It also gathered information about the planet's core, atmosphere, and magnetic field.

The latest probe sent to Mercury, *MESSENGER* (MErcury Surface, Space ENvironment, GEochemistry, and Ranging), was launched by the United States in 2004. The probe is scheduled to reach Mercury in 2011. Once in orbit, *MESSENGER* will conduct an in-depth analysis of the planet's geology, magnetic field, and other physical properties.

▶ EXPLORING THE OUTER PLANETS

Only the United States has sent space probes to the outer planets. *Pioneer 10*, launched in 1972, became the first probe to reach Jupiter. *Pioneer 11* followed about a year later. Relatively simple spacecraft, these probes helped pave the way for later, more advanced probes.

The *Pioneer*s were followed by *Voyager 1* and *Voyager 2*, both launched in 1977. When these probes reached Jupiter, they took highly detailed pictures of the planet's clouds and its largest satellites. They also discovered

The robotic rover *Sojourner* was deployed on the surface of Mars by the *Mars Pathfinder* space probe. The rover studied the planet's surface and atmospheric features.

a thin ring around Jupiter that was not visible from Earth. From Jupiter, *Voyager 1* sped on to Saturn, arriving in 1979. The probe took pictures of the planet and Titan, its largest satellite. The probe discovered that Titan had an atmosphere denser than the Earth's and composed mostly of nitrogen.

Voyager 1 was unable to visit more planets due to the course it followed to get a close look at Titan. *Voyager 2*, however, took a path that allowed it to study Saturn's rings more closely. That placed it on course for the more distant planets. When *Voyager 2* reached Uranus in 1986, it took pictures of the planet's rings, discovered ten new satellites, and detected a magnetic field on the planet. In 1989, *Voyager 2* arrived at Neptune. It discovered six satellites, several rings, and fascinating cloud features in the planet's stormy atmosphere.

The *Galileo* probe reached Jupiter in 1995. It deployed a probe of its own that penetrated the planet's thick clouds and analyzed the physical properties of the atmosphere. *Galileo* discovered strong evidence of liquid water on some of Jupiter's large moons, as well as noticeable surface changes on Io because of the moon's active volcanoes.

In 2004 the *Cassini* became the first space probe to orbit Saturn. Its four-year mission is to study the planet and its rings and moons. The probe soon found new moons and a new radiation belt. *Cassini* deployed another probe, the European Space Agency's *Huygens*, to study the moon Titan. The *Huygens* gathered valuable information as it descended through the moon's atmosphere and landed on its barren surface.

The first space probe sent to study Pluto, which is now considered a dwarf planet instead of a true planet, was launched in 2006. This probe, called *New Horizons*, is expected to reach Pluto in 2015.

▸ **OTHER PROBES**

When Halley's comet entered the inner solar system in 1986, the European Space Agency's *Giotto* approached to within about 370 miles (596 kilometers) of the comet's nucleus and provided the most revealing pic-

In 2005, the *Deep Impact* space probe rendezvoused with the comet Tempel 1. It deployed a device that collided with the comet's core, releasing a bright plume of debris.

tures of a comet to date. In 2004 the United States' *Stardust* rendezvoused with the comet Wild-2 and collected samples of dust from its coma. The probe returned the samples to Earth in 2006. The American space probe *Deep Impact* rendezvoused with the comet Tempel 1 in 2005. It deployed a device that collided with the comet's core and then analyzed the results of the impact.

In 2001 the American *NEAR* (*Near Earth Asteroid Rendezvous*) *Shoemaker* probe became the first spacecraft to land on an asteroid. In 2003, Japan and the United States launched *Hayabusa*. This probe landed on another asteroid and obtained samples. It will return to Earth with them by about 2010.

Space probes have also been sent to the sun to study its atmosphere, magnetic field, and other properties. The *Ulysses*, a joint project of NASA and the European Space Agency, was launched in 1990. It was the first probe to study the sun's polar regions. In 2001, *Genesis* was sent to collect samples of the solar wind, a stream of charged particles flowing from the sun. The probe returned to Earth in 2004. The samples it carried provided new insights into how the solar system evolved millions of years ago.

JOSEPH KELCH
Davis Planetarium
Maryland Science Center

See also OBSERVATORIES; SPACE EXPLORATION AND TRAVEL; SPACE TELESCOPES; articles on individual planets.

BALLET

Ballet is a French word that comes from the Italian verb *ballare*, which means "to dance." A ballet is performed in a theater for entertainment. It combines dance with other art forms, usually stage design and music. Ballets can tell stories, from fairy tales such as *The Sleeping Beauty* to modern topics. Or they can merely depict an idea or mood.

Ballet technique is strict, and the training is strenuous. But the result on stage is natural and beautiful. The movements are designed to display the human body in the most elegant and harmonious way possible.

Classical ballet is most often characterized by a female dancer, called a ballerina, dancing on pointe (on the tips of her toes). Sometimes she is assisted by a male partner, called a danseur. A danseur can lift the ballerina into the air and keep her steady as she turns. The principal dancers are called the prima ballerina and the premier danseur. When the two principal dancers perform alone together, the dance is called a pas de deux. A group of dancers, called a corps de ballet, often accompanies the principal dancers. The dance steps are created by a choreographer.

Clockwise from above: Mikhail Baryshnikov, known for his energy and astounding leaps, was one of the most celebrated premier danseurs of the 20th century. Prima ballerina Darcey Bussell performs *The Nutcracker* with Jonathan Cope at the Royal Ballet in London; an instructor teaches an aspiring ballerina the five basic positions of ballet; the part of Odette, the white swan in *Swan Lake,* is one of the most famous roles in the history of ballet.

A student demonstrates her work in pointe shoes (*detail below*) for her instructor. Ballet requires rigorous physical discipline.

Ballet began in Italy about the time of Columbus' voyages to America. It was quite different then from what it is today. At that time ballet was a court entertainment for the amusement of the nobility at lavish balls and banquets. The steps were modeled on the elegant but rather simple social dances of the day.

Ballet as we know it today is the product of many countries. The French organized the technique and gave it liveliness. The Russians added strength and passion. The English gave it delicacy and tenderness. The Americans gave it speed and variety.

▶ TRAINING

A ballet teacher must have a sound understanding of ballet technique and the human anatomy. He or she must also understand the relationship of rhythm to dance. This is known as musicality. The teacher guides the students through the basic movements that make up the classroom exercises. He or she should be able to give instructions to individual dancers as well as to the entire class. Finally, the teacher must be firm yet patient.

The Ballet Studio

The ideal ballet studio is a large room, preferably the size and shape of a stage. The floor should be sprung. This means it is specially built to absorb the weight of jumping. A sprung floor helps dancers avoid injury from high impact. If the floor is wooden, dancers may apply rosin (hardened pine sap) to their slippers to give them traction. Sometimes a rubberized surface is used.

One of the studio walls is covered in mirrors. This helps the students check their positions and alignment. Handrails, called barres, are placed at waist height. The dancer holds on to them with one hand for support while doing the exercises. Most studios have a piano or sound system for musical accompaniment.

Clothing

Dancers need to wear close-fitting clothes so that the teacher may check for correct placement. Girls wear a leotard and tights. Boys wear tights, usually with a white T-shirt tucked in. Soft, snug slippers of either canvas or leather are necessary. After age 10, if the

turnout, because doing so can lead to serious injuries. Port de bras, in which the arms pass from one position to another, is also practiced at the barre.

Barre Exercises. Warm-up exercises begin with a series of pliés, or knee bends. Pliés are followed by *relevés*. This is an opposite action, in which the dancer rises up onto the balls of the feet. Pliés, *relevés*, and *tendus* (foot "stretches") are followed by various battements (or "beatings"), where one foot beats against the other. In *battement tendu*, the foot is stretched along the floor until it is fully arched. The toes are lengthened into what is called a pointed foot. In *battement dégagé*, the foot passes through *tendu*. It then "disengages" by brushing a few inches off the ground into the air.

Next the dancer practices circling motions of the leg, called *rond de jambe à terre*. The dancer begins in fifth position, brushes the foot to *tendu* front, makes a half-circle along the floor to *tendu* back, and passes through

teacher feels a girl has become strong enough in her technique, she may begin to work on pointe.

A Typical Class

A ballet class normally lasts an hour and a half. It begins with exercises at the barre, using the five basic positions. Barre exercises help dancers develop strength and improve their turnout. Turnout is when the legs are rotated outward from the hip joint. The amount of one's turnout depends on flexibility in the hip socket. It is important not to force

The Five Basic Positions of Ballet (Arms and Feet)

| 1st position | 2nd position | 3rd position | 4th position | 5th position |

Above left: The French king Louis XIV became known as the Sun King for his performances as the Greek god Apollo. *Above:* Marie Carmargo shortened her skirts so audiences could better appreciate her footwork.

first position to begin again. The exercise is then reversed, starting to the back. This is followed by *rond de jambe en l'air.* One leg is lifted in second position at 90 degrees in the air. The raised foot then traces an oval shape as it comes in to the knee of the standing leg, and then stretches back out.

The dancers then practice *frappé,* which means "struck." The foot raises and flexes at the ankle, with its heel touching the front of the other ankle of the supporting leg. The ball of the raised foot sweeps the floor and ends with a straight gesture leg in a *dégagé.*

The last exercise at the barre is *grand battement,* or "big beating." Its motion is the same as the *dégagé,* but the foot continues into the air, taking the leg as high as it can without raising the hip.

Floor Exercises. The dancers then move to the center of the room, where they dance without the help of the barre. Center work generally begins with an adagio, which develops balance. This is followed by a grand waltz combination that includes various turns and other steps. Then comes a series of small, quick jumps known as *petit allegro.* The dancers end their practice with *grand allegro.* At this stage, they are ready to soar through the air with larger leaps and bigger jumps.

Révérence. When the class is over, dancers perform a *révérence* to show respect to their teacher and the pianist. This is done with a series of bows and curtsies to slow music, followed by applause.

▶ **HISTORY**

Ballet developed as an art form about 500 years ago, at the height of the period known as the Renaissance. In 1547, Catherine de Médicis of Florence brought Italian dancing masters to France when she married the French king Henri II. When they performed at court, many people were impressed by the richness of their elaborate ballets. Soon these spectacles came to represent the power and glory of France.

In the mid-1600's, ballet was performed at the royal palace of King Louis XIV. The king himself, along with members of his court, usually took part. Typically, these baroque-period ballets were based on stories from Greek mythology. Louis often danced the role of Apollo. As a result he became known as the Sun King. (For more information, see the Wonder Question in the biography of Louis XIV.) Louis took dancing lessons daily from his dancing master, Pierre Beauchamp. Beauchamp helped establish ballet technique. He defined the five basic ballet positions. He also formulated a dance notation system, which provided symbols for the steps and floor patterns to guide the dancers.

In 1961, American ballet choreographer Jerome Robbins adapted his Broadway dance sequences for the movie production of *West Side Story*, a modern retelling of *Romeo and Juliet*.

the moods and emotions of its characters. The ballet was considered a commentary on modern society. Another Ballet Theater choreographer, Agnes de Mille, created ballets based on American themes. Among the most famous were *Rodeo* (1943), and *Fall River Legend* (1948). She also developed the dance sequences for the popular Broadway musical *Oklahoma* (1943).

Jerome Robbins, a former co-director for New York City Ballet, was an inventive choreographer. He brought jazz, tap, and social dancing into his ballets. He also choreographed for Broadway musicals and films, such as *West Side Story* and *Fiddler on the Roof*.

In 1940, Lucia Chase and Richard Pleasant began the Ballet Theater in New York City. Now known as American Ballet Theatre (ABT), it is one of the most famous repertory companies in the world. Antony Tudor became one of its many choreographers. His *Lilac Garden*, first performed in 1936, showed

Modern Themes

As far back as the 1930's, ballet has been used to express modern themes. One early example is Kurt Jooss's anti-war ballet, *The Green Table* (1932). Many choreographers continue to use ballet to make a statement about society. British director and choreographer Matthew Bourne transformed the classic *Swan Lake* (1995) by replacing the swans, typically played by ballerinas, with an all-male cast. Mats Ek of Sweden choreographed a modern version of *The Sleeping Beauty* (1996) that deals with the problems of city life.

The blending of ballet with dance from around the world is also seen in the work of Jiri Kylian of the Nederlands Dance Theater. Kylian researched the dances of the Aboriginal tribes of Australia. He then used their movements in his ballet *Stamping Ground* (1983). In some instances, choreographers, such as William Forsythe of the Frankfurt Ballet, have used classical ballet in a stark, modern way in abstract dances that have no story. All these possibilities ensure that ballet will continue to move in many new directions in the years to come.

DORIS HERING
Critic-at-large, *Dance Magazine*

PATRICIA BEAMAN
Department of Dance
Tisch School of the Arts
New York University

The Dance Theatre of Harlem (DTH) was founded in 1969 by Arthur Mitchell, a veteran of the New York City Ballet. Mitchell was the first African American to dance principal roles for a major ballet company.

RODENTS

Rodents are among the most abundant animals on Earth. About 40 percent of all mammals in the world are rodents, which belong to the scientific order Rodentia. There are about 2,000 species of rodents divided into about 30 different groups, or families. They include familiar animals such as rats, mice, squirrels, beavers, guinea pigs, and woodchucks. Less well known rodents include cavies, capybaras, chinchillas, gundis, and pacas.

Rodents live on every continent except Antarctica. And they have successfully adapted to just about every kind of habitat. Some rodents, such as lemmings, thrive on the cold, harsh arctic tundra. Gerbils live in deserts. Beavers and muskrats live in and around water. Some kinds of squirrels rarely leave the trees. Mole rats spend their entire lives underground.

▶ **CHARACTERISTICS OF RODENTS**

The most distinguishing characteristic shared by all rodents is their teeth. They have two prominent front teeth, called **incisors**, which they use to gnaw, or chew. In fact, the term "rodent" comes from the Latin word *rodere*, meaning "to gnaw." Rodents gnaw on everything, including trees, seeds, tough grasses, and nut shells. They even gnaw on the electrical wiring in people's homes. They gnaw so much because their incisors grow throughout their lives and constantly need to be worn down. Rodents have no canine teeth behind their incisors. Instead, they have a space between their incisors and their chewing molars. When a rodent gnaws, it draws its lips into this gap. This prevents fragments of the material the animal is gnawing from getting into its mouth.

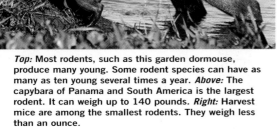

Top: Most rodents, such as this garden dormouse, produce many young. Some rodent species can have as many as ten young several times a year. *Above:* The capybara of Panama and South America is the largest rodent. It can weigh up to 140 pounds. *Right:* Harvest mice are among the smallest rodents. They weigh less than an ounce.

This article provides a general overview of the animals classified as rodents. For more information on specific kinds of rodents, see the articles BEAVERS; GUINEA PIGS, HAMSTERS, AND GERBILS; PORCUPINES; RATS AND MICE; and SQUIRRELS, WOODCHUCKS, AND CHIPMUNKS in the appropriate volumes.

Rodents typically have stout, compact bodies with short legs. Some South American rodents that live among tall grasses have longer, more sturdy legs than most rodents. Rodents have various kinds of tails. Burrowing species, such as prairie dogs and hamsters, have short tails. Tree-dwelling species, such as squirrels, have long furry tails that they use to balance themselves as they climb and jump. Beavers have broad, flat tails for swimming. Rats and mice have long, naked tails. The springhare, which hops about like a kangaroo, has a very long and bushy tail.

The capybara of Panama and South America is the largest rodent in the world. It can reach 24 inches (60 centimeters) tall at the shoulder and be as long as 53 inches (134 centimeters). A capybara can weigh up to 140 pounds (63 kilograms). Capybaras are social animals that spend a lot of time in the water. Their webbed feet help them swim. They communicate using barks and whistles.

Among the smallest rodents are pygmy mice, harvest mice, and pygmy jerboas. They weigh less than an ounce. Jerboas are desert animals. They have long tails and hop on their hind feet.

▶ LIVES OF RODENTS

Rodents are mainly vegetarians. They eat various kinds of plant food such as leaves, fruits, and nuts. Some will also feed on small animals such as grasshoppers and spiders. Squirrels sometimes eat bird eggs and nestlings (baby birds). A few rodents, such as the Australian water rat, eat only meat.

Rodents generally have very acute senses. Their sense of smell is very well developed. Burrowing rodents that spend much time underground often have small eyes. Their eyesight is poor. Rodents communicate by sight, sound, and smell. Many make loud whistles, and many species use smell in reproductive behavior. A rodent's whiskers are very sensitive to touch.

Rodents generally produce many young. Some species can have litters of up to ten offspring several times a year. When food is plentiful, rodent populations can soar. As many as 80,000 house mice have been recorded living within a single acre of land. Some species of rodents can reproduce when they are only a month old.

The life span of rodents varies widely. Some live less than two years. Others can live for twenty years. Generally, the smaller the animal, the shorter its life span.

The most distinguishing characteristic all rodents share is their large front teeth, or incisors. These teeth grow continuously, so rodents keep them worn down by gnawing on everything, including large nuts.

Rodents exhibit a wide range of behavior. Some are active during the day, others during the night. Some species are solitary, but others are very social. The most social rodents are naked mole rats, which live in underground colonies in Africa. Their social structure is similar to ants. The colony revolves around a single female, like a queen ant, who breeds with just a few males. The rest of the colony is divided into distinct groups, or castes. Small workers dig and gather food and

Prairie dogs are one of several species of rodents that live underground. Like other burrowing rodents, prairie dogs have short tails. These animals dig extensive burrows in which large family groups live.

in spring. Some, such as marmots, gather in family groups and curl up together to sleep through the winter. They wake about once a month to eliminate waste. For more information, see the article HIBERNATION in Volume H.

▶ RODENTS AND THEIR ENVIRONMENT

Rodents are an important part of the ecosystems in which they live. They are a source of food for many different animals, including hawks and other birds, foxes, and other mammals. People have raised guinea pigs as food for thousands of years. Beavers were a major part of the fur trade in colonial America. Nutrias and chinchillas are raised in captivity for their fur.

nesting materials. Another caste consists of a few larger adults that spend most of their time guarding the breeding female.

In areas where winters are long and cold, some rodents hibernate. In hibernation, the heart rate, breathing rate, and body temperature of the animal drop to low levels. This conserves energy. Some species, such as the common dormouse of Europe, hibernate for as long as nine months. Other species store food in their burrows and wake up now and then to feed during the winter. Others only eat the stored food when they first wake up

Because they are intelligent and easy to raise in captivity, some species of rodents make good pets. Guinea pigs, gerbils, hamsters, rats, and mice are especially popular. These same traits, as well as a rapid rate of reproduction, have also made rodents ideal for use in scientific research. For example, rodents have been vital to the development of vaccines for diseases and in studies of how animals learn and how genes work.

Their large numbers and adaptability, however, have also made some species of rodents serious economic pests. Every year, millions of dollars worth of crops are destroyed by rodents such as the house mouse, the roof rat, and the Norway rat. Some species of squirrels, wild hamsters, and voles also consume crops and damage property. Rodents can also carry diseases such as the plague and typhus.

Like other kinds of animals, many species of rodents are endangered today. This is mostly because of habitat destruction by people clearing land to grow crops or build homes. About 15 percent of all rodent species are considered either endangered or vulnerable to extinction. Many of these live in specialized or limited habitats in parts of the world where human populations are growing rapidly.

DOROTHY H. PATENT
Author, science and nature books for children

WONDER QUESTION

Are rabbits rodents?

Rabbits are not rodents, although they were once thought to belong to the order Rodentia. Like rodents, rabbits have large incisors that they use for gnawing. But they also have a second pair of incisors behind the gnawing ones. This difference is the primary reason scientists now classify rabbits in the order Lagomorpha. This order also includes hares and pikas. For more information about rabbits and their relatives, see the article RABBITS AND HARES in Volume QR.

349

RATS AND MICE

Rats and mice belong to the group of gnawing mammals called rodents. Scientists have debated for years about the best way to classify rats and mice within this group. But today rats and mice are usually placed in the Muridae family. This family of rodents includes more than 1,000 species. It also accounts for more than one-quarter of all

Like most rodents, rats and mice produce many offspring and have adapted to almost every kind of environment. *Above:* A deer mouse nurses her young. *Right:* A black rat rests on a pipe.

mammals worldwide. In addition to the animals commonly called rats and mice, this family also includes voles, lemmings, hamsters, muskrats, and gerbils. Some animals that are called rats or mice belong to different families of rodents. These include pocket mice and kangaroo rats.

Rats and mice are further divided into two groups. Old world rats and mice are native to Europe, Asia, and Africa. These animals include the Norway rat and the common house mouse. New World rats and mice live from northwestern Canada to the tip of South America. Members of this group include the deer, or white-footed, mouse and the Andean rat. Rats and mice are not native to Antarctica, New Zealand, and a few small islands. But wherever people have gone, rats and mice have followed. These rodents are now

found just about everywhere people are. And they have adapted to just about every kind of environment.

▶ CHARACTERISTICS OF RATS AND MICE

Most rats and mice have pointed muzzles, small eyes, and long whiskers. Most also have long tails that are hairless or covered with very fine hair. Species that live in trees usually have relatively long tails. Burrowing species have shorter ones.

Rats and mice have four sharp teeth, called incisors, at the front of the mouth. These incisors are used for gnawing, and they grow continuously throughout the animal's life. Gnawing wears away the incisors, keeping them from getting too long. Rats and mice also have twelve chewing molars. These are separated from the incisors by a toothless gap.

Generally, animals called rats are bigger than those called mice. Mice can be very tiny, such as the pygmy mouse. This animal weighs only ¼ ounce (7 grams) and is 2 to

RATS AND MICE AS PETS

Domestic rats and mice are popular pets. They are hardy and easy to care for. They can be tamed by frequent, gentle handling. With either species, it is best to keep two together for companionship. Rats are more intelligent and interactive pets. They require larger cages and more attention. You should handle a pet rat for at least an hour a day.

Glass aquariums and wire cages are both suitable for housing your pet. Aquariums should have tight-fitting screen lids. The bottom of the cage should be covered with appropriate bedding material, such as wood shavings (except cedar or pine, which can harm your pet). This should be changed at least once a week. You should also provide your pets with nesting material, such as strips of torn-up paper towels.

Make your pets' environment interesting and stimulating for them. Give them objects that they can climb on or crawl through. These objects can include cardboard tubes from rolls of toilet paper or paper towels. Larger tubes and tunnels for rats are

available at pet stores. An empty tissue box provides a safe place to hide or sleep.

Various kinds of pellet food for rats, mice, and similar animals are available at pet shops. These pellets provide all the proper nutrients your pets need. But rats and mice appreciate occasional treats of seeds or fresh fruits or vegetables. Your pets must also have a water bottle. The bottle should always contain fresh water. It should also be cleaned regularly.

3 inches (5 to 8 centimeters) long. Its tail is only about 1½ to 2 inches (4 to 5 centimeters) long. The largest rat is the rare slender-tailed cloud rat, which lives in the forests of the Philippines. It can weigh up to 4½ pounds (2 kilograms). Its body can measure 19 inches (48 centimeters) long. Its tail is an additional 13 inches (33 centimeters) long.

▶ LIVES OF RATS AND MICE

Like most rodents, rats and mice produce many offspring. There are often about twelve young in a litter. Some species can have several litters of young a year. The young mature quickly. Soon they can produce their own young.

Small mice live only a year or two, but large rats may live for several years. Rats and mice feed mostly on plant material. They use their sharp incisors to cut off blades of grass or crack the shells of seeds and nuts. A few species, such as the fish-eating rats, eat other animals.

Although some rats and mice can live in large groups, they are essentially solitary. They communicate with one another with squeaks and whistles. Their sense of smell is often used in mating behavior.

▶ RATS AND MICE AND THEIR ENVIRONMENT

Rats and mice play an important role in the ecologies of their environments. They are a major source of food for predators such as snakes and birds.

Some wild rats and mice are considered pests by people. These animals, particularly the roof rat, Norway rat, and house mouse, damage property, eat crops, and carry diseases. But domesticated forms of both the house mouse and the Norway rat have been important to science. They are used for research in animal behavior, genetics, and medicine.

DOROTHY HINSHAW PATENT
Author, science and nature books for children

SQUIRRELS, WOODCHUCKS, AND CHIPMUNKS

Squirrels, woodchucks, and chipmunks are rodents belonging to the scientific family Sciuridae. This family consists of more than 270 species, which also includes prairie dogs and marmots. These adaptable animals are found

Clockwise from above:
Woodchucks and other kinds of marmots are the largest members of the squirrel family. Chipmunks carry food by stuffing it into cheek pouches. Flying squirrels use membranes between their front and hind legs to glide through the air.

on every continent except Antarctica and Australia. They live in habitats ranging from wet tropical rain forests to hot, dry deserts to snowy rocky mountains. Many species live in trees. Others live in complex underground burrows.

▶ **CHARACTERISTICS OF SQUIRRELS, WOODCHUCKS, AND CHIPMUNKS**

Squirrels and their relatives typically have long bodies with short front legs and longer hind ones. They have large eyes with sharp vision. Tree-dwelling species have long bushy tails. They use their tails to balance themselves as they scurry and jump among branches. Burrowing squirrels, such as prairie dogs and ground squirrels, mostly have short furry tails. Flying squirrels have a furry membrane that stretches from the front legs to the hind legs on each side of the body. After leaping into the air, a flying squirrel does not truly fly. Instead, it spreads out its legs so that the membrane forms a wide kite-like parachute that slows the animal's descent. The flying squirrel controls its glide by moving its legs and using its tail as a rudder.

The smallest squirrel is the African pygmy squirrel. Its body measures about 3 inches (8 centimeters) long and its tail about 6 inches (15 centimeters). It weighs less than an ounce.

Woodchucks, also called groundhogs, are a kind of marmot. They have strong, stocky bodies and broad heads. They measure about 18 inches (46 centimeters) long with a 7-inch (18-centimeter) tail. They weigh about 10 pounds (4.5 kilograms). Woodchucks and other marmots are the largest members of the squirrel family.

Chipmunks are small squirrels with striped coats. They live mostly on the ground but climb trees for food. The common Eastern chipmunk is about 5 inches (13 centimeters) long with a 4-inch (10-centimeter) tail.

LIVES OF SQUIRRELS, WOODCHUCKS, AND CHIPMUNKS

Members of this family feed mostly on plant material. Some, like prairie dogs, eat grasses and herbs. Squirrels prefer nuts and seeds. Some tree squirrels and chipmunks also eat insects, bird eggs, and nestlings (baby birds). Many species have cheek pouches for carrying food.

These animals are often very vocal, making loud whistles and barks. Prairie dogs use calls to warn of danger. Marmots whistle loudly at intruders. Chipmunks make chirping sounds much like birds.

Young are born blind and naked. Litter size depends on the species and the mother's health. Litters range from just one or two young to as many as nine or more. In most species, the mother raises the young without help from her mate. In a typical species such as the red squirrel, the young grow fast. They are able to live on their own by 8 weeks of age.

Some species of marmots and ground squirrels live in colonies with large,

Bird feeders are commonly raided by squirrels. These intelligent—and agile—rodents are not easily kept from a food source.

complex underground burrows. Prairie dogs live in groups of families called **coteries**. A black-tailed prairie dog coterie consists of one male with from one to six females, their 1-year-old offspring, and the newest young. Coteries live together in larger groups called **towns**. Before the settlement of the American West, prairie dog towns with hundreds of thousands or even millions of animals were common.

During the winter, many members of the squirrel family that live in cold climates hibernate. They spend most of the time in a very deep sleep. During this sleep, their body temperature and heart rate are lowered. Now and then, their body temperature may rise and they wake up to feed on stored food. Some desert species will enter a similar state, called estivation, to survive periods of extreme heat or drought.

SQUIRRELS, WOODCHUCKS, AND CHIPMUNKS AND THEIR ENVIRONMENT

Squirrels, woodchucks, and chipmunks are often considered pests. They are particularly troublesome to farmers and ranchers. The animals eat crops, and the holes to their burrows can be hazardous to livestock, who may step in them and injure themselves. Their burrows can also damage irrigation channels. Squirrels are common visitors to bird feeders, eating the seeds and chasing away birds. Squirrels are intelligent and usually find a way around attempts to keep them off bird feeders. Squirrels may also kill trees by stripping bark from them. Some squirrels carry diseases such as bubonic plague and Rocky Mountain spotted fever.

But these animals also play an important role in their environment. They are a source of food for many predators, such as hawks, owls, coyotes, and foxes. Their tunneling circulates and aerates (adds air to) the soil. And some of the seeds they bury for winter food are left uneaten and grow into trees.

Around the world, fifty species in this family are considered endangered. These include some prairie dogs and marmots and many flying squirrels.

DOROTHY HINSHAW PATENT
Author, science and nature books for children

See also RODENTS.

353

AUTOMOBILE RACING

Automobile racing is a fast-paced, exciting sport in which two or more cars compete against each other. It is not just the speed of a car that determines the winner of a race. The skill and endurance of the driver are equally important.

Racing automobiles is a dangerous sport. Strict regulations govern the designs of the cars; the equipment worn by the drivers, such as helmets, suits, and restraints; and even the barriers separating the spectators from the track. These and other measures are meant to ensure a highly competitive race in a safe environment for all.

Automobile racing is popular around the world. Stock-car racing has been called one of the fastest-growing sports in the United States. It is better known by the name of its governing body, NASCAR. Every year, mil-lions of people across the country attend NASCAR races or watch them on television.

▶ KINDS OF AUTOMOBILE RACING

Automobile racing worldwide is governed by the Fédération Internationale de l'Automobile (FIA), headquartered in Paris, France. Separate governing organizations usually exist for each kind of racing as well. In addition to NASCAR, other popular kinds of automobile racing today include Formula One, Indy car, drag, off road, land speed, sprint and midget car, and endurance.

NASCAR

NASCAR (the National Association for Stock Car Auto Racing) is the most popular form of racing in the United States. The organization was founded in 1947, only a few years after stock-car racing developed in the southeastern United States. At first, drivers raced standard passenger, or stock, cars (with slight modifications to the engines). Modern stock cars look like standard passenger cars, but they are built specifically for racing. They have larger and more powerful engines, reinforced bodies, and many safety features.

Early tracks were small dirt ovals. As this form of racing grew in popularity,

Left: NASCAR is the most popular form of auto racing in the United States. *Below:* A pit crew services an Indy race car during the Indianapolis 500. The Indianapolis 500 is the most famous race for Indy cars.

WOMEN IN AUTOMOBILE RACING

Women have been racing automobiles almost as long as men have. For many years they struggled for acceptance from their fellow drivers and racing fans. Today women are earning respect for their determination and skill behind the wheel.

In 1949, Louise Smith became the first woman to race in NASCAR's championship. In 1977, Janet Guthrie became the first woman to compete in both the Daytona 500 and the Indy 500. Shirley Muldowney set a record for professional drag-racing championships won by a woman (18). (See the separate profile of Muldowney accompanying this article.)

Many women are making their mark in automobile racing today. In 2005, Katherine Legge became the first woman to win a major open-wheeled race in North America. Sarah Fisher has often placed in the top ten at NASCAR races. In 2006, drag-racer Erica Enders became the first woman to qualify first in the NHRA's Pro Stock division. And Danica Patrick is emerging as a top Indy driver. At her first Indy 500 in 2005, she became the first woman to lead the race (19 laps) and the first to finish as high as fourth place. She was named Rookie of the Year.

Danica Patrick is one of many women who are making their mark in automobile racing today.

more and more races were held on paved ovals. Today stock-car racing is held on a variety of paved racetracks and road courses. They range from ½ to 2½ miles (0.8 kilometer to 4 kilometers) in length. On the longer racetracks, stock cars can reach more than 190 miles (305 kilometers) per hour. All tracks have pit areas, where pit crews change tires, add fuel, and make quick repairs during the race.

NASCAR racing has different divisions, or series, for different kinds of vehicles. At the top is the **Nextel Cup Series**. These races are for the fastest cars and the most skilled drivers. The premier race in this series is the Daytona 500, which is also the premier race for stock-car racing in general. It is held at the Daytona International Speedway in Florida. The cars in the **Busch Series** are lighter and slightly less powerful than Nextel Cup cars. In the **Craftsman Truck Series**, drivers develop their racing skills in modified pickup trucks. The trucks are less powerful than Busch Series cars, and the races are slower.

Formula One

Formula One, or Grand Prix, racing originated in 1895. It is one of the most distinguished kinds of automotive racing in the world. It is conducted in a series of about 18 races, called a **circuit**, held on several continents. All races are held on courses that twist and turn like country roads. These courses also include pit areas. Formula One cars travel at speeds ranging from 30 miles (48 kilometers) per hour to more than 200 miles (320 kilometers) per hour. Only the world's best drivers are allowed to compete in Formula One racing events.

Formula One cars are constructed according to specifications set by the FIA. These specifications limit the weight, tire dimensions, engine size, and overall aerodynamic design of the cars. The cars are open-wheeled, mid-engine vehicles with special wings located at the front and rear. **Open-wheeled** means that no fenders surround the wheels. **Mid-engine** means the engine is located behind the driver but in front of the rear axle. The shape of the wings causes the air flowing over them to push down on the car and keep it firmly on the road. This is called **downforce**. Formula One race cars also have electronic traction control systems that limit rear wheel spin. These systems are similar to traction control systems installed on modern passen-

Profiles:

Mario Andretti (1940–), born in Montona, Italy, was one of the most versatile racers of all time. He moved to the United States at age 15 and began racing in 1959. In 1965 he finished third in his first Indy 500 and was named Rookie of the Year.

Dale Earnhardt

He was the first driver to win championships in three different kinds of racing: Indy (1965–66, 1968, 1984), stock car (1967), and Formula One (1978). Andretti won more than 100 races in his career before retiring in 1994. He was inducted into the International Motorsports Hall of Fame in 2000.

Dale Earnhardt (1953–2001) was born in Kannapolis, North Carolina. He was one of the most famous NASCAR racers of all time and brought great popularity to the sport. Known as the Intimidator because of his aggressive driving style, he won the NASCAR championship seven times (1980, 1986–87, 1990–91, 1993–94) and the Daytona 500 once (1998). Earnhardt was killed in a crash during the final lap of the 2001 Daytona 500. During his career he won 76 races and earned more than $40 million. He was inducted into the International Motorsports Hall of Fame in 2006. His son, **Dale Earnhardt, Jr.,** (1974–), is also a NASCAR driver. He won the Daytona 500 in 2004.

A. J. (Anthony Joseph) Foyt (1935–), born in Houston, Texas, was the first racer to win the Indianapolis 500 four times (1961, 1964, 1967, 1977). He won more than sixty Indy-car races during his career, as well as the 24 Hours of Le Mans (1967) and NASCAR's Daytona 500 (1972). He also won more than forty sprint- and midget-car races. He was inducted into the International Motorsports Hall of Fame in 2000.

Don Garlits (1932–), born in Tampa, Florida, was a top drag racer as well as a major innovator of drag-racing technology. He set a remarkable series of drag-racing speed records, becoming the first to surpass 170 miles per hour (mph)/274 kilometers per hour (kph) (1957), 180 mph/290 kph (1958), 200 mph/322 kph (1964), 240 mph/386 kph (1968), 250 mph/403 kph (1975), and 270 mph/435 kph (1986). He was the first racer to use special air deflectors to keep a dragster grounded at high speeds and the first to use motorcycle wheels on the front of a dragster. He also designed and built the first successful dragster with its engine mounted behind the driver. He was inducted into the International Motorsports Hall of Fame in 1997.

Shirley Muldowney (1940–) was born in Burlington, Vermont. She was a pioneer for women in automotive racing and one of the best drag racers in the history of the sport. She was the first woman to be licensed to drive Top Fuel (nitromethane-powered) dragsters for the National Hot Rod Association (NHRA). In 1976 she became the first woman to win a national professional title in drag racing. In 1977

ger cars. Formula One cars are fueled by gasoline.

Indy-Car Racing

Indy cars resemble Formula One race cars. They have slender bodies, front and rear wings, and open wheels. But unlike gasoline-powered Formula One cars, Indy cars use methanol or ethanol as fuel. Races range from 200 to 500 miles (320 to 800 kilometers) in length. They are held on a paved oval track or on a road course. Both have pit areas. The cars begin each race from a rolling start, slowly following behind a pace car for several laps. Indy cars can reach speeds of 225 miles (360 kilometers) per hour or more.

Indy cars are named for the Indianapolis Motor Speedway, where they compete in the Indianapolis 500. The Indianapolis 500 is the most famous race for Indy cars. It was first run in 1911 and has been held almost every year since. Thirty-three cars race 200 times around the 2½-mile track for a total of 500 miles.

Indy-car racing has two governing organizations, the Championship Auto Racing

The fastest cars used in drag racing are Top Fuel dragsters. These long, thin cars can reach more than 300 miles (480 kilometers) per hour.

she became the first woman to win the NHRA's Winston Top Fuel Championship. She later became the first driver—man or woman—to win that same championship twice (1980) and three times (1982). During her career, she won a record 18 NHRA titles. In 1977 the U.S. House of Representatives honored her with an Outstanding Achievement Award. She was inducted into the International Motorsports Hall of Fame in 2004.

Lee Petty (1914–2000) and **Richard Petty** (1937–), both born in Level Cross, North Carolina, were the most accomplished members of a family forever linked with NASCAR racing. Lee was one of the sport's first stars. He won the Winston Cup championship three times (1954, 1958, 1959) and the first Daytona 500, in 1959. He was inducted into the International Motorsports Hall of Fame in 1990. Richard, Lee's son, was known as the King for his record-setting career as a

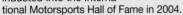
Shirley Muldowney

Richard Petty

NASCAR driver. Among the records he held at the time of his retirement in 1992 were for most total wins (200), most Daytona 500 wins (7), most Winston Cup championships (7, shared with Dale Earnhardt), and most wins in a season (27). His outgoing personality and popularity with racing fans made him a natural ambassador for the sport. Richard was inducted into the International Motorsports Hall of Fame in 1997.

Jackie (John Young) Stewart (1939–), born in Dumbartonshire, Scotland, was known as the Flying Scot for his success as a Formula One racer. During his career, he won 27 races and the World Driving Championship three times (1969, 1971, 1973). Stewart was also a strong advocate for increased safety in racing, a sport where injuries and fatalities were common. His efforts led to the adoption of seat belts, helmets that fully covered the driver's face, and other measures that increased safety for racers and spectators alike. He was inducted into the International Motorsports Hall of Fame in 1990 and was knighted in 2001.

Robert (Bobby) Unser (1934–) and **Al Unser, Sr.** (1939–), both born in Albuquerque, New Mexico, are members of one of America's most famous families of race-car drivers. The two brothers won more than 50 Indy-car races combined. In the Indianapolis 500, Al, Sr., is one of three four-time winners (1970, 1971, 1978, and 1987) and Bobby is a three-time winner (1968, 1975, and 1981). Bobby was inducted into the International Motorsports Hall of Fame in 1990. Al, Sr., was inducted in 1998. His son, **Al Unser, Jr.** (1962–), won the Indianapolis 500 in 1992 and 1994.

Teams (CART) and the Indy Racing League (IRL). The IRL runs only on oval tracks. CART runs on both ovals and road courses.

Drag Racing

Drag racing originated in the United States in the early 1950's. In this sport, two cars race side-by-side down a straight track ⅛ or ¼ mile (.2 or .4 kilometer) in length. The cars begin the race from a standstill, or a standing start. An electronic device featuring a row of colored lights starts each race. This device is known as the Christmas Tree. It is positioned in the center of the track slightly ahead of the starting line. The first vehicle to cross the finish line is declared the winner. In addition, the time it takes a car to run the course and the maximum speed reached when crossing the finish line (called the **terminal speed**) are recorded.

Many different kinds, or classes, of cars are used in drag racing. Cars race only against those in the same class. The fastest cars used in drag racing are Top Fuel dragsters. These long, thin cars have large rear wheels, small front wheels, and powerful engines fueled by

nitromethane. They can reach up to 330 miles (530 kilometers) per hour, crossing a quarter mile in 4.5 seconds.

The National Hot Rod Association (NHRA) is the largest governing body. It holds several meets across the country throughout the year. The largest event is the NHRA's U.S. Nationals held in Indianapolis on Labor Day weekend each year.

Off-Road Racing

Off-road races are primarily a North American sport. They are usually run on unpaved roads in rural areas. Many classes of cars compete in off-road racing. These include modified pickup trucks and unique types of buggies. The most famous off-road race is the Baja 1000 that takes place in Mexico. SCORE International is the governing body for this race. There is also a series of off-road races held in the United States. These races are run on small but challenging dirt road courses built within a baseball or football stadium or an indoor arena. These courses include many tight turns and jumps over uneven terrain.

In 1997, the jet-powered Thrust SSC became the first automobile to travel faster than the speed of sound.

on methanol and ethanol. They can accelerate very quickly. There are several regional sanctioning bodies for sprint cars.

Midgets are open-wheeled race cars that look like smaller versions of sprint cars. They are powered by highly modified four-cylinder engines that also run on methanol and ethanol. Midgets race on ¼-mile dirt or paved tracks and occasionally on special indoor tracks.

Endurance Racing

Endurance races are run on road courses and last for a specified length of time. The longest of these races is 24 hours. Several classes of cars usually compete in the same race. The most powerful cars in the race are "prototype" cars that are built by specialty race-car builders. For each race there is one overall winner and a winner for each class of car. During the race, the cars make pit stops for fuel, tires, and any mechanical repairs to keep them in the competition. Because of the length of the race, each race team has as many as four drivers that share the driving duties. Drivers are changed during pit stops. The most famous endurance races are France's 24 Hours of Le Mans and Florida's 24 Hours of Daytona and the 12 Hours of Sebring.

Land Speed Racing

The object of land speed racing is to achieve the fastest possible terminal speed. Unlike all other racing cars, land speed cars are raced individually. These races take place on immense flat areas such as the Bonneville Salt Flats, an ancient dry lake bed in Utah.

The first recognized land speed record, of 39.25 miles (63.2 kilometers) per hour, was set in France in 1898 in an electric-powered car. But most of the earliest land speed races were made using internal combustion engines to drive the car's wheels. Sir Malcolm Campbell set the first official record at Bonneville in 1935. He traveled 276.8 miles (445.6 kilometers) per hour in his Bluebird race car. Then in 1963, Craig Breedlove set a record of 407.5 miles (656.1 kilometers) per hour in a three-wheeled, jet-powered vehicle. Since then, an assortment of rocket- and jet-powered vehicles have set and reset speed records. In 1997 Andy Green, in the Thrust SSC, became the first driver to exceed the sound barrier. He reached a speed of 763.035 miles (1,228 kilometers) per hour. The fastest speed recorded for a wheel-driven vehicle is 417 miles (671 kilometers) per hour, set by Tom Burkland in 2004.

Sprint- and Midget-Car Racing

Sprint cars are small open-wheeled race cars designed to run on small dirt or paved oval tracks. These tracks range from ¼ to ½ mile in length. Sprint cars are powered by highly modified automobile engines that run

▶ CONTRIBUTIONS OF AUTOMOBILE RACING

Automobile racing has contributed greatly to the development of cars in general. The biggest innovation has been the increase in horsepower of the internal combustion engine. Improvements in fuel economy can also be directly traced to automobile racing. Passenger vehicles have benefited from advances in body design and braking systems (such as disc brakes) first developed on race cars. Automobile racing also introduced seat belts as a safety feature in the 1940's, long before they were offered in passenger cars. Today's durable tires are a direct result of the development of tires for race cars. Not everyone can become a race-car driver. But we all benefit from the many innovations racing has given to the passenger car.

ROBERT GENAT
Author, *American Drag Racing*

See also KARTING.

SOILS

Soils are mixtures of solid particles, air, and water. Some of the particles are bits of broken-down rocks and minerals. And some are bits of once-living things. These particles stay loosely packed because the spaces between them are filled by air and water. Soil also contains living organisms.

Soils are found on the surface of the Earth. They can be a few inches deep, or they can go down several feet. Our word "soil" comes from the Latin word *solum*, which means "floor" or "ground." The Latin root tells you something about the importance of soils. Soils provide the ground, or foundation, of all life on land. They support the plants on which people and other living beings depend.

Soils change all the time. They emerge from the ceaseless processes of geology and climate, as well as the actions of living things, including plants and animals. Although soils are constantly renewed, they develop very slowly. If soils are misused, they can take a long time to recover.

▶ CHARACTERISTICS OF SOILS

The soil in one place is never exactly the same as the soil in another place. Some soils are dark brown. Others are gray. Still others are yellow or reddish.

Color is just one way that soils differ. Some soils are gritty, and others are fine. Some are acidic. Some contain high proportions of certain minerals. These characteristics, and others, determine how well a soil supports plant growth. A soil's characteristics can even be used to predict which plants will thrive in that soil, and which will struggle.

An important soil characteristic is texture. It is determined by the relative amounts of clay, silt, and sand particles. Clay particles are the smallest. Silt particles are larger. And sand particles are larger still. Rocks are common in some soils, but they are not considered soil particles.

Tiny particles pack a lot more surface area into a given space than large particles. And more surface area means the soil has more places where it may come into contact with water. Clay-rich soils tend to hold water tightly. They may even hold water so well that water is unable to filter through to plant roots. Water passes through sandy soils easily.

Soil is a thin layer of loose material on the surface of the Earth. Soil is precious because it supports the plants on which people and other living things depend.

But they may not hold on to water long enough for plants to use.

If a soil has a fairly even mixture of sand, silt, and clay, it is called a **loam**. Loams are good at holding water, but they also drain well.

When a soil is moist, its texture can be felt. Sand feels gritty and rough. Silt feels smooth and powdery, like baby powder. Clay is hard when dry, and moldable and sticky when wet, like modeling clay. Clay particles have negative charges, like magnets, and attract nutrients with opposite charges. So soils containing clay can hold nutrients well, increasing their fertility.

The fertility of a soil also depends on how much organic matter it contains. Organic matter consists of decomposed plant and animal tissues. When this matter is thoroughly decomposed, it is called **humus**. Organic matter also has charges to hold plant nutrients. And it acts like glue, joining soil mineral particles together in clumps. It typically gives a darker color to the top layer of a soil than the deeper layers.

The composition of soil particles is important, too. Most soil particles are made of a mineral called quartz. But feldspars, micas, and many other minerals are common. Some clay particles are made of minerals that give them stronger charges. These particles hold more nutrients.

▶ CLASSIFICATION OF SOILS

People have classified soils since ancient times. They have also created maps showing the distribution of soils. The oldest map of soil types is the 3,000-year-old Altar of Land and Grain in China. The altar is a square area on top of a raised platform. It uses five colored areas to represent the soil types prevalent in five regions of China.

Since then, many classification systems for soils have been created. In 1975, the United States began using its Soil Taxonomy. This system defines more than twelve orders (major types) of soils. Each order includes several subdivisions. The lowest and most specific level in the Soil Taxonomy is the soil series. More than 20,000 soil series have been described.

A well-defined classification system makes it possible to conduct detailed surveys. These surveys help identify the strengths and weaknesses of land for different purposes. These purposes include farming, construction, and waste disposal.

▶ DEVELOPMENT OF SOILS

Soils form gradually over long periods of time. This is because the processes that create soil work very slowly. These processes act on **parent materials**, or starting materials. Parent materials may consist of broken-down bedrock or loose rock material. Loose material is often carried by glaciers, wind, or water before it builds up in a particular place. It can also slide down a hillside. Parent materials also include organic matter, such as the material that builds up in swamps or bogs.

One way that parent materials change is through weathering. Physical weathering reduces the particle size of rocks. For example, when water freezes, it expands. And when it expands, it can widen cracks within rocks. Chemical weathering reduces particle size, too. However, it also changes the minerals that make up the particles. For example, water reacts with some minerals, forming chemicals that break down yet other minerals. Parent materials are also affected by living organisms. As plants grow, die, and decay, organic matter accumulates in soil.

When parent materials develop over time, the soil that is created tends to form **horizons**, or layers. The most common horizons are named the A, B, and C horizons. The A horizon is the mineral surface, or topsoil. The B horizon is the subsurface horizon, or subsoil. Sometimes there are several B

GRAVEL	SAND	SILT	CLAY
0.08 in to 3 in (2 mm to 75 mm)	0.002 in to 0.08 in (0.05 mm to 2 mm)	0.00008 in to 0.002 in (0.002 mm to 0.05 mm)	<0.00008 in (<0.002 mm)

Much of soil consists of mineral particles of different sizes. These include sand, silt, and clay. Objects larger than grains of sand are not considered soil particles.

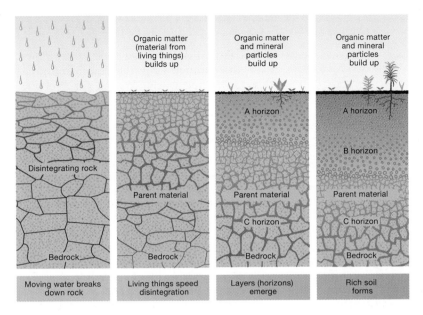

| Moving water breaks down rock | Living things speed disintegration | Layers (horizons) emerge | Rich soil forms |

Disintegrating rock · Bedrock · Organic matter (material from living things) builds up · Parent material · Bedrock · Organic matter and mineral particles build up · A horizon · Parent material · C horizon · Bedrock · Organic matter and mineral particles build up · A horizon · B horizon · Parent material · C horizon · Bedrock

Soil develops slowly. Over time, weathering breaks down rock. Distinct layers of broken-down minerals form, plants take root, and organic material begins to build up.

smaller animals, such as beetles and ants, millipedes and centipedes, slugs and snails, and spiders and mites, feed on organic matter. This starts the process of decay. The body wastes of these animals enrich the soil. The most important of all these animals are the earthworms. Like tiny plows, earthworms turn over the soil and improve it in many ways.

In addition, countless numbers of microorganisms are present in soil, feeding on particles of organic matter. As they feed they break the organic material into minerals, gases, and liquids. These decay products are broken down still further by other microorganisms. There result new combinations of the basic elements. Plants can then use the substances for growth.

horizons. The C horizon is the parent material. Beneath the C horizon is solid rock, or bedrock. All the horizons of a soil may be seen in a **soil profile**. A soil profile provides a vertical, cross-sectional view of the soil.

Some soils develop more quickly than others. For example, soils in regions with more rainfall tend to form faster than soils in dry regions. This is because rainfall promotes more plant growth. There are also forces that slow soil development. Soil develops slowly if topsoil is **eroded** (worn down and carried away). Soils develop when the formation processes occur more rapidly than erosion.

The youngest soils are probably at least 50 to 100 years old. The oldest soils are on landscapes that are many thousands of years old. But soils are not always as old as their landscapes. Weathering, erosion, deposition, and soil formation never stop.

▶ **LIVING ORGANISMS IN SOILS**

The soil contains many living things. All help the soil in some way. For example, the roots of plants grow down into the soil. Thus, plants hold the soil and prevent it from being blown or washed away.

Many kinds of animals live in the soil. Rodents, such as ground squirrels and moles, make their burrows there. Their tunnels and holes let more air and water into the soil. Still

Soil is fragile and can be destroyed or lost if it is misused. Poor farming practices can cause soil to be carried away by water. When this happens, soil erosion can be severe.

Special farming techniques can be used to conserve soil. One technique, no-till farming, avoids using machines that rake crop remains out of the soil.

Decay is important because it provides elements that are absent from air and water. Of the 16 elements that all plants need, just three are present in air or water. These are oxygen, hydrogen, and carbon. The other elements, which result from decay, include macronutrients and micronutrients. Plants need relatively large quantities of macronutrients. These are nitrogen, phosphorus, potassium, sulfur, calcium, and magnesium. Plants need just traces of micronutrients. These are boron, cobalt, copper, iron, manganese, molybdenum, and zinc.

Although decay can release every macronutrient, soils often need extra nitrogen, phosphorus, and potassium. These macronutrients are the main incredients in most commercial fertilizers. (Nitrogen is plentiful as a gas in the air, but plants cannot use nitrogen in this form.) Calcium and magnesium are often added when lime is spread over acidic soils.

▶ ROLE OF SOILS IN WATER, ROCK, AND CARBON CYCLES

Water, minerals, and other substances continuously move through soils. These movements are parts of larger cycles. Among these are the water, rock, and carbon cycles.

In one part of the water cycle, water flows over and through land. (For more information, see the article WATER in Volume WXYZ.) As soon as a stable landscape has water flowing through it, soils begin to form. This is because the moving water weathers rock, creating small mineral particles.

Water, together with wind and gravity, carries weathered rock material and soil to the sea. On the sea floor, this material builds up in layers of sediment, forming sedimentary rock. This rock can be transformed into other kinds of rock because of the temperatures and pressures deep within the Earth. Such transformations are an important part of the rock cycle. Eventually, these other kinds of rock can be exposed to weathering and the processes of soil formation. (For more information, see the article ROCKS in Volume QR.)

Another cycle involving soils is the carbon cycle. In this cycle, carbon dioxide in the atmosphere is used by plants to create plant tissues. When these tissues decompose, some carbon is returned to the atmosphere, while some remains within soil organic matter.

Some scientists are concerned that this cycle's balance of carbon could be disturbed. With rising global temperatures, decomposition could increase, releasing more carbon dioxide. This could enhance the greenhouse effect, which would worsen global warming. (For more information, see the article GLOBAL WARMING in Volume G.) Other scientists say a warmer environment might support more plant growth, which might help remove some carbon dioxide from the air.

▶ THE EFFECT OF HUMAN ACTIVITY ON SOILS

People may speed up or slow down the slow natural process of soil erosion. Unless we are careful, we can quickly destroy fertile soil that took thousands of years to develop. Fertile soil is not just fragile, it is also a limited resource. Just 12 percent of the Earth's land is suitable for crop production. Nearly all this land is currently used. The rest is too hot, too cold, too steep, too shallow, too wet, too dry, or has some chemical problem and cannot be used to grow crops.

Good soil is constantly covered over when houses, factories, and roads are built. Once roofs have replaced roots, the soil is lost. Each year, farmers must produce more crops on less land.

How to Make an Edible Soil Profile

When scientists study soils found in different locations, they often compare soil profiles. These profiles are cross-sectional views. They can be diagrams, photographs, or even models. These profiles usually highlight the horizons, or layers, from the bedrock to the surface.

You can create a model of a soil profile that is also a dessert! This model should be assembled in a glass bowl, so all the horizons are visible. Each layer includes a different set of dry ingredients. These ingredients represent soil components, and they are held in place with a pudding mixture. As the layers rise, the components are more finely broken down. This is how layers are ordered in real soils.

Use the following dry ingredients for each layer, from the bottom to the top:

- C horizon—coarsely broken graham crackers and chocolate chunks.
- B horizon—crushed graham crackers and chocolate chips.
- A horizon—finely crushed graham crackers and crushed chocolate cookie wafers.
- Topsoil—crushed chocolate cookie wafers.
- Organic matter—coconut flakes colored with green food coloring.

Organic matter
Topsoil
A horizon
B horizon
C horizon

To make the pudding mixture, combine roughly equal amounts of pudding (pre-made or instant) and whipped topping. In each layer, the pudding mixture may be placed in the middle, with the dry ingredients placed on the outside, against the inside of the glass bowl. Or the pudding mixture can be mixed with the dry ingredients.

When forests are cut down and replaced with crops, the soil is changed. With continual planting of the same crops, cleared forestland stops producing in five years. Crops exhaust (use up) the elements that took many years to build up. If the elements are not replaced, the soil loses its fertility. If the land is left bare between crops, winds and rains may carry off the topsoil.

In the United States, the mass of soil that is lost because of wind and water erosion is about six times the mass of food that is produced. To prevent such losses, the Department of Agriculture's Natural Resources Conservation Service helps people plan the wise use of the remaining soil.

Fertile land that is used to produce food crops can be **conserved**, or protected, in various ways. Erosion can be slowed by such things as contour plowing and crop rotation. Contour plowing follows the curve of the land, thus slowing down the flow of water—and soil—from the top of a slope to the bottom. Crops are rotated—that is, first one kind of crop is grown in a field, then another—so

that the repeated planting of the same crop will not exhaust minerals.

Another conservation practice is no-till farming. Tilling is the use of tractor-drawn implements to rake the soil. Tilling can remove weeds, mix in fertilizers, and create furrows for irrigation. However, it can also compact soil, kill soil organisms, and speed erosion. No-till farming avoids these problems by leaving soil intact and leaving crop remains in the fields.

Organic and chemical fertilizers are added to replace the minerals that are used up. Cover crops are grown to prevent soil erosion between crops. Various other measures are taken to control the floods and the droughts that are the result of the washing and blowing away of soil.

With good management, people can save and even improve the fertile topsoil on which our life depends.

CLAY ROBINSON
West Texas A&M University

See also BACTERIA; CONSERVATION; GEOLOGY; MINERALS; ORES; ROCKS; WORMS.

GRASSES AND GRASSLANDS

Grasslands are wide-open expanses. Although some grasslands are dotted with trees and shrubs, the plants that grow there are mostly grasses and wildflowers. Grasses have jointed stems, slender leaves, and tiny flower clusters. They usually lack woody tissue.

Grasses are used as food by grazing animals. In fact, many grasslands are populated by large herds of grazing animals.

Grasslands are so vast that they account for nearly a quarter of the Earth's vegetation. Many of the original grasslands now produce crops. These areas support cultivated grains such as corn or wheat, or they are used as pastures for hay or cattle production.

For North Americans, the most familiar grasslands are the prairies that once filled the vast middle of the continent. These were the "seas of grass" that first awed the pioneers who crossed them in wagon trains.

Prairies, however, are just one type of several great grassland regions of the world. These include the steppes of Russia and Asia, the veldt of southern African, and the South American pampas. In fact, grasslands are found on every continent except Antarctica.

Scientists believe that grasses first appeared in Africa and then spread around the world. First they spread to Europe and Asia, and then to South America. Finally, they spread from South America to North America.

All grasslands support a variety of plants. However, grasses dominate. Grasses are members of the family Poaceae. This family is similar to the sedge (Cyperaceae) and rush (Juncaceae) families. However, sedges are more characteristic of tundra, and rushes are more characteristic of wetlands.

▶ CHARACTERISTICS OF GRASSES

Grasses are plants that share several traits. Grasses have **culms** (stems) that are smooth, shiny, and mostly hollow. At regular spaces the culms have joints. The leaves are usually long and

Grasslands are found worldwide. *Above:* In Africa, there are grasslands called savannas that are famous for their wildlife. *Left:* The steppes of Russia and Asia have supported nomadic herders for thousands of years. *Below:* The North American prairie has been described as a sea of grass.

narrow. The veins in the leaves all run in the same direction.

One leaf grows at each joint. Each leaf consists of two parts, a sheath and a blade. The sheath is the lower part of the leaf. It fits closely around the culm. The blade is long and slender. No other plant family has exactly this kind of stem and leaf.

The flowers are at the top of the culm. They are usually small and not showy. They produce the seeds of the grass plant.

Annual and Perennial Grasses

Grasses are categorized as annual grasses or perennial grasses. **Annual grasses** germinate and grow for just one season. Near the end of the growing season, after flowering, they set seed and then die. New plants emerge the following season from seed. **Perennial grasses**, in contrast, survive from one season to the next. They survive because they rise from permanent underground structures. These structures include crowns and rhizomes. **Crowns** are where roots and stems meet. **Rhizomes** are underground stems that send shoots upward. They are called creeping stems because they grow sideways. Other creeping stems grow above the ground. They are called **stolons**.

There are two kinds of perennial grasses: sod-forming grasses and bunchgrasses. **Sod-forming grasses** develop a solid mat of grass over the ground. This mat becomes more dense and spreads out as the grass plants send out rhizomes and stolons. The dense network of roots holds soil together.

Bunchgrasses grow in distinct clumps. They spread by sending up sideshoots, or **tillers**. These emerge from the crown.

▶ **DEFINING GRASSLANDS**

Wherever there are grasslands, certain climate patterns and landscape features are found. The weather is unpredictable and changes from year to year. The terrain is level and open, or there are gently rolling hills. Because the landscape is so open, there are strong prevailing winds. These winds help explain why water is lost so quickly to evaporation. In fact, water is lost to evaporation faster than it is received through precipitation. Periodically there are severe droughts.

Usually 10 to 40 inches (25 to 100 centimeters) of rain falls each year. This rainfall is

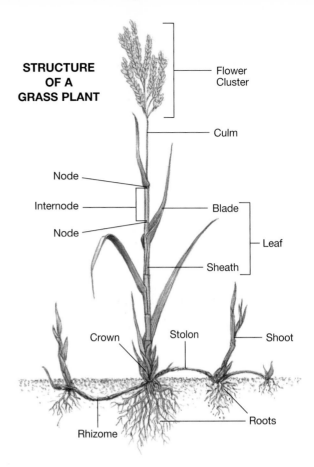

STRUCTURE OF A GRASS PLANT

Flower Cluster

Culm

Node

Internode

Node

Blade

Leaf

Sheath

Crown

Stolon

Shoot

Rhizome

Roots

balanced by water losses. Most of these losses occur because of evaporation and transpiration. **Evaporation** is when liquid water turns to vapor and rises into the air. **Transpiration** is when plants release water vapor.

The balance between rainfall and water losses can produce conditions that are too wet or too dry to support grassland. If conditions are too wet, forests grow. Somewhat drier conditions support oak savanna, a lightly forested grassland. Even drier conditions support tallgrass prairie and shortgrass prairie. If conditions are too dry for grassland, deserts occur.

Rainfall varies from year to year. In a wet year it can be four times as great as in a dry year. Most of the rain falls in summer during the peak of the growing season. Temperature ranges can be great, too. For example, in the tallgrass prairie region of Kansas, annual temperature may range from –35°F (–37°C) in the winter to 115°F (45°C) or more in the summer. In a single day, the temperature may range 70°F (40°C). All grasslands experience some seasonal cycle of drought. Some droughts may last for several years.

Factors besides climate help define grasslands. Many grasslands need to be renewed by periodic fires. These fires eliminate dead leaves that pile up and stifle new grass shoots. And they help recycle the nutrients contained in the dead leaves. In grasslands, dead plant material tends to rot into the soil very slowly. This is because grasslands are often dry, and dry conditions tend to slow the rotting of plant material. In grasslands, plant materials can also be broken down by fire.

Fire also prevents the grasslands from being invaded by trees and shrubs. After a fire, grasses recover quickly, unlike trees and shrubs, which are more likely to be destroyed. Without the occasional fire, tallgrass prairie eventually changes into woodland. The prevention of naturally occurring fires can sometimes harm grasslands. To avoid such harm, controlled burns are organized.

▶ TYPES OF GRASSLANDS

There are many ways to categorize grasslands. Perhaps the simplest way is to consider how wet they are. Two basic grassland types are moist grasslands and dry grasslands. A third type, savanna, is a special case. It can receive as much rainfall as moist grassland. However, savanna is often less able to retain this water. And some savannas have soil that is too poor to support vegetation that is less hardy than grassland.

Moist Grasslands

Moist grasslands are also called humid or subhumid grasslands. In these grasslands, rainfall is ample. It falls mostly during the warmer part of the year. These grasslands need periodic fires to clear away leaf litter.

Moist grasslands have produced the world's deepest, most fertile soils. This is because the plants in these grasslands have very deep roots. They help bring air, water, and organic matter deep below the surface.

Types of Plants. These grasslands typically support the lush growth of tall grasses during the growing season. They usually grow taller than 50 inches (125 centimeters). In wetter years, it is fairly common for the tallest grasses to exceed 6 feet (2 meters) in height. Other plants include broad-leafed plants as well as trees and shrubs. These plants tend to grow along streams and the lower slopes of hills.

Where They Are Found. Examples of moist grasslands are the tallgrass and mixed-grass prairies of North America, the Eurasian steppe, the eastern portion of the South American pampas, and the wetter parts of the grasslands of southern Africa and eastern Australia.

Human Activities. The climate and soils of moist grasslands are ideal for agriculture. As a result, moist grasslands have been almost entirely converted to fields of wheat, corn, soybeans, and other crops. Many are used as pastures for grazing livestock.

Dry Grasslands

In dry or arid grasslands, rain seldom falls. Annual amounts are less than 15 inches (38 centimeters). There are also high winds, which speeds evaporation. It is too dry for most tall grasses. Instead, grasses grow only 5 to 24 inches tall (13 to 60 centimeters). These areas are referred to as shortgrass plains.

Setting and carefully controlling fires can help preserve grasslands. These fires consume leaf litter that would otherwise stifle the growth of new grass shoots.

Over time, grasslands build up rich soil that is useful in agriculture. Native grazing animals have been replaced by domestic livestock such as cattle and sheep. And many grasslands have been converted to cropland.

Unlike many moist grassland plants, dryland grasses have shallow roots. They depend on moisture in the upper soil layers. Below these layers, there is a permanent dry zone that the roots never enter.

Even hotter and drier than the shortgrass plains are the desert grasslands. Rainfalls are brief and occur only during summer and winter. As little as 10 to 15 inches (25 to 38 centimeters) of rain falls each year.

Types of Plants. The dominant grasses of the shortgrass prairie are sod-forming species. Because of the dense sod, relatively few wildflowers grow on the shortgrass plains.

Desert grasslands are dominated by bunchgrasses but are dotted with mesquite woodland. Annual grasses germinate and grow only during the summer rainy season. However, annual broad-leafed plants grow mostly in the cool winter and spring months.

Where They Are Found. Arid grasslands occur worldwide. For example, there are the shortgrass plains and the desert grasslands of the western United States and the annual grasslands of California's Central Valley. Arid grasslands also occur in the drier grassy parts of South America, Africa, and Australia.

Human Activities. Dry grasslands generally need to be irrigated to support agriculture. With irrigation, corn, soybeans, and other crops can be grown. Much of the arid grasslands are grazed by cattle.

Dry grasslands are sensitive to human activities. These activities can even contribute to disaster. For example, much of the American shortgrass prairie suffered dust storms in the 1930's. They were caused by poor soil conservation, drought, and winds. They affected an area that became known as the Dust Bowl. Recovering from this disaster took decades.

Other factors damage dry grasslands. These include overgrazing by livestock, fire suppression, and erosion of the thin topsoil. They have allowed dry grasslands to be invaded by desert shrubs such as mesquite and creosote bush. Heavy grazing and competition from introduced species have caused California grassland plants to be replaced by non-native grasses. In other parts of the world, arid grasslands have been greatly altered by human activities. These include the use of chemical fertilizers and the introduction of non-native grasses to support sheep ranching.

Savannas

Savannas are tropical grasslands. Like other grasslands, they are wide-open expanses. They typically occur on level terrain, often on old flood plains.

The savanna's open landscape is maintained by both biological and physical forces. For instance, the plant-eating animals of the African savanna feed on all parts of the vegetation, from low-growing plants to the tops of trees. Fire also plays a crucial role in maintaining the savanna landscape.

Animals

Grasslands are home to many forms of animal life. These include mammals large and small, birds, reptiles, and a host of **invertebrates** (animals with no backbones). The most noticeable animals of the grasslands are mammals. Many of them are **herbivores**. That is, they eat only plants.

Large Grazing Animals. In most grasslands, the chief grazers are **ungulates**, or hoofed animals. They have special adaptations for a diet based on grasses. These adaptations include spade-like front teeth for grazing and broad molars for chewing and grinding tough plant matter. Another adaptation is a four-chambered stomach. Animals with such a stomach are called **ruminants**. They swallow food nearly whole and use the first two chambers of the stomach to partially digest it. Then the food is regurgitated (brought up) so that it can be chewed again. Finally, the food is swallowed again and passed to the second two stomach chambers.

The grasslands once supported huge herds of grazing animals. In North America, there were herds of hoofed mammals such as bison and pronghorn. In Europe and Asia, there were herds of wild horses and saigas (a medium-sized goat antelope). Perhaps the largest and most diverse communities of hoofed mammals developed on the East African plains. On these plains, herds of wildebeest, gazelle, and zebra still roam.

WONDER QUESTION

How old are grasses?

At one time, the best fossil evidence suggested that grasses became widespread only after dinosaurs became extinct. The fossils showed impressions of grass leaves and stems. They were no more that 55 million years old. But now older fossils have been found. And they show that dinosaurs fed on grasses. The new evidence consists of fossilized dinosaur droppings that were left behind about 65 million years ago. They contain mineral particles of the type produced by grasses. In fact, they contain traces of several types of grasses. As a result, scientists now suspect that grasses began to spread and diversify much earlier than previously thought.

Originally, the South American and Australian grasslands lacked large hoofed animals. On the pampas, the closest native equivalent is the capybara, a large grazing rodent that lives in herds. In Australia, the native grazer is a marsupial, the kangaroo. Today, herds of cattle and flocks of sheep have replaced most of the large native grazers.

Other Animals. Among the abundant and diverse invertebrates of the grasslands are insects, spiders, and worms. Invertebrates are found within every grassland layer. Beneath the ground, plant roots and vegetation support a host of plant-eating insects. At the soil surface, spiders hunt other insects and beetles feed on droppings and dead animals. In the vegetation above the ground, many insects pollinate wildflowers.

Animal Behavior. The large grazers of the open grassland lack hiding places. They protect themselves against predators by forming strong social groups. The large predators also form social groups. For example, the wolves of the steppes and prairies hunt in packs. Another important behavior for the large grazers is migration. It allows them to move to where food is abundant.

Many other animals exhibit special adaptations to grassland environments. Many small mammals and reptiles avoid the harsh sun, strong winds, and occasional fires by burrowing underground. Because of dense grass and lack of trees for song perches, some grassland birds perform showy flight songs to announce territory and attract mates.

Grassland animals share some other interesting traits. They often move around by hopping or leaping. Examples include grasshoppers, jumping mice, jackrabbits, and gazelles. These animals use their strong hind legs to leap upward, which lets them see above thick grass. Many grassland animals are capable of moving quickly. Some of the world's fastest mammals, such as antelopes and cheetahs, live in grasslands.

Soil

In the grasslands, the topsoil is typically dark and deep and contains high levels of organic matter. Grassland soils are formed over thousands of years by the turnover of decaying root material.

Within a single growing season, anywhere from 30 to 60 percent of new roots die and decompose. This decomposed organic matter accumulates over time and enriches the soil.

The soils of the humid grasslands are the world's richest, most productive soils. The soils of the arid grasslands are lighter brown and contain less organic matter. In most areas, these soils have been broken to support our present-day grain belts.

Some gas stations offer gasoline/ethanol blends. The ethanol comes from fermented plant material. The plants used include cereal grasses such as corn.

▶ HUMAN ACTIVITIES

Grasslands have probably always been essential to human welfare. Many anthropologists believe that human beings spent much of their early history in the African grasslands. This history includes the transition from nomadic to more settled life. At first, settled life involved the domestication of grazing animals. Later, with the invention of the plow, farmers first broke the sod. They began tapping into the fertile soils that had built up over thousands of years. Today the world's grasslands are among the world's most critically endangered biomes.

Modern agriculture has changed grasslands profoundly. Grasslands are now cultivated to grow grains and other crops. They are often planted with non-native pasture grasses. Grasslands feed much of the world. However, the fertility of grassland soils has been "mined" for many years. This has depleted soil nutrients and removed much of the organic matter from soils. To stay productive, farmers must use large amounts of fertilizers, pesticides, and herbicides. Energy sources are tapped to create and spread these substances, as well as to run farm machinery. In addition, irrigation is needed to support agriculture in arid grasslands, where rainfall is sparse and droughts are frequent.

Huge tracts of grassland support millions of domesticated livestock, mainly cattle. When hay is mowed for these animals, nesting habitat for small mammals and birds can be lost. Arid grasslands may be overgrazed. This can lead to soil erosion, the loss of native plant species, and the loss of native animal life.

Other human activities can impact the grasslands. For example, people protect their crops and livestock by preventing grassland fires. As a result, plants that would ordinarily be eliminated by fires begin to replace grassy vegetation. This can even lead to the growth of trees in the tallgrass prairie region.

▶ FUTURE OF THE GRASSLANDS

Several programs are restoring and protecting grasslands. These efforts also help preserve grassland plants and animals. For example, the Conservation Reserve Program in the United States pays farmers to retire cropland. Instead of crops, the land is planted with native prairie species. To prevent overgrazing, ranchers can move their animals from place to place. This is called holistic resource management. It mimics the way native hoofed animals migrate as they graze.

Worldwide, there is new interest in planting grassland areas back to their original form. This is called ecological restoration. Another development is natural systems agriculture. This is an agricultural system that uses mixtures of perennial grains. Farms that use this system resemble natural grasslands.

There is keen interest in finding ways to convert plant materials to ethanol fuel. One method is to harvest and ferment corn. Another method is to ferment cellulose, which makes up the hard, fibrous parts of plants. This technique could lead to the harvesting of native perennial grasses (such as switchgrass) to produce ethanol. This could help stretch dwindling gasoline supplies.

JON PIPER
Bethel College

See also PLANTS; WEEDS.

ROMANIES

Romanies are a people who first appeared in Europe about 700 years ago. Today they are found in every country in Europe, as well as in North and South America, Australia, and elsewhere. They have a fascinating history, their own language, their own customs, and traditions they have passed on from generation to generation.

▶ ORIGINS AND HISTORY

Romanies have often been called "Gypsies"—a name they dislike—because it was first mistakenly believed that they traveled to Europe from Egypt. In fact they originated in India and call themselves Romani people or Roma (the word "Roma" means "men"). Thousands of Indians left their homeland as a resisting army between A.D. 1000–1027. This was because India was being invaded by outsiders who were trying to spread Islam, the Muslim religion, toward the East.

The Indians moved through Persia and eventually reached the Byzantine Empire (where Turkey is located today). After staying there for more than two centuries, they crossed over into the Balkan Peninsula. Now they crossed not as an army but as a new population with its own language and identity. This move was once again because of the spread of Islam, this time toward the West. By 1500 there were Romanies in nearly every European country.

A Romani youngster carries the flag symbolizing the Romani people. The Stone Flower monument in the background is a memorial to the thousands of Romanies and others killed in the Nazi concentration camps of Jasenovac, Croatia.

For the most part, the Romanies were dark-skinned, with black hair. They traveled in long caravans. The men went on horse or on foot. The women and children, with their folded tents and their few belongings, traveled in wagons and carts. Wherever they went, people viewed them with curiosity and suspicion. This attitude often turned to hostility, because the Romanies differed greatly from the citizens of their host countries. They not only looked different but also kept to themselves. This occurred because their traditions did not allow them to socialize too closely with non-Romanies (whom they call *gadjé*). Most of all they were seen as outsiders. This was because they had no country or government of their own. And they were mistaken for the invading Ottoman Turks, the same ones responsible for the Romani move into Europe.

From the very beginning, the Romanies maintained their own way of life. They lived in the West but with an Asian language and culture. For this reason, their history has largely been one of repression and persecution. This was the case even in the 20th century, when an estimated 1.5 million Romanies were killed in Nazi concentration camps during the Holocaust. (The Holocaust is called the *Porraimos* in Romani, the language of the Romanies).

▶ LANGUAGE, CUSTOMS, AND TRADITIONS

Romanies have survived so long because they kept their language, customs, and traditions alive despite hostility from the outside world. Their language has a grammar and vocabulary that are similar in many ways to Hindi, the main language of northern India. All of Romani's basic words are Indian. But in their journey west, the Romani people also adopted words from other languages. Romani Americans have English words in their language, such as *juso* for "orange juice."

In earlier times, Romanies were kept on the move because of laws forbidding them to stop. And so their ways of making a living reflected those circumstances. They mended things, sold horses, told fortunes, and did other jobs that did not require a permanent base or fixed, heavy equipment. Some people trained performing bears or worked as circus performers. Others became famous boxers.

Frequently, Romanies employed their talents as musicians and sometimes actors. One of the best-known jazz artists, Django Reinhardt, was a Romani, as was the famous actor and director Charlie Chaplin. Today, only a tiny minority of Romanies travel permanently. Most have been settled for a very long time. In fact the biggest group of all, the Vlax Romanies, were forced to stay in one place, Romania, as slaves for more than 500 years.

A traditional Romani community is headed by one man, who is chosen for his age, experience, and wisdom. He sees that the standards by which the families live are maintained. And he deals with officials in the non-Romani world. He makes sure that everyone respects the Romani laws, customs, and traditions, which include rules concerning social behavior, eating habits, and cleanliness. For example, dishes cannot be washed in the same sink that is used for washing one's hands or clothing. Birth, marriage, and death are marked by strictly observed rituals.

▶ **ROMANIES TODAY**

Romanies are found in almost every part of the world. However, today the majority of them live in Europe and North and South America, with the largest numbers in the Balkans. There are about 12 million worldwide, about 7 million in all of Europe, and about 1 million in North America. There may be a Romani family on your street. If you are looking for storybook Gypsies with colorful caravans, though, you will not see any. That is because "real" Romanies are not at all like Esmeralda of *The Hunchback of Notre Dame* or other characters in fiction.

A teacher in a school in Russia helps Romani students with their lessons. Education is critical to improving the lives of the Romani people.

Romanies have kept up with the changing times by adjusting some of their ways. Like other people, they use cars, campers, and trailers instead of traveling in carts or wagons. Their skills as metalworkers and horse dealers are no longer as valuable as in the past. So, many Romani men have become expert at automobile repair. Fortune telling is still a popular occupation among Romani women. But there are also Romanies who are government officials, professors, and lawyers.

In 1979 the Romani people won representation at the United Nations. And today they have membership in the European Union. Many of the Romanies living in Europe find it difficult to break out of the poverty in which they live because of discrimination, lack of education, and poor health. Since Communism ended in Europe in 1989, the situation has become worse for the Romanies living there, because different ethnic groups have created new countries for themselves.

In 2005 eight countries in Central and Southeastern Europe—Bulgaria, Croatia, the Czech Republic, Hungary, FYR Macedonia, Romania, Serbia and Montenegro, and Slovakia—began the Decade of Roma Inclusion, 2005–2015. This program is intended to help close the gap in living conditions between the Romani and the non–Romani people in the eight countries. It includes measures to fight discrimination against Romanies and to provide them with better healthcare and education. The first steps being taken are through education. This includes teaching Romanies much-needed professional skills. It also involves educating the non-Romani world about the real history and experience of this enduring people.

Reviewed by IAN HANCOCK
Author, *We Are the Romani People*

GRAPES AND BERRIES

We all delight in eating ripe colorful fruits, maybe even picking them ourselves and popping them, warmed by the sun, right into our mouths. Grapes and the small fruits we call berries are delicious, ready-to-go foods packed with taste and vitamins.

Most people call almost any small, seed-filled fruit a berry. Scientists, however, are more strict. Before they decide a fruit is a berry, they consider its structure and how it develops from a flower. Scientists know of several types of berry. One type, called the true berry, includes the tomato. Another type includes the banana, the blueberry, and the cranberry.

The grape is a true berry. But we call a grape a grape—unless we are referring to dried grapes, known as raisins or sultanas. The strawberry, raspberry, and blackberry are not berries in the scientific sense. Because of their structures, scientists call these fruits aggregate fruits. But most people are happy to think of them as berries.

▶ GRAPES

Grapes are made into juice, wine, vinegar, jellies and jams. They are eaten fresh or dried, as raisins. Grapes originated in both halves of the globe, the Eastern and Western hemispheres. Today, however, a species of grape that originated in the Eastern hemisphere is the one that is most often grown around the world. Called *Vitis vinifera*, this species was first cultivated about 7,000 years ago near the Caspian Sea, in present-day Iran.

Originally people relied on grapes for the making of wine. The alcohol in wine acted as a preservative. As a result, it was far safer to drink than the often-contaminated water. And it went well with meals and the social gatherings of friends and family.

Grapevines spread throughout the Middle East. They had been planted in Greece by 1700 B.C. and in China at about the same time. By the first century B.C., the Greeks had carried vines to southwestern Europe and Italy. Grape growing soon became central to the Roman Empire.

Wine became a product traded across borders. New ideas and customs as well as wine were exchanged among the Greeks, Egyptians, Arabs, and Romans. Wine became central to religious ceremonies, too. The worship of assorted "gods of wine" became common.

Vitis vinifera did not grow in North America. But many other species of grape did. In 1000 A.D., Viking Leif Ericson sailed west from Iceland and came upon a place filled with wild grapes. He named it Vinland. Historians think Vinland was a region along coastal North America. It may have been in Canada or northern New England.

Native American grapes now named Concord, Catawba, and Niagara grew well in the Americas. However, vines transplanted from Europe had a tough time with frost and diseases. American grapes, while delicious, had a musky taste. Many felt that this taste did not translate well into wine. U.S. presi-

Grapes are harvested from grapevines. The fruit-bearing shoots on these vines are carefully pruned. This encourages the growth of large fruit clusters.

374

dent Thomas Jefferson repeatedly tried and failed to raise European wine grapes on his estate in Virginia.

Hearty native grapevines, all resistant to a destructive aphid-like insect called phylloxera, rescued European vineyard owners in the 1870's. Growers planted new vines created by grafting European cuttings on the stock of their sturdy American cousins.

The tending of vineyards has changed little since ancient times. Egyptian paintings from 3,500 years ago show people working in vineyards much in the same way as they do today. The hand labor required remains considerable.

Grapes grow on woody vines. Each vine is planted in well-worked soil about 6 to 8 feet (2 to 2½ meters) apart on stakes or trellises. The vine develops a main trunk, side branches called arms, and leafy stems called shoots. After a year, the shoots start bearing fruit and are called fruiting canes. Vineyard workers prune older canes yearly. This encourages the growth of large fruit clusters on the fruiting canes and the growth of new shoots.

Growers even prune out individual berries within a cluster of grapes to give the remaining fruit enough room to plump up. Within five years the vine is producing grapes ready for commercial use. Grapevines produce fruit at top capacity for about ten years. However, a few vines as old as 100 years are still in production in Europe.

▶ BERRIES

The world is abundant with berries, both wild and cultivated. Familiar berries include strawberries and raspberries. Exotic berries include Tibet's richly nutritious Goji berry and Brazil's acai, a berry produced by palms in the Amazon River basin.

Even "accidental" berries occur. One example is the boysenberry. This North American fruit is named for a southern California farmer named Rudolph Boysen. It sprang from a cross between a red raspberry and a blackberry. It became popular in the 1930's, when it was sold at Knott's Berry Farm, a roadside stand that grew into a theme park.

Strawberries were nicknamed for the plant's habit of strewing. This means the plant spreads out low to the ground.

Strawberries. Like the grape, strawberries originated in both hemispheres. The eastern version was most likely native to northern Italy and France. But today's most widely grown strawberry, *Fragaria ananassa*, is a cross between two western plants. One originated on the Atlantic Coast of North America. The other originated on the Pacific Coast of South America.

In 1714 an amateur botanist named Amédée-François Frézier first brought the Pacific strawberry home to his native France from Chile. By the 1740's, a strawberry plant long nurtured by native Americans along the east coast of the present-day United States was planted next to a descendant of the Chilean plant. The result was a hybrid, or offspring of two different species. This hybrid is the basis of the world's commercial strawberry crop.

Strawberries were nicknamed for the plant's habit of strewing. This means the plant scatters itself along the ground, growing low to the earth on runners that root and form new plants. Too much rain, strong wind, or high temperatures can damage strawberries. However, they remain the most profitable berry crop. Commercial strawberry plants are cultivated in raised beds, in holes poked through plastic mulch. The plants are kept moist by drip irrigation systems.

When the plants are 4 to 5 inches (10 to 13 centimeters) high, they are ready to harvest. In the United States, more than 20,000 migrant workers carefully handpick the berries.

Blueberries. The blueberry is native to northern North America and thrives in cool weather. Although cultivated blueberries are grown, many commercial products are made from the wild blueberry, or lowbush, plant. The blueberries from this plant are usually mechanically harvested.

Blueberries were prized by native Americans. The blueberries were eaten fresh or ground into a paste for mixing with cornmeal. Many Indians called the blue fruits "star berries" because the blossom end of the fruit forms a five-pointed star. Star berries were thought to be a gift from the Great Spirit to hungry children.

Raspberries and Blackberries. Like strawberries, raspberries are not true berries. They are a cluster of small fruitlets, each containing a seed.

Raspberries are native to both hemispheres. It is likely that the so-called European raspberry originated in Asia. Over 200 species of the plant grow there. The Roman general Pompey records bringing home raspberries picked in what is today Turkey.

Raspberries grow on woody stems called canes. As anyone who has ever picked berries from them knows, most canes contain thorns or prickles. The new canes produce blooms and fruit in their second year, then dry up and die. New canes grow each year.

The berries come in many different colors, from red to purple, black, or even yellow. Those not consumed fresh are made into wine, vinegar, and fruit spreads.

Blackberries are often mistaken for black raspberries. Blackberries, too, grow on canes and carry their seeds on the outside. To easily

The blossom end of the blueberry forms a five-pointed star. This is why the fruit has been called the "star berry."

tell a black raspberry from a blackberry, notice that the black raspberry leaves its center core behind when picked. The blackberry is plucked off whole, like a strawberry.

Cranberries and Other Berries. The cranberry is named for its flower, which resembles a crane's head. It is closely related to the blueberry, and it grows from a perennial evergreen vine. The cranberry is a native of North America, growing wild in sandy marshes.

The cranberry was important to native people as an ingredient in pemmican, a staple winter food made with wild game. Because the cranberry kept well, it was also one of the first foods to be shipped to Britain from the American colonies in the early 1700's.

At harvest time, commercial cranberry bogs are flooded with water. Picking machines gently shake free the fruits. The ripe red fruits then float to the surface, ready to be gathered together, or corralled, in wood frames.

Berries can be enjoyed in many ways. Try locally grown gooseberries with a bit of sugar in fresh plain yogurt. Sample red currant jams and jellies on toast. Sip Swedish lingonberry soda. And pour chokeberry syrup on your pancakes.

MEREDITH SAYLES HUGHES
Co-founder, The FOOD Museum

See also WINE.

SUPPLEMENT

Deaths

Independent Nations of the World

The United States

    Senate

    House of Representatives

    Cabinet

    Supreme Court

    State Governors

Canada and Its Provinces and Territories

June Allyson (with Peter Lawford)

DEATHS

Allyson, June. American actress; died on July 8, at the age of 88. With her perky character and her husky voice, Allyson became one of Hollywood's most-popular stars of the 1940's and 1950's. Her films included *Two Girls and a Sailor* (1944), *Little Women* (1949), *The Glenn Miller Story* (1953), and *Executive Suite* (1954).

Altman, Robert. American film director; died on November 20, at the age of 81. Altman directed such hit films as *M*A*S*H* (1970), *McCabe and Mrs. Miller* (1971), and *The Player* (1992). In 2006 he was given an honorary Academy Award "to honor a career that has repeatedly reinvented the art form and inspired filmmakers and audiences alike."

Auerbach, Red. American basketball coach, general manager, and club president of the Boston Celtics; died on October 28, at the age of 89. Auerbach built the Celtics into a basketball dynasty. As Celtics coach, he won nine NBA championships; as general manager, he helped lead the Celtics to six more championships; and as Celtics president, he saw the team take their 16th championship. He was inducted into the NBA Hall of Fame in 1969.

Bradley, Ed. American award-winning CBS television news reporter; died on November 9, at the age of 65. Bradley began his career at CBS in the 1960's in radio. He later switched to television, becoming White House correspondent and the anchor of the Sunday evening newscast. In 1981, Bradley joined the highly popular newsmagazine *60 Minutes*. One of the best interviewers on television, he won 19 Emmy Awards.

Red Buttons

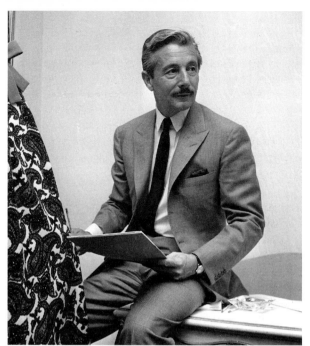

Oleg Cassini

Buttons, Red. American comedian and actor; died on July 13, at the age of 87. After working in burlesque and on Broadway, Buttons made his way into television. His comedy/variety show, *The Red Buttons Show*, was highly popular in the early 1950's. Buttons was also a fine dramatic actor. In 1957 he won the Academy Award for Best Supporting Actor for his role in the movie *Sayonara*.

Cassini, Oleg. French-born American fashion designer; died on March 17, at the age of 92. In 1936, Cassini moved to the United States, where he became a prestigious costume and dress designer. In the early 1960's Jacqueline Kennedy, wife of President John F. Kennedy, chose Cassini to design her wardrobe. The Jackie Kennedy look—A-line skirts, two-piece suits, and pillbox hats—was soon copied by women everywhere.

Douglas, Mike. American television host; died on August 11, at the age of 81. In 1961 he began hosting *The Mike Douglas Show*. Part talk show, part comedy, and part music, it was an instant hit, running through 1982. His star-studded guest list included President Richard Nixon, singer Barbra Streisand, and 3-year-old golf prodigy Tiger Woods.

Ford, Glenn. Canadian-born American actor; died on August 30, at the age of 90. From 1940 through the 1960's, Ford appeared in almost 100 Westerns, melodramas, and romantic films. He won the 1962 Golden Globe Award for Best Actor for his performance in *Pocketful of Miracles*. Among his other notable films were *The Teahouse of the August Moon* (1956), *Don't Go Near the Water* (1957), and *The Courtship of Eddie's Father* (1963).

Friedan, Betty. American feminist; died on February 4, at the age of 85. She was best known for *The Feminine Mystique* (1963), her groundbreaking book that attacked the then commonly held idea that women should be content with their roles as housewives and mothers. In 1966, Friedan cofounded the National Organization for Women (NOW), cementing her place in history as "the mother of American feminism."

Friedman, Milton. American economist; died on November 16, at the age of 94. Friedman advocated a free-market economy, in which

Betty Friedan

Steve Irwin

the economy was as close to "pure capitalism" as possible. His books included *Capitalism and Freedom* (1962) and *Free to Choose* (1980). Friedman was awarded the 1976 Nobel Prize in Economics.

Galbraith, John Kenneth. Canadian-born American economist; died on April 29, at the age of 97. Galbraith taught at Harvard University for some 30 years. His influence was felt beyond the academic world because of his best-selling books, including *The Affluent Society* (1958) and his 1981 memoir, *A Life in Our Times.* Galbraith served in government from the administration of Franklin D. Roosevelt to that of Lyndon B. Johnson and was awarded two Presidential Medals of Freedom.

Irwin, Steve. Australian conservationist and television personality nicknamed "The Crocodile Hunter"; died on September 4, at the age of 44. In 1996, Irwin and his wife, Terri, began hosting *The Crocodile Hunter* television show, which featured him in hair-raising situations with wild animals. The show became hugely popular around the world. His death occurred when he was struck by the poisonous barb of a stingray while filming a documentary on Australia's Great Barrier Reef.

King, Coretta Scott. American civil-rights activist and widow of civil-rights leader Dr. Martin Luther King, Jr.; died on January 31, at the age of 78. Following the 1968 assassination of her husband, Mrs. King founded and became head of the Martin Luther King, Jr., Center for Nonviolent Social Change, in Atlanta, Georgia. She worked on behalf of African Americans and other minorities, the poor, and women's rights.

Knotts, Don. American television comedy star; died on February 24, at the age of 81. Knotts became well known for his role as the bumbling Deputy Sheriff Barney Fife on the 1960's *Andy Griffith Show*—for which he won five Emmy Awards. After a two-year stint with his own *Don Knotts Show*, he joined the cast of *Three's Company* (1979–84), playing nerdy landlord Ralph Furley. He also starred in several motion pictures.

Coretta Scott King

Lewis, Al. American actor; died on February 3, at the age of 82. Lewis was best known for his role as Grandpa on the mid-1960's television comedy series *The Munsters*. Lewis began his show-business career in burlesque and vaudeville, and he went on to perform on Broadway, in movies, and on television. His first success on television was in the early 1960's series *Car 54, Where Are You?*

McGavin, Darren. American actor; died on February 25, at the age of 83. He is best known for his title role of hardboiled detective Mike Hammer in the 1950's television series, based on stories by Mickey Spillane. He gained more acclaim as a Chicago reporter in the TV horror series *Kolchak: The Night Stalker*. In 1990, McGavin won an Emmy Award (Outstanding Guest Star) for his role as Candice Bergen's father in the TV sitcom *Murphy Brown*.

Morita, Pat. Japanese-American actor; died on November 24, 2005, at the age of 73. Starting out as a stand-up comedian, Morita

Pat Morita

Don Knotts (with Andy Griffith)

worked his way into television, where he became popular as Arnold, the restaurant owner on the *Happy Days* sitcom (1974–84). His defining film role was that of the wise karate teacher in the 1984 movie *The Karate Kid* and three *Karate Kid* sequels.

Palance, Jack. American actor; died on November 10, at the age of 87. With his rugged face, high cheekbones, and menacing sneer, Palance became known for his roles as a Hollywood "bad guy," such as the evil gunfighter Jack Wilson in the classic Western film *Shane* (1953). But he won an Academy Award for Best Supporting Actor in 1992 for his role in the comedy *City Slickers*.

Parks, Gordon. American photographer, filmmaker, writer, and composer; died on March 7, at the age of 93. Parks was the first African-American photographer to be on the staff of *Life* magazine (1948–68). And he was the first African-American to produce and direct a major Hollywood film, the autobiographical *The Learning Tree*. The 1971 film *Shaft*, which Parks directed, was about an African-American private detective and was the first of

Gordon Parks

the "blaxploitation" films to hit movie screens in the 1970's. Parks was awarded the National Medal of Arts in 1988.

Pryor, Richard. American comedian and actor; died on December 10, 2005, at the age of 65. Richard Pryor's stand-up comedy was all about being black in America. His humor was often blunt—but it made blacks and whites laugh together. Pryor also starred in such movie comedies as *Silver Streak* (1976) and *Stir Crazy* (1980). His comedy albums won five Grammy Awards. In 1988, Pryor became the first comedian to receive the Kennedy Center's Mark Twain Prize for American Humor.

Rawls, Lou. American singer; died on January 6, at the age of 72. A versatile, smooth baritone, Rawls sang in a number of genres, from gospel and soul to blues, jazz, and pop. His first hit song, in 1966, was "Love Is a Hurtin' Thing." Ten years later, his biggest hit, "You'll Never Find Another Love Like Mine," was number-one on the rhythm-and-blues charts and number-two on the pop charts. He won three Grammy Awards during his career.

Reeve, Dana. American actress and singer; died on March 6, at the age of 44. When her husband, actor Christopher Reeve, fell from a horse and became paralyzed in 1995, she gave up her career to care for him, and also became a leading advocate for research into spinal-cord paralysis. The year after her husband's death in 2004, she announced that she had lung cancer, even though she had never smoked.

Spelling, Aaron. American television producer; died on June 23, at the age of 83. The most prolific producer in American television history, Spelling worked on almost 200 productions, including *The Mod Squad* (1968–73), *Starsky and Hutch* (1975–79), *Charlie's Angels* (1976–81), *The Love Boat* (1977–86), *Fantasy Island* (1978–84), *Dynasty* (1981–89), *Beverly Hills 90210* (1990–2000), and *Melrose Place* (1992–99).

Spillane, Mickey. American author of crime novels; died on July 17, at the age of 88. Spillane started his career writing for comic

Maureen Stapleton

Dennis Weaver

space satellite, which was launched in 1958. The two belts, which extend from about 400 miles (644 kilometers) above Earth to about 12,000 miles (19,320 kilometers), are called the Van Allen belts.

Weaver, Dennis. American actor; died February 24, at the age of 81. Weaver gained fame playing the role of Chester Goode, the loyal deputy to Sheriff Matt Dillon (James Arness) on the TV Western series *Gunsmoke* (1955–64). In the 1970's, he starred in another series, *McCloud*, playing a lawman from New Mexico who is placed on assignment in New York City. Weaver remained active through 2005, when he played the owner of a thoroughbred racing ranch in the TV series *Wildfire*.

Winters, Shelley. American actress; died on January 14, at the age of 85. Winters acted in some 200 films and television shows. Her roles in *The Diary of Anne Frank* (1959) and *A Patch of Blue* (1965) earned her Academy Awards for Best Supporting Actress. Other notable films include *A Place in the Sun* (1951) and *The Poseidon Adventure* (1972). In the 1990's, she played Roseanne Barr's grandmother on the *Roseanne* sitcom.

books. When one of his stories was rejected, Spillane turned it into a novel, with tough-guy detective Mike Hammer as the hero. The book, *I, the Jury* (1947), was an instant success. Thirteen other Mike Hammer novels followed, including *Kiss Me Deadly* (1955) and *The Girl Hunters* (1963), both of which were made into movies.

Stapleton, Maureen. American actress; died on March 13, at the age of 80. On the Broadway stage, she won a Tony Award (Best Featured Actress) for her role as an Italian widow in Tennessee Williams's *The Rose Tattoo* (1951). Her second Tony (Best Actress) was for her portrayal of an alcoholic in Neil Simon's *The Gingerbread Lady* (1971). In film, she won an Oscar (Best Supporting Actress) for her role as Emma Goldman, an anarchist, in *Reds* (1981).

Van Allen, James A. American physicist; died on August 9, at the age of 91. Using a Geiger counter, Van Allen discovered two belts of charged particles—cosmic rays—trapped in Earth's magnetic field. The Geiger counter was aboard *Explorer I*, the first U.S.

Shelley Winters

INDEPENDENT NATIONS OF THE WORLD

NATION	CAPITAL	AREA (in sq mi)	POPULATION (estimate)	GOVERNMENT
Afghanistan	Kabul	250,000	31,100,000	Hamid Karzai—president
Albania	Tirana	11,100	3,200,000	Alfred Moisiu—president Sali Berisha—premier
Algeria	Algiers	919,595	33,500,000	Abdelaziz Bouteflika—president
Andorra	Andorra la Vella	175	100,000	Albert Pintat—premier
Angola	Luanda	481,354	15,800,000	José Eduardo dos Santos—president
Antigua and Barbuda	St. John's	171	100,000	Baldwin Spencer—prime minister
Argentina	Buenos Aires	1,068,297	39,000,000	Nestor Carlos Kirchner—president
Armenia	Yerevan	11,500	3,000,000	Robert Kocharyan—president
Australia	Canberra	2,967,895	20,600,000	John Howard—prime minister
Austria	Vienna	32,374	8,300,000	Heinz Fischer—president Wolfgang Schüssel—chancellor
Azerbaijan	Baku	33,500	8,500,000	Ilham Aliyev—president
Bahamas	Nassau	5,380	300,000	Perry Christie—prime minister
Bahrain	Manama	240	700,000	Hamad bin Isa al-Khalifa—king
Bangladesh	Dhaka	55,598	146,600,000	Iajuddin Ahmed—president
Barbados	Bridgetown	168	300,000	Owen Arthur—prime minister
Belarus	Minsk	80,154	9,700,000	Aleksandr Lukashenko—president
Belgium	Brussels	11,781	10,500,000	Albert II—king Guy Verhofstadt—premier
Belize	Belmopan	8,867	300,000	Said Musa—prime minister
Benin	Porto-Novo	43,484	8,700,000	Yayi Boni—president
Bhutan	Thimbu	18,147	900,000	Jigme Khesar Namgyel Wangchuck—king
Bolivia	La Paz Sucre	424,165	9,100,000	Evo Morales—president
Bosnia and Herzegovina	Sarajevo	19,800	3,900,000	3-member presidency
Botswana	Gaborone	231,804	1,800,000	Festus Mogae—president
Brazil	Brasília	3,286,478	186,800,000	Luiz Ignácio Lula da Silva—president
Brunei Darussalam	Bandar Seri Begawan	2,226	400,000	Hassanal Bolkiah—head of state
Bulgaria	Sofia	42,823	7,700,000	Georgi Parvanov—president Sergei Stanishev—premier
Burkina Faso	Ouagadougou	105,869	13,600,000	Blaise Compaoré—president
Burma (Myanmar)	Rangoon (Yangon)	261,218	51,000,000	Than Shwe—head of government
Burundi	Bujumbura	10,747	7,800,000	Pierre Nkurunziza—president
Cambodia	Phnom Penh	69,898	14,100,000	Norodom Sihamoni—king Hun Sen—prime minister
Cameroon	Yaoundé	183,569	17,300,000	Paul Biya—president

NATION	CAPITAL	AREA (in sq mi)	POPULATION (estimate)	GOVERNMENT
Canada	Ottawa	3,851,809	32,600,000	Stephen Harper—prime minister
Cape Verde	Praia	1,557	500,000	Pedro Pires—president
Central African Republic	Bangui	240,535	4,300,000	François Bozizé—president
Chad	N'Djamena	495,754	10,000,000	Idriss Deby—president
Chile	Santiago	292,257	16,400,000	Michelle Bachelet—president
China	Beijing	3,705,390	1,311,400,000	Hu Jintao—president Wen Jiabao—premier
Colombia	Bogotá	439,736	46,800,000	Alvaro Uribe Vélez—president
Comoros	Moroni	838	700,000	Ahmed Abdallah Mohamed Sambi—president
Congo (Zaire)	Kinshasa	905,565	62,700,000	Joseph Kabila—president
Congo Republic	Brazzaville	132,047	3,700,000	Denis Sassou-Nguesso—president
Costa Rica	San José	19,575	4,300,000	Oscar Arias Sanchez—president
Croatia	Zagreb	21,829	4,400,000	Stipe Mesic—president
Cuba	Havana	44,218	11,300,000	Fidel Castro—president (incapacitated) Raúl Castro—acting president
Cyprus	Nicosia	3,572	1,000,000	Tassos Papadopoulos—president
Czech Republic	Prague	30,469	10,300,000	Vaclav Klaus—president Mirek Topolanek—premier
Denmark	Copenhagen	16,629	5,400,000	Margrethe II—queen Anders Fogh Rasmussen—premier
Djibouti	Djibouti	8,494	800,000	Ismail Omar Guelleh—president
Dominica	Roseau	290	100,000	Roosevelt Skerrit—prime minister
Dominican Republic	Santo Domingo	18,816	9,000,000	Leonel Fernández Reyna—president
East Timor	Dili	5,743	1,000,000	Kay Rala Xanana Gusmao—president
Ecuador	Quito	109,483	13,300,000	Rafael Correa—president-elect
Egypt	Cairo	386,660	75,400,000	Mohammed Hosni Mubarak—president Ahmed Nazif—premier
El Salvador	San Salvador	8,124	7,000,000	Elias Antonio Saca—president
Equatorial Guinea	Malabo	10,831	500,000	Teodoro Obiang Nguema Mbasogo—president
Eritrea	Asmara	45,405	4,600,000	Isaias Afewerki—president
Estonia	Tallinn	17,413	1,300,000	Toomas Hendrik Ilves—president
Ethiopia	Addis Ababa	426,372	74,800,000	Girma Woldegiorgis—president
Fiji	Suva	7,055	800,000	Josaia Voreqe Bainimarama—president
Finland	Helsinki	130,120	5,300,000	Tarja Halonen—president Matti Vanhanen—premier
France	Paris	213,000	61,200,000	Jacques Chirac—president Dominique de Villepin—premier
Gabon	Libreville	103,346	1,400,000	Omar Bongo—president
Gambia	Banjul	4,361	1,500,000	Yahya Jammeh—head of state
Georgia	Tbilisi	27,000	4,400,000	Mikhail Saakashvili—president

NATION	CAPITAL	AREA (in sq mi)	POPULATION (estimate)	GOVERNMENT
Germany	Berlin	137,744	82,400,000	Horst Köhler—president Angela Merkel—chancellor
Ghana	Accra	92,099	22,600,000	John Kufuor—president
Greece	Athens	50,944	11,100,000	Karolos Papoulias—president Costas Caramanlis—premier
Grenada	St. George's	133	100,000	Keith Mitchell—prime minister
Guatemala	Guatemala City	42,042	13,000,000	Oscar Berger Perdomo—president
Guinea	Conakry	94,926	9,800,000	Lansana Conté—president
Guinea-Bissau	Bissau	13,948	1,400,000	João Bernardo Vieira—president
Guyana	Georgetown	83,000	700,000	Bharrat Jagdeo—president
Haiti	Port-au-Prince	10,714	8,500,000	René Garcia Préval—president
Honduras	Tegucigalpa	43,277	7,400,000	Manuel Zelaya—president
Hungary	Budapest	35,919	10,100,000	László Sólyom—president Ferenc Gyurcsany—premier
Iceland	Reykjavik	39,768	300,000	Olafur Grimsson—president Geir H. Haarde—premier
India	New Delhi	1,269,340	1,121,800,000	A.P.J. Abdul Kalam—president Manmohan Singh—prime minister
Indonesia	Jakarta	735,358	225,500,000	Susilo Bambang Yudhoyono—president
Iran	Tehran	636,293	70,300,000	Ayatollah Ali Khamenei—religious leader Mahmoud Ahmadinejad—president
Iraq	Baghdad	167,925	29,600,000	Jalal Talabani—president Nouri Kamel al-Maliki—premier
Ireland	Dublin	27,136	4,200,000	Mary McAleese—president Bertie Ahern—prime minister
Israel	Jerusalem	8,019	7,200,000	Moshe Katsav—president Ehud Olmert—prime minister
Italy	Rome	116,303	59,000,000	Giorgio Napolitano—president Romano Prodi—premier
Ivory Coast	Yamoussoukro	124,503	19,700,000	Laurent Gbagbo—president
Jamaica	Kingston	4,244	2,700,000	Portia Simpson Miller—prime minister
Japan	Tokyo	143,751	127,800,000	Akihito—emperor Shinzo Abe—premier
Jordan	Amman	35,475	5,600,000	Abdullah II—king Marouf al-Bakhit—prime minister
Kazakhstan	Almaty	1,049,000	15,300,000	Nursultan A. Nazarbayev—president
Kenya	Nairobi	224,959	34,700,000	Mwai Kibaki—president
Kiribati	Tarawa	264	100,000	Anote Tong—president
Korea (North)	Pyongyang	46,540	23,100,000	Kim Jong Il—president Pak Pong Chu—premier
Korea (South)	Seoul	38,025	48,500,000	Roh Moo Hyun—president Han Myeong Sook—premier
Kuwait	Kuwait	6,880	2,700,000	Sabah al-Ahmad al-Jabir al-Sabah— head of state
Kyrgyzstan	Bishkek	76,641	5,200,000	Kurmanbek Bakiyev—president

NATION	CAPITAL	AREA (in sq mi)	POPULATION (estimate)	GOVERNMENT
Laos	Vientiane	91,429	6,100,000	Choummaly Sayasone—president Bouasone Bouphavanh—premier
Latvia	Riga	24,600	2,300,000	Vaira Vike-Freiberga—president
Lebanon	Beirut	4,015	3,900,000	Emile Lahoud—president Fouad Siniora—prime minister
Lesotho	Maseru	11,720	1,800,000	Letsie III—king Bethuel Pakalitha Mosisili—premier
Liberia	Monrovia	43,000	3,400,000	Ellen Johnson-Sirleaf—president
Libya	Tripoli	679,362	5,900,000	Muammar el-Qaddafi—head of government
Liechtenstein	Vaduz	61	40,000	Hans Adam II—prince
Lithuania	Vilnius	25,174	3,400,000	Valdas Adamkus—president
Luxembourg	Luxembourg	998	500,000	Henri—grand duke Jean-Claude Juncker—premier
Macedonia	Skopje	9,928	2,000,000	Branko Crvenkovski—president
Madagascar	Antananarivo	226,657	17,800,000	Marc Ravalomanana—president
Malawi	Lilongwe	45,747	12,800,000	Bingu wa Mutharika—president
Malaysia	Kuala Lumpur	127,317	26,900,000	Sultan Mizan Zainal Abidin—king Abdullah Badawi—prime minister
Maldives	Male	115	300,000	Maumoon Abdul Gayoom—president
Mali	Bamako	478,765	13,900,000	Amadou Toumani Touré—president
Malta	Valletta	122	400,000	Eddie Fenech Adami—president Lawrence Gonzi—prime minister
Marshall Islands	Majuro	70	100,000	Kessai Note—president
Mauritania	Nouakchott	397,954	3,200,000	Ely Ould Mohamed Vall—president
Mauritius	Port Louis	790	1,300,000	Anerood Jugnauth—president Navinchandra Ramgoolam—premier
Mexico	Mexico City	761,602	108,300,000	Felipe Calderón—president
Micronesia	Colonia	271	100,000	Joseph J. Urusemal—president
Moldova	Chisinau	13,000	4,000,000	Vladimir Voronin—president
Monaco	Monaco-Ville	0.6	30,000	Albert II—prince
Mongolia	Ulan Bator	604,248	2,600,000	Nambaryn Enkhbayar—president
Montenegro	Podgorica	5,415	631,000	Filip Vujanovic—president
Morocco	Rabat	172,413	31,700,000	Mohammed VI—king Driss Jettou—premier
Mozambique	Maputo	309,494	19,900,000	Armando Guebuza—president
Namibia	Windhoek	318,260	2,100,000	Hifikepunye Pohamba—president
Nauru	Yaren District	8	10,000	Ludwig Scotty—president
Nepal	Katmandu	54,362	26,000,000	Gyanendra Bir Bikram Shah—king
Netherlands	Amsterdam	15,770	16,400,000	Beatrix—queen Jan Peter Balkenende—premier
New Zealand	Wellington	103,736	4,100,000	Helen Clark—prime minister
Nicaragua	Managua	50,193	5,600,000	Daniel Ortega—president
Niger	Niamey	489,190	14,400,000	Mamadou Tandja—president

NATION	CAPITAL	AREA (in sq mi)	POPULATION (estimate)	GOVERNMENT
Nigeria	Abuja	356,667	134,500,000	Olusegun Obasanjo—president
Norway	Oslo	125,056	4,700,000	Harold V—king Jens Stoltenberg—premier
Oman	Muscat	82,030	2,600,000	Qaboos bin Said al-Said—sultan
Pakistan	Islamabad	310,404	165,800,000	Pervez Musharraf—president
Palau	Koror	192	20,000	Tommy Remengesau—president
Panama	Panama City	29,761	3,300,000	Martín Torrijos Espino—president
Papua New Guinea	Port Moresby	178,260	6,000,000	Michael Somare—prime minister
Paraguay	Asunción	157,047	6,300,000	Nicanor Duarte Frutos—president
Peru	Lima	496,222	28,400,000	Alan García—president
Philippines	Manila	115,830	86,300,000	Gloria Macapagal-Arroyo—president Noli de Castro—vice-president
Poland	Warsaw	120,725	38,100,000	Jaroslaw Kaczynski—premier
Portugal	Lisbon	35,553	10,600,000	Anibal António Cavaco Silva—president José Sócrates Carvalho Pinto de Sousa—premier
Qatar	Doha	4,247	800,000	Hamad bin Khalifa al-Thani—head of state
Romania	Bucharest	91,700	21,600,000	Traian Basescu—president Calin Popescu-Tariceanu—premier
Russia	Moscow	6,600,000	142,300,000	Vladimir V. Putin—president
Rwanda	Kigali	10,169	9,100,000	Paul Kagame—president
St. Kitts and Nevis	Basseterre	105	50,000	Denzil Douglas—prime minister
St. Lucia	Castries	238	200,000	John Compton—prime minister
St. Vincent and the Grenadines	Kingstown	150	100,000	Ralph Gonsalves—prime minister
Samoa	Apia	1,097	200,000	Malietoa Tanumafili II—head of state
San Marino	San Marino	24	30,000	Fiorenzo Stolfi—head of government
São Tomé and Príncipe	São Tomé	372	200,000	Fradique de Menezes—president
Saudi Arabia	Riyadh	830,000	24,100,000	Abdullah bin Abdul-Aziz al Saud—king
Senegal	Dakar	75,750	11,900,000	Abdoulaye Wade—president
Serbia	Belgrade	34,116	9,400,000	Boris Tadic—president
Seychelles	Victoria	107	100,000	James Michel—president
Sierra Leone	Freetown	27,700	5,700,000	Ahmad Tejan Kabbah—president
Singapore	Singapore	224	4,500,000	S. R. Nathan—president Lee Hsien Loong—prime minister
Slovakia	Bratislava	18,933	5,400,000	Ivan Gasparovic—president
Slovenia	Ljubljana	7,819	2,000,000	Janez Drnovsek—president
Solomon Islands	Honiara	10,983	500,000	Manasseh Sogavare—prime minister
Somalia	Mogadishu	246,200	8,900,000	Abdullahi Yusuf Ahmed—president
South Africa	Pretoria Cape Town Bloemfontein	471,444	47,300,000	Thabo Mbeki—president
Spain	Madrid	194,896	45,500,000	Juan Carlos I—king José Luis Rodríguez Zapatero—premier

NATION	CAPITAL	AREA (in sq mi)	POPULATION (estimate)	GOVERNMENT
Sri Lanka	Colombo	25,332	19,900,000	Mahinda Rajapaksa—president
Sudan	Khartoum	967,500	41,200,000	O. Hassan Ahmed al-Bashir—president
Suriname	Paramaribo	63,037	500,000	Runaldo Ronald Venetiaan—president
Swaziland	Mbabane	6,704	1,100,000	Mswati III—king
Sweden	Stockholm	173,731	9,100,000	Carl XVI Gustaf—king Fredrik Reinfeldt—premier
Switzerland	Bern	15,941	7,500,000	Micheline Calmy-Rey—president
Syria	Damascus	71,498	19,500,000	Bashar al-Assad—president Naji Otari—premier
Taiwan	Taipei	13,885	22,800,000	Chen Shui-bian—president Su Tseng-chang—premier
Tajikistan	Dushanbe	55,250	7,000,000	Oqil Oqilov—premier
Tanzania	Dar es Salaam	364,898	37,900,000	Jakaya Kikwete—president
Thailand	Bangkok	198,457	65,200,000	Bhumibol Adulyadej—king Surayud Chulanont—premier
Togo	Lomé	21,622	6,300,000	Faure Gnassingbe—president
Tonga	Nuku'alofa	270	100,000	George Tupou V—king Feleti Sevele—premier
Trinidad & Tobago	Port of Spain	1,980	1,300,000	George Maxwell Richards—president Patrick Manning—prime minister
Tunisia	Tunis	63,170	10,100,000	Zine el-Abidine Ben Ali—president
Turkey	Ankara	301,381	73,700,000	Ahmet Necdet Sezer—president Recep Tayyip Erdogan—prime minister
Turkmenistan	Ashkhabad	188,455	5,300,000	K. Berdymukhamedov—head of state
Tuvalu	Funafuti	10	10,000	Apisai Ielemia—prime minister
Uganda	Kampala	91,134	27,700,000	Yoweri Museveni—president
Ukraine	Kiev	231,990	46,800,000	Viktor A. Yushchenko—president
United Arab Emirates	Abu Dhabi	32,278	4,900,000	Khalifa bin Zayed al-Nahayan—president
United Kingdom	London	94,226	60,500,000	Elizabeth II—queen Tony Blair—prime minister
United States	Washington, D.C.	3,618,467	299,100,000	George W. Bush—president Richard Cheney—vice-president
Uruguay	Montevideo	68,037	3,300,000	Tabaré Vázquez—president
Uzbekistan	Tashkent	172,750	26,200,000	Islam A. Karimov—president
Vanuatu	Vila	5,700	200,000	Kalkot Matas Kelekele—president
Vatican City	Vatican City	0.17	900	Benedict XVI—pope
Venezuela	Caracas	352,143	27,000,000	Hugo Chávez—president
Vietnam	Hanoi	128,402	84,200,000	Nong Duc Manh—Communist Party secretary Nguyen Tan Dung—premier
Yemen	Sana	203,849	21,600,000	Ali Abdullah Saleh—president Abd al-Qadir Ba Jamal—premier
Zambia	Lusaka	290,585	11,900,000	Levy Mwanawasa—president
Zimbabwe	Harare	150,333	13,100,000	Robert Mugabe—president

THE CONGRESS OF THE UNITED STATES

UNITED STATES SENATE
(50 Democrats, 49 Republicans, 1 Independent)

Alabama
Richard C. Shelby (R)
Jeff Sessions (R)

Alaska
Ted Stevens (R)
Lisa Murkowski (R)

Arizona
John S. McCain III (R)
Jon Kyl (R)**

Arkansas
Blanche L. Lincoln (D)
Mark Pryor (D)

California
Barbara Boxer (D)
Dianne Feinstein (D)**

Colorado
Wayne Allard (R)
Ken Salazar (D)

Connecticut
Christopher J. Dodd (D)
Joseph I. Lieberman (D)***

Delaware
Joseph R. Biden, Jr. (D)
Thomas Carper (D)**

Florida
Mel Martinez (R)
Bill Nelson (D)**

Georgia
Johnny Isakson (R)
Saxby Chambliss (R)

Hawaii
Daniel K. Inouye (D)
Daniel K. Akaka (D)**

Idaho
Larry Craig (R)
Michael Crapo (R)

Illinois
Richard J. Durbin (D)
Barack Obama (D)

Indiana
Richard G. Lugar (R)**
Evan Bayh (D)

Iowa
Chuck Grassley (R)
Tom Harkin (D)

Kansas
Sam Brownback (R)
Pat Roberts (R)

Kentucky
Mitch McConnell (R)
Jim Bunning (R)

Louisiana
David Vitter (R)
Mary Landrieu (D)

Maine
Olympia J. Snowe (R)**
Susan Collins (R)

Maryland
Barbara A. Mikulski (D)
Ben Cardin (D)*

Massachusetts
Edward M. Kennedy (D)**
John Kerry (D)

Michigan
Carl Levin (D)
Debbie Stabenow (D)**

Minnesota
Norm Coleman (R)
Amy Klobuchar (D)*

Mississippi
Thad Cochran (R)
Trent Lott (R)**

Missouri
Christopher Bond (R)
Claire McCaskill (D)*

Montana
Max Baucus (D)
Jon Tester (D)*

Nebraska
Chuck Hagel (R)
Ben Nelson (D)**

Nevada
Harry Reid (D)
John Ensign (R)**

New Hampshire
Judd Gregg (R)
John E. Sununu (R)

New Jersey
Frank Lautenberg (D)
Robert Menendez**

New Mexico
Pete V. Domenici (R)
Jeff Bingaman (D)**

New York
Charles E. Schumer (D)
Hillary Rodham Clinton (D)**

North Carolina
Richard Burr (R)
Elizabeth Dole (R)

North Dakota
Kent Conrad (D)**
Byron L. Dorgan (D)

Ohio
George Voinovich (R)
Sherrod Brown (D)*

Oklahoma
Tom Coburn (R)
James M. Inhofe (R)

Oregon
Gordon Smith (R)
Ron Wyden (D)

Pennsylvania
Arlen Specter (R)
Robert P. Casey, Jr. (D)*

Rhode Island
Jack Reed (D)
Sheldon Whitehouse (D)*

South Carolina
Jim DeMint (R)
Lindsey Graham (R)

South Dakota
John Thune (R)
Tim Johnson (D)

Tennessee
Lamar Alexander (R)
Bob Corker (R)*

Texas
Kay Bailey Hutchison (R)**
John Cornyn (R)

Utah
Orrin G. Hatch (R)**
Robert F. Bennett (R)

Vermont
Patrick J. Leahy (D)
Bernie Sanders (I)*

Virginia
John W. Warner (R)
Jim Webb (D)*

Washington
Patty Murray (D)
Maria Cantwell (D)**

West Virginia
Robert C. Byrd (D)**
John D. Rockefeller IV (D)

Wisconsin
Herb Kohl (D)**
Russell D. Feingold (D)

Wyoming
Craig Thomas (R)**
Michael Enzi (R)

* elected in 2006
** re-elected in 2006
*** re-elected as an Independent
    in 2006
all others, incumbents

(D) Democrat
(R) Republican
(I) Independent

UNITED STATES HOUSE OF REPRESENTATIVES
(233 Democrats, 202 Republicans)

Alabama
1. J. Bonner (R)
2. T. Everett (R)
3. M. Rogers (R)
4. R. B. Aderholt (R)
5. R. E. Cramer, Jr. (D)
6. S. Bachus (R)
7. A. Davis (D)

Alaska
   D. Young (R)

Arizona
1. R. Renzi (R)
2. T. Franks (R)
3. J. B. Shadegg (R)
4. E. Pastor (D)
5. H. Mitchell (D)*
6. J. Flake (R)
7. R. M. Grijalva (D)
8. G. Giffords (D)*

Arkansas
1. M. Berry (D)
2. V. Snyder (D)
3. J. Boozman (R)
4. M. Ross (D)

California
1. M. Thompson (D)
2. W. Herger (R)
3. D. Lungren (R)
4. J. T. Doolittle (R)
5. D. O. Matsui (D)
6. L. C. Woolsey (D)
7. G. Miller (D)
8. N. Pelosi (D)
9. B. Lee (D)
10. E. O. Tauscher (D)
11. J. McNerney (D)*
12. T. Lantos (D)
13. F. P. Stark (D)
14. A. G. Eshoo (D)
15. M. M. Honda (D)
16. Z. Lofgren (D)
17. S. Farr (D)
18. D. A. Cardoza (D)
19. G. Radanovich (R)
20. J. Costa (D)
21. D. Nunes (R)
22. K. McCarthy (R)*
23. L. Capps (D)
24. E. Gallegly (R)
25. H. P. McKeon (R)
26. D. Dreier (R)
27. B. Sherman (D)
28. H. L. Berman (D)
29. A. B. Schiff (D)
30. H. A. Waxman (D)
31. X. Becerra (D)
32. H. L. Solis (D)
33. D. E. Watson (D)
34. L. Roybal-Allard (D)
35. M. Waters (D)
36. J. Harman (D)
37. J. Millender-McDonald (D)
38. G. F. Napolitano (D)
39. L. T. Sanchez (D)
40. E. R. Royce (R)
41. J. Lewis (R)
42. G. G. Miller (R)
43. J. Baca (D)
44. K. Calvert (R)
45. M. Bono (R)
46. D. Rohrabacher (R)
47. L. Sanchez (D)
48. J. Campbell (R)
49. D. E. Issa (R)
50. B. Bilbray (R)
51. B. Filner (D)
52. D. Hunter (R)
53. S. A. Davis (D)

Colorado
1. D. DeGette (D)
2. M. Udall (D)
3. J. Salazar (D)
4. M. N. Musgrave (R)
5. D. Lamborn (R)*
6. T. G. Tancredo (R)
7. E. Perlmutter (D)*

Connecticut
1. J. B. Larson (D)
2. J. Courtney (D)*
3. R. L. DeLauro (D)
4. C. Shays (R)
5. C. Murphy (D)*

Delaware
   M. N. Castle (R)

Florida
1. J. Miller (R)
2. A. Boyd (D)
3. C. Brown (D)
4. A. Crenshaw (R)
5. G. Brown-Waite (R)
6. C. Stearns (R)
7. J. L. Mica (R)
8. R. Keller (R)
9. G. M. Bilirakis (R)*
10. C. W. Young (R)
11. K. Castor (D)*
12. A. H. Putnam (R)
13. V. Buchanan (R)*
14. C. Mack (R)
15. D. Weldon (R)
16. T. Mahoney (D)*
17. K. B. Meek (D)
18. I. Ros-Lehtinen (R)
19. R. Wexler (D)
20. D. Wasserman Schultz (D)
21. L. Diaz-Balart (R)
22. R. Klein (D)*
23. A. L. Hastings (D)
24. T. Feeney (R)
25. M. Diaz-Balart (R)

Georgia
1. J. Kingston (R)
2. S. D. Bishop, Jr. (D)
3. L. A. Westmoreland (R)
4. H. Johnson (D)*
5. J. Lewis (D)
6. T. Price (R)
7. J. Linder (R)
8. J. Marshall (D)
9. N. Deal (R)
10. C. Norwood (R)
11. P. Gingrey (R)
12. J. Barrow (D)
13. D. Scott (D)

Hawaii
1. N. Abercrombie (D)
2. M. Hirono (D)*

Idaho
1. B. Sali (R)*
2. M. K. Simpson (R)

Illinois
1. B. L. Rush (D)
2. J. L. Jackson, Jr. (D)
3. D. Lipinski (D)
4. L. V. Gutierrez (D)
5. R. Emanuel (D)
6. P. Roskam (R)*
7. D. K. Davis (D)
8. M. L. Bean (D)
9. J. D. Schakowsky (D)
10. M. S. Kirk (R)
11. J. Weller (R)
12. J. F. Costello (D)
13. J. Biggert (R)
14. J. D. Hastert (R)
15. T. V. Johnson (R)
16. D. A. Manzullo (R)
17. P. Hare (D)*
18. R. LaHood (R)
19. J. Shimkus (R)

Indiana
1. P. J. Visclosky (D)
2. J. Donnelly (D)*
3. M. E. Souder (R)
4. S. Buyer (R)
5. D. Burton (R)
6. M. Pence (R)
7. J. Carson (D)
8. B. Ellsworth (D)*
9. B. Hill (D)*

Iowa
1. B. Braley (D)*
2. D. Loebsack (D)*
3. L. L. Boswell (D)
4. T. Latham (R)
5. S. King (R)

Kansas
1. J. Moran (R)
2. N. Boyda (D)*
3. D. Moore (D)
4. T. Tiahrt (R)

Kentucky
1. E. Whitfield (R)
2. R. Lewis (R)
3. J. Yarmuth (D)*
4. G. Davis (R)
5. H. Rogers (R)
6. B. Chandler (D)

Louisiana
1. B. Jindal (R)
2. W. J. Jefferson (D)
3. C. Melancon (D)
4. J. McCrery (R)
5. R. Alexander (R)
6. R. H. Baker (R)
7. C. Boustany (R)

Maine
1. T. H. Allen (D)
2. M. H. Michaud (D)

Maryland
1. W. T. Gilchrest (R)
2. C.A. Ruppersberger (D)
3. J. Sarbanes (D)*
4. A. R. Wynn (D)
5. S. H. Hoyer (D)
6. R. G. Bartlett (R)
7. E. E. Cummings (D)
8. C. Van Hollen (D)

Massachusetts
1. J. W. Olver (D)
2. R. E. Neal (D)
3. J. P. McGovern (D)
4. B. Frank (D)
5. M. T. Meehan (D)
6. J. F. Tierney (D)
7. E. J. Markey (D)
8. M. E. Capuano (D)
9. S. F. Lynch (D)
10. W. D. Delahunt (D)

Michigan
1. B. Stupak (D)
2. P. Hoekstra (R)
3. V. J. Ehlers (R)
4. D. Camp (R)
5. D. E. Kildee (D)
6. F. Upton (R)
7. T. Walberg (R)*
8. M. Rogers (R)
9. J. Knollenberg (R)
10. C. S. Miller (R)
11. T. G. McCotter (R)
12. S. M. Levin (D)
13. C. C. Kilpatrick (D)
14. J. Conyers, Jr. (D)
15. J. D. Dingell (D)

Minnesota
1. T. Walz (D)*
2. J. Kline (R)
3. J. Ramstad (R)
4. B. McCollum (D)

5. K. Ellison (D)*
6. M. Bachmann (R)*
7. C. C. Peterson (D)
8. J. L. Oberstar (D)

Mississippi
1. R. F. Wicker (R)
2. B. G. Thompson (D)
3. C. W. Pickering (R)
4. G. Taylor (D)

Missouri
1. W. L. Clay (D)
2. W. T. Akin (R)
3. R. Carnahan (D)
4. I. Skelton (D)
5. E. Cleaver (D)
6. S. Graves (R)
7. R. Blunt (R)
8. J. A. Emerson (R)
9. K. C. Hulshof (R)

Montana
    D. R. Rehberg (R)

Nebraska
1. J. Fortenberry (R)
2. L. Terry (R)
3. A. Smith (R)*

Nevada
1. S. Berkley (D)
2. D. Heller (R)*
3. J. C. Porter (R)

New Hampshire
1. C. Shea-Porter (D)*
2. P. Hodes (D)*

New Jersey
1. R. E. Andrews (D)
2. F. A. LoBiondo (R)
3. J. Saxton (R)
4. C. H. Smith (R)
5. S. Garrett (R)
6. F. Pallone, Jr. (D)
7. M. Ferguson (R)
8. B. Pascrell, Jr. (D)
9. S. R. Rothman (D)
10. D. M. Payne (D)
11. R. P. Frelinghuysen (R)
12. R. D. Holt (D)
13. A. Sires (D)*

New Mexico
1. H. Wilson (R)
2. S. Pearce (R)
3. T. Udall (D)

New York
1. T. H. Bishop (D)
2. S. Israel (D)
3. P. T. King (R)
4. C. McCarthy (D)
5. G. L. Ackerman (D)
6. G. W. Meeks (D)

7. J. Crowley (D)
8. J. Nadler (D)
9. A. D. Weiner (D)
10. E. Towns (D)
11. Y. D. Clarke (D)*
12. N. M. Velázquez (D)
13. V. Fossella (R)
14. C. B. Maloney (D)
15. C. B. Rangel (D)
16. J. E. Serrano (D)
17. E. L. Engel (D)
18. N. M. Lowey (D)
19. J. Hall (D)*
20. K.E. Gillibrand (D)*
21. M. R. McNulty (D)
22. M. D. Hinchey (D)
23. J. M. McHugh (R)
24. M.A. Arcuri (D)*
25. J. T. Walsh (R)
26. T. M. Reynolds (R)
27. B. Higgins (D)
28. L. M. Slaughter (D)
29. J. R. Kuhl, Jr. (R)

North Carolina
1. D. K. Butterfield (D)
2. B. Etheridge (D)
3. W. B. Jones (R)
4. D. E. Price (D)
5. V. Foxx (R)
6. H. Coble (R)
7. M. McIntyre (D)
8. R. Hayes (R)
9. S. W. Myrick (R)
10. P. T. McHenry (R)
11. H. Shuler (D)*
12. M. L. Watt (D)
13. B. Miller (D)

North Dakota
    E. Pomeroy (D)

Ohio
1. S. Chabot (R)
2. J. Schmidt (R)
3. M. R. Turner (R)
4. J. Jordan (R)*
5. P. E. Gillmor (R)
6. C. Wilson (D)*
7. D. L. Hobson (R)
8. J. A. Boehner (R)
9. M. Kaptur (D)
10. D. J. Kucinich (D)
11. S. T. Jones (D)
12. P. J. Tiberi (R)
13. B. Sutton (D)*
14. S. C. LaTourette (R)
15. D. Pryce (R)
16. R. Regula (R)
17. T. Ryan (D)
18. Z. Space (D)*

Oklahoma
1. J. Sullivan (R)
2. D. Boren (D)
3. F. D. Lucas (R)
4. T. Cole (R)
5. M. Fallin (R)*

Oregon
1. D. Wu (D)
2. G. Walden (R)

3. E. Blumenauer (D)
4. P. A. DeFazio (D)
5. D. Hooley (D)

Pennsylvania
1. R. A. Brady (D)
2. C. Fattah (D)
3. P. English (R)
4. J. Altmire (D)*
5. J. E. Peterson (R)
6. J. Gerlach (R)
7. J. Sestak (D)*
8. P. Murphy (D)*
9. B. Shuster (R)
10. C. Carney (D)*
11. P. E. Kanjorski (D)
12. J. P. Murtha (D)
13. A. Y. Schwartz (D)
14. M. F. Doyle (D)
15. C. W. Dent (R)
16. J. R. Pitts (R)
17. T. Holden (D)
18. T. Murphy (R)
19. T. R. Platts (R)

Rhode Island
1. P. J. Kennedy (D)
2. J. R. Langevin (D)

South Carolina
1. H. E. Brown, Jr. (R)
2. J. Wilson (R)
3. J. G. Barrett (R)
4. B. Inglis (R)
5. J. M. Spratt, Jr. (D)
6. J. E. Clyburn (D)

South Dakota
    S. Herseth (D)

Tennessee
1. D. Davis (R)*
2. J. J. Duncan, Jr. (R)
3. Z. Wamp (R)
4. L. Davis (D)
5. J. Cooper (D)
6. B. Gordon (D)
7. M. Blackburn (R)
8. J. S. Tanner (D)
9. S. Cohen (D)*

Texas
1. L. Gohmert (R)
2. T. Poe (R)
3. S. Johnson (R)
4. R. M. Hall (R)
5. J. Hensarling (R)
6. J. Barton (R)
7. J. A. Culberson (R)
8. K. Brady (R)
9. A. Green (D)
10. M. T. McCaul (R)
11. K. M. Conaway (R)
12. K. Granger (R)
13. M. Thornberry (R)
14. R. Paul (R)
15. R. Hinojosa (D)
16. S. Reyes (D)
17. C. Edwards (D)
18. S. Jackson-Lee (D)

19. R. Neugebauer (R)
20. C. A. Gonzalez (D)
21. L. S. Smith (R)
22. N. Lampson (D)*
23. C. D. Rodriguez (D)*
24. K. Marchant (R)
25. L. Doggett (D)
26. M. C. Burgess (R)
27. S. P. Ortiz (D)
28. H. Cuellar (D)
29. G. Green (D)
30. E. B. Johnson (D)
31. J. R. Carter (R)
32. P. Sessions (R)

Utah
1. R. Bishop (R)
2. J. Matheson (D)
3. C. Cannon (R)

Vermont
    P. Welch (D)*

Virginia
1. J. A. Davis (R)
2. T. D. Drake (R)
3. R. C. Scott (D)
4. J. R. Forbes (R)
5. V. H. Goode, Jr. (R)
6. B. Goodlatte (R)
7. E. Cantor (R)
8. J. P. Moran (D)
9. R. Boucher (D)
10. F. R. Wolf (R)
11. T. Davis (R)

Washington
1. J. Inslee (D)
2. R. Larsen (D)
3. B. Baird (D)
4. D. Hastings (R)
5. C. McMorris Rodgers (R)
6. N. D. Dicks (D)
7. J. McDermott (D)
8. D. G. Reichert (R)
9. A. Smith (D)

West Virginia
1. A. B. Mollohan (D)
2. S. M. Capito (R)
3. N. J. Rahall II (D)

Wisconsin
1. P. Ryan (R)
2. T. Baldwin (D)
3. R. Kind (D)
4. G. Moore (D)
5. F. J. Sensenbrenner, Jr. (R)
6. T. E. Petri (R)
7. D. R. Obey (D)
8. S. Kagen (D)*

Wyoming
    B. Cubin (R)

(D) Democrat
(R) Republican

* elected in 2006; all others re-elected
in 2006

UNITED STATES SUPREME COURT

Chief Justice: John G. Roberts, Jr. (2005)
Associate Justices:
John Paul Stevens (1975)
Antonin Scalia (1986)
Anthony M. Kennedy (1988)
David H. Souter (1990)
Clarence Thomas (1991)
Ruth Bader Ginsburg (1993)
Stephen G. Breyer (1994)
Samuel A. Alito, Jr. (2006)

UNITED STATES CABINET

Secretary of Agriculture: Mike Johanns
Attorney General: Alberto R. Gonzales
Secretary of Commerce: Carlos M. Gutierrez
Secretary of Defense: Robert M. Gates
Secretary of Education: Margaret Spellings
Secretary of Energy: Samuel W. Bodman
Secretary of Health and Human Services: Michael O. Leavitt
Secretary of Homeland Security: Michael Chertoff
Secretary of Housing and Urban Development: Alphonso Jackson
Secretary of the Interior: Dirk Kempthorne
Secretary of Labor: Elaine L. Chao
Secretary of State: Condoleezza Rice
Secretary of Transportation: Mary E. Peters
Secretary of the Treasury: Henry M. Paulson, Jr.
Secretary of Veterans Affairs: Jim Nicholson

After the November elections, Nancy Pelosi, the Democratic leader in the House of Representatives, was chosen to become the first woman Speaker of the House in U.S. history.

STATE GOVERNORS

Alabama	Bob Riley (R)**	Montana	Brian Schweitzer (D)
Alaska	Sarah Palin (R)*	Nebraska	Dave Heineman (R)**
Arizona	Janet Napolitano (D)**	Nevada	Jim Gibbons (R)*
Arkansas	Mike Beebe (D)*	New Hampshire	John Lynch (D)**
California	Arnold Schwarzenegger (R)**	New Jersey	Jon S. Corzine (D)
Colorado	Bill Ritter (D)*	New Mexico	Bill Richardson (D)**
Connecticut	M. Jodi Rell (R)**	New York	Eliot Spitzer (D)*
Delaware	Ruth Ann Minner (D)	North Carolina	Michael F. Easley (D)
Florida	Charlie Crist (R)*	North Dakota	John Hoeven (R)
Georgia	Sonny Perdue (R)**	Ohio	Ted Strickland (D)*
Hawaii	Linda Lingle (R)**	Oklahoma	Brad Henry (D)**
Idaho	C.L."Butch" Otter (R)*	Oregon	Ted Kulongoski (D)**
Illinois	Rod Blagojevich (D)**	Pennsylvania	Edward G. Rendell (D)**
Indiana	Mitch Daniels (R)	Rhode Island	Don Carcieri (R)**
Iowa	Chet Culver (D)*	South Carolina	Mark Sanford (R)**
Kansas	Kathleen Sebelius (D)**	South Dakota	Mike Rounds (R)**
Kentucky	Ernie Fletcher (R)	Tennessee	Phil Bredesen (D)**
Louisiana	Kathleen B. Blanco (D)	Texas	Rick Perry (R)**
Maine	John Baldacci (D)**	Utah	Jon Huntsman, Jr. (R)
Maryland	Martin O'Malley (D)*	Vermont	Jim Douglas (R)**
Massachusetts	Deval Patrick (D)*	Virginia	Timothy M. Kaine (D)
Michigan	Jennifer Granholm (D)**	Washington	Christine Gregoire (D)
Minnesota	Tim Pawlenty (R)**	West Virginia	Joseph Manchin III (D)
Mississippi	Haley Barbour (R)	Wisconsin	Jim Doyle (D)**
Missouri	Matt Blunt (R)	Wyoming	Dave Freudenthal (D)**

*elected in 2006   **re-elected in 2006   all others, incumbents   (D) Democrat (R) Republican

393

CANADA

Capital: Ottawa
Head of State: Queen Elizabeth II
Governor General: Michaëlle Jean
Prime Minister: Stephen Harper (Conservative)
Leader of the Opposition: Stéphane Dion (Liberal)
Population: 32,623,500
Area: 3,851,809 sq mi (9,976,185 km²)

PROVINCES AND TERRITORIES

Alberta
Capital: Edmonton
Lieutenant Governor: Norman L. Kwong
Premier: Ed Stelmach (Progressive Conservative)
Leader of the Opposition: Kevin Taft (Liberal)
Entered Confederation: Sept. 1, 1905
Population: 3,375,800
Area: 255,285 sq mi (661,188 km²)

British Columbia
Capital: Victoria
Lieutenant Governor: Iona Campagnolo
Premier: Gordon Campbell (Liberal)
Leader of the Opposition: Carole James
   (New Democratic Party)
Entered Confederation: July 20, 1871
Population: 4,310,500
Area: 366,255 sq mi (948,600 km²)

Manitoba
Capital: Winnipeg
Lieutenant Governor: John Harvard
Premier: Gary Albert Doer (New Democratic Party)
Leader of the Opposition: Hugh McFayden
   (Progressive Conservative)
Entered Confederation: July 15, 1870
Population: 1,177,800
Area: 251,000 sq mi (650,090 km²)

New Brunswick
Capital: Fredericton
Lieutenant Governor: Herménégilde Chiasson
Premier: Shawn M. Graham (Liberal)
Leader of the Opposition: Bernard Lord
   (Progressive Conservative)
Entered Confederation: July 1, 1867
Population: 749,200
Area: 28,354 sq mi (73,436 km²)

Newfoundland and Labrador
Capital: St. John's
Lieutenant Governor: Edward M. Roberts
Premier: Danny Williams (Progressive Conservative)
Leader of the Opposition: Gerry Reid (Liberal)
Entered Confederation: March 31, 1949
Population: 509,700
Area: 156,185 sq mi (404,517 km²)

Nova Scotia
Capital: Halifax
Lieutenant Governor: Mayann E. Francis
Premier: Rodney MacDonald (Progressive Conservative)
Leader of the Opposition: Darrell Dexter (New
   Democratic Party)
Entered Confederation: July 1, 1867
Population: 934,400
Area: 21,425 sq mi (55,491 km²)

Ontario
Capital: Toronto
Lieutenant Governor: James K. Bartleman
Premier: Dalton McGuinty (Liberal)
Leader of the Opposition: John Tory (Progressive
   Conservative)
Entered Confederation: July 1, 1867
Population: 12,687,000
Area: 412,582 sq mi (1,068,582 km²)

Prince Edward Island
Capital: Charlottetown
Lieutenant Governor: Barbara A. Hagerman
Premier: Patrick G. Binns (Progressive Conservative)
Leader of the Opposition: Robert Ghiz (Liberal)
Entered Confederation: July 1, 1873
Population: 138,500
Area: 2,184 sq mi (5,657 km²)

Quebec
Capital: Quebec City
Lieutenant Governor: Lise Thibault
Premier: Jean Charest (Liberal)
Leader of the Opposition: André Boisclair (Parti Québécois)
Entered Confederation: July 1, 1867
Population: 7,651,500
Area: 594,860 sq mi (1,540,700 km^2)

Saskatchewan
Capital: Regina
Lieutenant Governor: Gordon Barnhart
Premier: Lorne Calvert (New Democratic Party)
Leader of the Opposition: Brad Wall
  (Saskatchewan Party)
Entered Confederation: Sept. 1, 1905
Population: 985,400
Area: 251,700 sq mi (651,900 km^2)

Yukon
Capital: Whitehorse
Commissioner: Geraldine Van Bibber

Premier: Dennis Fentie (Yukon Party)
Leader of the Opposition: Arthur Mitchell
  (Liberal)
Organized as a Territory: June 13, 1898
Population: 31,200
Area: 186,299 sq mi (482,515 km^2)

Northwest Territories
Capital: Yellowknife
Commissioner: Antony W.J. (Tony) Whitford
Premier: Joseph Handley
Reconstituted as a Territory: Sept. 1, 1905
Population: 41,900
Area: 468,000 sq mi (1,170,000 km^2)

Nunavut
Capital: Iqaluit
Commissioner: Ann Meekitjuk Hanson
Government Leader: Paul Okalik
Organized as a Territory: April 1, 1999
Population: 30,800
Area: 797,600 sq mi (1,994,000 km^2)

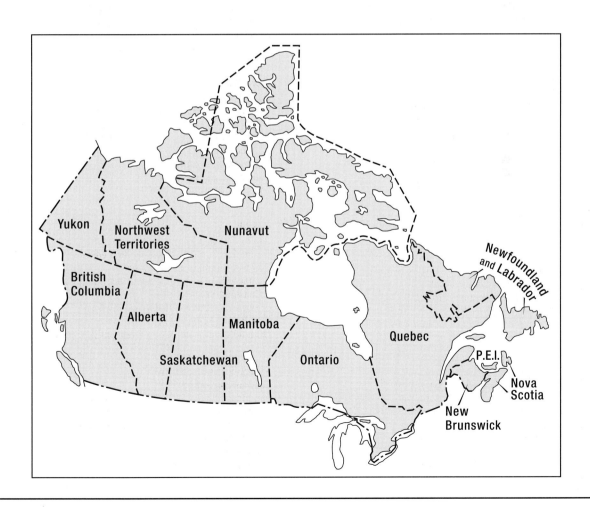

INDEX

A

C

N

Q–R

S

U–V

W

X–Y–Z

ILLUSTRATION CREDITS AND ACKNOWLEDGMENTS

The following list credits or acknowledges, by page, the source of illustrations and text excerpts used in this work. Illustration credits are listed illustration by illustration—left to right, top to bottom. When two or more illustrations appear on one page, their credits are separated by semicolons. When both the photographer or artist and an agency or other source are given for an illustration, they are usually separated by a slash. Excerpts from previously published works are listed by inclusive page numbers.

6　© Art Wolfe/www.artwolfe.com; © Michael Thompson/Animals Animals – Earth Scenes; © Kevin Winter/Getty Images

7　ESA-AOEX Medialab/AP/Wide World Photos; © Claudio Scaccini/AP/Wide World Photos; © Traudel Sachs/Phototake, Inc.

12-13　© Gerry Penny/epa/Corbis; © Patti Sapone/Star Ledger/Corbis

14　© Nabil Al Jurani/AP/Wide World Photos; © Ed Betz/AP/Wide World Photos

15　© Humayoun Shiab/epa/Corbis; © David Guttenfelder/AP/Wide World Photos

16　© William West/AFP/Getty Images; © Kiichiro Sato/AP/Wide World Photos

17　© Matt York/AP/Wide World Photos; © Matt Dunham/AP/Wide World Photos

18　© Ali Haider/epa/Corbis

19　© Pablo Martinez-Monsivais/Getty Images

20　© Fiona Hanson/AP/Wide World Photos

21　© Bruce Beehler

22　© Mandel Ngan/AFP/Getty Images

23　U.S. Treasury/AP/Wide World Photos

24　Courtesy, Center for Screen-time Awareness

25　© Sergey Dolzhenko/epa/Corbis

26　© David Longstreath/AP/Wide World Photos

27　© Keith Bedford/Reuters/Landov

28　© Science, Drs. Marian Vanhaeren and Francesco d'Errico/AP/Wide World Photos

29　© Kevin Schafer/Peter Arnold, Inc.; © BAVARIA/Taxi/Getty Images; © Kevin Schafer/Peter Arnold, Inc.

30　© Alexander Nemenov/Pool/epa/Corbis

31　© Ann Johansson/AP/Wide World Photos

32　© Matt Dunham/AP/Wide World Photos

33　© Bill Haber/AP/Wide World Photos

34　© Lealisa Westerhoff/AFP/Getty Images

35　© Don Emmert/AFP/Getty Images; © SPI, dbox via Getty Images

36　© Mark Wilson/Getty Images

37　© Torsten Silz/AFP/Getty Images

38　Courtesy, United States Mint

39　© Kiichiro Sato/AP/Wide World Photos

40　© Corbis

42　© Nabil Al Jurani/AP/Wide World Photos

43　© AFP/Getty Images; © Ali Haider/Getty Images

44　© Hadi Mizban/AP/Wide World Photos

45　© David Furst/AFP/Getty Images

46　© Jim Hollander/AFP/Getty Images; © Ali Ali/epa/Corbis; © Mohammed Abed/AFP/Getty Images

47　© David Guttenfelder/AP/Wide World Photos

48　© John Lawrence/Stone/Getty Images

49　© Corbis; Bettmann/Corbis

50　© Greg Wahl-Stephens/AP/Wide World Photos; © Gene J. Puskar/AP/Wide World Photos; © David H. Wells/Corbis; © West Rock/Taxi/Getty Images

51　© Danny Gawlowski/Dallas Morning News/Corbis; © Matt York/AP/Wide World Photos

52　© The Consulate General of Mexico/Getty Images; © Justin Sullivan/Getty Images

53　© Robyn Beck/AFP/Getty Images

54　© Beatrice Mategwa/Reuters/Corbis

55　© Ron Haviv/VII/AP/Wide World Photos; © Stephen Morrison/epa/Corbis

56-57　© Amr Nabil/AP/Wide World Photos; © Finbarr O'Reilly/Reuters/Corbis; © Shehzad Noorani/UNICEF via Getty Images

58　© Images.com/Corbis

59　© Buchholz/Taxi/Getty Images; © Time Life Pictures/Getty Images; © Creatas Images/PictureQuest

60　© William West/AFP/Getty Images

61　© Atta Kenare/AFP/Getty Images; © Vahid Salemi/AP/Wide World Photos

62　© Ed Betz/AP/Wide World Photos

63　© Binod Joshi/AP/Wide World Photos

64　© Petty Officer 1st Class Shane T. McCoy/epa/Corbis; © Humayoun Shiab/epa/Corbis

65　© Rusty Kennedy/AP/Wide World Photos

66　© Ed Wray/AP/Wide World Photos

67　© Michele Crosera/AFP/Getty Images

68　© Martial Trezzini/epa/Corbis; © David Karp/AP/Wide World Photos

69　AP/Wide World Photos; © Shaun Best/Reuters/Corbis

70　© Mark Wilson/Getty Images; © Martin Bernetti/AFP/Getty Images

71　© Farjana K. Godhuly/AFP/Getty Images; © Bob Bird/AP/Wide World Photos

72-73　© Stephen Dalton/Minden Pictures

74　© Art Wolfe/www.artwolfe.com

75　© Charles Palek/Animals Animals; © Ernest A. Janes/Bruce Coleman, Inc.

76　© Juergen & Christine Sohns/Animals Animals; © Art Wolfe/www.artwolfe.com

77　© Jim Brandenburg/Minden Pictures; © Laura Riley/Bruce Coleman, Inc.; © Wild & Natural/Animals Animals

78　© Mike Wilkes/npl/Minden Pictures; © Bill Beatty/Visuals Unlimited; © Breck P. Kent/Animals Animals

79　© Tom Vezo/Minden Pictures

80　© Gerry Ellis/Minden Pictures; © Frans Lanting/Minden Pictures

81　© Tom Brakefield/Corbis; © Schafer & Hill/Stone/Getty Images; © Stephen Dalton/Minden Pictures

82　© Nigel Dennis/Animals Animals; © D. MacDonald/OSF/Animals Animals

83　© J & B Photographers/Animals Animals

84　© Wendy Dennis/Visuals Unlimited; © Jorg & Petra Wegner/Animals Animals

85　© D. MacDonald/OSF/Animals Animals; © Wendy Dennis/Visuals Unlimited

86　© A. Fifis; IFREMER/AP/Wide World Photos; © Dr. Jean K. Krejca, Zara Environmental LLC

87　Courtesy of Carnegie Museum of Natural History; © Simon Lin/AP/Wide World Photos

88　© Shane Moore/Animals Animals

89　© Michael Durham/Minden Pictures; © Doug Allan/OSF/Animals Animals

90　© Jeffrey Lepore/Photo Researchers, Inc.; © Darren Bennett/Animals Animals

91　© McDonald Wildlife Photography/Animals Animals; © K. Gowlett-Holmes/OSF/Animals Animals

92　© Miriam Silverstein/Animals Animals

93　© Susan Beatty/Animals Animals

94　© Stephen Dalton/Minden Pictures

95　© Stephen Dalton/Animals Animals

96　© Supplied by WENN/Newscom; © Ann Batdorf/Smithsonian National Zoo/CNP/Corbis; © Ken Bohn/San Diego Zoo/AP/Wide World Photos

97　© Sabina Louise Pierce; © Daniel J. Cox/Corbis

98　© Australia Zoo/Handout/epa/Corbis; © Bikas Das/AP/Wide World Photos

99　© Kathy Willens/AP/Wide World Photos; © Mario Vazquez/AFP/Getty Images

100　© Ted Daeschler/AFP/Getty Images; © Shawn Gould/National Geographic/KRT/Newscom

101　© John Amis/epa/Corbis; © Barry Williams/Getty Images

102-03　© age fotostock/SuperStock

104　© Steve Dininno/Images.com/Corbis

105　© Hubert Boesl/dpa/Corbis; © ABC Television/Courtesy of Getty Images; © Hubert Boesl/epa/Corbis; Photo by Hulton Archive/Getty Images

106　© Hank Morgan/Photo Researchers, Inc.

107　© Kirsten Miller/Images.com/Corbis

108　© Jean-Pierre Pieuchot/The Image Bank/Getty Images

109　© Matt Houston/AP/Wide World Photos; © Doug Plummer/SuperStock

110　© Gary W. Carter/Corbis; © John Kaprielian/Photo Researchers, Inc.; © Will Crocker/The Image Bank/Getty Images; © Mary Clay/Taxi/Getty Images

111　© Susan Van Etten/PhotoEdit, Inc.

112　© Ben Margot/AP/Wide World Photos

113　© Christinne Muschi/Corbis

118　© Clive Nichols/The Image Bank/Getty Images

119　© The LuEsther T. Mertz Library, NYBG/Art Resource, NY; © Alexandra Day/Corbis

120-21　© Michael Thompson/Animals Animals – Earth Scenes; © Paul Miles, Jr./Bruce Coleman, Inc.; © Geoff Bryant/Photo Researchers, Inc.; © NancyRotenberg/Animals Animals – Earth Scenes; © Geoffrey Bryant/Photo Researchers, Inc.; © Nancy Rotenberg/Animals Animals –